READINGS
IN EDUCATIONAL
PSYCHOLOGY

This book is part of the
WORLD SERIES IN EDUCATIONAL PSYCHOLOGY
AND SPECIAL EDUCATION

Thomas E. Jordan
Consulting Editor

Other books in this Series

PERSPECTIVES IN THE EDUCATION OF DISADVANTAGED CHILDREN
Milly Cowles

EDUCATIONAL PSYCHOLOGY
Allen Jack Edwards and Dale P. Scannell

READINGS
IN EDUCATIONAL
PSYCHOLOGY

HAROLD W. BERNARD
AND WESLEY C. HUCKINS

Oregon State System of Higher Education
Division of Continuing Education

The World Publishing Company
Cleveland and New York

Published by The World Publishing Company
2231 West 110th Street, Cleveland, Ohio 44102

Published simultaneously in Canada by
Nelson, Foster & Scott Ltd.

First Printing

Library of Congress Catalog Card Number: 67–12074

Printed in the United States of America

FOREWORD

• This book is designed
for those students, so stimulating to professors, who seek to go beyond the
satisfying of minimum requirements and are pursuing learning for their
own sake. The kinds of articles recommended in the past and endorsed by
such students are the kinds contained within this volume. Many of the
articles have been recommended in courses other than educational psychology. We hope that professors will also find them of interest and value,
although they may not necessarily be new to them.

When teaching classes in educational psychology, we have often recommended that students read certain articles that emphasize or expand a
concept briefly presented in a text. The recommended article might be one
that shows how generalizations have been derived. It might be one that
controverts a viewpoint presented with either conscious or unintentional
bias. It might be one that reviews, consolidates, and evaluates many researches. On other occasions an article has been recommended because it
seemed desirable for students to become acquainted with some of the
leaders in the field; e.g., Bruner, Coladarci, Pressey, Rogers, Skinner, Torrance, and many others. Others have been recommended because they state
so cogently an idea that seemed significant to us. Still others have been
included simply because they combine a number of the foregoing criteria.

When making these recommendations, it was fully recognized that few
students could follow through. The sheer press of numbers at the library
reserve desk, as well as the limited quantity of bound or unbound periodicals, would immediately be discouraging. Many students who, it seemed,
sincerely wanted to read the recommended reference would report: "I
went over three times, but the book was out every time," or "The issue
I wanted was at the bindery."

The solution of the difficulty was to make selected articles available
through a relatively inexpensive book of readings. The student could,
through his individually owned book, come to see the nature of the source
of generalizations in educational psychology, could get to know some of
the frontier thinkers. Perhaps still more important, he could witness the

conflicting conclusions derived from data that are ostensibly the same. Thus he could realize that theory is theory and not yet law. These considerations were kept in mind as periodicals were reviewed in making the selections for this book.

An active selection process is a part of the learning activity of most people. They tend to choose from their environment certain things to which they attend and to overlook the remainder. Generally this is a cumulative process. The more an individual knows, the more it is possible for him to attend to and the more he can learn. The greater his fund of information, the more he can understand, integrate, and apply, and the more choices he can make toward increasing his knowledge. The old adage "The rich get richer and the poor get poorer" is particularly relevant to the learning process in this respect.

There are many points of view presented in these readings. They represent an intellectual environment in which the reader can build upon his own understanding and increase his ability to learn more. To do this most effectively, he will have to become active in the process and to consider and weigh each idea to see how it fits and how it can be associated with what he already knows. In other words, the person who is actively engaged in his own learning is continually recognizing dilemmas and questions and looking for answers. One really makes knowledge his when he applies it, or at least makes plans to apply it.

Those who plan to teach others have a double responsibility. They need to establish effective learning procedures for themselves, and they need to be able to show others how this can be done. One cannot teach what he does not know. We urge readers to take advantage of the opportunity presented by these readings to become conscious of their own learning and to become active in improving the process by which they do it.

Although an attempt was made to include a preponderance of the most recent articles in the field, we were less successful at this than we had hoped to be. The issues that were foremost a number of years ago have been solidly incorporated into educational psychology (transfer of learning, nature of adolescence, "schools" of psychology) and, although essential to the whole, are of relatively little current research interest. New sets of problems (creativity, group processes, culturally disadvantaged pupils, and machine teaching) have become the current foci.

No claim is made that the articles selected are necessarily the best ones in the area covered. Excellent articles were rejected because of their length. This is especially true of many of the articles that appear in various yearbooks of the National Society for the Study of Education. We began by listing the topics generally covered in educational psychology courses and then read some five hundred articles to guide the choices finally made. Certainly, choice is a highly personal matter, and we admit that in many instances we chose an article because it appealed to us—it supported our biases. However, the considerations mentioned above were the bases for initial selection. If either of us questioned the merit of an article nominated by the other, we discarded it—because others who might so question would not have the chance for dialogue that we had.

Considering the fact that the typical student of educational psychology is an underclassman, we have generally avoided articles that have been stated largely in statistical terms. When statistical concepts do appear in the articles, the terms have been briefly defined in the introductory comments.

Because there is both intentional and unintentional bias in most presentations; because two sides are sometimes presented; because teaching techniques must ultimately be individually unique, we ask students to become *active* readers. It is suggested that they try to decide why they approve of a particular thesis. They might try to find some defect in the thesis and to test the idea against some popular belief. At least occasionally, students would do well to read our comments and questions, then check to see if they would have introduced the articles somewhat differently.

This collection is oriented toward the practical; that is, implications for the classroom teachers are immediate and perceptible in most of the articles. Theoretical underpinnings of classroom practice are not ignored, but they are regarded as being the "supporting cast" to the "star performers" —pupils and teachers. Practicality has been complemented by controversy. There are many issues that are controversial, such as the nature and development of intelligence, the role of programed instruction, the complementary nature of readiness, and instructional content and procedures. We have tried to present various views but must admit that our biases very probably are still present.

Our hope is that students will find in the volume a partial realization of our goal—to introduce them to the men and the ideas that constitute the substance of educational psychology. Through this acquaintance, it is hoped that enough lively interest will have been stimulated that the student will be a reactive reader of future articles relating to educational psychology.

HAROLD W. BERNARD

WESLEY C. HUCKINS

Portland, Oregon
April, 1967

TABLE OF CONTENTS

READINGS
IN EDUCATIONAL
PSYCHOLOGY

THE FIELD
OF EDUCATIONAL
PSYCHOLOGY

• The student who is beginning to read in the field of educational psychology can be expected to have questions concerning the scope of the area he is starting to study. He will have questions about how the information can be applied in practical situations. For a number of reasons, these questions cannot be answered with assurance. In the first place, it makes a difference whether the subject of educational psychology is perceived to be limited to formal or school learning situations. The type of material the student encounters is determined by whether individuals are viewed as reacting as whole and integrated organisms or believed to function in a more atomistic fashion, and by whether education is believed to be mostly an intellectual function. Furthermore, the dynamic and changing nature of the society toward which education and learning are being oriented prevents a stabilization and a description of the field of educational psychology.

Each of the three readings included in this section serves in one way or another to illustrate the dynamic and growing nature of the field of educational psychology. Graffam does this by describing the manner in which ideas and procedures from a number of disciplines can be synthesized into a new and productive approach to learning. From a primary concern with the manner in which individuals commit, retain, and apply information, the educational psychologist now may be required to familiarize himself with the dynamics of the interaction and relation of individuals within groups. He may find it necessary to investigate how to use groups

1

as human-relations laboratories and how to help people learn social competences from group processes.

Berg also makes this point. He emphasizes that changes in the culture demand that man's attitudes and methods of relating to his fellows become of paramount concern to education. Unfortunately, they have not always been. The extent of the emphasis and concern now needed may well be proportional to education's previous neglect of this basic human need.

Much of what was believed to be appropriate for education ten years ago may no longer be accorded so much emphasis, and much of what is pertinent today may be less so in another decade. The testing of hypotheses advocated by Coladarci and his statement that "the teacher must be a continuous inquirer into the validity of his own procedures" serve to emphasize both the changing and the developing nature of what we think we know. This is as it should be. When one comes to believe he has the answer, he tends to stop looking. To be effective in the school of the future, teachers, as Graffam indicates, "should possess the willingness and courage to depart from the authoritarian role of the dispenser of knowledge. . . ." They need to become partners with the student in the learning process. Unless each functions as a learner and unless the teacher views his role as growing with his students, he is likely to become an inhibitor rather than a facilitator of the learning process.

It appears essential that both the teacher and the student, now and in the future, approach their task with some realization of the transitory nature of the information with which they deal and which they hope to apply. The teacher, in particular, needs to appreciate that probably only a fraction of what can be found out about education and learning is known and available at present. Further, he needs to realize that even though this knowledge is both dynamic and incomplete, there probably is much more known than we now put to use. Not only do we need to learn more about the learning process in all types of environments, but we need more rigorous application of what we do know.

This is a riddle for which the reader perhaps can find an answer. Why is it that many recognized educational inadequacies exist concomitantly with the techniques and knowledge for their removal? Perhaps part of the answer to the question resides in Graffam's comments on how educational psychology might be taught more effectively. He says, in effect, "Let's engage in education as a *process of learning* rather than as a simple accumulation of facts." This too is part of the message of Coladarci, when he advises the teacher to proceed "on the basis of the best information now available. . . ." Considered, even though tentative, positions on issues of education might well be the kind of preparation pupils need to greet the change which is immanent—and again the pertinence of Berg's statements is perceived.

The student of educational psychology can make this course more interesting and more valuable when he (1) realizes the broad implications of educational problems, (2) heeds the specific suggestions for daily functioning, and (3) is involved in the process of his own education.

DONALD T. GRAFFAM

Professor, Department of Education and Psychology, Dickinson College

1 · WHY NOT TEAM LEARNING?

● During the past few years, considerable publicity has been given to a new development in educational methodology known as team teaching. During the past eight years at Dickinson College, the writer and a succession of his classes in educational psychology have been engaged in evolving another new concept and method of teaching-learning which bears some interesting comparisons to team teaching. This development, which has come to be labelled *team learning*, is grounded in pragmatic philosophy of education, wholistic learning theory in psychology, and principles of group dynamics in sociology. The experience and testimony of the various participants in this eight-year enterprise, comprising more than six hundred students, fifty cooperating elementary school teachers and principals, and six consultants, indicate that team learning can provide a powerful key for stimulating individual motivation and class morale for better and faster learning.

Actually, the first experimentation with team learning by the writer goes back to the late thirties in a high school elective course (consumers education) for juniors and seniors, but no formal attempt was made at that time to work out a definite philosophy and methodology (3). Changes of occupation brought about by World War II prevented the writer from experimenting further with the method until he began to teach the course in educational psychology at Dickinson College in 1954. Since that time more than twenty classes have participated in a venture which may prove to be as significant a contribution to educational methodology as team teaching.

Journal of Teacher Education, 15: 289–292, 1964. Used by permission of the original publisher, *Journal of Teacher Education*, NEA, Washington, D.C.

Educational psychology provides fertile ground for cultivating and crossing the best aspects of competing philosophies of education and psychological theories of learning and of principles of group dynamics in sociology; furthermore, the subject itself is concerned with the improvement of teaching and learning. Application of the principles of team learning has not been limited to classes in educational psychology; it has been extended to other courses in the department of education and psychology and conceivably could also be extended to many courses offered in secondary schools and colleges. Discussion here, however, is concerned with (a) how team learning operates in our educational psychology classes; (b) some comparisons with team teaching; and (c) some general principles derived from our experience that can be applied to other courses.

The course in educational psychology at Dickinson College employs a dual approach incorporating (a) an accelerated traditional treatment and (b) a field study program. The former prepares the students to conduct the latter in groups of five or six members acting as team-learning units. Typically, the course is offered in two sections each semester. Each class, limited to thirty upper-division students, meets in a classroom in which the only special equipment is tables large enough to accommodate six or eight persons each.

In the first or second session, students are assigned alphabetically to groups of five or six members. This procedure has proved in the long run to be the simplest method for achieving random selection of ability and preventing the formation of cliques. In order to hasten the process of getting acquainted, the members of each group complete and exchange a personal data sheet and autobiographical sketch. Later on, each group elects a chairman (or co-chairmen) whose main functions are to weld the members into a team and provide leadership in the field study program. The nature of the course is discussed in the light of three educational philosophies—idealism, realism, and pragmatism—and their methodological implications, as presented by Thut (5). Examination of case studies of previous classes lends reality to the course description and serves as an effective motivational factor.

The first (essentialistic) phase of the semester's work consists of an accelerated program of study in order to provide the theoretical and factual bases of the course and furnish the necessary background for the second (pragmatic) phase in which each group employs team learning in making a case study of an elementary school child. Instruction begins in the traditional manner of lectures and assignments in two basic textbooks (1,4). Coaching in special reading and study techniques is given as a stimulus to extensive reading in current educational and psychological journals in the library. Selected reports of readings are incorporated into the course content through class discussions. Students are willing to go along with this crash program in anticipation of the team-learning aspect of the course and in the realization that considerable familiarity with the subject matter of educational psychology is a necessary preparation for field work.

The essentialistic phase continues for about two months. During this period, emphasis is placed on ideas and principles (idealism) and on facts and the scientifically developed content of educational psychology, together with a working knowledge of the scientific method and its application in observing individual behavior (realism). Learning during this stage is more a matter of individual, competitive enterprise than of team learning.

The pragmatic phase is interposed about the fourth week when each team is introduced to a cooperating teacher and her school principal in one of the six local elementary schools in order to conduct a case study of a pupil selected by the teacher. By the end of the eighth week, the role of the professor has changed from that of instructor to resource person or consultant, and team learning has been substituted for the traditional competitive striving of individuals. The nature of the group has changed from an aggregation of members into a *team* possessing psychological unity because of mutually perceived goals. As for control of class conduct, it is henceforth shared by the team chairman, two elected class leaders, and the teacher, all of whom are jointly responsible for scheduling the completion of case studies and final reports of these studies to the class.

The manifestations of change in attitude and morale of the class members from this point on are strikingly observable. Enthusiasm mounts, morale soars, as the teams gather anecdotes and other data on their "subjects" through scheduled visits to their respective elementary school classrooms. Class periods are utilized for the discussion, analysis, and organization of data by each team working as an independent learning unit in the attempt to apply knowledge gained from textbooks, lectures, the library, and their own experience toward the goal of trying to understand the behavior of a flesh-and-blood learner—their own subject. Here, indeed, is group dynamics at work! In addition to the required course work and regular class sessions, some teams schedule as many as ten or fifteen meetings on their own time in order to work on their case studies. Team learning thus stimulates transfer of learning from textbooks to real life situations.

The tangible goal of our teams is the case study—"The Record of Frannie Fidget" or "Boldilocks and the Three R's," for example—and its sociodramatic presentation to the class. The typical product, containing about seventy pages, is organized into sections including a foreword, table of contents, explanation of team learning and its underlying pragmatic philosophy, an anecdotal record of samples of the child's behavior, data from school records and other sources, and notes on library research appropriate to the age and characteristics of the subject. The final section contains recommendations for the improvement of the subject's learning efficiency and adjustment. Several copies of the record are made, one copy being retained by the instructor and one being presented to the cooperating teacher. All copies are classified as confidential materials, and all parties participating in the program are pledged to abide by a code of ethics to protect the anonymity of the children being studied. This in itself is a valuable kind of training for adult responsibility.

Team learning as here conceived and presented is not to be confused with committee work, group projects, etc., ordinarily encountered in high school and college classes as temporary arrangements to meet some aspect of a course. Nor is it similar in purpose or method to team teaching. Team learning entails a definite philosophy and methodology which must be understood by the instructor and explained to students who are mature enough to meet the responsibilities required for participation in independent group activity. Like team teaching, it requires careful preplanning. On the other hand, complicated administrative arrangements, time-consuming conferences with colleagues and other personnel, and specially designed environment and equipment are not necessary. All the work can be done by the instructor and his committees of students.

In team learning, the whole emphasis is on the learners and learning, not on teachers and teaching. The spotlight is where it belongs on the stars of the play, not on the authors, directors, the stage setting, props, or crew. Education is conceived of as a democratic leading-forth process in which learners have a stake in their total growth, especially in the creative development of their social and cognitive abilities, and not as a method of imparting information by experts to tyros. Team learning is based on wholistic learning theory which implements competence in dealing with the environment and accountability for those dealings, not on stimulus-response psychology. It recognizes that growth through individual effort can be augmented through group process. It places as high a premium on the teacher's empathy as on his mastery of a subject field. Finally, team learning is not designed as an economy measure or as a device to handle more students or reduce teacher load. It costs neither more nor less than conventional instruction and does not invite the possibility of being expanded into an expensive affair. The sole aim is the improvement of learning.

A number of principles have emerged from our experience which may be helpful to instructors who would like to experiment with team learning. First, there should be a readiness on the part of both teacher and learners to try it. The teacher should have a knowledgeable background in educational philosophy, psychology, and sociology to support a conceptual understanding of what is to be undertaken. If he lacks this background, he can prepare himself by studying the references in this paper or any of the standard works in the three fields. Moreover, he should possess the willingness and courage to depart from the authoritarian role of dispenser of knowledge and have faith in his students' ability, after an initial period of guidance, to organize and direct their own learning effectively toward clearly defined and accepted goals. At the same time, the learners must have the potential maturity to accept the role of responsible group membership.

Second, the objectives of the course must be worked out carefully by the teacher and communicated to the students in ways that encourage their acceptance. Both parties can then decide cooperatively which objective or objectives lend themselves to team learning and which ones can be handled better by traditional methods of instruction. It is to be noted that team learning does not displace the teacher or diminish his ultimate authority and responsibility.

Third, team learning can acquire an organic continuity once it has been applied in a course. Succeeding classes can be made to sense their participation in a creative stream of development by drawing upon their predecessors' experience and by adding modifications of their own. Students on our campus who have had the course usually accept with enthusiasm an invitation to serve present groups as resource persons.

Fourth, the composition and leadership of the teams are important factors. The alphabetical method of selection mentioned above has worked out successfully in our case, but some teachers might find it desirable to structure the class into balanced or homogeneous groups by means of sociometry or the use of tests. Each team must have a leader or chairman. Experience has taught us that having each committee elect its own chairman (or co-chairmen), after an initial period of getting acquainted, is a better way to secure effective leadership than either early election or teacher selection.

Fifth, everything possible should be done to promote cohesiveness and cooperative effort within each team. Psychological unity may be facilitated by informing members that they will be given the same grade based on the quality of the team's product. The soundness of this principle has not only been established theoretically and experimentally by Deutsch (2) but has been verified by our experience. Democratically determined leadership also promotes cohesiveness.

Sixth, the learning activities of each team should culminate in some tangible product which can be evaluated in terms of the specific goals of the group and the total objectives of the course. A tangible goal materializes group purpose and accelerates the motivation of the members as they move toward it.

The increasing complexity and interdependence of our society and the rapid multiplication of new knowledge demand new and better techniques of teaching and learning which will produce citizens who are able to work effectively in groups and who are skilled in the process of group decision making. Team learning is designed to accomplish these ends, and it is thus appropriate to the needs and trends of our times. Furthermore, it is easy and inexpensive to implement, it harmonizes with the latest theories in psychology and sociology pertinent to education, and it comes directly to grips with the enduring central problem in our schools—the improvement of learning.

REFERENCES

1. Cronbach, Lee J. *Educational Psychology.* Second edition. New York: Harcourt, Brace & World, 1963.
2. Deutsch, Morton. "The Effects of Cooperation and Competition upon Group Process." *Group Dynamics: Research and Theory.* (Edited by Dorwin Cartwright and A. F. Zander.) White Plains, New York: Row, Peterson & Co., 1953. pp. 319–53.
3. Graffam, Donald T. "Helping Students Plan for Economic Security." *California Journal of Secondary Education* 15: 225–29; April 1940.
4. Prescott, Daniel A. *The Child in the Educative Process.* New York: McGraw-Hill Book Co., 1957.
5. Thut, I. N. *The Story of Education: Philosophical and Historical Foundations.* McGraw-Hill Book Co., 1957.

IRWIN A. BERG
Professor and Chairman of Department of Psychology, Louisiana State University

2 · CULTURAL TRENDS AND THE TASK OF PSYCHOLOGY[1]

• In newspapers, magazines, radio, and television much has been made of the technological aspects of cultural change, and there is much to fire the imagination in man's continuing conquest of the material world. There is something for everyone. The small boy can daydream of being an astronaut, the physician can read about space medicine, the engineer can envision strange, new devices made of unique alloys, the housewife can see a home full of robot servants—and so it goes. The impact on our daily lives is indeed far-reaching; yet the changes are far, far greater than the oft-discussed space flights, electronic computers, and the like. If there is much to fire the imagination in our new technology, there is much more to sear the soul. Therefore, it seems essential that we pause to review some of the nonhardware implications of cultural change, particularly with reference to our profession of psychology. Three aspects merit a particularly close look: the population explosion, the impact of automation, and man's violence toward man. This is not to say that the world's population growth (nor automation nor violence, for that matter) has been ignored, or even in any way slighted as a source of national concern. Much has been said and written of burgeoning mankind and its eventual destiny of starvation. Therefore, we need not dwell lengthily on this topic. But we must give some consideration to it, if only because the

American Psychologist, 20: 203–207, 1965. Copyright © 1965 by the American Psychological Association, and reproduced by permission.

[1] Presidential Address delivered at Southwestern Psychological Association, San Antonio, Texas, April 1964.

soaring rate of population growth compounds and intensifies the problems psychologists will face. John D. Rockefeller, III, Chairman of the Board of the Population Council, has noted that to reach a world population of one billion, it took mankind the entire period of recorded history until the early nineteenth century. It took only another 100 years to add the second billion and but 30 more years to add the third billion. Only 15 years will be needed to reach four billion. Somewhere around this point in the world's population the moment of crisis will be reached; and if cultural change by plan has not preceded the crisis, it will very likely be achieved by cataclysm. C. G. Wrenn quoted a vivid description of the problem as described by mathematician J. D. Williams. He asked us to think of the earth as a partly flooded cellar 25 × 25 feet. Only one-fourth of the cellar is dry and 16 persons are on this dry portion. One of the 16 is an American and he has a spot 2 × 6 feet. He also has about half the food and other good things in the cellar. The American and all of the other 15 dwellers in the cellar are armed with powerful weapons; yet 10 of them are incredibly poor and hungry. Because of his past history, the American feels snugly isolated in the cellar. The other 15 know that he is not.

As Rockefeller points out, the answer does not lie in nuclear suicide. The answer can only reside in world population control. Yet the obstacles to such control are immense, for they include illiteracy, religious convictions, ancient social customs, economic needs, etc. These obstacles are chiefly attitudinal in nature and, as such, their removal will become a task for the psychologist. At present, we know something of attitudes and how to measure them. Now we must discover how to change them efficiently. We shall have to gain this knowledge rapidly and we shall have to work against difficulties inherent in our own culture which are raised against such studies. One difficulty, for example, will very likely be sharp criticism of proposals to "waste" good American dollars on research for changing attitudes in foreign lands—after all, attitudes are not important. Perhaps it will help to remind such critics that attitudes toward meat as a food have caused many thousands of people in India to die of starvation rather than eat the Brahma cattle which were grazing in their grain fields. Critics or not, psychologists must accept the challenge of producing attitude change. The alternative is an atomic Armageddon or starvation.

While the world's population is increasing in geometric proportion, the overall need for manpower in our culture is decreasing rapidly as a result of automation. The impact of these technological changes in our culture is only beginning to be felt. Automation as such is not new, of course, for its roots go back at least to the beginning of the Industrial Revolution. What *is* new is the number and variety of jobs being taken over by automatic operations and what is happening, as a result, to the structure of our society. Previously, only the relatively simple jobs were heavily affected and those persons thrown out of work were chiefly the marginal workers such as laborers, migratory workers, etc. In our expanding economy many of those persons could be absorbed elsewhere in the labor market, often in somewhat better jobs as a result of retraining. The others were the socially voiceless ones who accepted welfare payments silently if grimly. These latter were not a threat to the orderly functioning of our society, for illiterate or semi-literate people do not write convincing letters to the newspapers or to Congress, nor do they organize powerful protests. Now, however, the jobs under assault are not just the simple jobs which require muscle but little skill. The skilled and semiskilled tradesmen, the experienced office workers, and even some professional persons are feeling the initial pressure of decreased annual earnings and declining job opportunities. This pressure will mount and eventually become overwhelming as the new machines become more widely used. The painters, carpenters, electricians, and plumbers, for example, have direct knowledge of what prefabricated housing does to their jobs. What of the future when houses are molded in plastic units that need no painting and have fixtures and wiring already installed? Accountants have seen bank clerks replaced by computers that swallow magnetic-ink checks and post individual totals, all without benefit of coffee break or sick leave. What of the future when auditing practices are standardized and the machines with suitable programs are cheap enough for the smallest bank or business firm? While still largely experimental, we have machines that can type directly from the spoken word without the aid of a human typist and other machines which can translate printed material from a foreign language into English. While the spelling and sentence structure is idiosyncratic, the meaning of the translation is clear enough and the meaning for many white collar workers is even clearer.

We are shaping a new robotized culture in which *many people will be surplus amidst an economy of abundance.* These people will not starve, of course, for I feel sure we shall meet the acid test of a true civilization embodied in the question, "How do people in this society treat other people?" We have some distance to go in meeting this test; yet we have already come a long way. But if there is no starvation, there will be problems—very serious problems which cannot be solved by tear gas or fire-hoses. Of course, we can and will institute palliatives like 20-hour work weeks, early retirement, youth programs, and the like. These will help, but only in the sense that a corn plaster eases an aching toe. The fact remains that many people will be surplus and, furthermore, they will know it. They will not be the silent, bowed men of toil but rather the trained persons who have up to now been mainstays in our society, who have skills to offer but skills which society no longer needs. Eventually we shall find a solution, but the period of searching for an answer, the period we are just now entering, will be a time of increasing upheaval and social torment. It seems highly probable that we shall be faced with problems of delinquency and crime beside which our present problems in these areas will be dwarfed almost to invisibility. It also seems highly probable that the frequency of disorders such as alcoholism, depressions, neurotic reactions, etc., will vastly increase. What happens to self-respecting young people whose rosy dreams of youth are confined to a make-work program or to idleness? What happens to workers retired at 50, no matter what the size of the pension check? What happens to a man who works but 20 hours a week, year after year? For every one such who can make a successful and mature response to the challenge of vacant time there will very likely be another who develops a serious mental health problem.

The best guess one can make is that in 15 or 20 years half the population will be supporting the other half in enforced leisure or make-work jobs unless a world war intervenes. The working half will be engaged in activities essential to our strange, automated culture. These are the people who can manage the new society, who can wield the concepts essential to our new technology, who can invent, improve, and maintain the new machines. There will be no 20-hour week for them, and with the pressures inherent in their critical role it seems likely that stress reactions and other adjustment difficulties will sharply rise for this group also. Thus there will be two social groups and both will experience serious adjustment difficulties, although in varying degree. In this connection it may be noted that we seem to be heading toward a two-class society: the *essential* and the *surplus* citizens. There is nothing new about surplus human beings in a particular society, for there have always been 3 or 4% who could not or would not work although eligible for gainful employment. What is new in our evolving culture is that we shall have 10 or 15 times 3 or 4%, and most all of these people will want to work, to feel needed in the scheme of things as they did in decades past. How will two such groups view each other? That is more than a question, for it implies a threat of class warfare.

I think there is an approach in the search for an answer which lies in the behavioral sciences. I am admittedly professionally ethnocentric when I assert that psychology and its sister sciences of behavior can, if given the chance, come up with programs which initially can ease but not eliminate the wrenching agony, that is now upon us, of the transition from one culture pattern to another. Then, after the transition, I believe psychologists can participate actively in a new world centered primarily on people, not on technology—if given the chance.

The transition activities will probably be focused on the things psychologists are already doing, but the level and extent of activity will rise— such things as psychotherapy, community mental health, work with the aged, with children, with the handicapped, with the industrial worker, etc. These activities will not shield our society from the blows its surplus members will receive during the transition period. But they will cushion the impact and buy time for research and planning. They could buy time for research which would eventually enable us to understand our changing culture and help guide it from a machine-centered value system to one centered on mankind. That is a very big order, proposing that psychologists and their confreres in the behavioral sciences should try to understand and assist in reorientating a civilization that, as an English writer put it, will pay 40 millions for a bomb and 40 shillings for a poem. But somehow it must be done, for the alternatives are unthinkably disgusting, of the order of Orwell's *1984* or Huxley's *Brave New World.*

The alternatives are beginning to appear, although the emerging pattern is thus far seen primarily among the surplus citizens of our society. The pattern seems to be shaping toward an abrogation of law with resort to physical violence by some people who are directly affected by the current social and technological changes. Churches, homes, and railway trains have been bombed, human beings have been stoned, shot, and mobbed by those who rebelled at the portents of cultural change. Psychologically, I see evidence of generalization in such events. That is, if anything is disliked, the response seems to center more and more frequently in violence. Yet such violence is commonplace at a time when we have only *just entered the period of rapid cultural change.* What will it be like when the shock wave of change is full upon us? Obviously, society cannot be dedicated to the rule of law and at the same time permit violence in defiance of law to continue indefinitely. This will surely be at once the critical test of our society and the first signpost of the road we shall follow. If violence is met with violence, we shall probably be on our way to Orwell's *1984* and a society of iron regimentation.

Thus, as I see it, the central problem during the period of cultural transition now upon us is the handling of violence. That is the emerging task of psychology and other behavioral sciences. If our society fails in this task, the traditional patterns of violence as a tool will prevail, and our world is well schooled in these techniques. Hitler managed to incinerate 6,000,000 Jews, Stalin succeeded in killing 3,000,000 Kulaks by carefully engineered starvation—one can go on and on. Clearly, the task of psychology will have to involve a complete restructuring of attitudes toward other human beings. This will require profound changes in our social structure and our social interaction but I believe it can be done. It must be done if we are to avoid humanity in straitjackets, a humanity which would be less important than the robots which serve the society. If it can be done, the prospect is entrancing—for it can mean a golden age of individual creativity where mankind, freed from the burden of toil, can beautify the world physically, socially, and spiritually.

The task and the goal, therefore, become one, that of *proscribing violence in all forms of man toward man.* This will involve generalization of behavioral changes that permeate every fiber of the warp and the woof of our social structure and of our personal dynamics. Take our laws with respect to assault on a person's property and on his body as a case in point. If you hold up a man and take his money at the point of a gun, you may go to prison for life. If you have no designs on his money, but simply beat him and, let us say, knock out a few teeth, you probably will be fined about $100, and may also have to pay for some dental repairs. It is highly unlikely that you will go to jail at all unless you make a practice of assault and battery. Similarly, if you burglarize a bank or rob the United States mails, officers of the law will search, if necessary, for years to apprehend you. But the search will probably last only a month or two if your crime was stabbing a person in the eye. If caught, your punishment for the attack on property will be much heavier than for the attack on a human being. Obviously, this value system will have to be reversed if we are to develop a culture centered on people instead of machines and property.

Formidable as this proposed change in the law is, the necessary changes in our recreational activities will be even more so. Physical assault or brutality will have to be viewed as understandable only when occurring in young children who do not yet know any better, or by a person defending his very life, or by one who is mentally deranged. This would mean that sports which injure, maim, or kill human beings through physical assault must be outlawed. Boxing and football are cases in point. Incidentally, at least one Scandinavian country has or is about to outlaw boxing, apparently as a result of publicity given to the deaths of 165 fighters all over the world who died during a 9-year period as a result of ring injuries. Proper sports would be ones like handball, tennis, golf, swimming, and, with minor changes, baseball, basketball, etc. It may seem utterly absurd to suggest seriously that this can be done, even if we allow a generation or two for its achievement. It must have seemed equally absurd to ancient Romans who were told that their flesh-rending gladiatorial combats should be abolished. A few centuries ago our forebears were probably angry at the loss of a popular spectator sport and at the same time quite sure that a crime wave would follow the absurd abolition of branding, ear-cropping, hand-lopping, and drawing and quartering for criminal offenses. Our culture has changed in the kind and amount of violence it will tolerate and the record indicates that even greater changes in the future should be quite feasible. As a case in point, compare the orderly Scandinavian of today with his blood-lusting Viking ancestors. The control and eventual abolition of violence of man against man if taken seriously, *as it must be if we are to escape Brave New World,* is probably not the Herculean task it appears to be at first glance. There will be the jeers, jibes, and other assaults that always accompany far-reaching changes. But my estimate is that such evidence of opposition and social upheaval would be less than we went through when slavery or child labor was abolished.

But our task cannot stop with the elimination of actual physical violence by man against man. It must in time include verbal and gestural violence as well. Words and gestures which betoken physical violence to another human being must come to be regarded as vulgar in the extreme, as capable of being uttered only by an incredible boor, by a mentally disturbed person, or by a child who has not yet learned. This does not mean a rejection of our present literature which admittedly abounds in examples of violence in all forms. Rather such literature would come to be regarded much as we now regard the earthier passages of Chaucer and Shakespeare—characteristic of a bygone age.

As for the feasibility of psychologists and other behavioral scientists successfully completing this task, I should have to ask, "What kind of feasibility?" There are at least three kinds of feasibility. We certainly have the necessary skills right now to achieve such a program with individuals. To do it on a mass basis would require a great deal of research, but we know how to go about that, too. Given the necessary manpower and support, I should say it is quite feasible in this sense. A second feasibility is subject to the willingness of our legislative bodies to embrace such a program as that briefly sketched here. The past record of such bodies is not encouraging in terms of support given for studying man's behavior, certainly not when compared to support given to farm-produce prices, foreign aid, or space exploration. Yet it seems to me that, when the issue was clear, our Government has always responded with appropriate remedial action.

Such action, unfortunately, is sometimes predicated on fear of what could happen if the necessary steps were not taken. Nevertheless, the steps *were* taken. Thus I would predict that violence in labor disputes, racial strife, etc., will become more widespread, that delinquency, crime, and mental illness will sharply rise, and that the social upheaval associated with auto-mation-produced joblessness will increase. Then, after this trying period, our legislators will act to provide a broad, coordinated program, as they are beginning now to do in piecemeal programs for the aged, school dropouts, the mentally retarded, the retrainable jobless, etc. Accordingly, I feel rather optimistic with respect to the eventual feasibility of a program dealing with cultural change in this sense.

A last feasibility is that of *time*. Will we have time to train the necessary behavioral scientists, time to do the research, and institute the program before an orgy of atomic annihilation engulfs us? This is the factor that must give us pause. Sober reflection makes us aware that broad programs which would change the status quo are rarely welcomed. If accompanied by Cassandra-like warnings of impending evil, they are almost always assailed. Witness Winston Churchill's warning of Nazism before World War II and the calumny he endured. If one seeks a more appropriate and current example, consider the situation of the American Psychological Association Past President, Charles Osgood. He has been writing and talking about ways and means of achieving world peace—something that virtually every-one favors if I read the newspapers correctly. Several years ago, he proposed a method of reducing world tensions. One step was aimed at inducing reciprocation and required particular unilateral actions to be announced publicly by one world power and identified as part of a deliberate policy of reducing tension. No requirements, such as "if you do this, then we will do that," were to be involved—just a positive gesture of good faith and hope that the other power would eventually respond on a similar plane. Osgood was called a "Peacenik," and his proposal was variously labeled "surrender by degrees" and "graduated surrender." Be that as it may, any broad pro-gram involving cultural change will probably be slow in starting because of bitter opposition. This opposition will take time to soften. As a result I am not highly optimistic that a new age, rooted in man's humanity to man, will come about *before* we move up the path that leads to Orwell's *1984* or to nuclear devastation. There is, of course, the very definite possibility that behavioral scientists *will* be given the chance to reshape attitudes toward human violence. At the moment, however, the odds seem to favor the missiles and bombs.

Thus on the basis of reason and a cold appraisal of world events it does seem likely that another world war will intervene before the first steps can be taken toward achieving a golden age for mankind. Emotionally, however, I do not feel pessimistic, and it may be that such emotional factors which run counter to all reason are related to man's emergence from the cave and his strivings for a better place in the sun. This point is illustrated in a telephone conversation I had the day before I delivered this address. I talked with Karen Kirby, a young matron who only hours before had delivered a daughter, Kathleen Kirby. She talked quite animatedly of just-arrived Kathleen, of Christopher Kirby, her 2-year-old son, of her husband, and of her mother. She was looking to the future with pleasant expectancy and, somehow, her attitude communicated hope for the future to me, too. You see, Karen is my daughter and Kathleen and Christopher my grandchildren.

ARTHUR P. COLADARCI
Professor of Education and Psychology, Stanford University

3 · THE RELEVANCY OF EDUCATIONAL PSYCHOLOGY

● The relevancy of an applied area depends in part upon the definition of the process, institution, or event to which it is applied. The contribution that can be made by *educational* psychology is partially a function of the particular meaning invested in "education." This statement is not merely the usual innocuous preface to an extended discussion. Indeed, it is our major thesis. Too many teachers and administrators have thought of educational psychology as consisting only of an ordered catalogue of educational prescriptions, which, together with those provided by the other foundational fields in education, "tell" the teacher "how to teach" and the administrator "how to administer." The fallacy lies not only in the much too complimentary respect for the status of our knowledge in these areas but, more fundamentally, in the conception of education as a collection of successful recipes—the teacher or administrator is a person who has been armed with a bag-of-tricks into which he reaches for a decision regarding any given specific professional problem. Although this unfortunate orientation becomes an increasingly less frequent one, it still exists and may be partially attributable to the turn-of-the-century efforts to make education "scientific" by attempting to make it merely more *factual* (1).

If one, however, thinks of the nature of the educator's role in another way, educational psychology, and education generally, become more power-

Educational Leadership, 13: 489–492, May, 1956. Reprinted with permission of the Association for Supervision and Curriculum Development and Arthur P. Coladarci. Copyright © 1956 by the Association for Supervision and Curriculum Development.

ful, exciting and rigorous. The conception we have in mind can be described by beginning with a rather coarse but generally acceptable definition of the educator's role: to help the learner change his behavior in specified desirable directions. Although the definition is too ambiguous for detailed analysis, it serves to point out the two basic factors involved: a *process* ("behavior change") and a *criterion* ("specified desirable directions"). Suppose that the educator has clearly specified what he means by "desirable" behavior changes in the form of operationally stated educational goals (2). It appears, now, that the focal task for the teacher is to so interact with his pupils, and to so arrange the conditions and materials, that these pupils will change in the hoped-for ways. Put in these terms, the teacher's task can be seen as one of manipulating the learning situation in such a way that the *predicted* behavior changes actually do occur. If, at this point, the educational psychologist could say that we now know which manipulations will produce the desired changes, no problem would exist—we have only to apply the correct recipe. However, educational psychology cannot do this. Any particular combination of teacher-pupil-class-group-community-available materials, etc., is somewhat different from any other combination. There is no general prescription that can be considered to be clearly valid for particular cases. The teacher, then, *must be an active, continuous inquirer into the validity of his own procedures.* As Corey puts it:

> Most of the study of what should be kept in the schools and what should go and what should be added must be done in hundreds of thousands of classrooms and thousands of American communities. The studies must be understood by those who may have to change the way they do things as a result of the studies. Our schools cannot keep up with the life they are supposed to sustain and improve unless teachers, pupils, supervisors, administrators, and school patrons continuously examine what they are doing. Singly and in groups, they must use their imagination creatively and constructively to identify the practices that must be changed to meet the needs and demands of modern life, courageously to try out those practices that give better promise, and methodically and systematically gather evidence to test their worth (3).

At the risk of belaboring the point, let us put it in somewhat different form before considering the relevancy of educational psychology. The educator's decisions about methods, materials and curricular procedures should be thought of as *hypotheses* regarding the way in which the desired behavior changes can be brought about. These hypotheses must be *tested* continuously by inquiring into the degree to which the predicted behavior changes actually occurred. This view has been referred to elsewhere by the writer (4) as "teaching behavior defined as the-testing-of-hypotheses behavior." The crucial element is *tentativeness*; ideas and decisions about method and curriculum are to be held hypothetically, continuously tested, and continuously revised if necessary.

Contribution of Educational Psychology

Given this conception of the educator's role, how can educational psychology be brought to bear on it in helpful ways? The contribution can be broken down into two related categories. First, educational psychology, as a body of information and an arena of research activity, can help in the generation of the educational hypotheses. Intelligent hypotheses are not chosen randomly nor are they found full-blown. An intelligent hypothesizer thinks along the lines of the following model: "*On the basis of the best information now available to me,* I hypothesize that this procedure will produce this result." To translate this into the context of education, we might say, for instance: "*On the basis of what I now know* about individual differences and the reading process, I hypothesize that this kind of grouping-for-reading will lead to the kind of pupil progress in reading that I would like to bring about."

Educational psychology, as a source of information, contributes to the "on-the-basis-of-what-I-now-know" portion of the statement. It helps provide information on which to base hypotheses for particular purposes and particular children. The teacher or administrator who takes this point seriously will understand that one cannot merely "take a course in educational psychology," but that he must constantly keep informed about those developments in this area that are most relevant to his particular educational responsibilities. The reader may also note that this conception of the interaction between educational psychology and the teacher means that every teacher can *contribute* to educational psychology in the process of testing his hypotheses.

A second kind of contribution which educational psychology can make is that of helping teachers and administrators to acquire the attitudes and skills necessary to intelligent hypothesizing and the testing of hypotheses. Limitations of space preclude an explication of this. Generally, what is involved is learning such skills as how to interpret data intelligently, how to observe accurately, how to avoid common logical fallacies in making inferences, how to make adequate decisions regarding what data should be gathered, ways in which data can be gathered and recorded, etc.

Both of these contributions of educational psychology are shared by all the fields represented in this symposium. In the writer's view, this is the *raison d'être* of any field that purports to be "foundational" in professional education. Educational psychology, of course, has many additional and somewhat unique values for the educator. We have chosen to overlook those in this discussion since they are covered comprehensively and in detail in the available published literature. Those who are interested are invited to examine the published reports of a committee organized by the Executive Committee of the National Society of College Teachers of Education. The first report (5) discussed the ways in which educational psychology relates to curriculum development; the second (6) considers the nature of educational psychology and its general place in teacher education; the third (7) gives detailed attention to the ways in which specific areas of educational psychology can be helpful to the prospective teacher; the last report (8) describes present practices and developments in the teaching of educational psychology.

It is appropriate, in this case, that the final comment should be cautionary as well as benedictory. The writer has stated his position as though there are no responsible competing alternatives to it. Any dogmatic flavor in the statement is more a consequence of brevity than of intent. Many persons will hold that such a conception of education as we have presented here is both impractical and not valuable. Our response would be that the orientation is at least practical in the sense that many, many educators have learned to behave as inquirers; the orientation appears to be valuable in that where one finds such an educator he usually finds him to be valued by his colleagues, ego-involved in his profession, and able to criticize his procedures rationally. In short, such educators do exist and they appear to make the profession a better one by their membership in it.

REFERENCES

1. B. Othanel Smith. "Science of Education," in W. S. Monroe (editor), *Encyclopedia of Educational Research*. Macmillan, 1950. p. 1145–52.
2. Robert M. W. Travers. *Educational Measurement*. Macmillan, 1955. p. 19–36.
3. Stephen M. Corey. *Action Research to Improve School Practices*. Bureau of Publications, Teachers College, Columbia University, 1953. p. viii.
4. Arthur P. Coladarci. "Are Educational Researchers Prepared to Do Meaningful Research." *California Journal of Educational Research*. 1954, 5, 3–6.

5. "The Psychological Basis of the Modern Curriculum," *Journal of Educational Psychology*. 1948, 39, 129-69.

6. "Educational Psychology in the Education of Teachers," *Journal of Educational Psychology*. 1949, 40, 257–94.

7. "Educational Psychology for Teachers," *Journal of Educational Psychology*. 1950, 41, 321–72.

8. "Current Practices and Innovations in the Teaching of Educational Psychology," *Journal of Educational Psychology*. 1952, 43, 1–30.

THE NATURE AND COURSE OF LEARNING

• Educators, and teachers in particular, can be considered to be applied psychologists in a very meaningful sense. Although the theorist and the researcher have been more active in developing and testing new ideas and concepts that relate to education and learning, it is the teacher who puts them into practice in the classroom and influences their success and degree of application.

It has been said that there are many ways to get from here to there. That this is also true of the learning process there can be little doubt. As a result, the student of educational psychology can expect to find numerous explanations of the manner in which learning occurs and many opinions concerning the ways in which it best can be expedited. It is doubtful that any one way can be expected to work best for all learners. No two teachers, because of their own differences as individuals and the differences of their students, can expect to teach or to facilitate learning in the same way, nor can they expect to employ the same methods and techniques with comparable results in all situations.

Skinner stresses the fact that learning in the schools could be greatly improved if teachers knew more about the fact of reinforcement and would apply their knowledge. In the past, he says, educational control was aversive—children learned because of threats and to avoid either psychological or physical punishment. Reinforcement works; and it works surprisingly well, as has been demonstrated on laboratory animals. At this point some people protest that children are not the same as laboratory animals. But

Skinner has anticipated the objection and goes on to say that for gaining some skills the work of the teacher should be supplemented by mechanical devices, which can more consistently and quickly give impetus to effective learning. However, there still remain some questions. Do we know enough now that it will suffice to teach children only those things that can be scheduled and programed? (See Section XVII). How do creativity and problem-solving fit with the concept of reinforcement?

An explanation of the learning process appears to depend upon the way in which its developer comes to look at the learner. Whether the learner is viewed as a person or as an organism, whether he is seen to be capable of directing and organizing his own learning experiences, and whether control of the learning process is believed to be regulated by the learner or regulated by the teacher or by a machine are basic to the view of learning that is evolved. Both points of view purposely were included in this section. Skinner quite obviously favors external control of the learner through manipulation of the manner in which his behaviors are rewarded, while Weir just as obviously emphasizes internal control by the learner, in his insistence that if the pupil finds no meaning in a situation, he will learn nothing from it.

Beauchamp states five principles of learning that the reader might well examine in terms of the propositions forwarded by Skinner. Far from regarding learning as a mechanistic process, Beauchamp states that learning is organismic and cannot be reduced to an aggregation of parts. Maturity is fundamental; so too is meaning. Learning is an individual matter, but it is rooted in culture—one learns those things that are important in the culture. What then happens in the matter of choice? Both choice and acculturation are facts, and thus teachers and learners must seek to reduce the ambiguity of the incompleteness of their own knowledge at the same time that teachers must proceed to teach on the basis of tentative hypotheses.

As a matter of conjecture, it well may be that the most effective learning can be expected to occur when the learner can be made aware, through an understanding of himself, of the manner in which he learns. Because the self-direction and development so essential to the individual in our society probably are not possible without self-understanding, learning how he learns is perhaps the most important thing which the school can help a youngster to discover.

B. F. SKINNER

Edgar Pierce Professor of Psychology, Harvard University

4 · THE SCIENCE OF LEARNING AND THE ART OF TEACHING[1]

● Some promising advances have recently been made in the field of learning. Special techniques have been designed to arrange what are called "contingencies of reinforcement"—the relations which prevail between behavior on the one hand and the consequences of that behavior on the other—with the result that a much more effective control of behavior has been achieved. It has long been argued that an organism learns mainly by producing changes in its environment, but it is only recently that these changes have been carefully manipulated. In traditional devices for the study of learning—in the serial maze, for example, or in the T-maze, the problem box, or the familiar discrimination apparatus—the effects produced by the organism's behavior are left to many fluctuating circumstances. There is many a slip between the turn-to-the-right and the food-cup at the end of the alley. It is not surprising that techniques of this sort have yielded only very rough data from which the uniformities demanded by an experimental science can be extracted only by averaging many cases. In none of this work has the behavior of the individual organism been predicted in more than a statistical sense. The learning processes which are the presumed object of such research are reached only through a series of inferences. Current preoccupation with deductive systems reflects this state of the science.

Harvard Educational Review, 24: 86–97, Spring, 1954. Used by permission of the *Harvard Educational Review* and B. F. Skinner.

[1] Paper presented at a conference on Current Trends in Psychology and the Behavioral Sciences at the University of Pittsburgh, March 12, 1954.

Recent improvements in the conditions which control behavior in the field of learning are of two principal sorts. The Law of Effect has been taken seriously; we have made sure that effects *do* occur and that they occur under conditions which are optimal for producing the changes called learning. Once we have arranged the particular type of consequence called a reinforcement, our techniques permit us to shape up the behavior of an organism almost at will. It has become a routine exercise to demonstrate this in classes in elementary psychology by conditioning such an organism as a pigeon. Simply by presenting food to a hungry pigeon at the right time, it is possible to shape up three or four well-defined responses in a single demonstration period—such responses as turning around, pacing the floor in the pattern of a figure-8, standing still in a corner of the demonstration apparatus, stretching the neck, or stamping the foot. Extremely complex performances may be reached through successive stages in the shaping process, the contingencies of reinforcement being changed progressively in the direction of the required behavior. The results are often quite dramatic. In such a demonstration one can *see* learning take place. A significant change in behavior is often obvious as the result of a single reinforcement.

A second important advance in technique permits us to maintain behavior in given states of strength for long periods of time. Reinforcements continue to be important, of course, long after an organism has learned *how* to do something, long after it has acquired behavior. They are necessary to maintain the behavior in strength. Of special interest is the effect of various schedules of intermittent reinforcement. Charles B. Ferster and the author are currently preparing an extensive report of a five-year research program, sponsored by the Office of Naval Research, in which most of the important types of schedules have been investigated and in which the effects of schedules in general have been reduced to a few principles. On the theoretical side we now have a fairly good idea of why a given schedule produces its appropriate performance. On the practical side we have learned how to maintain any given level of activity for daily periods limited only by the physical exhaustion of the organism and from day to day without substantial change throughout its life. Many of these effects would be traditionally assigned to the field of motivation, although the principal operation is simply the arrangement of contingencies of reinforcement.[2]

These new methods of shaping behavior and of maintaining it in strength

[2] The reader may wish to review Dr. Skinner's article, "Some Contributions of an Experimental Analysis of Behavior to Psychology as a Whole," *The American Psychologist*, 1953, 8, 69–78.

are a great improvement over the traditional practices of professional animal trainers, and it is not surprising that our laboratory results are already being applied to the production of performing animals for commercial purposes. In a more academic environment they have been used for demonstration purposes which extend far beyond an interest in learning as such. For example, it is not too difficult to arrange the complex contingencies which produce many types of social behavior. Competition is exemplified by two pigeons playing a modified game of ping-pong. The pigeons drive the ball back and forth across a small table by pecking at it. When the ball gets by one pigeon, the other is reinforced. The task of constructing such a "social relation" is probably completely out of reach of the traditional animal trainer. It requires a carefully designed program of gradually changing contingencies and the skillful use of schedules to maintain the behavior in strength. Each pigeon is separately prepared for its part in the total performance, and the "social relation" is then arbitrarily constructed. The sequence of events leading up to this stable state are excellent material for the study of the factors important in nonsynthetic social behavior. It is instructive to consider how a similar series of contingencies could arise in the case of the human organism through the evolution of cultural patterns.

Cooperation can also be set up, perhaps more easily than competition. We have trained two pigeons to coordinate their behavior in a cooperative endeavor with a precision which equals that of the most skillful human dancers. In a more serious vein these techniques have permitted us to explore the complexities of the individual organism and to analyze some of the serial or coordinate behaviors involved in attention, problem solving, various types of self-control, and the subsidiary systems of responses within a single organism called "personalities." Some of these are exemplified in what we call multiple schedules of reinforcement. In general a given schedule has an effect upon the rate at which a response is emitted. Changes in the rate from moment to moment show a pattern typical of the schedule. The pattern may be as simple as a constant rate of responding at a given value, it may be a gradually accelerating rate between certain extremes, it may be an abrupt change from not responding at all to a given stable high rate, and so on. It has been shown that the performance characteristic of a given schedule can be brought under the control of a particular stimulus and that different performances can be brought under the control of different stimuli in the same organism. At a recent meeting of the American Psychological Association, Dr. Ferster and the author demonstrated a pigeon whose behavior showed the pattern typical of "fixed-interval" reinforcement in the presence of one stimulus and, alternately, the pattern typical of the very different schedule called "fixed ratio" in the presence of a second stimulus. In the laboratory we have been able to obtain performances appropriate to *nine* different schedules in the presence of appropriate stimuli in random alternation. When Stimulus 1 is present, the pigeon executes the performance appropriate to Schedule 1. When Stimulus 2 is present, the pigeon executes the performance appropriate to Schedule 2. And so on. This result is important because it makes the extrapolation of our laboratory results to daily life much more plausible. We are all constantly shifting from schedule to schedule as our immediate environment changes, but the dynamics of the control exercised by reinforcement remain essentially unchanged.

It is also possible to construct very complex *sequences* of schedules. It is not easy to describe these in a few words, but two or three examples may be mentioned. In one experiment the pigeon generates a performance appropriate to Schedule A where the reinforcement is simply the production of the stimulus characteristic of Schedule B, to which the pigeon then responds appropriately. Under a third stimulus, the bird yields a perform-ance appropriate to Schedule C where the reinforcement in this case is simply the production of the stimulus characteristic of Schedule D, to which the bird then responds appropriately. In a special case, first investigated by L. B. Wyckoff, Jr., the organism responds to one stimulus where the rein-forcement consists of the *clarification* of the stimulus controlling another response. The first response becomes, so to speak, an objective form of "paying attention" to the second stimulus. In one important version of this experiment, as yet unpublished, we could say that the pigeon is telling us whether it is "paying attention" to the *shape* of a spot of light or to its *color*.

One of the most dramatic applications of these techniques has recently been made in the Harvard Psychological Laboratories by Floyd Ratliff and Donald S. Blough, who have skillfully used multiple and serial schedules of reinforcement to study complex perceptual processes in the infrahuman organism. They have achieved a sort of psycho-physics without verbal instruction. In a recent experiment by Blough, for example, a pigeon draws a detailed dark-adaptation curve showing the characteristic breaks of rod and cone vision. The curve is recorded continuously in a single experi-mental period and is quite comparable with the curves of human subjects. The pigeon behaves in a way which, in the human case, we would not hesitate to describe by saying that it adjusts a very faint patch of light until it can just be seen.

In all this work, the species of the organism has made surprisingly little difference. It is true that the organisms studied have all been vertebrates, but they still cover a wide range. Comparable results have been obtained with pigeons, rats, dogs, monkeys, human children, and most recently, by the author in collaboration with Ogden R. Lindsley, human psychotic subjects. In spite of great phylogenetic differences, all these organisms show amazingly similar properties of the learning process. It should be emphasized that this has been achieved by analyzing the effects of reinforcement and by designing techniques which manipulate reinforcement with considerable precision. Only in this way can the behavior of the individual organism be brought under such precise control. It is also important to note that through a gradual advance to complex interrelations among responses, the same degree of rigor is being extended to behavior which would usually be assigned to such fields as perception, thinking, and personality dynamics.

From this exciting prospect of an advancing science of learning, it is a great shock to turn to that branch of technology which is most directly concerned with the learning process—education. Let us consider, for example, the teaching of arithmetic in the lower grades. The school is concerned with imparting to the child a large number of responses of a special sort. The responses are all verbal. They consist of speaking and writing certain words, figures, and signs which, to put it roughly, refer to numbers and to arithmetic operations. The first task is to shape up these responses—to get the child to pronounce and to write responses correctly, but the principal task is to bring this behavior under many sorts of stimulus control. This is what happens when the child learns to count, to recite tables, to count while ticking off the items in an assemblage of objects, to respond to spoken or written numbers by saying "odd," "even," "prime," and so on. Over and above this elaborate repertoire of numerical behavior, most of which is often dismissed as the product of rote learning, the teaching of arithmetic looks forward to those complex serial arrangements of responses involved in original mathematical thinking. The child must acquire responses of transposing, clearing fractions, and so on, which modify the order or pattern of the original material so that the response called a solution is eventually made possible.

Now, how is this extremely complicated verbal repertoire set up? In the first place, what reinforcements are used? Fifty years ago the answer would have been clear. At that time educational control was still frankly aversive. The child read numbers, copied numbers, memorized tables, and performed operations upon numbers to escape the threat of the birch rod or cane. Some positive reinforcements were perhaps eventually derived from the increased efficiency of the child in the field of arithmetic and in rare cases some automatic reinforcement may have resulted from the sheer manipulation of the medium—from the solution of problems or the discovery of the intricacies of the number system. But for the immediate purposes of education the child acted to avoid or escape punishment. It was part of the reform movement known as progressive education to make the positive consequences more immediately effective, but any one who visits the lower grades of the average school today will observe that a change has been made, not from aversive to positive control, but from one form of aversive stimulation to another. The child at his desk, filling in his workbook, is behaving primarily to escape from the threat of a series of minor aversive events—the teacher's displeasure, the criticism or ridicule of his classmates, an ignominious showing in a competition, low marks, a trip to the office "to be talked to" by the principal, or a word to the parent who may still resort to the birch rod. In this welter of aversive consequences, getting the right answer is in itself an insignificant event, any effect of which is lost amid the anxieties, the boredom, and the aggressions which are the inevitable by-products of aversive control.[3]

Secondly, we have to ask how the contingencies of reinforcement are arranged. When is a numerical operation reinforced as "right"? Eventually, of course, the pupil may be able to check his own answers and achieve some sort of automatic reinforcement, but in the early stages the reinforcement of being right is usually accorded by the teacher. The contingencies she provides are far from optimal. It can easily be demonstrated that, unless explicit mediating behavior has been set up, the lapse of only a few seconds between response and reinforcement destroys most of the effect. In a typical classroom, nevertheless, long periods of time customarily elapse. The teacher may walk up and down the aisle, for example, while the class is working on a sheet of problems, pausing here and there to say right or wrong. Many seconds or minutes intervene between the child's response and the teacher's reinforcement. In many cases—for example, when papers are taken home to be corrected—as much as 24 hours may intervene. It is surprising that this system has any effect whatsoever.

A third notable shortcoming is the lack of a skillful program which moves forward through a series of progressive approximations to the final complex behavior desired. A long series of contingencies is necessary to bring the organism into the possession of mathematical behavior most efficiently. But the teacher is seldom able to reinforce at each step in such a

[3] Skinner, B. F. *Science and Human Behavior.* New York: Macmillan, 1953.

series because she cannot deal with the pupil's responses one at a time. It is usually necessary to reinforce the behavior in blocks of responses—as in correcting a work sheet or page from a workbook. The responses within such a block must not be interrelated. The answer to one problem must not depend upon the answer to another. The number of stages through which one may progressively approach a complex pattern of behavior is therefore small, and the task so much the more difficult. Even the most modern workbook in beginning arithmetic is far from exemplifying an efficient program for shaping up mathematical behavior.

Perhaps the most serious criticism of the current classroom is the relative infrequency of reinforcement. Since the pupil is usually dependent upon the teacher for being right, and since many pupils are usually dependent upon the same teacher, the total number of contingencies which may be arranged during, say, the first four years, is of the order of only a few thousand. But a very rough estimate suggests that efficient mathematical behavior at this level requires something of the order of 25,000 contingencies. We may suppose that even in the brighter student a given contingency must be arranged several times to place the behavior well in hand. The responses to be set up are not simply the various items in tables of addition, subtraction, multiplication, and division; we have also to consider the alternative forms in which each item may be stated. To the learning of such material we should add hundreds of responses concerned with factoring, identifying primes, memorizing series, using short-cut techniques of calculation, constructing and using geometric representations or number forms, and so on. Over and above all this, the whole mathematical repertoire must be brought under the control of concrete problems of considerable variety. Perhaps 50,000 contingencies is a more conservative estimate. In this frame of reference the daily assignment in arithmetic seems pitifully meagre.

The result of all this is, of course, well known. Even our best schools are under criticism for their inefficiency in the teaching of drill subjects such as arithmetic. The condition in the average school is a matter of widespread national concern. Modern children simply do not learn arithmetic quickly or well. Nor is the result simply incompetence. The very subjects in which modern techniques are weakest are those in which failure is most conspicuous, and in the wake of an ever-growing incompetence come the anxieties, uncertainties, and aggressions which in their turn present other problems to the school. Most pupils soon claim the asylum of not being "ready" for arithmetic at a given level or, eventually, of not having a mathematical mind. Such explanations are readily seized upon by defensive teachers and parents. Few pupils ever reach the stage at which automatic reinforcements follow as the natural consequences of mathematical behavior. On the contrary, the figures and symbols of mathematics have become standard emotional stimuli. The glimpse of a column of figures, not to say an algebraic symbol or an integral sign, is likely to set off—not mathematical behavior—but a reaction of anxiety, guilt, or fear.

The teacher is usually no happier about this than the pupil. Denied the opportunity to control via the birch rod, quite at sea as to the mode of operation of the few techniques at her disposal, she spends as little time as possible on drill subjects and eagerly subscribes to philosophies of education which emphasize material of greater inherent interest. A confession of weakness is her extraordinary concern lest the child be taught something unnecessary. The repertoire to be imparted is carefully reduced to an essential minimum. In the field of spelling, for example, a great deal of time and energy has gone into discovering just those words which the young child is going to use, as if it were a crime to waste one's educational power in teaching an unnecessary word. Eventually, weakness of technique emerges in the disguise of a reformulation of the aims of education. Skills are minimized in favor of vague achievements—educating for democracy, educating the whole child, educating for life, and so on. And there the matter ends; for, unfortunately, these philosophies do not in turn suggest improvements in techniques. They offer little or no help in the design of better classroom practices.

There would be no point in urging these objections if improvement were impossible. But the advances which have recently been made in our control of the learning process suggest a thorough revision of classroom practices and, fortunately, they tell us how the revision can be brought about. This is not, of course, the first time that the results of an experimental science have been brought to bear upon the practical problems of education. The modern classroom does not, however, offer much evidence that research in the field of learning has been respected or used. This condition is no doubt partly due to the limitations of earlier research. But it has been encouraged by a too hasty conclusion that the laboratory study of learning is inherently limited because it cannot take into account the realities of the classroom. In the light of our increasing knowledge of the learning process we should, instead, insist upon dealing with those realities and forcing a substantial change in them. Education is perhaps the most important branch of scientific technology. It deeply affects the lives of all of us. We can no longer allow the exigencies of a practical situation to suppress the tremendous improvements which are within reach. The practical situation must be changed.

There are certain questions which have to be answered in turning to the study of any new organism. What behavior is to be set up? What reinforcers are at hand? What responses are available in embarking upon a program of progressive approximation which will lead to the final form of the behavior? How can reinforcements be most efficiently scheduled to maintain the behavior in strength? These questions are all relevant in considering the problem of the child in the lower grades.

In the first place, what reinforcements are available? What does the school have in its possession which will reinforce a child? We may look first to the material to be learned, for it is possible that this will provide considerable automatic reinforcement. Children play for hours with mechanical toys, paints, scissors and paper, noise-makers, puzzles—in short, with almost anything which feeds back significant changes in the environment and is reasonably free of aversive properties. The sheer control of nature is itself reinforcing. This effect is not evident in the modern school because it is masked by the emotional responses generated by aversive control. It is true that automatic reinforcement from the manipulation of the environment is probably only a mild reinforcer and may need to be carefully husbanded, but one of the most striking principles to emerge from recent research is that the *net* amount of reinforcement is of little significance. A very slight reinforcement may be tremendously effective in controlling behavior if it is wisely used.

If the natural reinforcement inherent in the subject matter is not enough, other reinforcers must be employed. Even in school the child is occasionally permitted to do "what he wants to do," and access to reinforcements of many sorts may be made contingent upon the more immediate consequences of the behavior to be established. Those who advocate competition as a useful social motive may wish to use the reinforcements which follow from excelling others, although there is the difficulty that in this case the reinforcement of one child is necessarily aversive to another. Next in order we might place the good will and affection of the teacher, and only when that has failed need we turn to the use of aversive stimulation.

In the second place, how are these reinforcements to be made contingent upon the desired behavior? There are two considerations here—the gradual elaboration of extremely complex patterns of behavior and the maintenance of the behavior in strength at each stage. The whole process of becoming competent in any field must be divided into a very large number of very small steps, and reinforcement must be contingent upon the accomplishment of each step. This solution to the problem of creating a complex repertoire of behavior also solves the problem of maintaining the behavior in strength. We could, of course, resort to the techniques of scheduling already developed in the study of other organisms but in the present state of our knowledge of educational practices, scheduling appears to be most effectively arranged through the design of the material to be learned. By making each successive step as small as possible, the frequency of reinforcement can be raised to a maximum, while the possibly aversive consequences of being wrong are reduced to a minimum. Other ways of designing material would yield other programs of reinforcement. Any supplementary reinforcement would probably have to be scheduled in the more traditional way.

These requirements are not excessive, but they are probably incompatible with the current realities of the classroom. In the experimental study of learning it has been found that the contingencies of reinforcement which are most efficient in controlling the organism cannot be arranged through the personal mediation of the experimenter. An organism is affected by subtle details of contingencies which are beyond the capacity of the human organism to arrange. Mechanical and electrical devices must be used. Mechanical help is also demanded by the sheer number of contingencies which may be used efficiently in a single experimental session. We have recorded many millions of responses from a single organism during thousands of experimental hours. Personal arrangement of the contingencies and personal observation of the results are quite unthinkable. Now, the human organism is, if anything, more sensitive to precise contingencies than the other organisms we have studied. We have every reason to expect, therefore, that the most effective control of human learning will require instrumental aid. The simple fact is that, as a mere reinforcing mechanism, the teacher is out of date. This would be true even if a single teacher devoted all her time to a single child, but her inadequacy is multiplied many-fold when she must serve as a reinforcing device to many children at once. If the teacher is to take advantage of recent advances in the study of learning, she must have the help of mechanical devices.

The technical problem of providing the necessary instrumental aid is not particularly difficult. There are many ways in which the necessary contingencies may be arranged, either mechanically or electrically. An inexpensive device which solves most of the principal problems has already been constructed. It is still in the experimental stage, but a description will suggest the kind of instrument which seems to be required. The device consists of a small box about the size of a small record player. On the top surface is a window through which a question or problem printed on a paper tape may be seen. The child answers the question by moving one or more sliders upon which the digits 0 through 9 are printed. The answer appears in square holes punched in the paper upon which the question is printed. When the answer has been set, the child turns a knob. The operation is as simple as adjusting a television set. If the answer is right, the knob turns freely and can be made to ring a bell or provide some other conditioned reinforcement. If the answer is wrong, the knob will not turn. A counter may be added to tally wrong answers. The knob must then be reversed slightly and a second attempt at a right answer made. (Unlike the flash-card, the device reports a wrong answer without giving the right answer.) When the answer is right, a further turn of the knob engages a clutch which moves the next problem into place in the window. This movement cannot be completed, however, until the sliders have been returned to zero.

The important features of the device are these: Reinforcement for the right answer is immediate. The mere manipulation of the device will probably be reinforcing enough to keep the average pupil at work for a suitable period each day, provided traces of earlier aversive control can be wiped out. A teacher may supervise an entire class at work on such devices at the same time, yet each child may progress at his own rate, completing as many problems as possible within the class period. If forced to be away from school, he may return to pick up where he left off. The gifted child will advance rapidly, but can be kept from getting too far ahead either by being excused from arithmetic for a time or by being given special sets of problems which take him into some of the interesting bypaths of mathematics.

The device makes it possible to present carefully designed material in which one problem can depend upon the answer to the preceding and where, therefore, the most efficient progress to an eventually complex repertoire can be made. Provision has been made for recording the commonest mistakes so that the tapes can be modified as experience dictates. Additional steps can be inserted where pupils tend to have trouble, and ultimately the material will reach a point at which the answers of the average child will almost always be right.

If the material itself proves not to be sufficiently reinforcing, other reinforcers in the possession of the teacher or school may be made contingent upon the operation of the device or upon progress through a series of problems. Supplemental reinforcement would not sacrifice the advantages gained from immediate reinforcement and from the possibility of constructing an optimal series of steps which approach the complex repertoire of mathematical behavior most efficiently.

A similar device in which the sliders carry the letters of the alphabet has been designed to teach spelling. In addition to the advantages which can be gained from precise reinforcement and careful programming, the device will teach reading at the same time. It can also be used to establish the large and important repertoire of verbal relationships encountered in logic and science. In short, it can teach verbal thinking. As to content instruction, the device can be operated as a multiple-choice self-rater.

Some objections to the use of such devices in the classroom can easily be foreseen. The cry will be raised that the child is being treated as a mere animal and that an essentially human intellectual achievement is being analyzed in unduly mechanistic terms. Mathematical behavior is usually regarded, not as a repertoire of responses involving numbers and numerical operations, but as evidences of mathematical ability or the exercise of the power of reason. It is true that the techniques which are emerging from the experimental study of learning are not designed to "develop the mind" or to further some vague "understanding" of mathematical relationships. They are designed, on the contrary, to establish the very behaviors which are taken to be the evidences of such mental states or processes. This is only a special case of the general change which is under way in the interpretation of human affairs. An advancing science continues to offer more and more convincing alternatives to traditional formulations. The behavior in terms of which human thinking must eventually be defined is worth treating in its own right as the substantial goal of education.

Of course the teacher has a more important function than to say right or wrong. The changes proposed would free her for the effective exercise of that function. Marking a set of papers in arithmetic—"Yes, nine and six *are* fifteen; no, nine and seven *are not* eighteen"—is beneath the dignity of any intelligent individual. There is more important work to be done— in which the teacher's relations to the pupil cannot be duplicated by a mechanical device. Instrumental help would merely improve these relations. One might say that the main trouble with education in the lower grades today is that the child is obviously not competent and *knows it* and that the teacher is unable to do anything about it and *knows that too.* If the advances which have recently been made in our control of behavior can give the child a genuine competence in reading, writing, spelling, and arith- metic, then the teacher may begin to function, not in lieu of a cheap machine, but through intellectual, cultural, and emotional contacts of that distinctive sort which testify to her status as a human being.

Another possible objection is that mechanized instruction will mean technological unemployment. We need not worry about this until there are enough teachers to go around and until the hours and energy demanded of the teacher are comparable to those in other fields of employment. Mechanical devices will eliminate the more tiresome labors of the teacher but they will not necessarily shorten the time during which she remains in contact with the pupil.

A more practical objection: Can we afford to mechanize our schools? The answer is clearly yes. The device I have just described could be produced as cheaply as a small radio or phonograph. There would need to be far fewer devices than pupils, for they could be used in rotation. But even if we suppose that the instrument eventually found to be most effective would cost several hundred dollars and that large numbers of them would be required, our economy should be able to stand the strain. Once we have accepted the possibility and the necessity of mechanical help in the classroom, the economic problem can easily be surmounted. There is no reason why the school room should be any less mechanized than, for example, the kitchen. A country which annually produces millions of refrigerators, dishwashers, automatic washing-machines, automatic clothes-driers, and automatic garbage disposers can certainly afford the equipment necessary to educate its citizens to high standards of competence in the most effective way.

There is a simple job to be done. The task can be stated in concrete terms. The necessary techniques are known. The equipment needed can easily be provided. Nothing stands in the way but cultural inertia. But what is more characteristic of America than an unwillingness to accept the traditional as inevitable? We are on the threshold of an exciting and revolutionary period, in which the scientific study of man will be put to work in man's best interests. Education must play its part. It must accept the fact that a sweeping revision of educational practices is possible and inevitable. When it has done this, we may look forward with confidence to a school system which is aware of the nature of its tasks, secure in its methods, and generously supported by the informed and effective citizens whom education itself will create.

EDWARD C. WEIR

Associate Professor of Education, University of Pittsburgh

5 · THE MEANING OF LEARNING AND THE LEARNING OF MEANING

• Educators have been increasingly engaged in recent years in discussion and experimentation which point to systematic thinking as both process and goal in teaching and learning. Some of our academic brethren—those who have finally come realistically to grips with the questions of what to teach and how to teach— are beginning to come around to the point of view that in teaching our emphasis should be not so much on assimilation of thought as it is on thinking. This discussion has centered largely on methodological approaches to helping students to discover (or create), analyze, and test ideas which they can use to solve problems and to explain and order the phenomena of existence. Emphasis is upon the "problem of warranted belief, and how teachers may help students determine whether there is any warrant for holding certain beliefs."[1] The methodology depends heavily on principles of formal logic. With regard to the organization of the curriculum, it is urged that ". . . the curriculum of a subject should be determined by the most fundamental understanding that can be achieved of the underlying principles that give structure to that subject."[2]

In what follows, it is not at all our intent to disparage this "new" focus in educational thought. We are most heartily receptive to any effort which

Phi Delta Kappan, 46: 280–284, 1965. Reprinted by permission of Phi Delta Kappa.

[1] L. E. Metcalf, "The Reflective Teacher," *Phi Delta Kappan*, October, 1962.

[2] Jerome S. Bruner, *The Process of Education.* Cambridge, Mass.; Harvard University Press. 1960, p. 51.

conceives of the human entity as an awareness and a seeking after meaning, a disposition to order and control experience. Such efforts are especially fortuitous at this particular time when the behavior of rats is seriously being proposed as the model for explanations of human behavior and technological and curricular gadgetry as the nostrum for the ailments of education. In view of these developments, it is gratifying to realize that dedicated educational thinkers and researchers are working diligently and without the doubtful advantage of great fanfare under the assumption that humanness is a unique phenomenon in the world and that the potential of the human consciousness unfolds through continuing experiences in reflective choice-making with regard to the dilemmas of existence.

However, it is our feeling that, in giving attention to the development of a logicalistic methodology for teaching and learning, we may overlook the *person* who is to teach and the *person* who is to learn. We need to remind ourselves of the ultimately *subjective* nature of thinking and learning, of knowledge and meaning. Principles of logic do not objectively exist; they only exist in *persons* who understand, accept, and use them in their thinking and learning. Knowledge exists in someone knowing. Concepts exist in someone conceptualizing. Meaning is not objectively *in* the universe; it exists in a particular individual *person's* awareness as he perceives his own identity and relatedness. Reflective thinking, which is an attribute of the highest order of human behavior, obviously can only occur in persons who are *subjectively* disposed and able to think reflectively. Critical examination of one's beliefs and behavior is not merely an operation in logic; it is an operation requiring a high degree of psychological competence. By the same token, the reflective teacher is not merely a logician; he is a *person* who is able to function reflectively as a person within the intricate complex of meanings and motivations, dreams and disappointments, hates and hopes and fears and loves that exist in the persons he is to teach. If he is to teach—that is, if he is to help his students to grow in their ability to function reflectively—it is important that he have competence in logic and that he have profound intimacy with the structure of his subject. However, it is at least of equal importance that he be the kind of human being who can relate personally to his students in such a way that they become psychologically free to create themselves, to engage themselves fully and courageously in the hazardous project of examining and reconstructing the meaning of their own living.

A man is an idea; he is what he perceives himself to be and what he perceives himself as becoming. An idea is a man; it comes into being as a man discovers it or creates it and employs it in shaping the essence of his living.

Translated into a concept of learning, this statement means that an individual has learned when he integrates into himself a new meaning, a meaning that has such personal significance in his awareness that the quality and direction of his existence are in some way different than they were before.

What do we mean by "meaning"? We suggest a subjective definition.

Meaning is the order imposed upon experience by the individual as he becomes aware of the interrelationships between the self and the phenomena encountered in his experience. An examination of some common usages of the term in its verb form may help to clarify our definition.

When in response to some fact or event, I say, "Now *that* really *means* something!", I am actually saying that the fact or event has significance for *me,* that it fits in or perhaps reinforces my way of looking at things, that it somehow serves what I conceive to be the purposes of *my* thinking and doing. My statement indicates that I have a fairly sharp awareness of how I should relate my own behavior to the fact or event. When, on the other hand, I respond to a friend's statement of an idea with the query, "Now, just what do you *mean* by that?", I am not only asking my friend what the statement means to him. I am also requesting a rephrasing or clarification of the intent of the statement so that I can see how it relates to me and thus determine the "sense" of the statement. And, of course, if the friend is not able to explain his statement so that I can catch at least a fleeting awareness of the relatedness of what he is saying to my own unique perceptions of reality, then the statement will never have meaning for me. Or, to illustrate with another common usage, when we say we "mean" to do a certain thing, we are saying that we shall henceforth impose an order upon certain of our experiences in the light of our intent, and the quality of the meaning in those experiences will be determined by the nature of our intent and the order which that intent dictates.

Perhaps a description and analysis of a little introspective experience on the part of the author will serve to illustrate our concept of the "meaning of meaning."

I sat before my desk a short while ago "staring into space" as I attempted to organize my thoughts in the direction of a statement of the concept of meaning being employed in this paper. My eyes chanced to hit upon an object whose meaning was very familiar to me—a box of facial tissues atop a filing cabinet in the far corner of this room. The meaning of the object was very familiar to me, but from the instant my eyes touched upon the object, its meaning began to change. It began to change because my eye had not actually "chanced" to hit upon the box of tissues. I was looking for something to use in my efforts to think through an adequate explanation of the nature of meaning. Looking upon the thing and thinking about it in this way caused it to take on a greatly different meaning than if I were looking for something to wipe my nose or mop up a puddle of spilled ice water. The meaning of the very tangible box of facial tissues began to take on a highly abstract quality as I struggled to identify the elements which determine the meaning of the object for me and to formulate these elements into the generalizations essential to an adequate explanation of meaning—as I sought, in other words, to impose a new order upon the object in the light of a newly perceived relationship between the object and a purpose I had defined for myself. I began to see, for example, that the meaning, "box of facial tissues," is determined by the object's relationships to a whole host of other objects—the ways in which it is the same as or different than other objects. But I also began to see that this relationship is an organization which *I* apply in trying to integrate this object into the structure of meanings which other objects have for me. Furthermore, it seemed to me that however abstract or tangible any experiential phenomenon may be, its meaning depends upon the way *I* perceive its function for *me* in the particular situation in which I experience it. A head cold?—the box becomes a container of nose-massagers. Surrounded and outnumbered by the enemy?—a flag of surrender. Watching a favorite TV program?—a commercialized interruption of a pleasant diversion resulting in trips to bathroom or refrigerator. Thinking about meaning?—a system of abstractions. Trying to explain a concept of meaning?—the box of facial tissues becomes a graphic device which may serve illustrative purposes. The particular way I react to an object in a particular situation signifies the meaning the object has for me in that situation.

As expressed by Lewin, "The 'meaning' of an event in psychology may be said to be known if its psychological position and its psychological direction are determined. In Mark Twain's *Life on the Mississippi,* the passengers on the boat enjoy the 'scenery,' but for the pilot the V-shape of the two hills, which a passenger admires, means a signal to turn sharply, the beautiful waves in the middle of the river mean dangerous rocks. The psychological connection of these 'stimuli' with actions has changed, and therefore the meaning has changed."[3]

It is true that the order I impose upon a given experiential situation may be an objectively illogical order, completely or partially out of conformity with reality. I may completely or partially misinterpret the rela-

[3] Kurt Lewin, "Field Theory and Learning," in Nelson B. Henry (ed.), *The Psychology of Learning,* 41st Yearbook, Part II, National Society for the Study of Education. Bloomington, Ill.: Public School Publishing Co., 1942, p. 229.

tionship the event or object has with my goals and values, so that my behavior, as a result, will be seen by others to be inappropriate. But it is the relationship *I* see, the order *I* impose, and to me, therefore, my behavior will seem quite appropriate—until such time as my pattern of meanings takes on a new and perhaps more realistic configuration. Herein, of course, lies the task of education—*to help the young to discover and take into themselves increasingly more realistic and encompassing meanings with concomitantly increased efficiency of behavior.* Rigorous application of principles of logic, together with understanding of the fundamental structure of organized knowledge, are essential in the development of a pattern of subjective meaning that is consistent and whole, but one must also be psychologically consistent and whole if he is to recognize the inappropriateness of his perceptions of reality.

If it were not for the fact that personal meaning can be distorted and inconsistent with reality, it would be almost a tautology to say that the task of education is to help the young to discover and incorporate increasingly more adequate meanings into their experience. Meaning, as we have defined it, is present in some degree in all learning. And conversely, if the individual can find no meaning in a situation, he will learn nothing in that situation.

In the often-used example of the child touching the hot stove, the evidence of learning lies not in the fact of withdrawal from the source of pain but rather in the subsequent consistency of the child's avoidance behavior with respect to the stove. From this subsequent consistency of behavior, we can infer that for the child the stove has taken on a new meaning. The stove signifies pain, and sharp physical discomfort is the quality of relationship which the child "sees" between the stove and himself. He thus discriminates the stove from other objects in the room; it takes on a more precise configuration for him. He also generalizes about the object he has thus discriminated, and, for this reason, is able to behave appropriately with respect to the object when he encounters it again. The world has become a little more meaningful for the child. He has learned, and his living, therefore, becomes a little more efficient. If he were not able to discriminate and generalize in this way from his experiences with this object, his experiences with the stove might well be disastrous.

The relationship that the child has discovered and the order he has imposed on his experience are not the results of "systematic reasoning." The new meaning was acquired at a relatively low level of cognitive activity. Nevertheless, there was a "sensing" of, a conscious awareness of, new relationships, and this meets the requirements of our definition of meaning. The phenomenon of intuitive creation of new meaning, however, is not always evidence of childishness of thought. A powerful new idea frequently emerges in the consciousness of the creative thinker prior to the application of logic and often in the face of what appears to be logical. The procedures of logic are needed to test and validate the new idea, but perhaps we need to give more attention to the pre-logical processes which operate so mysteriously in our children and in our Einsteins and Beethovens to produce a new richness of meaning where no meaning existed before.

All learning, then, involves an increase in the learner's store of personal meanings or a shift or re-patterning of perceptual structure and is accompanied or followed by relevant changes in behavior.

The reasonableness of this statement is clear. A situation must mean something to the individual if he is to respond to it. If it means nothing to him, he will not respond to it (except at the level of reflex action which does not involve learning). Psychologically, it is impossible for him to respond to it. If he cannot respond to the situation, he obviously cannot learn from it. "Through perception we learn," Kingsley and Garry declare, and "without perception there could be no learning except possibly that of the most primitive and meager sort."[4] And Hartmann, several years ago, stated the case even more strongly.

> . . . it should be stressed that no experience or stimulus is ever meaningless or valueless in a strict sense. It may have little meaning, a distorted meaning, or an ugly meaning, but anything that affects a person and provokes a reaction from him cannot be strictly devoid of meaning. . . . An experience with zero meaning is psychologically nonexistent. Rote learning, the curse of all inadequate instruction, defines one end of the meaning continuum and "logical" or "systematic" learning the other; but absolutely it is present all along the line.[5]

The "meaning continuum" mentioned by Hartmann is a useful device. It helps to explain learning which occurs in situations which are apparently meaningless, or almost meaningless, such as the acquisition of motor skills or arbitrary associations through procedures of drill and rote memorization. Much of our learning is of this type. We learn to bat a baseball or use a typewriter, we commonly think, through repetition of the movements involved in batting and typing, and this activity is neurophysical rather than

---

[4] Howard L. Kingsley and Ralph Garry, *The Nature and Conditions of Learning.* Englewood Cliffs, N. J.: Prentice-Hall, 1957, p. 329.

[5] George W. Hartmann, "The Field Theory of Learning and Its Educational Consequences," in Nelson B. Henry (ed.), *The Psychology of Learning*, 41st Yearbook, National Society for the Study of Education. Bloomington, Ill.: Public School Publishing Co., 1942, p. 190.

cognitive. There is no reasonable relationship among the letters of the alphabet, nor is there any reason why a combination of certain letters of the alphabet should signify the object "house" any more than there is for the fact that the symbol "2" should mean "two." These are arbitrary associations, pure and simple, and it is argued therefore that there is little sense in cluttering up the learning process by trying to make them meaningful. Efficiency of learning, some might say, requires that we simply repeat the associations a sufficient number of times so that they become fixated into the neurological system.

If we look more carefully into these situations, however, we will find that some degree of cognitive activity *is* involved, some degree of meaning, some association, form, or order is imposed by the learner. Furthermore, the more thoughtful, the more meaningful the learner's behavior in such situations, the more effective the learning will be. It is not a question of meaningful learning or non-meaningful learning. It is rather a matter of levels of meaningfulness in learning.

Our own experiences in requiring graduate and undergraduate students as an initiatory activity in the study of principles of instructional method to learn sets of nonsense syllables or numbers series have borne this out. Invariably, when students report and analyze the procedures they used in learning the material they indicate that they imposed some order—frequently unique or humorously "illogical"—upon the material in order to learn it.

When attempting to evaluate the effectiveness of learning we usually refer to two basic criteria: Has the learning significantly affected the learner's behavior? Will the learner be able to use the learning in life situations other than that in which the learning has occurred? There are no yes or no answers to these questions. For if any learning at all has occurred, there is some effect, however inconsequential, upon the learner's behavior; there will be some degree of transfer, however transitory. If the student memorizes the assigned facts in a history lesson in order to recite them and please the teacher, during the next day's recitation he is able to answer questions he was not previously able to answer. And if the teacher provides him with the "opportunity" of taking a "surprise quiz," he will probably be able to transfer much of the material from the recitation situation to the quiz situation. It is true that the facts he has learned may have little if any effect on the student's basic patterns of thinking and living. It is also true that he may find little use for the facts in other life situations —even if he is able to retain them beyond the classroom situation in which they were required.

Similarly, a student who has been exercised in logic may be able to repeat the procedure in analyzing generalizations and problems on an examination. He has learned that much; but if he does not perceive the applicability of the precedures to *his* problems and *his* explanations of existence, the learning remains superficial.

The point is that learning ranges along a continuum of effectiveness. The position of a given learning situation on the continuum is a function of the transferability of the learning and of the effect of the learning on the individual's behavior. And, in turn, it is the quality of personal meaningfulness, as we have defined it, which determines transfer and effect.

It will be recalled that in our definition of meaning we emphasized the individual's awareness of the interrelationships *between the self and the phenomena encountered in experience.* Such self-identification with phenomena is necessary not only in a learning situation; it is equally necessary in a transfer situation. The individual must see that the new situation has relationship to his own self-concept, to his own life purposes, values, and interests. If the student memorizes the facts of the history assignment or dutifully repeats the formulae of logic in order to accomplish the purpose of pleasing a teacher he likes, or merely as a titillating intellectual pastime, he is unlikely to transfer this learning to other situations in which the teacher is not present or intellectual titillation not his urgent concern. The individual must *see* the applicability of the learning in the new situation, and he must *want* to make the transfer.

In summation, what we have been saying is that learning is the self-incorporation of meaning into the subjectivity of the learner. The more deeply personal the meaning acquired through a learning experience, the more effective and lasting the learning will be. If allowances are made for the "intuitive hypothesis," the processes of systematic thinking are probably productive of the most highly dependable and fruitful meanings. We need to remember, however, that learning occurs only to the extent that these processes are internalized into the personality structure of the learner as an integral part of a way of living. The objective, in other words, must be subjectivized. This is not to imply a dichotomy between the objective activity of systematic thinking and the subjective activity of perception. It is rather to suggest that, since these two types of activity are inseparable in the dynamics of teaching-learning, there is need for exploring the possibilities of merging the thought and efforts of the proponents of both approaches to the study of the problems of teaching and learning.

MARY BEAUCHAMP
Assistant Professor of Education, New York University

6 · HOW SHOULD WE LOOK AT LEVELS—FROM THE PSYCHOLOGY OF LEARNING

> • *"Matt is not reading up to grade level." "Barbara is not working up to normal capacity." "Pete is too immature for this grade."*

We have yet to find a teacher who can relate the meaning of these oft-used cliches to what happens when a child learns. A dismaying proportion of school practice rests upon the premises that child growth and development can be standardized, that learning takes place *alike* in all children, that chronological age and grade level are valid concretenesses. These premises have been nullified by what we know about child growth and development and about how learning occurs. The only concept of levels that can be justified is that of the individual's recognition of his own levels of understanding, responses, insights, and comprehensions.

We shall attempt to state five principles of learning that belie the traditional levels concept in education, to identify briefly a few practices that urgently need examination, and to suggest some beacons of hope for the schools of the immediate future.

Principles of Learning

At least five important principles of learning, widely accepted in educational psychology, urge us to reconsider our practices in regard to levels.

Childhood Education, 32: 165–167, 1955. (From *Childhood Education*, December, 1955, Vol. 32, No. 4. Reprinted by permission of the Association for Childhood Education International, 3615 Wisconsin Avenue, NW, Washington, D.C. 20016, and the author, Mary Beauchamp Lane.)

The child learns with his whole body and the process cannot be reduced to an aggregation of parts. Kurt Lewin established that the child thinks with his whole body. His early experimentation, so ably validated by Arnold Gesell's work, depicts the whole organism responding with acceptance or rejection. James Harvey Robinson states this principle thus: "But no such mind, exempt from bodily processes, animal impulses, savage traditions, infantile impressions, conventional reactions, and traditional knowledge, ever existed."[1] Physiological differences—especially reaction time; temperament; stamina; reservoir, release, and control of energy—affect integrally the quality of learning.

The following authors have reported most forcibly the significance of physiological differences and the wide range of differences at any one age:

Boole, Mary E. *The Preparation of the Child for Science.* Oxford, England: Clarendon Press, 1904.
Child, C. M. *Physiological Foundations of Behavior.* New York: Henry Holt and Co., 1924.
Coghill, G. E. *Anatomy and the Problem of Behavior.* Cambridge, England: Cambridge University Press, 1929.
Ogden, R. M. "The Education of the Whole Child." *Educational Trends,* April–May, 1938, issue.
Olson, Willard C. *Child Development.* Boston: D. C. Heath and Company, 1949.
Prescott, Daniel. *Emotion and the Educative Process.* Washington, D.C.: American Council on Education, 1938.

Psychological differences are so intimately related to the physiological that as yet our efforts to analyze them separately have yielded us little. The experimentation being pursued in the area of perception has raised tremendously significant questions about what we once assumed was the commonality of our psychological worlds.

We are admonished today by pioneer thinkers to keep the parts wholly related to and integrated with the whole. The human being is more than a bundle of cells, neurons, a mass of systems—he is a unique individuality, an integrated personality. He is process. This process of learning with the whole body demands that levels, as they have been applied to standardized procedures, be scuttled for recognition of the concept of individual differences.

The whole organism must reach a stage of maturity before learning can be integrative. This is the second principle of learning belying levels. This stage cannot be hurried without serious damage to the total personality.

---

[1] James Harvey Robinson, *Mind in the Making.* New York: Harper and Brothers, 1950, p. 33.

Cobb[2] has attributed the high percent of insanity to getting abstract concepts in the cortex before their meaning has been taken in by the whole body. Thus when a child is ready to read, he reads, if he is among people who read. When he is ready to feed himself with a spoon, he picks up the spoon and begins stuffing the food in. Practice *after* the stage of maturity is reached improves the function. Practice *before* retards growth in the function and usually damages personality. The best cue to a stage of readiness is interest. The child tells us what he is ready for. We don't tell him— but we do if our emphasis is on a reading readiness program, if we require workbooks in kindergarten, or memorization of the nines in grade three.

Learning is largely a process of acculturation and takes place on an unconscious (unaware) level. One's language, ways of moving, gestures, habits, manners, and ways of relating are a result of his unique interaction with other human beings. Even if we could standardize human beings, we should still have to standardize culture if we were to pay homage to grade levels. Plant says: "It is disturbing to realize how little the schools recognize that their twelve grades should be one, single, meaningful process."[3] Boole wisely stated: "The process should always be learned through experience unconsciously, the principle involved coming to consciousness later." Experience, so diverse in a democratic culture, is crucial in enriching the learning that takes place unconsciously. The teacher's role is to contrive deep and broad enriching experiences—to which individuals may relate as their own uniquenesses dictate.

The distinctively human levels of learning—comprehensions, understandings, and insights—derive their quality from the meaningfulness of learning at lower levels. If organismic learning (described by "growth, differentiation, and performance of the manifold local functions") or neurological learning (described by functioning of reflexes, conditioning, adaptive adjustments, mass movements of the body as a whole) are faulty the quality of the human levels will be inferior. The interdependence of all levels of learning demands attention to the uniqueness of one's growth pattern. A human being can "respond to more kinds and gradations of environmental changes and with responses which are more rapid, more complex, more variable, more integrated, and finally more adaptive."[4] This is true only if the uniqueness of the individual is respected and held inviolate.

[2] Stanley Cobb, *A Preface to Nervous Diseases.* Baltimore: William Wood and Company, 1936.

[3] James Plant, "The Individual and His Environment," *Educational Trends,* April–May, 1938, issue.

[4] R. W. Gerard, "Higher Levels of Integration," *Biological Symposia.* Vol. VIII. Lancaster, Pa.: Jacques Cattell Press, 1942. p. 72.

Each must do his own learning. This fifth principle of learning requires serious attention. Learning cannot be coerced. The teacher may assign, may motivate, may demand. But the child learns only what he chooses to learn. If we are to succeed in teaching higher levels of aspiring, of valuing, of sharing and of communicating, we must take the trouble to recognize what Allport[5] calls the life-style of the individual. We must learn to regard the child as he regards himself. We must strike the right note and when we do, learning occurs. Our goal is so to work that each step "is an expression of the child's own plan of being and becoming."

Re-examination of Practices

The foregoing principles operate within the child, but many present practices hamper their functioning and result in an inferior quality of learning. Space allows us only a mention of these.

The concept of grade levels is perhaps our biggest harassment because this practice is so firmly entrenched. No place else in our culture do we limit associations to a span of a chronological year. This method of organization lends itself to standardization of method and content and to the concept of learning as a "funneling in" process.

An extension of the grade level concept is that of ability grouping. In its virulent form it appears as three levels of reading groups within a grade, or homogeneous grouping by grades. Such practices are antithetical to the wholeness concepts so vital to mental health. Gerard states: ". . . the problem is to keep them (men in a group) sufficiently different so that they have something unique and worthwhile to communicate to one another."[6]

A third practice that must be reconsidered is the system of rewards and punishments used as extraneous motivations for effort. The word incentive comes from a root word meaning to sound an instrument. We must abandon grades (often used as threats), competitive practices, and motivation-to-outdo for incentive if we are to expect quality in our human relationships.

The standardized content that comes from limiting teaching to basal texts and syllabi is another practice that stamps the misconception of levels upon our educational practices. Wholeness and uniqueness are fostered as we utilize a variety of materials, see that a wealth of interests is represented in those materials, and respect a wide margin of error in "trying out" as those materials are used.

[5] Gordon Allport, *Becoming*, Yale Univ. Press, 1955.
[6] Gerard, *op. cit.*, p. 83.

Beacons of Hope

And now a word about the other side of the coin. The beacon lights of schools designed and planned with and for children are spreading. Many primary schools are functioning so that children may achieve high levels of wholeness, and so that learning is integrative. We are learning that too much pressure, too soon applied, delays the acquisition of skill. A few schools are experiencing the challenge of grouping children representing an age span of three or four years—known as inter-age grouping. Thousands of teachers are recognizing that child study is one of the most productive inservice programs. And parents are likewise forming discussion groups to understand all children—not just *my child*. We are beginning to realize that the mind cannot be up-to-date by looking backwards during the period of schooling.

As we speak of levels, we advocate that we first recognize the fallacy of levels except as it applies to the individual's own recognition of his own internal growth factors and that we expand a concept of individual levels to include those really significant human functions of sharing, appreciating, valuing, communicating. These are functions not confined by verbal facility. They are the stuff of human relationships and give purpose to living and learning. As we help each child realize his own potentialities in satisfying his desires for communicating, for associating, for relating positively to others, for understanding himself and for sharing his own self, we shall be reaching higher and higher levels of learning. For as Lao-tzu said, "The way to do is to be."

EDUCATIONAL IMPLICATIONS OF TRANSFER

• Knowledge is accumulated by small steps and close examination of restricted phenomena as well as by brilliant and inclusive insights. In this section are cited some examples of the examination of a restricted phenomenon. Transfer of learning has been a focus of concern ever since the organization of educational psychology as a distinct discipline. It will remain a concern, because without transfer the advantage of formal education would be small. There is just too much to be learned by all of us, teachers and pupils, to perform necessary learnings in every specific instance. Transfer simply means that once something is learned in situation A, the time required is lessened or the strength of acquisition improved when learning situation B.[1]

The article by McIntyre and Dingman serves not only to show how the classical conditions of transfer—the nature of the material, the methods of teaching, and the characteristics of the learner—influence transfer, but also to show how detailed experiments in learning must be. Reading the article tends to remind us of how slowly accurate knowledge accumulates.

The article introduces some measurement terms that will be encountered again and again—here and elsewhere in professional literature. The reader is asked to pause long enough to make these terms understandable.

Mean—the arithmetical average. The sum of the scores divided by the number of cases (pupils).

[1] Harold W. Bernard, *Psychology of Learning and Teaching*, 2nd ed. (New York: McGraw-Hill Book Company, 1965), p. 59.

N—number of cases.

Standard deviation (SD)—a statistic used to express the extent the deviations, or variations, from the mean of a distribution. The first example in the article, 3.10, means that in approximately 68 per cent, or two-thirds of the cases, the IQ would fall within plus or minus one SD from the mean, i.e., plus or minus 3.1 on either side of 125 and within the range 121.9 to 128.1.

The article by Johnson and Stratton uses the foregoing statistical terms plus the term *reliability*. This refers to the extent to which one measurement, or score, will duplicate a repeated measurement of the same thing on the same person. The extent is indicated by a coefficient of correlation between the two measures. The statistics are there to tell a story, and the reader will see that while it takes several pages to present the material in a discourse, a table presents the same material in half a page. This is another way of saying, "Don't run away from those statistics, but learn to understand them and save yourself time in reading other educational and psychological literature." An important generalization that stems from the article is that learning by several methods results in greater transfer than does learning by any one method.

ROBERT B. McINTYRE
University of Southern California
HARVEY F. DINGMAN
Pacific State Hospital, Pomona, California

7 · MENTAL AGE *vs.* LEARNING ABILITY: AN INVESTIGATION OF TRANSFER OF TRAINING BETWEEN HIERARCHICAL LEVELS

● In developing and testing methods of programmed instruction, much attention has been paid to the internal aspects of the program (Skinner, 1958). Programs have been written using small increments of information and others using large learning steps or branching, multi-track methods. Attention has also been paid to the criteria used in evaluating learning (e.g., Gagne & Dick, 1962). Evaluation of learning in terms of performance in the program has been used, as well as external evaluations based on the learner's ability to transfer his skills to other situations.

Relatively unexplored as yet have been the characteristics of the learner as they relate to programmed instruction and teaching machines. An individual's past experience with particular learning areas, for example, should be positively related to his learning in these areas. Simply stated, an individual tends to learn with greater ease in those areas with which he has some familiarity. This past experience in school related learning has traditionally been measured in some form of developmental level expressed in grade or age equivalents. Another individual characteristic related to an individual's ability to do well in complex school type learning is his general intelligence.

American Journal of Mental Deficiency, 68: 396–403, November, 1963. Reprinted by permission of the senior author and the *American Journal of Mental Deficiency*.

The purpose of this paper was to investigate the effects of these two individual characteristics as they related to an individual's ability to transfer training from one level of problem complexity to another. Specific predictions were:

1. There would be a complex interaction between problem difficulty level, intelligence, and past learning.

2. At some levels, intelligence would be related to learning and, at other levels, past learning would be related.

That is, those subjects with higher intelligence should do better than those with lower intelligence except where their past level of achievement compensates for lower ability. Conversely, at some problem level, success would be related to past achievement rather than intelligence.

Method

MEASURES

Standard intelligence test scores were used as a measure of intelligence (IQ). Available IQs were used and consisted of individual test results obtained by the psychology staff of Pacific State Hospital. The tests used were primarily WISCs and WAISs and all test scores were less than four years old.

Since the stimuli used dealt with number concepts, a measure of past achievement in the area of number and arithmetic concepts was used. The development and validation of this test, the Pacific State Hospital Number Concept Test, has already been reported in the literature (Shotwell, Dingman, Tarjan, 1956). This test yields an Arithmetic Age (AA) score, which may be considered as a type of mental age score with only one specific area sampled. The authors report a validity coefficient of .93 between Binet MA and arithmetic test score expressed in total number of items correct.

SUBJECTS

Subjects were drawn from a pool of hospitalized male retardates with tested IQs above fifty and primary diagnoses of familial or undifferentiated mental retardation. Only those Ss who showed no obvious visual or motor defect were given the pre-training series. Of the 29 Ss who were tested, 20 reached criterion on the pre-training. These 20 constituted the experimental sample.

These 20 Ss were dichotomized on the basis of recorded IQ scores. Those with IQs above 60 were placed in the high IQ group. Each IQ group was separately dichotomized on the basis of its tested AA scores. The 9 rejected Ss consisted of 3 each from all groups except the high IQ, high AA group. The composition of the four groups thus formed is shown in Table I.

Table I. Composition of Experimental Groups by Age, IQ, and Arithmetic Age (N = 20)

Group (Each = 5)	Chronological age in years		IQ		Arithmetic age in years	
	Mean	SD	Mean	SD	Mean	SD
High IQ, high AA	24.32	3.10	67.8	5.42	8.60	.95
High IQ, low AA	21.12	6.50	71.8	7.73	7.40	.90
Low IQ, high AA	17.38	2.86	54.4	2.15	7.58	1.06
Low IQ, low AA	21.64	6.67	55.0	2.28	4.92	.56
Rejected subjects (N = 9) .	23.90	5.07	58.9	7.62	6.41	1.81

STIMULI

The stimuli used consisted of a series of number problems, prepared on 35 mm. transparencies. These problems were of graded difficulty levels established on the basis of similarity to items at specific AA levels on the Pacific State Hospital Number Concept Test. At the level equivalent to Arithmetic Age four, the problem consisted of responding to groups of dots. At AA five the problem was numeral recognition. Arithmetic Age six level involved simple addition using either the digit one or two. Problems at AA 7 were simple subtraction using the numbers one or two; and problems at AA 8 involved subtraction using the tens column. Table II shows the stimuli used at leach level. At each problem level there were three slides so that the responses three, four, and six were each correct for one slide at each level.

At each level the stimulus slides were put in the same prearranged order. Each consecutive trial block of three slides contained all three stimuli with the stimuli randomly arranged within trial blocks. Trial blocks were randomly arranged within series. No stimulus was presented twice consecutively since previous work had suggested that some retarded subjects do not perceive the beginning of a new trial unless the stimulus has changed. All stimuli were presented to all Ss.

Table II. Stimuli Used at Each Problem Difficulty Level

Arithmetic age level	Stimuli (presented in random order within arithmetic age levels)		
AA 4	.	. .	. . .
	. .	. .	. . .
AA 5	3	4	6
AA 6	2	3	4
	+1	+1	+2
	⎯	⎯	⎯
AA 7	4	6	7
	−1	−2	−1
	⎯	⎯	⎯
AA 8	6	10	14
	−3	−6	−8
	⎯	⎯	⎯

EQUIPMENT

Stimuli were presented on an 8 inch by 11 inch milk glass screen by an automatic slide projector. A candy delivery tube was mounted to the left of the screen. Three telegraph keys were mounted in front of the screen. For each stimuli, one of the keys would bring a reward of one candy, signifying and reinforcing a correct response. Either of the other two keys would sound a buzzer and light a red light for five seconds, signifying and negatively reinforcing an incorrect response. A subject was allowed to continue responding until he did make a correct response which then ended that particular trial. None of the keys were operative while the buzzer was sounding. For all trial series the left key was associated with the response 3, the middle key with 4, and the right key with 6.

The stimulus on the screen was changed automatically when the *S* pressed a white telegraph key mounted at the far right of the *S*'s position and designated as the ready key. Time to first response and time to correct response were measured by electronic clocks calibrated to 1/100 of a second. The number of times each response key was pressed was accumulated by three additional counters.

PROCEDURE

Each *S* was tested individually by the same *E*. Subjects were told that the equipment would show pictures and give out candy if the *S* did well.

The S was told that the purpose of the experiment was to find out about the machine. The Pacific State Hospital Number Concept was administered first before presentation of any of the stimuli. Subjects were then seated in front of the apparatus and instructed in the use of the ready key and the response keys. The buzzer and candy delivery were demonstrated prior to the pre-training trials.

All Ss were then presented with the pre-training stimuli, consisting of three geometrical figures: circle, square, and triangle. For the first fifteen trials, if necessary, E gave direct assistance in the form of verbal reinforcement of correct responses, calling of stimuli names and direct manipulation of S's hand to the correct key. After the first fifteen trials, E sat out of S's direct line of vision and gave no further assistance. Criterion of pre-training learning was established as eight consecutive correct responses. All Ss who had not reached criterion after 45 trials were eliminated from the experiment. (See Table I.)

Results

The number of error free trials for each 15 trial block, which constituted one problem level, was used as the criterion score for analysis. Positive transfer of training was indicated by any increase in error free trials from problem level to problem level. The scores were treated by analysis of variance in a mixed higher order design such that IQ and AA and IQ $\times$ AA interaction effects were between-subjects comparisons. Problem difficulty level, with all of its interaction effects, was based on within-subject comparisons (Lindquist, 1953). The results of this analysis and the significant lower-order effects from the necessary subanalyses are presented in Table III.

As predicted, there was a significant interaction between IQ, AA and difficulty level. This indicates that the relationship between IQ and difficulty level is related to AA and that the AA and difficulty level relationship is related to IQ.

Analysis of the effects of IQ and AA at each difficulty level shows that the high AA Ss do significantly better on the level 4 problems than do the low AA Ss, while IQ is not significant here. However, at level 6 AA is not significant but high IQ Ss do significantly better than low IQ Ss. No IQ by AA interaction effects are significant. The experimental prediction that both past experience (AA) and intelligence (IQ) would be significantly related to transfer of training but at different levels was therefore confirmed.

Using only the low IQ Ss for subanalysis, the difficulty levels were found

Table III. Over-all Analysis of Variance and Significant Lower-Order Interaction and Simple Effects

Source of variance	Σx^2	df	s^2	F	P<
Between subjects	737.05	79	....	....	....
IQ	75.69	1	75.69	11.87	0.001
AA	176.89	1	176.89	27.75	0.001
IQ x AA	0.01	1	0.01	0.00	....
Error (between)	484.46	76	6.37	....	....
Within subjects	449.46	320	....	....	....
Difficulty level	48.06	4	12.02	11.05	0.001
Level x IQ	43.06	4	10.76	9.90	0.001
Level x AA	11.26	4	2.82	2.59	0.05
Level x AA x IQ	16.74	4	4.18	3.85	0.01
Error (within)	330.34	304	1.09	....	....
Total	1186.51	399	....	....	....
Subanalyses					
Low AA Ss only					
Level x IQ	24.48	4	6.12	4.84	0.005
Error (within)	40.40	32	1.26	....	....
Low AA, low IQ Ss only					
Between subjects	197.84	4	49.46	14.83	0.001
Level x subjects	53.36	16	3.34	....	....
Low IQ Ss only					
Difficulty level	75.40	4	18.85	6.01	0.005
Error (within)	100.44	32	3.14	....	....
Difficulty level 4 only					
AA	68.45	1	68.45	6.97	0.025
Within	150.00	16	9.06	....	....
Difficulty level 6 only					
IQ	68.00	1	68.00	6.80	0.05
Within	160.80	16	10.05	....	....

to be significantly different. As shown in Table IV, these differences were caused by a sharp drop in performance from level 5 to level 6 and a subsequent rise from level 7 to level 8. There was no significant level effect with the high IQ Ss.

Analysis of the data for each AA level separately shows a significant interaction between IQ and Level among the low AA Ss only. This effect

Table IV. Differences Between Mean Scores at Each Difficulty Level
Using Low IQ Ss Only
(Critical D t. 995 = 1.79)

	Problem difficulty level			
	—AA 5	—AA 6	—AA 7	—AA 8
AA 4	—1.60	1.60	1.10	—1.10
AA 5	....	3.20*	2.70*	.50
AA 6	....	....	—.50	—2.70*
AA 7	....	....	....	—1.80*

* Dtp $<$.01 (Lindquist, 1953, p. 93).

is primarily due to significant differences between subjects in the high IQ, low AA group.

The performance curves across difficulty levels are presented in Figure 1. Similar curves were obtained by plotting latency scores. Figure 2 shows the same curves, using the reciprocal of latency in seconds for time to correct solution, less buzzer time.

As may be seen from the graphs, the lower IQ Ss ended the series showing positive transfer from level to level, even though the problems were becoming harder and out of these Ss' ability range. The higher IQ Ss showed either no increase or a slight decrease in performance as the problems become more difficult.

Discussion

In this experiment, the relationships between intelligence, past learning, and type of problem to be learned were shown to be complexly inter-related. Although all Ss were theoretically capable of solving the discrimination problem presented at AA level 4, those Ss in the high AA groups did significantly better than those in the low AA groups. In transferring this training to the next level, AA 5, all groups showed some improvement, although this was not statistically significant.

When the problem involved simple arithmetic skills, such as addition at level AA 6, a sharp difference was displayed between IQ groups. The high IQ Ss showed no significant decrement in performance, while the low IQ Ss dropped significantly in accuracy and showed an increase in response time. The problems at this level were such that most Ss were familiar with the form and had attempted to solve arithmetically similar problems on the arithmetic test previously administered.

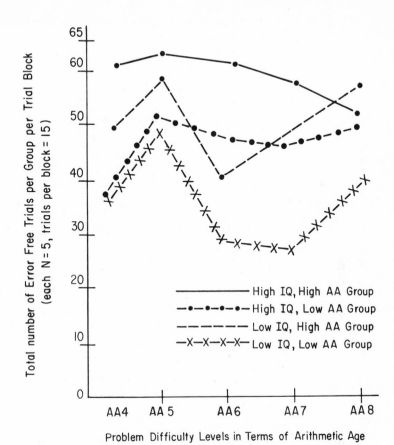

FIGURE 1. Number of Error Free Trials per Experimental Group at Each Problem Difficulty Level.

After this drop in performance, the low IQ *Ss* began to show positive transfer again and made a significant gain in performance from level AA 7 to AA 8. The problems at level AA 8 were beyond these *Ss'* arithmetical skill yet they showed improvement.

For the high IQ groups, the results were approximately what would be expected, with the amount of transfer of training decreasing gradually as the stimuli become increasingly difficult.

In the low IQ group however, there appeared to be two types of transfer involved. When dealing with simple dots and numerals, these *Ss* were able to transfer training from one problem level to another. As the prob-

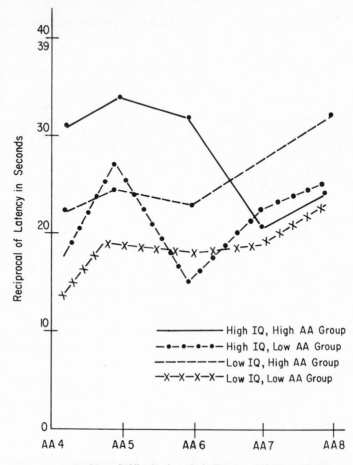

FIGURE 2.   Reciprocal Latency in Seconds at Each Problem
Difficulty Level.

lems became more complex and reached the limits of the *S*'s abilities, an interference in transfer takes place. Once the problem difficulty level exceeded the limits of these *Ss*' abilities, a significant positive transfer of training was again found.

It is suggested here that these lower IQ *Ss* are able to deal with the AA level 4 and 5 material in a verbally mediated manner. They recognize and verbally label the stimuli as three, four, etc. Upon reaching levels 6 and 7 however, their attempts to use abstract processes are unsuccessful due to their inability to deal with this level of complexity. Their attempts to solve the problems arithmetically result in incorrect responses and an increase in latency. Once they stop dealing with the material as a series of number problems, they respond to the experimental situation as a simple three-choice discrimination learning problem and are able to show increased learning while operating at this lower level of mental functioning.

These results point up some of the individual differences which relate to automated instruction. Given identical training situations, some Ss deal with the problems on an abstract verbal level. Other Ss use more concrete associative processes. If the objective of this teaching procedure had been rote learning of specific number combinations, it would have been more effective with the duller retardates. Had the objective been the development of general number concepts, the brighter group would have proved superior.

In developing programs it would seem to be necessary to consider the possible strategies available to the learner. Where the programmed task involves associative and abstract learning and the learner has the necessary associations in his behavior hierarchy, the program may be an effective one. Similarly when simple S-R conditioning is called for, and the learner does not have other response modes competing with this learning, the efficiency of the program should be high. However, where the strategy called for by the program differs from that used by the learner, it is doubtful that maximum learning takes place.

Summary

A series of three-choice discrimination problems using arithmetical content was presented to a group of retarded male Ss. Intelligence, past learning, and problem difficulty level were found to interact with each other. Both intelligence and past learning were significantly related to transfer of training but at different levels. Lower IQ Ss showed significant transfer of training when dealing with arithmetic problems which were beyond their achievement level. It is suggested that these Ss treated the experimental situation as a simple three-choice learning problem when the stimuli became too complex for them to handle on a verbal level. Implications were discussed for program development based on knowledge of the learner's available modes of response.

REFERENCES

Gagne, R. M., and Dick, W. Learning measures in a self-instructional program in solving equations. *Psychol. Report*, 1962, 10, 131–146.

Lindquist, E. F. *Design and analysis of experiments in psychology and education.* Boston: Houghton Mifflin, 1953.

Shotwell, Anna M., Dingman, H. F., and Tarjan, G. A number test for mental defectives. *Amer. J. Ment. Defic.*, 1956, 60, 589–594.

Skinner, B. F. Teaching machines. *Science*, 1958, 128, 969–977.

DONALD M. JOHNSON
Michigan State University
R. PAUL STRATTON
Michigan State University

8 · EVALUATION OF FIVE METHODS OF TEACHING CONCEPTS[1]

• Most concept experiments require the subject (S) to learn to classify objects by practice with positive and negative instances and to label the positive instances with a nonsense syllable. Theoretical discussions often take this procedure as typical of concept learning. Carroll (1964) has questioned the relevance of such experiments to concept learning in school because the label is usually a standard word with a network of associations, and because teachers use several methods, some of which are more deductive than inductive. Serra (1953) was able to list a variety of methods by which teachers introduce concepts in elementary school, and inspection of a college textbook will also disclose a diversity of methods. There are at least three, in addition to the classification method, that have been frequently used by teachers and textbooks, but have not been experimentally evaluated: defining a concept, using it in a sentence, and giving synonyms.

Experimental evaluation of these methods requires different tests of concept achievement appropriate to each, and different types of test item have been devised for regular testing of concept achievement in school also. Cronbach (1942) described several types of test item for diagnostic vocabulary testing. Hastings (1941) constructed six tests, each of a different

Journal of Educational Psychology, 57: 48–53, 1966. Copyright © 1966 by the American Psychological Association, and reproduced by permission.

[1] Supported in part by a grant from the National Science Foundation for undergraduate research participation. Thanks are due to Henry Askew for expert assistance in scoring.

item type, for testing achievement of 35 standard mathematics concepts and attained good reliabilities for each test. These studies have been concerned with blocks of related concepts within an area of knowledge, rather than single concepts, but the results suggest that achievement of single concepts may also be evaluated by different tests which correspond to different teaching methods.

Evaluation of different teaching methods raises the critical question of amount of transfer. Classification practice may build up specific associations that suffice for a classification test, but lack the generality needed for a definition test. However, a recent experiment with 12-year-old children (Johnson & O'Reilly, 1964) found more transfer from classification training to definitions, when the definitions were carefully scored, than previous research had indicated. Since a set to learn concepts facilitates concept achievement (Reed, 1946), college Ss, who are used to studying concepts, may show even more transfer. The question can be systematically investigated by giving all tests to all Ss. This study proposes, therefore, to construct four tests of a few concepts, to teach these concepts by four corresponding methods and by a combination of the four, and to compare achievements on all tests following all teaching methods.

Test Construction and Analysis

Only standard concepts, designated by words, are relevant. The results of a preliminary study with a definition test and a multiple-choice synonym test gave some indication of suitable levels of difficulty. Words with Thorndike-Lorge frequency counts between 11 and 14 could be expected to be easy for college students. Words with counts between 1 and 6 could be expected to be difficult.

Selection was based on frequency and suitability to the four tests to be described. Only nouns, verbs, and adjectives with four synonyms could be used. Words with more than one meaning in an abridged dictionary and technical words that some Ss might currently be studying were rejected. From the two pools of items that survived editing the experimenters arbitrarily chose four easy words: controversy, vile, rustic, and vicinity, and four difficult words: alacrity, altercation, chide, and opulent.

TESTS

There were two tests of the open-end or free-response type and two of the objective or multiple-choice type.

Definitions. Each word was printed with space for a short response. The instructions were: "There are four words to be defined. Explain briefly what each word means. Try each one even if you have to guess."

Sentences. The incomplete-sentence technique is a way of embedding a word in connected discourse. The instructions were: "Here are some incomplete sentences to be finished. Please add a few words to give each sentence a meaningful ending. Try each one even if you have to guess." There were two sentences for each concept, and the eight sentences were printed in irregular order. Two examples follow: "A controversy ceases when —————————————." "Something rustic would probably be found —————————."

Classification. Four short phrases were written to describe objects or events classifiable under each of the four concepts, together with four unrelated phrases. These 20 items appeared in irregular order with the following instructions:

> Most, but not all, of the following items can be classified under four concepts: rustic, vile, controversy, vicinity. Read each item and mark each on your answer sheet thus: rustic 1, vile 2, controversy 3, vicinity 4, none of these 5.

Three sample items follow: "Two men of differing opinions discuss the social value of a book." "A weathered old barn." "An ex-criminal becomes a respected member of the community."

Synonyms. This conventional vocabulary test requires S to choose a synonym, but 10 choices were presented rather than the usual 5 in order to increase the reliability of the single item. Four such items were constructed for each concept; the 16 items appeared in blocks of 4, one for each word, in alphabetical order.

The tests were administered in the order given above to reduce the opportunity for learning from the alternatives on the multiple-choice tests. The two free-response tests were printed on separate sheets; each sheet was collected when completed. Time required was about 40 minutes.

SUBJECTS

Group 1, which had the easy concepts, consisted of 63 students in two classes in general psychology at Michigan State University. Group 2, which had the difficult concepts, consisted of 75 students in abnormal psychology. One foreign student was eliminated from each group.

RESULTS

The definitions were rated on a scale of 0–4 by two judges, using ordinary dictionary entries as criteria. The two sentence completions for each concept were treated as a unit and rated on a scale of 0–4 by the two judges because evaluation of a response seemed to be more stable when it was read in conjunction with another response related to the same concept. The criteria of judgment were based on the instructions to write meaningful endings and the assumption that Ss would try to demonstrate their knowledge. For both easy and difficult concepts, and for both definitions and sentences, the correlations between scorers were satisfactory for present purposes, ranging from .60–.97 with a median of .78. The sums of the two ratings were used in the analysis; hence the scores for each test ranged from 0–8.

The data from Classifications and Synonyms were treated as four-item tests with reliabilities computed by Kuder-Richardson Formula 20. For the easy concepts errors were infrequent, and reliabilities ranged from .19–.72 with a median of .48. For the difficult concepts the range was .65–.89 with a median of .79. The scores were doubled so that the range of scores on each test extended from 0–8.

Evaluation of Teaching Methods

A comparison of methods requires that each be used separately. Therefore four sets of teaching materials or programs, corresponding to the four tests, were prepared for teaching the four more difficult concepts. A mixed program was also prepared. Mean scores on the four tests of the four difficult concepts ranged from 2.6–5.2 as compared to a maximum of 8, hence there is room for improvement on each.

MATERIALS

Definitions. Definitions were written, with the help of several dictionaries, to characterize each term in a specific way and to place each in a higher-order class. An example follows:

> When two or more people express different opinions, get excited, and contradict each other, the event is called an *altercation.* Thus an

altercation is a social interaction characterized by heated exchange of opposing arguments. Now write a definition of *altercation* in your own words.

The four definitions, with spaces for the responses, were printed on one side of one sheet of paper; hence all the material remained in view.

Sentences. Russell and Fea (1963) point out that wide reading is universally recommended as a method of building vocabulary, but that direct research on the value of reading in increasing vocabulary has yielded disappointing results. And the reason, they suggest, is the practice of trying to learn unfamiliar words from unfamiliar context.

For present purposes a short story of 174 words was written in which each of the four words appeared twice. The instructions were to read the story and learn the four words. Following Russell and Fea, the context was made easy; to most college students only the four words were unfamiliar. Then Ss were given four incomplete sentences with the request to finish them, using each of the four words once. All the material remained in view.

Classifications. Short descriptions of objects and events, similar to the test materials, were arranged in blocks of five, one classifiable under each of the four concepts, and one irrelevant. The four words and "none" were printed at the top of each block with instructions to classify each item by writing the appropriate word on a blank line next to the item. One such block appeared on the first page of a booklet, and the next page gave the answers to the first block, followed by a second block of five items. There were six blocks of 30 events to be classified, and correct answers were given to all. The arrangement of the booklet made it easy to turn back and check answers.

Synonyms. The first page of the booklet for the synonym training told Ss that their task was to learn the meanings of four concepts. Four short statements appeared next: "Alacrity means eagerness." "Altercation means squabble." "Chide means to criticize." "Opulent means luxuriant." Then each of the four concepts appeared next to a blank space, and four other synonyms were given, namely, reproach, quarrel, lavish, and promptness, to be matched with the four concepts by writing one synonym in each blank. The next page gave the answers to these and another block of four synonyms to be matched to the same four concepts. Four blocks of four synonyms were given, followed by answers on succeeding pages. The arrangement of the booklet facilitated checking of answers.

Mixed Program. The review by Serra (1953) reported that teachers commonly use several methods together. Johnson and O'Reilly (1964) found that children with practice in classifying birds and defining the class learned more than children with only classifying practice. It is reasonable to suppose that, even if the amount of training is equated, a combination of methods would be more efficient than any single method.

The Mixed Program was constructed of materials used in the other four programs with necessary modifications. The definitions were abridged. Each concept appeared only once in the context of a sentence. Two synonyms and one example were given. An illustration follows:

> To chide someone is to talk to him to get him to correct his mistakes. Chide means to criticize or reproach. Thus a mother might chide her children for fighting with each other. An example might be a group of fellows poking fun at a boy with dirty clothes. Now write in your own words what chide means.

This was followed by one block of synonyms for matching and one block of events for classification, with correct answers.

The plan of the experiment required the formulation of certain rules in the preparation of the materials. The four teaching methods should be distinct. The definitions should not include synonyms. The words in context should not include definitions or examples to be classified. In respect to sentences, classifications, and synonyms the items used for teaching and testing should be different. This rule does not apply to the scoring of definitions because memorizing a definition is an accepted part of this teaching method. Each program should be an equally good representative of the method it embodies. This last is a goal that cannot be attained, but the attempt was made to make each program maximally effective.

Each program should require the same time for completion. Differences in reading speed and care make this criterion difficult to attain also, but after some preliminary trials and adjustments it was expected that each program would require about 12 minutes for most college students.

PROCEDURE

Teaching and testing were conducted in a class of about 200 students in general psychology. The five sets of teaching materials, together with an irrelevant set of materials for a control group, were passed out serially so that approximately one-sixth of the class received each set, and neighboring Ss had different sets. Work was stopped and papers were collected at the end of 12 minutes. Nearly all Ss had finished.

The tests were given 9 days later. Absence of Ss on either day reduced the number in the five method groups to 22–28. The control group was increased to 40 by the addition of Ss who were present on the test day but absent on the teaching day. Scoring of the Definitions and Sentences was carried out by the two judges who had attained the interjudge agreement mentioned above. The sums of the two ratings were used.

RESULTS

Table 1 shows the scores obtained by all groups on the separate tests and also the totals. The maximum score on any test of the four concepts is 32, and the maximum total is 128. In respect to total score all method

Table 1. Means and Standard Deviations Obtained on Four Tests of Concept Achievement by Six Groups with Different Training Methods

Method groups	N	Achievement scores				
		Def.	Sen.	Class.	Syn.	Total
Definitions	28	20.2	23.0	28.0	27.9	99.1
		8.4	8.3	5.3	5.3	22.6
Sentences	26	23.6	25.2	28.4	28.7	105.8
		7.9	5.4	4.0	4.0	17.1
Classifications	24	21.4	24.2	28.4	28.8	102.8
		8.2	6.6	5.6	4.5	21.0
Synonyms	25	19.9	24.3	26.1	27.6	97.9
		9.2	6.8	4.4	4.6	22.1
4 groups pooled	103	21.3	24.1	27.7	28.3	101.4
		8.5	6.2	4.4	4.6	20.8
Mixed program	22	26.5	27.4	29.3	30.5	113.6
		6.5	5.3	3.2	2.0	11.4
Control	40	12.8	17.6	23.5	23.4	77.2
		9.9	8.3	8.0	9.0	31.3

groups exceeded the control group. These differences are large and, as Table 2 shows, highly significant.

The group that received the Mixed program achieved higher total scores, as expected, than any group that received a single kind of training. These differences are significant with the exception of the group that had training on sentences, and this difference would be significant by a one-tailed test. Within the four groups that received a single kind of training there are no significant differences. For this reason these groups were pooled to form a group of 103 with a mean total of 101.4. The difference between this mean and that of the mixed group is highly significant.

Table 2. Significance of Differences between Totals Shown in Table 1

Method groups	Sen.	Class.	Syn.	Mixed	Control
Definitions	1.23	0.61	0.20	2.95*	3.34*
Sentences	...	0.55	1.42	1.88	4.75*
Classifications	...	...	0.80	2.19†	3.89*
Synonyms	...	...	...	3.12*	3.10*
4 groups pooled	...	...	...	2.66*	6.00*
Mixed program	...	...	...	...	6.56*

$* p < 0.01$ $† p < 0.05$.

The results for separate tests are similar to those for total scores, but the differences are not so clear-cut. All groups did better than the control group on all tests, and the mixed group did better than any single-method group. On the Definitions test no single-method group is significantly superior to any other, but when the four groups are pooled, the mean of the pooled group is superior to the control group $(p < .01)$, and the mixed group is superior to the pooled group $(p < .01)$. The same statements can be made for the Sentences test and the Synonyms test. On the Classifications test the difference between the pooled-group mean and the control-group mean is significant $(p < .01)$, and the difference between the mixed-group and the pooled-group mean yields a t of 1.56. In general it is safe to say that each kind of training was effective in raising scores on all tests above the control group and that the mixed training was best.

Another way to look at the data is to examine the mean scores on each test of each concept. Each of the 16 concept means for the pooled group exceeded the corresponding mean for the control group, and 15 of the 16 means for the mixed group exceeded the corresponding means for the pooled group.

Discussion

The results show that construction of short tests of single concepts is feasible. The tests of the more difficult concepts yielded 16 reliable scores in about 40 minutes; each score measures knowledge of a single concept by a different response, and each is sensitive to the improvement resulting from a small amount of practice. The small standard deviations for the mixed group on Classifications and Synonyms suggest a ceiling effect, but this effect was not serious enough to prevent this group from exceeding the others.

Concepts of this kind can be taught to college students equally well by different programs of instruction which require different responses. The superiority of the Mixed program supports the common practice of teachers and textbook writers.

The question about transfer may be phrased in this form: How much of what was learned by one method transferred to the tests constructed of materials used in the other methods? Since transfer effects are usually small, one might assume that each of the four single-method groups would get its highest score on the test corresponding to that method. The results of Table 1 do not support this assumption. The group that had practice in writing definitions actually was below the pooled-group mean on the Definitions test, but above the pooled-group mean on Classifications. The synonyms group was the lowest of the four on Synonyms; it was above the pooled-group mean only on Sentences. Over-all, there is no evidence of specific relations between training method and test achievement; the picture is one of 100% transfer.

One interpretation for the large transfer effect is that S sets concept acquisition as his goal, varying his methods on his own initiative and testing himself so that the intended differences between training methods vanish. Thus each method takes over some of the advantages of the mixed method. Another possibility is that the transfer occurs on the testing day when S treats the four tests as problems and uses whatever he can recall to solve them. One with training on sentences may recall the story, for example, and use this information to formulate a definition or to choose a synonym. Probably transfer occurs during both learning and testing.

The matter of interference should be mentioned. One might suppose that if S is given a definition or a synonym, there would be no more for him to learn. But he is given four definitions, or four synonyms, as well as verbal instructions; hence some interference can be expected. This may explain why the Sentences method, which depends on learning from context, usually considered inefficient, was as good as any. The continuity of the story probably reduced the amount of interference.

REFERENCES

Carroll, J. B. Words, meanings and concepts. *Harvard Educational Review*, 1964, 34, 178–202.

Cronbach, L. J. Analysis of techniques for diagnostic vocabulary testing. *Journal of Educational Research*, 1942, 36, 206–217.

Hastings, J. T. Testing junior high school mathematics concepts. *School Review*, 1941, 49, 766–776.

Johnson, D. M., and O'Reilly, C. A. Concept attainment in children: Classifying and defining. *Journal of Educational Psychology*, 1964, 55, 71–74.

Reed, H. B. Factors influencing the learning and retention of concepts: I. The influence of set. *Journal of Experimental Psychology*, 1946, 36, 71–87.

Russell, D. H., and Fea, H. R. Research on teaching reading. In N. L. Gage (Ed.), *Handbook of research on teaching*. Chicago: Rand McNally, 1963. Pp. 865–928.

Serra, M. C. How to develop concepts and their verbal representation. *Elementary School Journal*, 1953, 53, 275–285.

PROBLEM-SOLVING
AND CREATIVITY

• There are points of
similarity and difference between the concepts of problem-solving and
creativity presented in this section and the phenomenon of transfer considered in the preceding one. In transfer, ideas and learnings from familiar
situations are applied to similar situations, calling on the learner's ability
to perceive relationships, associations, similarities, and samenesses between
ideas and objects. Creative thinking depends more upon re-combining and
synthesizing experience into something different, for the purpose of visualizing new situations. It also differs from the type of thinking employed in
problem-solving in its emphasis upon reasoning in divergent and often
nonconforming ways sometimes unacceptable to teachers, peers, and even
parents.

To think creatively, the individual must be different. He is often considered peculiar and eccentric and has difficulty gaining acceptance in peer
groups and classrooms. As a matter of fact, it has been common practice
to equate the divergent thinker, the creator, and the genius with maladjustment and neuroticism to the point where a certain amount of emotional and mental disturbance has been expected and felt to be necessary.
Fortunately, this view is being changed. Dr. Lawrence Kubie,[1] who has
published extensively in this area, feels that while access to the unconscious
is essential for divergent and creative thought, such access may be obtained
more readily by the very emotionally sound person, because of his comparative absence of ego defenses, than by the neurotic, whose defenses are
unable to deny unconscious material. This is borne out by those who have

---

[1] Lawrence Kubie, *Neurotic Distortion of the Creative Process* (University of
Kansas: Noonday Press, 1961), pp. 6, 58–61.

studied the creative process. Torrance[2] reports research that identifies peaks of creativity in children at ages four-and-one-half and nine. It is significant that these are times of maximum feelings of psychological security. Lows in ability to think creatively coincide with ages three, six, and eleven—times of insecurity for youngsters.

In contrast to creative thinking, problem-solving generally employs accepted and tested methods of reasoning and does not rely so much upon the insightful, "Ah-ha!" experience or the intuitive hunch. The technique of problem-solving can usually be called up on demand, while the creative insight is more elusive and is more likely to pop into awareness unexpectedly. Although it is generally accepted that high intelligence is associated with superiority in problem-solving, the ability to think creatively occurs over a wider range of intellectual ability. Getzels and Jackson,[3] for example, worked with a group of students who scored in the top 20 per cent in measures of creativity but were *below* the top 20 per cent in IQ. Interestingly enough, their school achievement was equal to that of another group of students picked for high IQ but low creativity.

This gives rise to some rather sobering thoughts concerning conventional educational and testing procedures. First: It may be that the commonly used measures of determining the IQ really are based upon the individual's willingness to feed back the expected answers, to think in a conforming rather than in a divergent manner. Second: It may be that schools tend to reward, and hence to perpetuate, conventional behaviors and ways of thinking to the degree that the creative production of new and different ideas is actually discouraged. By the time youngsters are graduated from high school, they may have been conditioned to think in a conforming fashion habitually and may find it quite difficult to develop novel and divergent concepts. The educator who is interested in promoting creative thinking needs to realize that it is not easy to be different and that group, peer, classroom, and other societal pressures are almost always brought to bear upon the divergent individual. Both individual strength and exterior support are needed before the person may be able to dare to be, as phrased by Torrance, "the minority of one" necessary for generating and presenting the novel and the different idea.

There is little marketable value for the commonplace in thinking. No

[2] E. Paul Torrance, *Constructive Behavior: Stress, Personality and Mental Health* (Belmont, California: Wadworth Publishing Company, Inc., 1965), pp. 101–3.

[3] Jacob W. Getzels and Philip W. Jackson, *Creativity and Intelligence* (New York: John Wiley and Sons, Inc., 1962), p. 24.

one pays for ideas that have already been assimilated and applied by the culture. One brilliant thinker and one revolutionary idea can make more difference than thousands of mediocre ideas. Influence, prestige, and confidence in the future are possible to the nation and the school system that can produce such thinking. The key to the universe will not be discovered by the conforming thinker.

E. PAUL TORRANCE
Professor of Educational Psychology, University of Georgia

9 · PROBLEM-SOLVING ATTITUDES AND SELF CONCEPTS OF BEGINNING JUNIOR HIGH SCHOOL STUDENTS

● For years, many teachers have observed that young people seem to lose much of their creativity and problem-solving ability at about the time they enter junior high school in the seventh grade. Recently, there have been a few empirical studies that have shown that, as measured by tests of creative thinking ability, there are rather marked drops in creative functioning at this time (2, 4). Some have explained these drops in terms of the adolescent's increased concern for peer approval and a beginning interest in the approval of the opposite sex. Others have explained them on the basis of the onset of adolescence and physiological changes which seem to overwhelm some young people at about this time. Still others have explained these decrements in creative functioning on the basis of the increased formality of education, departmentalization, and decreased attention to the learner as self-acting.

Contrary to a number of current investigators, the author has maintained that the drop in creative functioning among many youngsters at about the time they enter junior high school should be of concern to teachers and guidance workers. He has suggested that some of the same forces involved in the decreases in creative functioning may also be involved in school dropout, delinquency, and mental illness—problems that are apparently

Guidance Journal, 4: 74–86, 1966. Used by permission of the *Guidance Journal,* Ohio State University.

being more widely recognized as concerns of the junior high school. Studies of high school dropouts are beginning to show that many youngsters who achieve and behave exceptionally well in elementary school, suddenly begin failing and misbehaving when they enter junior high school (1).

In this article, the author will explore the possibility that some of the problems just outlined may be related to erroneous concepts about the nature of effective problem solving and a lack of confidence in one's own ability as a problem solver. This exploration will consist of an examination of the problem-solving concepts and self concepts of samples of seventh graders from three different localities and data from an experiment of a preventive nature and two of a remedial nature.

Procedures

The subjects which provide the basic data concerning the problem-solving concepts and self concepts were 114 seventh graders in a medium-sized town in Georgia; 104, in a middle-class suburb in Minnesota; and 79, in a university laboratory school in Minnesota.

The potential dropouts were 45 seventh graders enrolled in a school located in an economically and culturally disadvantaged neighborhood. These youngsters had been identified by their teachers as likely to drop out of school. A random half of them were placed in an experimental program with a special staff of teachers, a half-time counselor, and a principal. The others continued undisturbed in the school's regular program.

The subjects of the other experimental remedial program were 52 seventh graders who met in small groups (6 to 10) throughout the school year to discuss their problems under the school's guidance and counseling staff. Their controls were 27 seventh graders in the same school who continued with the school's usual program.

The subjects of the preventive program were 101 beginning seventh graders who had participated as fourth graders in an experimental program of creative development (3). Their controls were 117 seventh graders who had also served as controls in the original fourth-grade study.

The instrument used to obtain concepts concerning the nature of creative problem solving and self concepts of one's self as a problem solver was developed by Martin Covington and Richard Crutchfield at the University of California, Berkeley and used with their permission. The inventory is introduced with the following problem:

> Some engineers want to run a heavy television cable through a pipe. The pipe is 500 feet long and 6 inches in diameter. The pipe

is about 10 feet below the ground, but it is open at both ends so the engineers can work on it. The pipe is not straight, but is made up of sections that twist and curve.

The engineers have already tried to push the television cable through from the ends of the pipe, but each time the cable twists and gets stuck after only a few feet.

The problem is to think of ways to run this particular television cable through this pipe, but without ripping up or digging down to the pipe.

In the section dealing with concepts about the nature of effective problem solving, there are thirty "Yes" or "No" statements preceded by the following instructions:

Let's pretend that your class has been given this problem to solve. Here are some things children might say about this problem, or problems like it. Circle "Yes" if you agree with a statement, or "No" if you disagree. Remember there are no right or wrong answers.

The section designed to elicit self concepts regarding one's problem-solving ability consists of 22 similar items preceded by the following instructions:

Now we would like to know how you, yourself, might feel when working on the problem of getting the television cable through the pipe. Remember, these questions are about how *you* think and feel, so there are no right or wrong answers.

Results

PREOCCUPATION WITH THE ONE BEST ANSWER

Three items were designed to assess the extent to which subjects accept the idea of the "one best answer" to all problems. The following percentages of "yes" responses were obtained for the total "general population" sample of seventh graders and for the potential dropout for these three items:

	General Sample	Dropout Sample
There is probably only one answer to a problem like this one.	12%	45%
Although several answers may be suggested, there is usually only one best answer.	41%	65%
There is probably only one way that is best for solving a problem like this one.	27%	70%

It may be surmised from these data that a large majority of seventh graders (88 percent) recognize that there may be more than one answer to a problem such as this one, but that a relatively large proportion of them believe that "there is usually only one best answer" (41 percent) or "only one way that is best" (27 percent). In all cases, however, the potential dropouts are far more preoccupied with the "one best answer" concept (statistically significant at better than the .01 level).

In the group guidance program for seventh graders, there seems to have been a reduction in the prevalence of this concept. On the first item above, ten percent of the experimentals and 26 percent of the controls answered "Yes." On the third item, 23 percent of the experimentals and 52 percent of the controls answered "Yes." In both cases, the differences in proportions are statistically significant at better than the .05 level. Little change in these concepts seems to have resulted from the experimental program for potential dropouts. The experimental fourth-grade program in creative development, however, seems to have produced differences concerning this concept that persisted to the seventh grade. Thirty-five percent of the experimentals and 46 percent of the controls answered "Yes" to the second item. A similar but not statistically significant trend was noted for the other two items.

AUTHORITY OF THE PEER MAJORITY

It has frequently been observed that most adolescents are so concerned with the authority of the peer majority that they abandon their moral and other values as guides to behavior and do not make an honest search for the truth. The following three items elicit attitudes about the "authority of the peer majority":

	General Sample	Potential Dropouts
In a problem like this one, the best answer should be the one that most members of the class think is right.	55%	58%
In a problem like this one, the best answer will be the one that most of the class decides is right.	50%	70%
If someone gets an idea that is different from everyone else's, the idea is probably not very good; otherwise others would have thought of it too.	5%	43%

From these data it would appear that over one-half of both dropouts and seventh graders in general think that "the best answer *should* be the one that most members of the class think is right." Differences between the general sample and the potential dropouts emerge, however, with the potential dropouts more frequently subscribing to the idea that the majority answer *is* the right one and more frequently suppressing ideas that are different from those suggested by classmates.

The experimental programs seem to have had little influence in modifying concepts about the authority of the peer majority. The only significant difference occurred in one of the schools that had participated in the experimental program of creative development where only 34 percent of the experimentals compared with 50 percent of the controls thought that "the best answer should be the one that most members of the class think is right."

AVERSION TO DIVERGENT IDEAS

It is generally recognized that healthy groups give consideration to divergent ideas and as a result are more productive, make better decisions, and function more effectively than groups where there is intolerance of such ideas. The following are the results obtained for the general and potential dropout samples on the five items dealing with divergent ideas:

	General Sample	Potential Dropouts
New ideas should be tried out only after older ideas that have worked before fail to bring an answer.	69%	90%
In solving problems, one should consider the silly as well as the ideas that have worked before.	68%	45%
Ideas that are wrong don't need to be suggested, because they only waste time.	29%	53%
Problems are not fair if they make you keep looking for new ideas in order to solve them.	15%	28%
The best workers will get one good idea and stick with it rather than think of many ideas, which might confuse them.	57%	78%

It will be noted here that there are marked differences between the general sample and the potential dropouts (all differences statistically significant at the .05 level or better), with the dropouts expressing a stronger aversion to new or different ideas. There is also reflected considerable conservatism regarding the consideration of such ideas. There seems, however, a willingness to accept problems that require them to keep looking for new ideas.

The experimental group guidance program seems to have created a greater willingness to consider new ideas and a greater intolerance of "wrong ideas." Thirty-five percent of the experimentals and 63 percent of controls favored giving consideration to many ideas rather than just sticking with one idea. Thirty-five percent of the experimentals and 15 percent of the controls feel that it is a waste of time for the students to suggest "wrong ideas." This result suggests that some of the groups did not develop the skills of using constructively wrong ideas, learning from them, and using them as a basis for thinking of new ideas (hitchhiking).

The fourth-grade program in creative development seems to have produced some differences that seem to have persisted to the seventh grade. In one of the schools, 75 percent of the experimentals and 45 percent of the controls were favorable to the consideration of silly ideas as well as those that have worked before. The Georgia children were generally more favorable than the Minnesota children to consider a variety of possibilities.

The experimental program for potential dropouts seems to have had little effect in modifying ideas in this area.

SUPPRESSION OF IDEAS

The following are the results obtained from the four items dealing with the desirability of suppressing rather than expressing ideas that might be different or incorrect:

	General Sample	Potential Dropouts
If someone gets an idea that no one else has thought of, he should keep it to himself.	16%	43%
Anyone who suggests a lot of ideas usually keeps others from giving their ideas.	29%	68%
It is best to make sure that an idea is a good one before it is suggested to the class.	75%	93%
Someone who keeps working on a problem that no one else in the class can solve is stubborn and selfish.	7%	25%

Especially notable in these data are the large differences between the general sample and the potential dropout group and the unfavorable attitudes of the potential dropouts (all of the differences between the two groups are statistically significant at better than the .01 level). In working with the potential dropouts in the testing situation, the author and his assistants were intensely aware of the sanctions being exercised even in this situation against those who continued working on problems beyond a period of time when the majority pretended to have finished. In smaller groups, the leader might have been able to lighten these sanctions or even prevent their occurrence, but in a large group the power of the sanctions is so great and the forces of regression so strong that the leader was helpless in doing so.

None of the experimental programs seemed to have a great deal of influence on ideas concerning the suppression of ideas. The group guidance project seems to have been more successful than any of the others in this respect. This was especially true concerning the idea that the expression of a large number of ideas by one member of a class robs others of the opportunity of giving their ideas; 31 percent of the experimentals and 48 percent of the controls subscribed to this idea. There was a general tendency for the Georgia seventh graders to feel a need for suppressing one's ideas; 85 percent of the experimentals and 90 percent of the controls believe that one should make sure that "an idea is a good one before it is suggested to the class." This is a problem that might be of special significance to guidance workers in certain communities or regions.

THE INNATENESS OF PROBLEM-SOLVING ABILITY

The following results were elicited by the three items dealing with the concept of the innateness and unchangeability of the problem-solving abilities.

	General Sample	Potential Dropouts
Boys and girls can learn to read and do arithmetic, but they cannot learn to think better or get better ideas.	17%	28%
If someone is not very good at thinking and solving problems by the time he is my age, then it is too late.	23%	43%
Some people are naturally born to be better thinkers than others and there is nothing that can be done.	31%	63%

It will be noted that in all three instances a larger proportion of the dropouts than of the general sample of seventh graders accept the concept of the idea that thinking and problem-solving skills cannot be learned. It is still remarkable, however, that almost one-third of the general group believe that there is nothing that can be done to become a better thinker.

The group guidance project seemed to have no influence on the attitudes in this area. The other two projects, however, seemed to have some slight effects. Only three percent of the youngsters who had as fourth graders participated in the creative development project accepted the statement that boys and girls "cannot learn to think better or get better ideas," compared with 12 percent of their controls, 23 percent of the general group, and 43 percent of the potential dropouts. Only 15 percent of the experimental subjects in the dropout project accepted this statement compared with 28 percent at the beginning and 30 percent for their controls at the end of the seventh grade. Fifty-five percent of them still maintained the notion that thinking ability is inborn and that there is nothing that can be done to improve it, however.

In the second section of the instrument, there is another item dealing with the unchanging nature of thinking and problem-solving abilities (Do you feel that you are one of those people who is not very good at thinking and solving problems?). Twenty-six percent of the general sample and 40 percent of the potential dropouts answered "Yes." The group guidance experience did not seem to affect this self-concept but the other two programs seem to have had some positive influence. In the creative development project, only 18 percent of the experimentals compared with 36 percent of the controls expressed this feeling about themselves at the time they entered the seventh grade. In the project for potential dropouts, 40 percent of the experimentals compared with 65 percent of the controls expressed this self concept at the end of the seventh grade. In both instances, the differences in proportions is statistically significant at the .01 level.

FEAR OF BEING RIDICULED

Results obtained from three items dealing with fear of being ridiculed are as follows:

	General Sample	Potential Dropouts
Do you feel that your ideas might be laughed at?	44%	73%
Although others might not laugh out loud at your ideas, do you still feel that they would not like them?	47%	73%
Do you think that many times your suggestions and ideas are not taken seriously by the rest of the class?	74%	95%

These data reveal problems that might well become a major concern of guidance workers in junior high schools. Even in the fairly affluent and progressive suburban, laboratory, and medium-sized schools from which the general sample was drawn, almost one-half of the students say that they are afraid that their classmates will laugh at their ideas and about three-fourths of them think that many times their suggestions and ideas are not taken seriously by the rest of the class. Perhaps most impressive, however, is the fact that among the potential dropouts 95 percent feel that their ideas and suggestions are not taken seriously. One senses that many of them have given up and have stopped thinking and making suggestions.

All three of the experimental programs seem to have had some influence on self-concepts in this area. In the group guidance program, 65 percent of the experimentals compared to 74 percent of the controls feel that their classmates frequently do not consider their ideas and suggestions. The experimentals, however, more frequently (33 percent) than their controls (22 percent) feel that their ideas might be laughed at. It must be remembered that they more frequently exposed their ideas to their peers than those in the control group. In the suburban school, 28 percent of the experimentals and 52 percent of the controls feel that their classmates do not like their ideas. In the potential dropout project, 100 percent of the experimentals at the beginning of the project felt that the rest of the class would not consider their ideas and suggestions. At the end of the seventh grade, only 65 percent of them expressed this feeling.

NOT KNOWING HOW TO START

Sixty-one percent of the general sample and 60 percent of the dropouts indicated that they would not know how to get started on the problem posed. In all three experimental projects, however, the experimentals tended to show slight but not statistically significant advantages in this respect over their controls.

FEAR OF ASKING QUESTIONS

Twenty percent of the general sample and 35 percent of the potential dropouts indicated that they feel that one should not ask too many questions about problems in class. Again, we find in each of the experimental projects slight but statistically insignificant gains in favor of the experimental subjects.

HOPELESSNESS OF ACHIEVING SUCCESS

Nineteen percent of the general sample and 40 percent of the potential dropouts expressed feelings of hopelessness for success in solving the problem posed at the beginning of the test. In the group guidance program, the experimental subjects more frequently than their controls expressed doubts about their ability to solve problems like this (33 and 15 percent respectively). In the creative development project, four percent of the experimentals and 20 percent of the controls expressed such doubts. In the school located in a medium-sized southern town, 60 percent of the experimentals and 66 percent of the controls expressed feelings of hopelessness about solving this kind of problem. It is interesting to note that the suburban children feel less hopelessness about solving this kind of problem than the other groups, especially their counterparts in the medium-sized southern town. It may be that suburban children are more familiar with this particular problem than the other groups. In the potential dropout project, 35 percent of the experimentals and 50 percent of the controls expressed hopelessness about being able to solve the problem. This amounted to a net gain of 40 percent for the experimentals over the controls.

Conclusion

Many youngsters in the beginning year of junior high school express concepts about creative problem solving and self-concepts that would seem to limit seriously their ability to learn on their own and solve problems. Many of them apparently feel rather keenly that their ideas are not given serious consideration by classmates and are likely to be ridiculed. Many seventh graders are handicapped by beliefs in one best answer to all problems, the authority of the peer majority, an aversion to new and divergent ideas, suppression of ideas, the innateness of problem-solving ability, and the unresponsiveness of these abilities to practice and education. Fortunately, however, many of these attitudes and concepts are amenable to change through preventive and remedial projects such as the ones described briefly in this paper. If guidance workers are alert to the existence of erroneous ideas about the nature of problem-solving skills and self concepts as problem solvers, they will probably be more effective in helping youngsters achieve more accurate concepts at the beginning of their junior high school careers.

REFERENCES

1. Lichter, Solomon O., Rapien, Elsie B., Seibert, Frances M., and Sklansky, M. A. *The Drop-Outs*. New York: Free Press of Glencoe, 1962.
2. Torrance, E. Paul. *Guiding Creative Talent*. Englewood Cliffs, N.J.: Prentice-Hall, 1962.

3. Torrance, E. Paul, and Gupta, R. K. *Development and Evaluation of Recorded Programmed Experiences in Creative Thinking in the Fourth Grade.* Minneapolis: Bureau of Educational Research, University of Minnesota, 1964.

4. Yamamoto, Kaoru. "Development of Ability to Ask Questions Under Specific Testing Conditions," *Journal of Genetic Psychology,* CI (September, 1962), 83–90.

J. W. GETZELS
Professor of Educational Psychology, University of Chicago
P. W. JACKSON
Professor of Educational Psychology, University of Chicago

10 · THE MEANING OF "GIFTEDNESS"—AN EXAMINATION OF AN EXPANDING CONCEPT

• When a concept becomes the focus of critical concern it is almost inevitable that its original meaning will simultaneously be expanded and differentiated. The concept of "giftedness" is, of course, of critical concern at this time, and the purpose of this paper is to examine the transformations this concept is presently undergoing and to suggest some additional modifications in its application.

"Giftedness" as related to children has most frequently been defined as a score on an intelligence test, and typically the study of the so-called gifted child has been equated with the study of the single I.Q. variable. Involved in this unidimensional definition of giftedness are several types of confusion, if not outright error. First, there is the limitation of the single metric itself, which not only restricts our perspective of the more general phenomenon, but places on the one concept a greater theoretical and predictive burden than it was intended to carry. For all practical school purposes, the term "gifted child" has become synonymous with the expression "child with a high I.Q.," thus blinding us to other forms of excellence. Second, within the universe of intellectual functions themselves, we have behaved as if the intelligence test represented an adequate sampling of *all* these functions. For example, despite the growing body of literature concerning intellectual processes which seem closely allied to the general concept of "creativity," we tend to treat the latter concept as applicable only to performance in one or more of the *arts*. In effect, the term "creative

Phi Delta Kappan, 40: 75–77, 1958. Permission to reprint granted by Phi Delta Kappa.

child" has become synonymous with the expression "child with artistic talents," thus limiting out attempts to identify and foster cognitive abilities related to creative functioning in areas other than the arts. Third, there has been a failure to attend sufficiently to the difference between the *definition* of giftedness as given by the I.Q. and the variations in the *value* placed upon giftedness as so defined. It is often taken for granted, for example, that the gifted child is equally valued by teachers and by parents, in the classroom and at home; that he is held an equally good prospect by teachers and by parents to succeed as an adult; and that children themselves *want* to be gifted. It can be demonstrated that none of these assumptions regarding the value of the gifted child can be held without question. Empirical data related to these assumptions indicate that the gifted child is *not* equally valued by teachers and by parents, in the classroom and at home; he is *not* held to be an equally good prospect by teachers and parents to succeed as an adult; and children themselves do *not* necessarily want to be gifted, at least not in the traditional sense of the word.

Despite its longevity, there is nothing inevitable about the use of the I.Q. in defining giftedness. Indeed, it may be argued that in many ways this definition is only an historical happenstance—a consequence of the fact that early inquiries in this field had as their context the classroom and its attendant concern with academic progress. If we moved the focus of our inquiry from the classroom setting, we might identify qualities defining giftedness for other situations just as the I.Q. did for the classroom. Indeed, *without* shifting our focus of inquiry, if we only changed the original criteria of learning, we might change the qualities defining giftedness even in the classroom. For example, if we recognize that learning involves the production of novelty as well as the remembrance of course content, then measures of creativity as well as the I.Q. might become appropriate in defining characteristics of giftedness.

A research project, under the direction of the authors, is now being conducted at the University of Chicago in order to provide empirical data related to the considerations outlined above.[1] As subjects of our research we have used a group of approximately 500 adolescents attending a Midwestern private school. The grade range covered by our group extends from the end of the sixth grade to the end of the senior year in high school. Because of the broad purpose of the research, we have inaugurated an extensive testing program involving the assessment of traditional qualities, such as intelligence and psychological health, and including attempts to assess

[1] This project is supported by a grant from the U.S. Office of Education.

less conventional dimensions such as creativity, morality, and the like. The study to be discussed here is but one small aspect of the larger investigation and concerns specifically a description of two of our experimental groups: one which we shall label the "highly intelligent" group, and the other the "highly creative" group.

Two Groups Mutually Exclusive

Our "highly intelligent" subjects were defined as those who were in the top 20 per cent of the sample population on conventional I.Q. measures, but who were *not* in the top 20 per cent on measures of creativity. Our "highly creative" subjects were defined as those who were in the top 20 per cent of our sample population on measures of creativity, but who were *not* in the top 20 per cent in I.Q. The groups comprised twenty-eight and twenty-four subjects respectively, with approximately an equal proportion of boys and girls in each.

Limitation of space does not permit a complete description of the instruments included in the creativity battery. However, an adequate understanding of the way in which the term "creative" is used in the material to follow requires at least passing comment concerning these tests.[2] Most briefly, all of the tests in the creative battery involved facility in dealing with verbal and numerical symbol systems, and object-space relationships. Some instruments called for rapid verbal associations to stimulus words; others called for the ability to structure quickly an incomplete or distorted perceptual stimulus; still others required remote, or clever, or original responses to complex verbal situations (e.g., supplying last lines to a fable). In one test the subject was to respond to a complex paragraph involving numerical values by suggesting all of the mathematical problems which could be solved with the information in the paragraph.

It should be noted that we did not include in our experimental groups those children who were high in *both* creativity and intelligence, and there were many such individuals. Our attempt was to isolate the two qualities under study from each other as much as possible in order to examine the

[2] Some of these instruments were adapted from the more inclusive test batteries of J. P. Guilford, professor of psychology at the University of Southern California, and R. B. Cattell, professor of psychology at the University of Illinois. Others were developed by the staff of the research project. A more complete description of these instruments is given in J. W. Getzels and P. W. Jackson, "The Highly Creative and the Highly Intelligent Adolescent: An Attempt at Differentiation," paper read at the American Psychological Association Meetings, Washington, D. C., August, 1958.

relative contribution of each to the functioning of the child. Those in-dividuals who excelled in both areas are the objects of further investigation still in progress.

Having identified our two experimental groups, we compared them to each other and to the population from which they were drawn on a number of relevant variables, including: school performance as measured by stand-ardized verbal and numerical achievement tests appropriate to each grade level; teacher preferences as measured by teacher ratings of the pupils on how much they "liked to have them in class"; the preferences of the children themselves for personal qualities they would like to possess; the children's perception of the personal qualities they believed would lead to success in adult life and those they felt teachers would most prefer in children. In addition, the children were asked to write four-minute stories in response to six pictures flashed on a screen for twenty seconds each. An examination was made of the differences in the writing "style" of the two groups.

Experiment Subjects Equal in Achievement

The results of these comparisons may be summarized as follows:

First, with respect to school achievement, despite a difference of twenty-three points between the *mean* I.Q.'s of the two groups, they were *equally* superior in school achievement to the student population as a whole.

Second, when asked to rate the children on the degree to which they would like to have them in class, the teachers exhibited a clear-cut prefer-ence for the high I.Q. child. The ratings given the high I.Q. group were significantly higher than those of the total student body; the ratings given the high creativity group did not differ significantly from those of the total student body. This occurred despite the fact, as we have seen, that *both* the high I.Q. and the high creative groups were *equally superior* to the other students in school achievement.

Third, comparing the personal aspirations of the children as reflected in the personal qualities they would like to possess, we find that the creative child himself rates high marks, I.Q., pep and energy, character, and goal-directedness *lower* than do members of the highly intelligent group, and that he rates wide range of interests, emotional stability, and sense of humor *higher* than do members of the highly intelligent group. The last item, sense of humor, is particularly noteworthy since the value which the creative child puts upon this quality so far exceeds the ranking it receives from high I.Q. children as to make it one of the outstanding differences between the two groups, and indeed sets the creativity group apart most sharply from *all* our other groups.

Fourth, the groups show distinct differences in the degree to which they aspire for "success" in adult life. The high I.Q. child desires to possess those qualities *now* which he believes will lead to success in adult life; the creative child does not seem to use this remote goal as criterion in the selection of his present aspirations.

Fifth, the relationship between the child's own personal aspirations and those qualities which he believes teachers prefer is quite different for the two groups. The high I.Q. child holds to a self-ideal which is consonant with the one he believes teachers will most readily approve; the self-ideal of the creative child is not only *not* consonant with what he believes to be the teacher approved model but shows a slight *negative* correlation with such model.

Sixth and finally, in their written responses to our six stimulus pictures, the creative students exhibited a degree of imagination and originality (not by any means the same as correct grammatical construction) unmatched by the high I.Q. students. Compared to the latter group, the creative students produced stories which seemed to "spring from" the stimulus rather than appeared to be "tied down" by it. Their stories made abundant use of humor, novel situations, and unexpected endings. They seemed to "play with" the picture stimulus for the pleasure of invention rather than "labor" the stimulus in order to find the "correct" theme.

Some Important Implications

There is, it seems to us, a consistency and unity even in these preliminary findings which may have important implications for defining and identifying so-called gifted children in the educational setting. We believe the high academic performance of our creative children coupled with the related lack of recognition which they may receive from teachers points to the core of the problem of expanding the present conception of "giftedness," and of breaking the bonds that the I.Q. has on this concept in the school situation. The personal qualities of such presently neglected groups as our creatives which tend to estrange teachers from them may very well derive from the very neglect which these children suffer in the educational setting. With respect to our creative students, for example, the quality of "disillusionment" which appears to be reflected in the discrepancies between their personal aspirations and the aspirations they believe to be valued by teachers and by society in general may be a function of just the neglect to which we have been pointing. Despite their exceptional talents, they may miss identification by the usual I.Q. instrument; and despite their superior achievement, they may fail to gain the same personal preference from teachers that the high I.Q. children seem to have. We venture to suggest that a consideration of these discrepancies may deepen our appreciation at once of the need for expanding the concept of giftedness in the school setting and of the very real difficulties involved in such expansion.

A Challenge for Educators, Researchers

Once we set a precedent by allowing an exception to the practice of labeling only high I.Q. children as "gifted," the possibility of expanding the concept to include other potentially productive groups becomes a genuine challenge to both educators and research workers. The not inconsiderable dangers inherent in the possibility of expanding the concept to a point where it becomes meaningless seem to us to be compensated by the possibility of increasing the effectiveness of our education for *all* children.

E. PAUL TORRANCE
Professor of Educational Psychology, University of Georgia

11 · THEIR STORIES TELL
THEIR FEELINGS: PROBLEMS
OF HIGHLY CREATIVE CHILDREN

● Inescapably, the individual who thinks of a new idea is, in the very beginning, a minority of one. Since creativity involves independence of mind, nonconformity to group pressures, or breaking out of the mold, it is inevitable that highly creative children experience some unusual problems of adjustment.

The highly creative child must either repress his creativity or learn to cope with the tensions which arise from being frequently a minority of one. Repression of creative needs may lead to personality breakdowns. Their expression frequently leads to loneliness, conflicts, and other problems of adjustment. Educators of gifted children need to understand these problems.

It is important to the educator that he understand the way children see society's sanctions against divergency. One of our studies furnished us with many insights in this respect. We asked 5,000 children in grades 3 through 6 to write imaginative stories concerning animals or persons with some divergent characteristic. One story written by a sixth-grade girl will illustrate this.

The protagonist was a flying monkey named "Pepper." Well-educated and unusual in that he ate peppers rather than bananas, Pepper was an individual to the point that he made a decision to go to America, which was unheard of in his society. In America, Pepper found himself an object of scorn and ridicule and wound up in a zoo cage. The story continues:

Education Digest, 27: 40–42, November, 1961. Condensed from *The Gifted Child Quarterly*, 5: 31–34, 1961.

Now Pepper was sad. He didn't like the cage they put him in. He made a vow that if he ever got out he would never be different again and 10 minutes later he saw some bent bars big enough to fly through . . . and in two days was back in the jungle. He kept his promise too. He was never different again. He was a good little flying monkey.

It would be safe to assume that Pepper also ate his bananas.

About two-thirds of the stories tell similar tales of conformity or of destruction. However, some cultures are more indulgent of divergency than others. In stories written by gifted children in special classes, the flying monkey is in some way able to persist in his flying in about 70 percent of the stories. Stories written by children in a small town populated with Indians, Whites, and a few Negroes also reflect this tolerance. The flying monkey succeeds in about 74 percent of the stories.

Another area that demands understanding by those working with gifted children is that these children are not always the well-rounded all-American types. The highly creative child is likely to have lagged in some phase of his development. Verbal abilities frequently will be below some of their other abilities.

Our society places high value on verbal skills and tremendous pressures are exerted on children to excel in this respect. The relentlessness of these pressures is symbolized in a story written by one of these children.

The plot dealt with the problems of a duck named Glob-Blob, who could not quack. Glob-Blob's life was made miserable by quackers of the Ladies Duck Aid Society who pursued him relentlessly, determined to beat into him an ability to quack. Finally, they succeeded in beating him to death.

. . . "That's life," Glob-Blob said to himself as, slowly but surely, failing, he dropped to the ground. The quackers, very pleased with themselves, sat down for a chat.

Many children must consider their counselors, teachers, and parents as "quackers" when we work so hard to make them become "better rounded personalities."

Another point that needs some attention and understanding is that many creative children prefer to work and learn on their own. Schools have been slow in providing such opportunities.

Last year we conducted a study and found that children would do a great deal of writing on their own, if properly motivated. In another study we found that gifted children in a split-shift school showed more growth in language development, science, and social studies than under a full-day schedule. I have seen learning situations "accidentally" left "open" a sufficient number of times to feel excited about what would happen if we should do so more frequently.

Attempt Hard Tasks

Highly creative children have a strong desire to move far ahead of their classmates in some areas. They like to attempt difficult tasks, and they make us afraid that they are not "ready." A frequent theme in our imaginative stories is related to this problem. The young animal or fowl asks, "When can I roar? When can I crow? When can I fly?" Almost always the answer is, "When you are a little older." We are always afraid that the young one might not be ready to learn and would be forever scarred by even a temporary failure.

A common experience in the lives of many outstanding individuals has been their ability to cope with failure and frustration. Had they not attempted difficult tasks, it is likely that their great ideas would not have been born. Fortunately, educators of gifted children are revising their concepts about what can be taught at various levels of education.

It is often said of outstanding creative achievers that they seemed to be possessed by a purpose and were "men of destiny." Creative children are searching for and do need a purpose worthy of the enthusiastic devotion they are capable of giving. Some of this need is portrayed in another story. It is an account of a monkey who didn't know what, who, or why he was. He identified with, and thought of himself as, the airplanes that flew over the jungle habitat. He even named himself, "Buzz."

> Now we all know that monkeys can't fly, but he didn't know this. Why he didn't even know that he was a monkey, so he kept trying and trying—and you know what? He flew!

The above may have implications concerning the need for helping children discover their potentialities and for helping them achieve their self-concepts creatively rather than by authority.

Counselors and teachers may become irritated with children who seem to create problems for themselves by trying consciously to be different—searching for their uniqueness. One authority maintains that creative individuals reject the demands of their society to surrender their individuality because "they want to own themselves totally and because they perceive a shortsightedness in the claim of society that all its members should adapt themselves to a norm for a given time and place."

One way in which the creative individual searches for his uniqueness is through his vocational choice. A recent study found that the highly creative responded with a greater number of different occupations, and more unusual or rare occupations, than did the highly intelligent subjects. Attitudes toward adult success were also different, the highly creative being less concerned with conventional standards.

In no group thus far studied have we failed to find clear evidence of the operations of pressures against the most creative members of the group, though they do vary widely in degree of severity.

In each classroom, three characteristics stand out as identifying the highly creative children: There is a tendency for them to gain a reputation for having wild or silly ideas. (Their teachers and their peers agree on this.) Their work is characterized by its productivity of ideas "off the beaten track." (This explains one difficulty of teachers and peers in evaluating their ideas and perhaps why the creative show up no better than they do on traditional intelligence tests.) And, the highly creative are characterized by humor and playfulness. All these characteristics help explain both the psychological estrangement and the creativity.

FACTORS THAT FACILITATE LEARNING

• As the editors indicated in the introduction, one reads more effectively from a frame of reference or a point of view. He interprets his reading and integrates it into his experience according to his way of looking at things. There it serves to increase his capacity to understand and appreciate subsequent reading and experience. Because of this, it often is possible to reread a selection after a period of time from a broader frame of reference and to find that much more has become meaningful. Burton's and Riessman's articles, in particular, lend themselves to this kind of rereading. With a notable exception, they furnish the reader with a condensed but fairly comprehensive treatment of what may be done to facilitate the learning process. The exception is the area of motivation. The explanation that one learns those behaviors that are rewarded and seeks always to return to a homeostatic balance fails to account for the urge to do new things and to explore strange and sometimes dangerous places. Menninger[1] speaks of heterostatic drives—the tendency of an organism to effect change, to initiate disturbances, and to learn. Homeostasis fails to furnish an acceptable explanation for the insatiable curiosity which drives the two-year-old youngster to manipulate and to investigate all the environment of which he becomes aware.

A more plausible explanation, though less amenable to statistical treatment and measurement, may well be that people learn because they have

[1] Karl Menninger, with M. Mayman and P. Pruyser, *The Vital Balance* (New York: Viking Press, 1963), pp. 84–85.

an urge to learn—as a plant pushing upward through a crack in a cement walk has an urge to grow. If this is the case, and motivation to learn, to change, and to become something better is innate, the removal of inhibiting factors and blocks to learning ought to be of more concern than a system of rewards, which do not work very well in the first place and probably would not be needed at all if natural curiosity could be encouraged rather than discouraged.

It is significant that with much known about the subject of learning there is so little conscious application of this information in the average classroom. Two of the most outstanding examples of this neglect are emphasized in the included selections. We know, first, that learning is a function of the entire organism, yet teachers have a tendency to overlook the pupil's feeling or emotional condition as a factor in promoting effective learning. And we also know that individuals are different and unique, yet teachers tend to expect learning to occur for all individuals with similar teaching and classroom experiences.

Reed's article dealing with the manner in which teacher attitude and interpersonal tension within the classroom affects the learning process and Burton's emphasis that intense emotional states are distracting are illustrative of the first example. The general lack of concern evidenced by education and by teacher-preparing institutions with the effect of the pupil-teacher relationship on learning also is illustrative of this. While it is customary for teacher preparation to include both subject-matter and method emphases, it is much less usual for teachers to be instructed in, and to understand, the dynamics of interpersonal relationships. That this may be a case of putting the cart before the horse is evidenced by the hierarchy of needs developed by Maslow.[2] He arranges human needs in a hierarchy of potency and indicates that such requirements as food, safety, psychological security, belongingness, and love must be met before the individual can be expected to focus upon the need to learn. In other words, the security of the self must be assured, both physically and psychologically, before it can be developed and enhanced. It seems to us that if what the teacher does in an interpersonal sense makes it impossible for the pupil to listen to him, his competence with the informational and methodological aspects of teaching may be wasted.

The second example of omitting what is known about learning from the classroom is evidenced by Riessman's concern with the necessity for understanding the style or way in which each pupil learns. If, as he indicates,

[2] Abraham H. Maslow, *Motivation and Personality* (New York: Harper and Row, 1954), pp. 80–122.

what is happening in the classroom can be antithetical to, or can fail to complement, the learning style of the pupil, it is essential that the areas of dissonance be identified and that some attempt be made to bring them into congruence. While considerable success has been experienced in identifying and describing self-defeating behavior patterns as far as social competence is concerned, this does not appear to have been done for learning. We see no reason why an astute observer could not do this for learning styles and patterns and for the dynamics of pupil-teacher interaction within the classroom. Perhaps learning styles and behavior patterns will be found to be interrelated. Perhaps a better understanding of one will facilitate an understanding of the other.

WILLIAM H. BURTON

Former Director of Apprenticeship Teaching, Harvard Graduate School of Education

---

12 · BASIC PRINCIPLES IN A GOOD
TEACHING-LEARNING SITUATION

Differences among Theorists

● A simple definition will be adequate for the summary here presented: Learning is a change in the individual, due to the interaction of that individual and his environment, which fills a need and makes him more capable of dealing adequately with his environment. A technical definition satisfactory to leading theorists in the field would be more difficult to state and is not necessary for our purposes.

The effort to summarize principles of learning which underlie desirable teaching situations is seriously complicated by the fact that there are approximately a dozen learning theories available. No one has yet formulated a systematic theory satisfactory in all respects. But many facts about learning are known and accepted. There is also agreement on the place of experimental procedures for the demonstration of facts and principles. Serious differences between the various theories remain regarding the nature of certain facts, the primacy of other facts, and the interpretation of facts. These differences must, of course, affect any statement of basic theory and principle.

The differences between theorists are due in part to differences in basic viewpoint and accepted premises. Sometimes two or more theories deal with different types of learning problems, different motivations, or other factors, without sufficient attention to, or development of, a systematic theory to cover more ground. Sometimes, even, disagreements will cut across the

---

Phi Delta Kappan, 39: 242–248, 1958. Permission to reprint granted by Phi Delta Kappa.

groupings of theorists so that some in one camp are in agreement with some in the rival camp and in disagreement with their colleagues. These differences cannot, in the present state of knowledge, be shrugged off when we are dealing with efforts at systematic theory. We can, however, get on with a more limited job of setting up a reasonably consistent statement of principles useful in everyday teaching.

Hilgard[1] has reduced the confusion considerably by classifying the ten or a dozen theories into two basic groups which he labels *stimulus-response* (connectionism, conditioning, behaviorism) and *cognitive* (Gestalt, organismic, sign-significate). Some theories do not fit clearly within either group. He goes on to point out that although no single systematic inclusive theory is as yet available, the situation is not as bad as it seems. He avoids premature systematization on the one hand, and naive eclecticism on the other, showing that something can be learned from the serious efforts of each group of theorists. In any practical situation, as contrasted with efforts to build a systematic theory, this is a sensible view. Pure theory, an absolute necessity for full understanding, is not available. We therefore accept any facts and principles which have been carefully demonstrated and which aid us in understanding and promoting learning.

The succeeding chapters in this symposium will undoubtedly reflect some of the differences in basic theory. The present chapter, assigned as an overall summary, will follow Hilgard's view and include principles which promise to be useful, regardless of theoretic origin. Every effort will be made, however, to maintain internal consistency in the statement.

Agreements among Theorists

Textbooks on learning and on teaching carry, among them, a considerable list of principles of learning basic to good teaching. It may come as something of a shock to the so-called practical schoolman to discover that learning theorists agree on only a limited number of these principles. Two excellent summaries[2] of agreement among theorists are available. The fifteen or so agreed-upon principles are not reproduced here, since they will be included within the various summaries to follow.

[1] Ernest R. Hilgard. *Theories of Learning*, revised edition. New York: Appleton-Century-Crofts, 1955. Chapter 1.

[2] Ernest R. Hilgard, *ibid.*, pp. 485–487, and T. R. McConnell, "Reconciliation of Learning Theories," Chapter 7 in *The Psychology of Learning* (Forty–First Yearbook, Part II, National Society for the Study of Education.) Bloomington, Ill.: Public School Publishing Co., 1942.

I. THE GENERAL PURPOSES OF LEARNING

The overall purposes of learning are relevant to the social order within which they operate. We believe in the democratic way of life with its emphasis on (a) opportunity for the fullest development of the unique capacities of the individual, and (b) a socially oriented group within which the individual may realize his destiny. This means that one goal of learning will be the development of creativity, individual initiative and responsibility, and leadership. The other will be the development of social skills and good human relations. The use of experts and of experimentation will be learned within the democratic social process. An extended list of democratic values could be made. The following brief list may be taken as guides for learning, and particularly for teaching:

1. The dignity and worth of the individual is a primary tenet of Judeo-Christian democracy. Respect for the individual is a corollary.

2. The common good of the group is a social aim of democracy. A proper balance should be maintained between the development of the independent individual and the social individual.

3. Obligations as well as rights are inherent in a democracy. The development of a "democratic conscience" in the individual is necessary to such a society.

4. A flexible functioning of the group with freedom for all to contribute is essential to democracy, and hence to the democratic learning process.

5. The process of group discussion, deliberation, and decision on common problems is the process of democracy. Decisions are based on consensus preferably, or on tentative majority decisions when consensus cannot be achieved. (Detailed principles governing group process are summarized separately later.)

II. GENERAL PRINCIPLES OF LEARNING[3]

The principles of learning are worded differently by various psychologists. Readers may substitute any wording or listing they prefer for the composite one given here.

1. The learning process is experiencing, doing, reacting, undergoing. The actual pattern to be learned is the chief aim, but a multitude of varied

[3] It is not possible in a short article to cite research background for each principle listed. The two research summaries already noted (Hilgard, and the Forty–First Yearbook, Part II, N.S.S.E.), together with several dozen individual research studies, were consulted. Texts in psychology and in principles of teaching were checked, though these are secondary sources. The two summaries contain bibliographies, Hilgard's alone covering over thirty pages.

learning activities and outcomes also occur. Active participation by a learner is preferable to the kind of passive reception usually involved in listening to a lecture or watching a motion picture.

2. Responses during the learning process are modified by their consequences.

3. The learning situation is dominated by a purpose or goal set by the learner, or accepted by him, and should lead to socially desirable results. The purposes and goals arise in the life of the learner.

4. The learning situation, to be of maximum value, must be realistic to the learner, meaningful, and take place within a rich and satisfying environment.

5. The learning process occurs through a wide variety of experiences and subject matters which are unified around a core of purpose.

6. The learning experience, initiated by need and purpose, is likely to be motivated by its own incompleteness, though extrinsic motives may sometimes be necessary. (See later summary on motivation.)

7. The learner will persist through difficulties, obstacles, and unpleasant situations to the extent that he deems the objectives worth-while.

8. The learning process and achievement are materially affected by the level of aspiration set by the learner. Individuals need practice in setting realistic goals for themselves, goals neither so low as to elicit little effort, nor so high as to foreordain failure. Realistic goal-setting leads to more satisfactory improvement than unrealistic goal-setting.

9. The learning process and the achievement of results are materially related to individual differences among the learners. The capacity of the learner is a critical factor in deciding what is to be learned and by whom. Brighter pupils can learn things that less bright ones cannot learn; older children can, in general, learn more rapidly than younger ones. (Any decline in adult years depends upon what is being learned.)

10. The learning process proceeds most effectively when the experiences, materials, and desired results are carefully adjusted to the maturity and background of experience of the learner. (See later summary on readiness.)

11. The learning process proceeds best when the learner can see results, has knowledge of his status and progress, when he achieves insight and understanding. That is, information about the nature of a good performance, knowledge of his own mistakes, and knowledge of successful results, aid the learner.

12. The personal history of the learner—for example, his reaction to authority (many other factors might be cited)—may hamper or enhance his ability to learn from a given teacher.

13. Tolerance for failure is best taught through providing a backlog of success that compensates for experienced failure.

14. The learning process proceeds most effectively under that type of instructional guidance which stimulates without dominating or coercing; which provides for successes rather than too many failures; which encourages rather than discourages.

15. The learning process in operation is a functioning unity of several procedures which may be separated arbitrarily for discussion.

16. The learning products are socially useful patterns of action, values, meanings, attitudes, appreciations, abilities, skills. The products are interrelated functionally but may be discussed separately.

17. The learning products accepted by the learners are those which satisfy a need, which are useful and meaningful to the learner.

18. The learning products are incorporated into the learner's personality slowly and gradually in some instances, and with relative rapidity in others. The realness of the conditions under which the learning takes place and the readiness of the learner contribute to integration.

19. The learning products when properly achieved and integrated are complex and adaptable, not simple and static.

20. Transfer to new tasks will be better if, in learning, the learner can discover relationships for himself, and if he has experience during learning of applying the principles within a variety of tasks.

21. There is no substitute for repetitive practice in the over-learning of skills (for instance, the performance of a concert pianist) or in the memorization of unrelated facts that must be automatized.

22. Spaced or distributed recalls are more advantageous in fixing material that is to be long retained.

III. GENERAL PRINCIPLES OF RE-LEARNING[4]

The learning of new social values and behavior is often a matter of re-learning, complicated by the presence of undesirable values and patterns of action.

1. The processes and principles governing the acquisition of socially

[4] Kurt Lewin and Paul Grabbe, "Conduct, Knowledge, and Acceptance of New Values," *The Journal of Social Issues*, August, 1954, pp. 56–64. Available also in Kenneth Benne and Bozidar Muntyan, *Human Relations in Curriculum Change.* New York: Dryden, 1951, pp. 24–33. See also Kurt Lewin, "Field Theory and Learning," in *The Psychology of Learning*, Forty–First Yearbook, Part II, National Society for the Study of Education, pp. 215–242. The principles here are reworded and rearranged from the original statement.

acceptable learning and of learning detrimental to society are basically alike.

2. Re-education is the achievement of changes in the learner's knowledge, belief, and values.

3. Re-education affects the cognitive structure of the individual, his perception of the physical and social worlds, that is, it changes his knowledge, beliefs, and expectations.

4. Re-education modifies the learner's personal values with respect to group and interpersonal relations.

5. Re-education influences the learner's behavior in social situations.

6. First-hand experience does not guarantee correct concepts; the total learning situation must be conducive to a change in cognition.

7. An individual's perception of the facts and values of a situation affects his behavior.

8. The possession of correct facts in the face of false perceptions does not assure change in inadequate social stereotypes.

9. Inadequate stereotypes are as difficult to obliterate as are incorrect concepts stemming from ignorance and misinformation.

10. Changes in emotional reaction do not necessarily follow acquisition of correct factual information.

11. A change in the "culture of the individual" is equivalent to a change in values, a change in the perception of social relationships, a change in "action-ideology."

   a. Hostility to re-education may stem from loyalty to old values.

   b. The new set of values must be freely chosen and accepted if re-education is to be successful.

12. Emotional acceptance of the new set of values must be a gradual process.

13. The new set of values necessary to change behavior is acquired frequently with belongingness to the group subscribing to the new values. A strong "we feeling" aids in changing values.

(At this point a few other principles might be listed, but they would be repetitions of, or obvious inferences from, general principles of learning.)

IV. GROUP PROCESS AND LEARNING

The use of group process obviously facilitates the learning of skills of communication, or participation and cooperation, of discussing evidence and conclusions. Recent research shows that, contrary to some common beliefs, pupils working in pairs or small groups do better in other areas also than when working individually. Results were superior in paragraph writing, solving algebra problems, improving reading ability, as well as in some of the tasks usually thought of as individual.[5]

1. Group process, properly applied, establishes communication and promotes interaction within a group of learners and between groups.

   a. The psycho-physical setting for group activities should enhance effectiveness in sharing information and ideas.

   (1) Books, audio-visual materials, and all other aids to learning should be assembled for the convenience of the learners.

   (2) The meeting places for large and small groups should be arranged to promote freedom of discussion.

   (3) Experts and consultants—resource persons—may be called in for various purposes.

   (4) Direct training in group process helps to facilitate its use.

   (5) Accurate records should be kept of process and results.

   b. Group process should create a social system of channels of communication between any group of learners and other groups, and with the community within which the school is located.

2. Group process should deal with the problems of the learner within the group, problems common to small groups within the class, and with problems of interest to the whole class.

   a. The readiness of the group should determine what type and level of problem and of learning experiences are to be used.

   b. Clarification and definition of purposes and problems, the selection of activities and materials, provision for evaluating progress, should be accomplished through free participatory discussion.

   c. Experts and consultants may aid in clarifying problems, in opening up new ways of solving them.

   d. Experimentation and simple tryout should be utilized.

   e. Evaluation of the process and its achievements, and of the degree of participation should be continuous. This often aids in clarifying or extending purposes, or in discovering new ones.

3. Leadership in group process should foster initiative and interaction as widely as possible for members of the group. Group process provides for wide sharing and changing of leadership in place of fixing authority in one person.

   a. Individuals who participate in a functioning and productive group are likely to develop desirable attitudes, social skills, and understandings.

   b. Leadership is substituted for authority in effective group process.

[5] David F. Russell, *Children's Thinking.* New York: Ginn & Co., 1956, pp. 266-267.

c. Authority, when used, is derived from the group and is the authority of the group over itself. Democratic authority may be delegated to any individual or committee to be exercised for the good of the group; it may be revoked when not so used.

4. Group process used for a sufficient time should modify the thinking and behavior of all participating learners.

a. The individual learns both as an individual and as a group member when he reorganizes his thinking and behavior toward problems which are of group concern.

b. The individual will learn the value of group activity as he participates in extensive continuing opportunity to make decisions.

c. The individual should be accorded respect and will learn many individual behaviors when he presents sincere arguments in disagreement with the majority of the group.

5. Group process used for a sufficient time should develop desirable social skills and human relations, with accompanying ability to effect changes of social value.

a. The learner will see the value of uncoerced consensus and action based on group decision.

b. Changes in persons, with resultant changes in institutions or procedures, may be effected.

V. PRESERVING THE LEARNER'S SECURITY

Distrust, fear, and insecurity are quite normal reactions to change. The abandonment of old and trusted knowledges and values with the acceptance of new values and behavior patterns is a serious matter for learners at all levels. The older the learner the more he has identified with his knowledges and values and the more necessary it is to conduct learning enterprises so that security and mental health are preserved. The need for security, being normal, must be respected by teachers and not sneered at, as we sometimes unhappily see. The general strategy is to begin with the known and to proceed with challenges likely to beget success; to proceed slowly enough that the learner may develop insight and understanding and may achieve appropriate skills for operating new knowledge and values. The discussion here is related to the more remote principles of re-learning set forth in summary No. III earlier.

1. Begin with problems real to the learners involved, but which contain challenge. Dealing with the familiar and with a challenge which is not overwhelming reduces tension.

2. Begin with problems which will likely yield success. Failure on a self-selected problem is not so devastating as is failure on an imposed task.

3. Allow time for development of understanding and for achievement of new skills and behaviors.

4. Develop a strong group feeling, but with full respect for the individuals within the group. (See earlier discussion of group process.)

5. Provide an atmosphere of freedom and spontaneity. An emotional climate free from tensions contributes to confidence and security.

6. Provide support in the form of recognition for contributions, praise for results.

7. Provide assurance that individual learners may contribute freely, may differ with the majority, may suggest new leads. Creative activities when accepted not only aid the learner in achieving results, but contribute to security.

8. Recognize and build upon differences in interests and special abilities within the group. A favorable effect results from aid given to learners in understanding themselves, both their capabilities and limitations, and in understanding their relationship with others and with the group.

9. Adjust the pace carefully to the individuals and the group. Slow acceptance and development are natural.

VI. THE MOTIVATION OF LEARNING

1. A motivated learner learns more readily than one who is not motivated. Motives may be general or specific, intrinsic or extrinsic.

2. Motivations which are too intense (especially pain, fear, anxiety) may be accompanied by distracting emotional states and by undesirable learning products.

3. Excessive motivation may be less effective than moderate motivation, especially for certain kinds of tasks.

4. Learning under intrinsic motivation is preferable to learning under extrinsic motivation.

5. Purposes and goals which make sense to a learner, which meet a need, which restore the natural equilibrium of the learner, are effective.

6. Purposes and goals should be geared to the interests, activities, and maturities of the learners.

7. Extrinsic motivations operate as follows:[6]

a. Motivation by reward is generally preferable to motivation by punishment, motivation by success preferable to motivation by failure. Marks, rewards, punishments operate as follows:

[6] Learning theorists differ considerably among themselves on these points. The summary here is an effort to give such guidance as is possible lacking a final systematic theory.

(1) Marks, rewards, and punishments not functionally related to the learning situation will beget learning, but it is learning soon lost and accompanied by detrimental concomitant learnings.

(2) The more closely the mark, reward, or punishment used as motive is a natural outcome of the learning process, the better effect it has. Learning is stimulated and undesirable concomitants are at a minimum.

(3) The more clearly the learner sees that the mark, reward, or punishment is an inherent aspect of the learning situation, not artificial and imposed, the better the learning which results.

b. Social motives of competition and rivalry operate as follows:

(1) Routine skills and factual information are readily acquired under these motives without immediate detrimental results.

(2) Certain conversational skills and more general types of thinking may be encouraged, but may have detrimental concomitants.

(3) Creative work—imaginative work generally—is not affected favorably.

(4) Individual mental hygiene and social welfare generally can suffer severely under motives of rivalry and competition. Unhappiness, frustration, and cheating may result with the individual; exploitation, social injustice, and waste may result with the group.

c. The newer social motives of cooperation, recognition by one's fellows, opportunity for participation in planning and decision making, seem to have very beneficial effects upon immediate and later learning. (A considerable revolution in human thinking concerning competition and cooperation, both in world affairs and in individual concerns, is underway. Data are appearing from time to time which should be noted.)

d. Commendation and praise for work well done are excellent incentives. Indiscriminate or undeserved praise has a detrimental effect. Praise is better than condemnation, but the latter is preferable to ignoring the learner's efforts.

e. Success achieved by the learner in adjusting his levels of aspiration to possible achievements is valuable.

f. Goals and levels of aspiration set by the learner's family or social class may be effective, but may also have serious ill effects.

g. Liking for the teacher seems to be a safe incentive with very young learners. With older learners liking must be combined with respect. The teacher's personality should be used sparingly as an incentive, since this type of motivation can invite detrimental concomitants.

h. Sarcasm and ridicule secure only the most undesirable and detrimental learning outcomes. (Continued use of sarcasm can only result from stupidity on the part of the teacher, or as an outlet for a frustrated personality.)

8. Learning without purpose and learning to do difficult, unpleasant, distasteful tasks under compulsion and coercion does not train the learner to persist with unpleasant learnings in real life. This does not mean that difficulty is to be eliminated from learning experience. Learners will persist through serious difficulties if the objective is deemed worth-while. That is, learning under purpose is the best guarantee of persistence in learning to overcome difficulties.

9. The maintenance of interest (or motivation) is important in learning. This can be done by several means, of which the following are illustrations:

   a. Use a variety of learning activities or experiences.

   b. Adapt closely to individual differences, especially in group work.

   c. Make use of success and recognition by the group.

   d. Adapt to levels of maturity and experimental background.

   e. As the teacher, manifest sincere enthusiasm.

   f. Take stock and re-plan from time to time.

VII. THE PRINCIPLE OF READINESS

1. Readiness is the stage in a learner's development when he can learn easily, effectively, and without emotional disturbance. Readiness is one of the most important factors in adjusting learning opportunities and experiences to the learner.

2. Readiness is not a separate and disparate trait; it is a condition brought about by many factors: the individual's rate of growth or maturing, background of experience, mental capacity, attitudes and interests, oral language development, emotional and social adjustments, health, kinesthetic coordination, and others.

3. Readiness for various types of learning and learning experience appears at different times. There is a succession of readinesses.

4. Readiness cannot be forced in advance of natural growth, but programs of experience which compensate for limited experience, which make up deficiencies in certain of the items listed in (2) above, are useful.

5. Readiness or the lack of it should not be assumed without investigation or tryout of certain activities. Observation of the learner's reaction to opportunities to learn is the safe guide to determining whether readiness is present or not.

*   *   *

Because of space limitations, we have omitted summaries of:

The learning of problem-solving skills.

The acquisition of meanings, generalizations, concepts.

The achievement of attitudes and appreciations.
The development of skills and abilities.

VIII. PRINCIPLES OF TEACHING

A list of principles of teaching would consist of a list of inferences drawn from the principles of learning set forth in the preceding pages. Any reader can derive these principles for himself through inspection of the summaries on learning. Instead of presenting a semi-repetition, there is substituted a listing of the characteristics of the learner himself, paralleled by a listing of the characteristics of a setting for learning which would fit the learner. The statements under "Setting for Learning" are directives for teaching.

The Learner

1. The learner, like all living organisms, is a unitary, integrating whole.

2. The learner, like any other living organism, seeks always to maintain equilibrium or balance.

3. The learner is a goal-seeking organism, pursuing aims to satisfy needs, thus to maintain equilibrium.

4. The learner is an active, behaving, exploratory individual.

5. The learner has a pattern and rhythm of growth peculiar to the individual. Notable differ-

The Setting for Learning

1. The desirable setting for functional learning experiences will provide for natural integration of feeling-doing-thinking.

2. Desirable learning experiences will provide opportunity for success in meeting needs and solving problems, but will also give constant challenge to go beyond immediate situations.

3. The desirable setting for learning will be dominated by purposes and goals set up by the learner or learners, either by themselves or with appropriate guidance from the total group, including consultants.

4. The setting must provide freedom to explore, to construct, to question, to differ, to make mistakes: freedom to develop creative contributions. The limits of freedom are democratic controls, rights of others, and good taste.

5. Widely varied types of learning experiences should be provided, adaptable to levels of maturity,

ences exist between individuals, in speed of learning, energy output, depth of feeling, facility of insight.

6. The learner brings with him a personality, a set of aims, values, social habits.

7. A learner may be quite immature in relation to one set of standards and experiences, and quite mature in relation to another.

8. The learner is a social animal, if normal, and naturally seeks activities involving other persons.

to different rates, interests, abilities, and so forth.

6. The purposes and experiences established should arise out of and be continuous with the life of the learner. The family background, and social-class status, as well as the individuality of the learner, must be taken into account.

7. Learners need sympathetic guidance while building an awareness and personality within their own experiences. They need protection from situations in which they can not yet act intelligently; protection from fears and anxieties; protection sufficient to insure security and status on various levels; plus challenge to grow, to conquer problems, to develop self-reliance. The learner needs guidance from consultants who know and understand the problems of a growing personality; who see learning as a developmental process. Guidance must be free from domination or coercion.

8. The setting must provide many varied opportunities to work in "we" relationships, developing eventually into self-directed group activity. The whole range of interactive human relationships, the co-operative group process, is essential to the development of mature socialized personality.

FRANK RIESSMAN
Professor of Educational Sociology, New York University

13 · STYLES OF LEARNING

● In any classroom, probably no two pupils learn the same things in the same way at the same pace. Some learn most easily through reading; others through listening; still others through doing things physically. Some prefer to work under the pressure of deadlines and tests; others like a more leisurely pace. Some learn by being challenged by people ahead of them; others learn best by helping people behind them.

Everyone has a distinct style of learning, as individual as his personality. These styles may be categorized principally as visual (reading), aural (listening), or physical (doing things), although any one person may use more than one. Some persons, for example, find it much easier to pace the floor while reading an assignment than to sit perfectly still at a desk. Their style may be more physical.

A common characteristic of the disadvantaged child is his physical approach to learning. He has been exposed to very little reading because his parents rarely have the time to read to him. For this reason, it may be easier for him to learn to read by acting out the words than by hearing them spoken by his teacher. This is borne out by the fact that children at a school in one of New York City's poorest neighborhoods are learning to read effectively by singing and dancing to the words. Since songs and physical movement have been incorporated into the teaching of reading, the percentage of retarded readers in the school has reportedly been cut in half.

For a long time now, teachers and guidance workers have tended to ignore the concept of different styles of learning. They have, instead, focused their attention on emotion, motivation, and personality as causes for learn-

NEA Journal, 55 (No. 3): 15–17, March, 1966. Used by permission of the *NEA Journal* and the author.

ing or failure to learn. When confronted with an intellectually able student whose learning fails to measure up to his learning potential, they have tended to attribute this failure to an emotional block or personality conflict. Little attention has been given to how a pupil's learning could be improved simply by concentrating on the way he works and learns.

I believe that a careful analysis of the way a child works and learns is of greater value than speculation about his emotional state. He may indeed feel sibling rivalry or certain irrational fears, but these conditions may not affect his learning as much as the methods his teacher uses to teach him. The important consideration, in my opinion, is whether the methods of learning imposed by the teacher utilize sufficiently the strengths in a child's style of learning.

Most teachers, unfortunately, have been trained to look upon learning in a general way. Their preparation, which may include no more than a few survey courses in educational psychology, neglects the idiosyncracies involved in learning.

For example, most teachers probably assume that the best way to study a reading assignment is first to survey the chapter. This is what they have been taught from the early grades through college because it is the way most people learn best. Some students, however, become so anxious and disturbed at being told to take an overall view of a chapter that they cannot function. Their style calls for reading a chapter slowly, section by section. Requiring such a person to skim the entire chapter first makes no more sense than telling a person who can't resist peeking at the last chapter of a mystery that he must read the book straight through.

The general recommendation that one must have a quiet place to study may be equally lacking in validity. Strangely enough, some people do their best studying in a noisy place, or with certain sounds such as music or even traffic in the background. The textbooks do not talk about this because, for the "average" person, peace and quiet are more conducive to learning.

Style is also very much involved in taking tests. For some individuals, the prospect of a test operates as a prod that stimulates them to absorb a great deal of material they need to master. On the other hand, being faced with a test causes many people to become disorganized, overanxious, and unable to work. After a test, some pupils are so upset over their mistakes that they develop an emotional block about remembering the correct answers to the questions on which they erred. Consequently, they repeatedly miss the same questions. For others, finding out that they gave wrong answers aids recall and challenges them to master the problems.

Each classroom is likely to include students whose styles of learning vary widely. Although the teacher cannot cater completely to each student's particular style, he can attempt to utilize the strengths and reduce or modify the weaknesses of those in his classes.

An individual's basic style of learning is probably laid down early in life and is not subject to fundamental change. For example, a pupil who likes to learn by listening and speaking (aural style) is unlikely to change completely and become an outstanding reader. I am not suggesting that such a pupil will not learn to read and write fluently but rather that his best, most permanent learning is likely to continue to come from listening and speaking.

Since the student is the person most vitally concerned, the first step is to help him discover his particular style of learning and recognize its strengths and limitations.

In identifying a style, it is extremely important to ascertain the person's work habits as precisely as possible. If a youngster is in despair because he cannot get any work done during the study time allowed in class or in the study hall, teachers should question him carefully about his routine. What does he do first when study time is announced? How does he try to make himself concentrate? What disturbs him?

Perhaps his answer will be: "At first I'm glad we have time to do the work at school so that I will be free when school is out. I open my book to the assignment, but it's noisy because kids are asking the teacher questions or flipping through their books or whispering. I go sharpen my pencils while I'm waiting for it to get quiet.

"By the time things settle down, I know I don't have too much time left and that I have to hurry or I won't get done. I try to read fast, but the words all run together and mean nothing. Some of the smart kids are already through, and I haven't even started. I usually give up and decide I may as well do it all at home like all the other dumb bunnies do."

A number of things may be involved in this boy's problem. Possibly he is a physical learner (sharpening the pencils may show some need for movement) who has difficulty with visual learning. Apparently he warms up slowly and works slowly, for when he tries to hurry, he finds he can do nothing.

The physical learner generally gets his muscles into his work, and this takes time. Such a student must realize that attempts to rush himself are of no avail, but that this does not make him a "dumb bunny." Once he gets past his warm-up point and begins to concentrate on his work, he may work very well for long periods of time.

If this student is made aware of the way he learns, he can schedule any work requiring concentration for longer periods of time, and use short periods for something less demanding, perhaps a review of the day's school-work. Probably his warm-up period will gradually decrease as he becomes less anxious about failing to keep pace with his fellow students.

A pupil can take advantage of the strengths inherent in his style of learning to balance his weaknesses. For example, consider the pupil who has to learn to read, although his learning style is physical rather than visual.

In order to teach reading to a youngster for whom reading is stylistically uncongenial, the teacher may want to try role playing, which is related to a physical style of learning. The pupil is more likely to be able to read about something that he just role played.

By teaching reading in this way, the teacher is not helping the pupil develop a reading style; he is helping the pupil develop a reading skill.

In a sense, the teacher is overcoming the pupil's difficulty with reading by making use of the pupil's strength, whether it be physical, aural, or whatever.

The challenge to every teacher is first how to identify the learning strengths in his pupils and then how to utilize them to overcome weaknesses. This is the central problem in the strategy of style.

HORACE B. REED
Chairman, Education Department, Skidmore College

14 · THE EFFECTS OF TEACHER WARMTH

● The inadequacies of teacher competence research have received considerable airing during the past ten years. This article is not an attempt to deprecate such healthy self-criticism. For the fact of the matter is that of the 1,300 to 1,400 studies that have been reported in this field during the past sixty years, only a small proportion are mature in design. Further, attempts to make any over-all collation of findings demonstrate that we are far from having sufficient scientific evidence for identifying competent teachers.

The point should be emphasized, however, that progress has been made. The identification of competent teachers requires accurate information about a web of component, interacting parts. It is the purpose of this article to call attention to four independent studies which provide coherent evidence concerning one of these parts. It should be made explicit, therefore, that the question at this stage is not whether we can now scientifically identify the competent teacher. The question is: Can we present scientific evidence immediately relevant to any part of the over-all problem?

Historical References

Selected characteristics of teachers have particular effects upon their students; yet only within the past twenty-five years could sufficient quantitative evidence be produced to show that there are important differences among the behaviors of teachers; that these differences produce differences in classroom atmosphere; and that classroom atmosphere is related to pupil behaviors. The research on teachers' classroom personalities by Anderson

Journal of Teacher Education, 12: 330–334, 1961. Used by permission of the *Journal of Teacher Education*.

and Brewer,[1] and the research on leadership and group life headed by Kurt Lewin[2] demonstrated clearly that children behave differently while under the training of different "types" of adults. Withall demonstrated the existence of different psychological climates produced by different teachers, with the same group of children.[3] These studies, and several other teacher competence researches on social climate, provided an objective basis upon which has been built more definitive researches.

A Collation of Four Researches

The four researches discussed here have a bearing upon the problem of the relationship between the variable of teacher warmth and the criterion of pupil change. There are four major features common to these researches which make feasible a collation of findings: each is statistically mature in research design; each has direct relevance to the antecedent teacher variable of warmth[4]; each depends upon pupil perception as a measure of the antecedent teacher variable; and each selects pupil change as the criterion. The necessity of mature research designs is obvious. The antecedent teacher warmth variable is a sufficiently broad concept to be important to educational theory, it is sufficiently specific to be clearly delineated, and there is a tenable rationale for predicting its effects. Using pupil responses to measure the antecedent teacher behaviors provides more accurate information about the way pupils see the teacher (as contrasted to measures which tell us what the teacher or school administrator thinks is the way the pupils see the teacher). Finally, selection of pupil change as the criterion for teacher competence makes educational sense and conforms to the consensus of most researchers in the field; the fact that each of the four researches utilizes a variety of pupil changes provides an opportunity to check on the uniformity of effect of the teacher variable.

Brookover investigated the correlation between friendly teacher-pupil relationships and pupils' informational achievement gains in a United States

[1] Harold H. Anderson and Joseph E. Brewer, *Studies of Teachers' Classroom Personalities, II* (Stanford, California: Stanford University Press, 1946).

[2] Ronald Lippitt and Ralph White, "An Experimental Study of Leadership and Group Life," *Readings in Social Psychology* edited by G. Swanson, T. Newcomb, and E. Hartley (New York: Henry Holt, 1952) p. 340–55.

[3] John G. Withall, "Assessment of the Social-Emotional Climates Experienced by a Group of Seventh Graders as They Moved from Class to Class," *Educational and Psychological Measurement* 12:3:440–51; 1952.

[4] The term warmth refers to teacher behaviors which relax interpersonal tension between teacher and pupil. It is with this reference in mind that the antecedents are comparable.

history course.[5] His sample included sixty-six male teachers and their 1,275 eleventh-grade pupils. He found a moderate, negative correlation ($r =$ $-.22$; significant at less than the .05 level) between pupils' rating of the warmth of teacher relationships with pupils and the subject-matter achievement criterion. Brookover explains this finding by stating:

> . . . the traditional relationship [in the classroom] is one of struggle—or at least of restricted cooperation—in which the teacher must maintain the dominant role if the interaction is to continue in an orderly fashion. High school students are accustomed to this situation and expect the teachers to force them to learn. If this domination is not present to a considerable degree, the student may react on the assumption that learning is not expected or not necessary. With the student behaving in traditional ways, the customary role of the dominative teacher may possibly stimulate more learning. . . .[6]

Brookover makes the implicit (and prevalent) assumption that a teacher who reduces interpersonal tension through a friendly approach to pupils also reduces tension concerning school work. However, Reed[7] found in his research that the teacher variable of warmth is independent of the teacher variable of demands for high standards of pupils' performance on school tasks (the intercorrelation of the two teacher variables is nearly zero and is not significant). We would suggest an alternative set of explanations concerning Brookover's findings. With eleventh-grade pupils the motivation of marks is a major factor in determining the gains that are made in an achievement such as information in United States history, while the motivational effects of teacher warmth may be negligible for such specific learnings. In fact, one of Skinner's teaching machines might be expected to provide equally good or better results. As concerns Brookover's obtained negative correlation, there is the added possibility that the teacher who spends some class time in maintaining a relaxed interpersonal climate may actually sacrifice some degree of informational achievement for other types of objectives; the less warm teacher may use this class time for informational, subject-matter emphasis.

If this set of explanations is somewhat correct, one would predict that any positive effect of a warm teacher would show up with the more comprehensive and/or attitudinal pupil changes. These learnings are less

[5] Wilbur B. Brookover, *A Sociology of Education* (New York: American Book Company, 1955).

[6] *Ibid.*, p. 305.

[7] Horace B. Reed, "Anxiety: the Ambivalent Variable," *Harvard Educational Review* 30:141–53; Spring, 1960.

directly affected by such motivators as marks for they seldom form important parts of examinations. They are therefore more likely to be dependent upon motivations associated with selected characteristics of the teacher. The following three researches, each independently executed, strongly confirm this prediction.

The research project directed by McCall is one of the most exacting and comprehensive in the field of teacher competence.[8] His sample included seventy-three sixth-grade teachers and 2,164 pupils, from rural and urban, Negro and white schools. Commissioned by the state of North Carolina, McCall was in a position to conduct an extensive study of many teacher factors and make a comprehensive measurement of pupil growth. The following quotation illustrates several strong elements of the project:

> [The general plan of research was] to measure comprehensively the growth produced in each class by the teacher of that class, to weigh the elements of the growth according to importance, to secure a single composite figure for all the growths made by each class, to correct this weighted crude growth for the capacity of the class to grow and for differences in class size if the latter appeared to influence growth, and then to correlate a large number of measures of the teachers' traits with this purified criterion of each teacher's worth as a teacher.[9]

One antecedent was the pupils' rating of their teachers on a scale which included the variable of kindness (a synonym for warmth). After obtaining weak positive, negative, or no relationships for the criterion and many other traits, as rated by several sources, McCall found that pupils' judgments of teachers' kindness was one moderately strong predictor of pupil growth. The mature, highly skilled design and execution of McCall's project compels serious consideration of the positive effect of warmth upon comprehensive learnings.

The teacher competence research by Cogan[10] is an excellent model, for it incorporates the major components suggested by Goethals[11] as essential in a scientific analysis of school problems. One of Cogan's antecedent teacher variables is termed inclusiveness. By this Cogan means pupils'

[8] William McCall, *Measurement of Teacher Merit* (Raleigh, North Carolina: North Carolina State Superintendent of Public Instruction, 1952).

[9] *Ibid.*, p. 10.

[10] Morris L. Cogan, "Behaviors of Teachers and the Predictive Behavior of Their Pupils," *Journal of Experimental Education* 27:89–124; December 1958.

[11] George W. Goethals, "A Framework for Educational Research," *Harvard Educational Review* 28:29–43; Winter, 1958.

perceptions of teacher behaviors which are expressive of the teacher's integrative, affiliative, and nurturant needs. While inclusiveness encompasses additional behaviors, a major factor is the relaxation of interpersonal tension between teacher and pupil. The criteria of his study are amounts of required and of self-initiated school work performed by the pupils. These criteria are pervasive in nature for they are relevant to many types of comprehensive school objectives. Cogan conceives his criteria as intervening between the teacher antecedents and such comprehensive criteria as McCall utilized. Predictions are based upon the theory that pupils see teacher behaviors as cues for the arousal of the different drives of anxiety or of liking, with the deduction that pupils will respond to anxiety by avoiding, and to liking by approaching learning activities. In a sample consisting of thirty-three eighth-grade teachers and 987 pupils, significant (.01 level) within-group positive correlations were found for inclusiveness and pupils' scores on self-initiated work ($r = .35$), and for inclusiveness and pupils' scores on required work ($r = .28$).

A third confirmation of McCall's and of Cogan's findings has been presented by Reed.[12] The latter theorized that the teacher's warm relationships with the pupils would help satisfy pupils' needs for emotional security. Warmth would therefore serve as a rewarding experience for the pupils. Since they associate many classroom learning activities with their teacher, they will tend to find such activities more or less rewarding as a function of more or less warmth between teacher and pupils. This should be especially true for a criterion such as pupils' interest in the subject, where the motivation for such school objectives may often not be provided by other sources. Reed's antecedent variable of warmth refers to pupils' perceptions of teacher behaviors which relax interpersonal tension between teacher and pupil; there is a consequent reduction in the frequency of pupils' problems concerning "getting along with the teacher," but not necessarily in the frequency of problems concerning subject-matter tasks. His criterion variable is interest in science as measured by the Reed Science Activity Inventory, a seventy-item inventory of the pupil's voluntary science activities carried out during the current school year. The sample included 1,045 ninth-grade boys and girls and their thirty-eight general science teachers from nineteen public schools. The within-class positive correlation between teacher warmth and pupils' interest in science was .20 for the boy sample and .28 for the girl sample, significant at the .001 level.

[12] Horace B. Reed, "Teacher Variables of Warmth, Demand, and Utilization of Intrinsic Motivation Related to Pupils' Science Interests: A Study Illustrating Several Potentials of Analysis of Variance and Covariance," *Journal of Experimental Education* 29:205–29; March 1961.

Conclusions from the Collation

Teacher competence research reviewers have repeatedly discussed the difficulties of comparing significant findings because of the basic dissimilarities among the studies. The four researches collated here have common major factors in design and intent, which makes comparison feasible and the formulation of constructs reasonable.

It appears valid to state with considerable confidence this generalization concerning the relationship between pupils' perceptions of teacher behaviors that relax interpersonal tension (warmth) and pupil change criteria: when the criteria are comprehensive and/or attitudinal in nature, the correlation will be significant, positive, and of moderate strength.

It appears plausible to state a second more tentative generalization concerning the relationship between teacher warmth and pupil change criteria: when the criteria are informational in nature and are school goals that are rewarded by the marking system, there will be low correlations or a negative relationship. For criteria of this nature, one would predict that the direction of effect of teacher warmth will change from positive to zero or negative as the pupil age increases.

Further Implications

A profitable area for further research would be an investigation of the origins of teachers' abilities to produce a warm classroom atmosphere. Seibel[13] and Bush[14] have each reported on attempts to analyze the components of teacher warmth and to trace some of its antecedents. Seibel, utilizing mature statistical procedures, identified several components (support, verbal and material rewards, solicitation, etc.) but found few meaningful leads as to origins. Bush offers several techniques as effective in increasing the warmth of the teacher-pupil relationship, although his work is of an exploratory nature and is not intended to be rigorous in design. Several of his suggestions might be valuable leads: the teacher's acquisition of information on the varied needs and capacities of the pupils, the teacher's conscious efforts to develop a warm classroom atmosphere, the matching of teachers and pupils as regards social beliefs and interests. Sheldon, Coale, and Copple have provided some evidence that the teacher variable of

---

[13] Dean W. Seibel, "The Prediction of Qualities of Interaction Between Apprentice Teachers and Pupils," (Unpublished doctoral dissertation, Harvard Graduate School of Education, 1955).

[14] Robert N. Bush, *The Teacher-Pupil Relationship* (New York: Prentice-Hall, 1954).

warmth is positively related to such teacher characteristics as higher intelligence, less authoritarianism, higher need for affiliation, and less need for succorance.[15] If these characteristics are important "origins" of warmth, perhaps the warmth variable is not easily amenable to change through teacher training experience; pre-training screening would then become a necessary device.

This discussion has focused upon only one part of the total problem of identifying the competent teacher. A word of caution is therefore necessary. It is probable that the warmth variable will shift in its effects, and in its importance, as a function of the types of criteria. Also, whether a teacher rates high or low on warmth may be of valuable practical information only when one knows more about other characteristics of the teacher. For example, Reed[16] found that the two teacher variables of warmth and of utilization of intrinsic motivation were separate variables but strongly intercorrelated. This may be interpreted to mean that in the training of teachers, instructions in the utilization of intrinsic motivation are more likely to be successful if the student teacher already possesses the attributes of warmth. Such permutations are to be expected with the gain of additional scientific evidence. The resulting picture of the practical implications of the warmth variable will undoubtedly have many other nuances, some of which are not now completely clear or obvious.

[15] M. Stephen Sheldon, Jack M. Coale, and Rockne Copple, "Concurrent Validity of the 'Warm Teacher Scales,' " *Journal of Educational Psychology* 50:37–40; February 1959.

[16] *Op. cit.*

LANGUAGE DEVELOPMENT

• During his study of these selections, the reader can expect to be impressed by a number of statements and ideas and relatively unaffected by others. He will accept only a part of what is read. He will be unable to accept other parts, because they do not fit or make sense in his field of experience. Further aspects will be held in abeyance until increasing knowledge and experience make them meaningful. The remainder, and perhaps a sizable portion, may remain unnoticed, unintegrated, and unlearned because the interpretative background of the reader does not permit him to recognize the idea or to classify it as important or significant. He is not, in other words, ready to learn this particular fact, technique, or piece of information.

The above is the principle of readiness which is mentioned in several of the included selections. From them, and from other selections, the conviction grows that the manner in which readiness has been traditionally perceived is changing. No longer is it believed to depend so exclusively upon physical and mental maturity; readiness depends also upon the type and variety of antecedent learning and experience. Burrows, in emphasizing the strategic importance of the early years for language development, and Hodges and Metz, in stating that behaviors learned early in life condition the individual's capacities for later learning, are all attesting to this.

The concept of developmental tasks also serves to emphasize the crucial nature of the early years. It helps to recognize that there are certain best times or ages for developing specific behaviors. It also helps to realize that if these tasks are not accomplished and these behaviors are not developed during certain times, the effective learning of essential future behaviors will be less possible. For these reasons the conviction is mounting that the preschool years can no longer be ignored if maximally effective individuals are to be developed. The realization is growing that learning is hierarchical in nature. Furthermore, remediation can never be more than a poor substitute for an adequate development during the time when the individual is able to be most receptive. Hence, there is a trend for learning experiences to be presented to younger and younger children. This is especially true of the learnings which can be considered as tools for gaining other learnings.

All of the means of communicating appear to be of this nature. Without an adequate means of receiving and expressing ideas to others, the individual is limited in his learning to what he can experience directly. To the extent that he can communicate, he can learn from the experiences of everyone else. Man has been a verbal animal for a long time. It has even been hypothesized that his ability to verbalize ideas has been more responsible for his superior brain and reasoning power than his superior intellect has been responsible for his ability to express himself verbally. However that might be, we are considerably more certain that much of our thinking is of a verbal nature and that we use words and the concepts they symbolize for us in all types of reasoning and thinking. No wonder vocabulary and verbal tests constitute the most valid and reliable measure of intelligence that we have been able to develop.

The child who is deprived, because of inadequate learning experiences, cultural encapsulation, or emotional pressures, of the opportunity to develop verbal fluency lacks not only the means of thinking but the means of developing and increasing his intellect. Studies have been conducted that show the cumulative effect of such deprivation. Intelligence quotients have been known to become progressively lower with age when the child's tools for discovering things are not on a par with those of his fellows. Conversely, IQ's have been raised, in some instance by over 20 points, by changes to more stimulating environments.

Metz's assertion that speech improvement must be self-improvement points up the interdependent relationship of communication skills, learning ability, and what Burrows refers to as "positive self-image." While it can be readily accepted that confidence in self is a requisite for learning, it probably is just as true that the ability to communicate with others and relate to them is needed in order for these positive feelings to be generated. None of the three is likely to develop fully without some attention being paid to the others.

ALVINA T. BURROWS
Professor of Education, New York University

15 · CHILDREN'S LANGUAGE: NEW INSIGHTS FOR THE LANGUAGE ARTS

● In the last decade, the disciplines of linguistics and of child study have been vigorous in their exploration of children's language. Many new insights have emerged. Some are being critically tested, and some are now waiting to be tested. Of the array of findings available for action, two major ideas will be presented in this article.

Linguists from widely differing schools proclaim the primacy of oral language. *Oral symbols are the language.* Written symbols stand for oral symbols—not for things, sensations, actions, or experience. The far-reaching implications of this principle will be indicated later.

A second basic idea comes from studies of child development and offers fresh reinforcement of long held views. The early years of life—the pre-school years, commonly—are optimal for language learning. Indeed, they appear to be so strategic that it is debatable whether deprivation in these years can be linguistically redeemed at later periods, even by elaborate enrichment programs.

Infancy and Syntax

We have known for a long time that kindergarten children coming from homes in which a literate level of English is spoken use all the major types

---

The National Elementary Principal, 45:16–21, September, 1965. Copyright ©
1965, Department of Elementary School Principals, National Education Association.

of sentences that have evolved in our language.[1] Without knowing grammatical terms, these children use simple, compound, complex, and compound-complex sentences. They speak and respond to sentences of considerable involvement and variety of pattern. Nor is their vocabulary a negligible achievement, whether one refers to the most generous estimates of recent students or to the more modest figures suggested by earlier observers.

How, without formal instruction, have school beginners learned this formidable array of skills in so short a time! A few spotlights have been directed on this learning drama; many more are needed.

From a report by Brown and Bellugi on the early language of two children, we find that these young talkers concerned themselves with syntax in remarkably efficient ways.[2] Two children, a boy and a girl aged twenty-seven and eighteen months, respectively, imitated their mothers' sentences, and though they left out words, they never changed the original order of words they repeated. "'Frazer will be unhappy" became "Frazer unhappy." "He's going out" became "He go out." Words and parts of words that carry meaning were retained in these and other samples from the systematically made records. "No, you can't write on Mr. Cromer's shoe" was condensed to "Write Cromer's shoe." It was never "Shoe write Cromer." The investigators remind us that in speaking such sentences as "Frazer will be unhappy," the adult spontaneously stresses *Frazer* and *unhappy*. This is of the very essence of the nature of our language. We do, indeed, stress the meaning-bearing words. Children learn the stress system as they learn to talk. Infinite numbers of repetitions make it automatic.

Of equal potential in this small study—small in the sense of being a record of only two children—is the record of how the mothers quite naturally taught language.[3] The examples given show that they added words and endings to their children's utterances but kept intact their word order and obvious meaning.

Although these two children were learning language in two homes of high educational status, informal observation on many playgrounds and in a number of homes tends to confirm the idea that similar methods are in quite general use. Parental reduction and addition to infant sentences, keeping the child word order and stress, seems to be an almost intuitive communication between parent and child. A great many replications of

[1] Fisher, Mary Shattuck. *Language Patterns of Pre-School Children.* Monograph No. 15. New York: Teachers College, Columbia University, 1934.

[2] Brown, Roger, and Bellugi, Ursula. "Three Processes in the Child's Acquisition of Syntax." *Harvard Educational Review* 34:133–51; Spring 1964.

[3] *Ibid.*

this basic study need to be done in homes of many different kinds. At what educational or literacy level is such teaching not done? Is this the kind of teaching, with variations of sensitivity to children's need for emotional identification and support, that characterizes the homes from which four- and five-year-old children bring the speech accomplishments noted earlier? If so, perhaps we have important clues to use in establishing early schools for "disadvantaged" youngsters.

Apparently, word order as a grammatical *sine qua non* is learned so thoroughly that parents unconsciously apply this knowledge in teaching their children—even parents who do not consciously know that English is this kind of language. Further substantiation for this belief is to be found in the studies of oral language of school-age children. Strickland found that even quite limited children—limited as to intelligence and socioeconomic status—used the common structural patterns of the language and a goodly number of their variations.[4] They could manipulate some movable parts of sentences in conversation without risk to the "kernel" sentence in which word order must remain fixed. Long hours of self-assigned drill that young children experience in monologue, in dramatic play, in talking with friends and family—in the constant chatter of normal youngsters—pay dividends. Infant babbling followed by practice on stressed words in meaningful order appears to result in what we call ability to communicate. The values of this early learning must not be taken for granted.

Thought Before Language

It is easy enough to sense young children's struggles to report on the activity of the moment, to convey wants, fears, and other facts and ideas. But can children think about these and other matters before they can talk? For the past few decades most students have thought not. Now, observations by Vygotsky, for example, suggest that pre-verbal thought is an actuality.[5] In similar vein, Carroll delineates some of the sequences by which children form concepts at a pre-verbal stage—concepts relating to food, to toys, to persons; concepts that are responses learned from direct experience.[6]

The relationship between these primary concepts and those acquired as

[4] Strickland, Ruth G. "The Language of Elementary School Children." *Bulletin of the School of Education, Indiana University,* Vol. 38; July 1962.

[5] Vygotsky, L. S. *Thought and Language.* (Edited and translated by Eugenia Hanfmann and G. Vakar.) Cambridge, Mass.: M.I.T. Press, 1962.

[6] Carroll, John B. "Words, Meanings and Concepts." *Harvard Educational Review* 34:178–202; Spring 1964.

part of verbal learning is not precisely clear. Perhaps verbal concept formation is in some measure the rearrangement of first-hand experiences and their resultant concepts into new and variant patterns. The instructional value of direct contact with things, events, and activities was supported by Eskridge's study of how inaccurately children learn concepts from reading.[7]

Although he was investigating the acquisition of geographic terms and their meanings, the processes appear sufficiently common to recall the dangers of shallow verbalism in other areas as well.

Children and Vocabulary

The field of vocabulary has been a battleground in educational research. Estimates of six-year-olds' average vocabulary have varied from as few as 2,500 words[8] to as many as 20,000 words.[9] The scholarly critique of Lorge and Chall directed toward the word sampling procedure in the later (and larger) study recommends a reduction of one-half to three-quarters.[10] If even this latter estimate is sustained by subsequent studies, we shall do well to find out how children's learning before the age of six can be so prodigious. And further, the range from the least verbal to the most verbal pupils assembled in a class intensifies the challenge to provide decently individualized programs of teaching as well as to discover reasons for such great differences among children.

What concepts do children possess for the meanings they can assign to so many words? Carroll defines differences between concepts and meanings.[11] Concepts appear as individual abstractions emerging from experience. Word meanings are societal agreements within a language community. That there are factors common to both is immediately apparent. Individual experience is the matrix of conceptualization, whether "real" or vicarious experience is the key.

[7] Eskridge, Thomas J., Jr. "Growth in Understanding of Geographic Terms in Grades IV–VII." *Research Studies in Education*, No. 4. Durham, N. C.: Duke University Press, 1939.

[8] Smith, Medorah E. "An Investigation of the Development of the Sentence and the Extent of Vocabulary in Young Children." *Studies in Child Welfare*, Vol. 5, No. 5. Iowa City: State University of Iowa, 1926. pp. 28–71.

[9] Smith, Mary K. "Measurement of the Size of General English Vocabulary Through the Elementary Grades and High School." *General Psychology Monograph*, Vol. 24, part 2, 1941.

[10] Lorge, Irving, and Chall, J. "Estimating the Size of Vocabularies of Children and Adults: An Analysis of Methodological Issues." *Journal of Experimental Education* 32:153; Winter 1963.

[11] Carroll, John B., *op. cit.*

Observing the exploratory behavior of young children, one is impressed by their drive to find out the make-up of things, to experience the environment. Olson calls this urge *seeking behavior.*[12] He describes the reinforcement given by a mother to the sounds made by infants, the adult repeating the sound often in a word. The child may again make the sound he made earlier in association with the activity at hand. Olson calls this process "circular stimulation."[13]

Thus in meaningful relationship to reality and to other human beings, children's learning of words, sounds, meanings, and concepts becomes blended in a highly efficient system of exercise and reinforcement.

Principles into Practice

What practical applications can be made from the two insights proposed by the disciplines of linguistics and child development? One admonition leaps out beyond most others: *Use the oral efficiency that children bring to school as the means of developing a complementary efficiency in reading and writing.* To extend, refine, and enhance the oral arts and skills children already possess is the first obligation.

Unconscious wisdom has linked direct experience with things—material substances, operations, events, and conditions—to oral language in the early school years. How much and what kinds of direct experience should be a component of work in middle and upper grades is somewhat less clear. That there should be some is obvious; that there should be more than is provided in most schools is equally obvious to many qualified observers. Taking trips, setting up and labeling exhibits, making models and illustrations, manipulating equipment, doing experiments and demonstrations add zest to learning. They fill an equally important function in furthering concept development.

Social situations implied in the first-hand contacts noted above also demand different kinds of language response. Children's ability to respond with appropriate language to social needs, remarkable though it is, requires continued practice and guidance. This requires conversation and discussion; it likewise requires informal reporting and, at times, carefully structured, formal reporting. Sensitivity to an audience can be furthered only by experiencing many diverse audience situations. Analysis after the experience can also help: "What held the attention of the large audience in the auditorium

---

[12] Olson, Willard C. *Child Development.* Boston, Mass.: D. C. Heath & Co., 1959. p. 402.

[13] *Ibid.*, p. 125.

when we gave our reports on air and water pressure? Where did we lose some of them? Were the illustrations clear enough for the things we couldn't tell in words? Did we talk slowly enough for new ideas to start to work?" Critical questions such as these point to some of the skills to be applied in a world that communicates increasingly through oral and graphic symbols.

Children need the release of dramatics, both informal spontaneous play and planned and practiced plays for an audience. After planning and playing an episode, whether a made-up one about a lost valentine or one developed around Robinson Crusoe's meeting with Friday, children need to lift to consciousness the varied ideas that different groups used to convey feeling as well as fact. Here again, discussion and conversation center around experience. Oral language is the warp and woof of the language arts curriculum, basic to extending meanings, to reading, and to writing. Talk is not time wasted!

The route from oral language to reading and writing is traveled by many a pupil with far greater success than headline hunters would credit to the modern school. By whatever method of approach, however, the relationship between oral language and the symbols for it must be experienced and made nearly automatic. Early reading, it would appear, should exploit prior oral accomplishments. It should convey a meaning richly imbedded in experience. It should be contained in sentence patterns fairly close to those that children speak, edited only as much as is necessary to conform to rudimentary requirements of written prose. Obviously, children's word order should be respected as in the earliest stages of oral learning.

With these parallels in mind, it is quite understandable why the language-experience approach to reading, of which children's dictation is the core, has many advocates. Linkage between his own experience and the words and tones conveying that experience is extended to linkage with their symbols on paper or chalkboard. Word order, so early imprinted by hearing and saying in the pre-reading years, assists in the location of discrete word symbols. Word recognition techniques, derived from "old" words and applied to "new" words, assist in the gradual learning of independence.

Hearing many good stories and much fine verse read aloud, even after considerable independence has been attained, is an essential. Beauty of language is learned through exposure to beautiful language. Recordings are excellent and some should be used, but they are no substitute for the mutuality of teachers and pupils sharing their pleasure in literature. "Feedback" is a term often heard along with "immediate reinforcement." No machine is so gifted in this reciprocal relationship as the face-to-face literary situation developed when the race was young and maintained in some form by every generation for thousands of years.

Children's Writing—When Not to Correct It

One of the acknowledged tasks of the elementary school years is to further the pupil's self-concept. Few experiences in school have so effectively destroyed a positive self-image as has the teaching of composition. Excessive correction has thwarted the pencils of many a beginner. In other cases, no correction at all has been offered for fear of cramping self-expression. When to correct and when not to correct children's writing has been a dilemma for many teachers.

Solutions arrived at in both England and America reveal surprising agreement. Correction is applied to children's practical writings—letters, reports, records, and other forms of factual prose in which the written paper itself is seen by an audience.[14] A British study reaching essentially the same conclusion calls these business-like forms "recording writing."[15]

Pride in achieving correct form is developed in these more objective examples. On the other hand, imaginative expression is for entertainment. Story and verse are to be read aloud to one's class, either by the author or by the teacher, and need not be corrected or re-written. After being enjoyed by an audience, they are filed privately; their physical form is relatively unimportant. They have already served their purpose in oral communication. Here again the oral basis for learning to write operates with real efficiency. Only when stories or verse are to be made public in a class newspaper or school publication must they be edited and re-written. Indeed, when they are made public they must be put into good form. This is an obligation to others as well as a mark of self-respect.

Correction of any writing is best done orally by teacher and pupil in an editing conference, taking turns reading aloud. Thus they apply the oral-auditory facility established long before to the newer learnings of writing and reading.

When writing is an opportunity to reveal one's own feelings and imagination without fear of criticism and with the assurance of respectful listeners, the pupil's picture of himself is enhanced. Not being on the defensive, he can appreciate the good writing of others, both peers and professionals. He can enjoy what is worthy in his teacher's eyes because he, too, is worthy

[14] Burrows, Alvina T.; Jackson, Doris C.; and Saunders, Dorothy O. *They All Want To Write.* New York: Holt, Rinehart & Winston, 1964.

[15] Clegg, A. B. *The Excitement of Writing.* London: Chatto and Windus, 1964.

as a writer. Both his listening audience and those who see his corrected public writing fortify his pleasure and his pride in writing and in himself.

Grammar in the School Program

Grammar is another aspect of the language program that has benefited from fresh insights. Children bring an array of grammatical skills to school. They use the word order system that is the very essence of English syntax. They begin and end sentences and other units of communication with appropriate tonal patterns. They know that one does not always talk in complete sentences.[16] "How long will it take to hatch these eggs?" is appropriately answered with "Twenty-one days." Using this superb economy of conversational style does not detract from sentence sense, which is a highly complex matter with no one monolithic pattern of response.

Children are seen to apply meaningful intonation even though their dialect may differ considerably from what the school covets. Telling children, whether directly or by constant correction, that their home language is bad has proved unproductive. One wonders that schools have so long persisted in such a fruitless attempt. Nor does the memorization of so-called "rules of grammar" merit any better results in the improvement of speech and writing.

By respecting home language, the new one presented in school has a much better chance of winning adherents. If new language patterns are identified with receptive teachers and administrators, with satisfaction in conversation and discussion, with taking part in plays and reporting on the exciting world outside of school and the hopefully fascinating one discovered in school, with reading and writing that are significant to the learner—if these kinds of identification and feelings of success surround the new language, then by the middle grades children can take on the discipline of practicing new conventions. But picking children's language apart in the primary grades, before they have even grown accustomed to a new speech community, can only widen the chasm between child and school.

Concern for the disadvantaged child raises questions about earlier and earlier schooling. Starting before the accustomed age for kindergarten offers a hope for more chance to influence language before it is too late. How late is too late remains to be seen. In view of the age at which children develop language facility in favored homes, even three or four years may

[16] Loban, Walter D. *The Language of Elementary School Children.* Research Report No. 4. Champaign, Ill.: National Council of Teachers of English, 1963.

be too late. There are data suggesting that in homes of low literacy, the whole scale of speech acquisition is delayed. Moreover, if speech training at home depends in part upon frequent one-to-one language contacts, then school groups even as small as fifteen per teacher may be much too large. Perhaps a family-size group of different ages is the basic language laboratory. How far we can stray from this social matrix of speech remains to be seen. Systematic records should be made in early opportunity groups across the country at this strategic period of expansion down the age scale.

Insights presented here are but a few of the many that could be discussed. The curriculum can now draw upon additional discoveries in the disciplines related to children's languages. Their application to learning can point toward new horizons for children and toward new vistas for teachers.

RICHARD E. HODGES
University of Chicago

16 · LINGUISTICS, PSYCHOLOGY, AND THE TEACHING OF ENGLISH

● The expanding production of knowledge is creating one of the most pressing educational problems of our time. Traditional certainties regarding the world in which we live are being shaken by emerging insights into the nature of knowledge in general and into the nature of the disciplines that comprise knowledge. Even a hurried examination of current educational literature reveals that both the content and the processes of formal education are undergoing considerable revision.

The natural sciences and mathematics, partly because of their preciseness and partly because of societal pressures, have been, and are being, explored for better ways of devising instructional programs. The hope is to insure that pupils will acquire basic understandings and competencies in these domains of knowledge.

One approach to this end is the concept of *structure*. A structural approach assumes that the interrelationships among the central, unifying ideas of a given domain of knowledge constitute the essential learnings expected of each pupil. The task of curriculum specialists is to identify these basic ideas in particular subject-matter fields and to formulate instructional strategies that will engender pupils' understandings of these ideas in increasingly complex form.

The concept of *structure* is not unique to mathematics and the natural sciences, however. We may assume that other domains of knowledge also possess structures that would provide pupils with frameworks within which these subjects might be investigated more comprehensively and with greater

Elementary School Journal, 66:208–213, 1966. Reprinted from the *Elementary School Journal* by permission of The University of Chicago Press. Copyright © 1966 by the University of Chicago.

depth than in traditional "factual" programs. Language is one such content field and one in which increasing attention is being given to structure. The structure of language as identified by linguists comprises a fundamental source for improving the teaching and the learning of language.

The concept of *structure* in a given subject-matter field concerns curriculum content primarily; however, the modes of inquiry employed by specialists in such fields also have important implications for the processes of learning. At all levels of education it is essential to consider both content and processes in formulating effective curriculum and instructional practices.

Secondary-school programs have incorporated innovations in subject-matter areas more readily than elementary-school programs have. The reasons are twofold: first, secondary-school curriculums are typically content-oriented. Second, high-school students about to enter adult society presumably have more immediate need to apply their formal school learnings than elementary-school children do.

Current curriculum developments in mathematics and in the natural sciences illustrate these conditions. Elementary-school programs in science and mathematics are only now beginning to change in the light of innovations in mathematics and science at the secondary-school level. These conditions are also becoming evident in English instruction as linguistic insights into the structure and the function of language are increasingly being applied to secondary-school English programs.

Surely, such efforts are to be commended. Yet certain difficulties may be expected to arise as a result of changes that are being made in the content and the methods of English programs.

English courses of study in the secondary schools may become inadequate as curriculum workers adapt linguistic concepts to elementary-school English programs.

Throughout the grades, attention is being given to the improvement of the teaching and the learning of grammar and composition. But grammar, in its broadest definition, is a description of the total language system. A balanced English program considers each of the basic components of the structure of English.

A balanced English program also considers all the data sources that are relevant to curriculum construction. Thus, there is a need to consider not only what the structure of language is, but also how knowledge of this structure is used, and how language generally is learned. These elements, in combination, are basic prerequisites for improving English programs throughout the grades.

Let us examine in greater detail the implications these difficulties suggest for English programs of study in elementary schools.

The Study of Language Throughout the Grades

Ideally, the scope and the sequence of language instruction at the elementary-school level are determined by the verbal habits children bring to the teaching-learning situation and the degree to which the content taught extends their knowledge of English and its uses. Obviously, English programs of study at the elementary- and the secondary-school levels are related. Alterations in content at any instructional level affect other levels as well. Consequently, there is a danger that as linguistic concepts are introduced into elementary-school programs, many of the learnings now being included in secondary-school English instruction will become redundant.

There is a patent need to design a total course of study for English throughout the grades, a course of study that will help the pupil to explore, to understand, and to apply relevant concepts that linguists have identified concerning the structure of his language. Elementary- and secondary-school language specialists need to co-operate in designing a total language experience for pupils throughout the grades. Such a co-operative undertaking is not only wise but essential if repetition and extraneous language learnings are to be avoided in developing an improved English program based on linguistic concepts.

Structure and Function of Language

The emphasis being given to improving instruction in grammar and composition suggests that other basic structural components of language have little relevance in the total English curriculum. Let us see how linguists view the structure of language.

THE STRUCTURE OF LANGUAGE

Linguists generally recognize three major elements in the structure of language. *Phonemes* (the distinctive sound features of language) are the basic building blocks of speech. *Morphemes* (the smallest units of meaning of language) are phonemes and phoneme combinations that are traditionally thought of as words and affixes. *Syntax* (the combining of morphemes into larger units of speech) is commonly thought of as the patterning of words into sentences.

The linguist's model of language structure illustrates the fact that structures are hierarchical. In linguistic structure preceding elements are included as parts of the elements that follow. Phonemes combine to form syllables and morphemes; and morphemes in turn combine in orderly patterns that permit intelligible communication. In this model, the grammar of a language is a description of the total structure of the language, its elements and the rules of ordering these elements into meaningful oral speech.

It should be noted that linguistic descriptions of these structural elements are stated in terms of oral language. To the linguist, the oral language is primary and basic, while the written form of language is secondary and derived. Yet written language is substantially a reflection of the spoken form, although in written English—as in the written form of all languages— this reflection is blurred. Linguists see this blurring of the oral code in its written form as a failure of the written language to obtain a one-to-one correspondence with the structure of oral language.

In written English, for example, this lack of "fit" with speech can be noticed at each of the several levels of language structure: the phonemes (sounds) of speech are not consistently represented by graphemes (letters); written syllabication does not reflect precisely the syllables of spoken English; the pitch, stress, and juncture phonemes of spoken language have few representations in writing; the syntactic patterns of written English are measured against more rigid standards than are the syntactic patterns of spoken discourse.

Yet the fact that the written code reflects the oral code, although im- perfectly, indicates that the same basic structural elements underlie both systems and that these elements, when understood, have advantages for instruction in both spoken English and written English. Once understood, these basic elements provide measures by which pupils can note departures from language norms in both speaking and writing.

The typical child entering school for the first time already has an implicit knowledge of the oral structure of his language. He speaks the language with some fluency and intelligibility. Formal language instruction should help the pupil to make explicit his knowledge of oral language and intro- duce him to written communication and the ways in which it reflects and departs from spoken language. Perhaps the most significant contribution linguists have made to formal English instruction is to point out that the child does not begin to learn his language when he enters school, but that he begins to learn to use it with greater sophistication and in new forms.

THE FUNCTION OF LANGUAGE

Linguists have provided another important distinction for English cur- riculum-planners: the idea that the communicative act entails skills in both producing and receiving intelligible verbal discourse. These skills involve the ability to encode, or to communicate meaningfully to others; and the ability to decode, or to interpret verbal communications from others. To encode, one must be able to produce acceptable speech and writing; to decode, one must be able to listen and read with facility.

Thus, effective communication involves skills in both the production and the reception of language and, in our culture, in both its oral and its written forms. When language usage is described as a total communicative act in the manner linguists indicate, it becomes apparent that English programs that separate reading from writing and speaking from listening are artificial and inconsistent with the functions of language. Whether explicitly or implicitly, effective verbal habits require that users understand what the structural elements of language are and how they interrelate in spoken and written communication.

In this light, the concept of the *language arts* is misleading. Language usage is not simply an "art," but the application of basic skills and under-standings of the system of language we use. Perhaps one peripheral benefit that will result from including linguistic concepts in the English curriculum is the elimination of the inaccurate term *language arts* and the substitution of a term that more accurately reflects the motives underlying language instruction.

The Learning of Language

Linguistics, however, is inadequate as a single data source for designing an effective English program. A well-conceived total English program needs to consider not only the nature of the subject but also the nature of the learner. A brief exploration of how language is learned may help illustrate the fact that the content and the processes of language instruction are inseparably related.

Just as the structure of language is hierarchical, so also does the learning of language develop in increasingly complex form. From the infant's first confrontation with the sounds in his environment to his awareness that some human sounds convey meanings, the learning of language proceeds from the simple to the complex, from the undifferentiated to the discrete. In the course of language development the young child learns to identify not only the basic structural components of his verbal code but also the operational rules that enable him to combine these elements into mean-ingful verbal discourse.

The child's learning of the elements of language structure and the rules for transforming these elements into verbal behavior occurs in different linguistic environments. Thus, dialect differences develop. Depending on the region, the socioeconomic standing, and the unique family speech patterns that comprise the language model which the child replicates, the language learner acquires not only an implicit knowledge of the structure of language but of a variant form as well. Dialect differences can occur at all levels of the structure of language—phonological, morphological, and syntactical. But to the young child, the dialect is *the* English language.

Dialect differentiation is a normal, inherent aspect of language usage. "Acceptable" language standards vary according to the group and the situation in which communication occurs. Accordingly, the conventional patterns of English that constitute formal language instruction represent only one use of English—ordinarily that of literary English.

Obviously, the patterns of literary English constitute essential learnings for pupils. However, the realities of verbal discourse clearly illustrate that this standard has particular uses in particular situations. A total language program also needs to account for informal uses of language and for the basic dialect differences that exist in our dynamic system of verbal communication.

Insights into the nature of learning in general also have important implications for English instruction. It is becoming increasingly evident that behaviors learned early in life condition the individual's capacities for later learning. Since many, if not most, of the essential verbal habits are acquired before adolescence, we may assume that to delay essential linguistic learnings until the pupil enters secondary school diminishes the influence these learnings might have in improving his language habits. Unquestionably much more research is needed to verify this assumption. Yet the available evidence suggests that increasing attention must be given to the development of basic language habits at the time in the pupil's school life when instruction will have maximum effect.

What implications does this discussion have for English curriculums and instruction in the elementary school?

First, if an effective program of language instruction is to emerge, a program that rationally explores both the structure and the function of language, the total formal language program must be considered, from its inception in the first grade to its completion in the twelfth grade. Such a program can be designed only if elementary- and secondary-school language specialists co-operate in exploring the problem. This kind of co-operative effort is not yet prevalent.

A second implication: the notion that the communicative act is a total process that involves abilities in encoding and decoding spoken and written

English suggests that increasing efforts are needed to integrate what are, in most classrooms, disassociated language experiences. The task of integration is complex and difficult. Yet the nucleus for integrating the interrelated aspects of communication—speaking, listening, reading, and writing—is contained in the notion that language is structured.

An integrated language curriculum might be developed to help the pupil explore the structure of oral language in increasing depth at succeeding levels. The curriculum might juxtapose oral elements that are reflected in the written form at each level of language structure. In any event, instruction concerning the grammar of our language should include experiences in which pupils are helped to identify and apply basic generalizations concerning the structural elements that comprise our grammatical system— phonology, morphology, and syntax.

A third implication: basic structural concepts underlie all language usage, regardless of the variations in language usage that exist in our dynamic society. Since intelligible communication occurs in different regional and socioeconomic groups, it is unrealistic to impose a single standard of language usage. The truism that "form follows function" applies directly to language usage. For some children, learning formal language patterns is similar to learning a second language. In fact, experimentation is now underway in which the methodologies of second-language instruction are being applied to formal English instruction among children whose dialect patterns are widely divergent from conventional language usage.

A fourth implication: the child's introduction to formal language learning in the early elementary-school grades basically affects how much meaning later language instruction will have for him. It follows that initial experiences with linguistic concepts in the total English program should begin early in the pupil's school career. By using the knowledge the child applies daily in his verbal interactions, and by helping him make this knowledge explicit in increasingly complex form, it may be supposed that the content as well as the processes of English programs will be improved.

Certainly there is a pressing need to improve current English programs in the light of evidence from several data sources, particularly linguistics and psychology. An examination of this strand of the curriculum is necessary if we are to have a balanced, effective English program throughout the grades, a program that considers the subject matter as well as the learner.

F. ELIZABETH METZ

Head Speech and Hearing Clinician, Phoenix (Arizona) Public Elementary School District

17 · POVERTY, EARLY LANGUAGE DEPRIVATION, AND LEARNING ABILITY

● For objective consideration of children's linguistic limitations, language should be subdivided into at least three of its definable aspects:

1. Lexical—relating to words or the vocabulary of an language as distinguished from its grammar or construction.
2. Phonetic Structure—relating to spoken language or speech sounds patterned within words.
3. Syntactic Structure—relating to the way in which words are put together or patterned to form phrases, clauses, or sentences in a connected or orderly system or arrangement—i.e., *grammar*.

Typical Limitations in the Lexical Aspects of Language

The acquisition of vocabulary is dependent upon two mental processes, abstraction and symbolization. A child who calls a *ladder* a *get-up* is demonstrating inability in symbolization, or the knowledge of names or signs to stand for objects, acts, qualities, attitudes, and relationships. When a child calls a *horse* a *doggy*, he is failing in symbolization and also in abstraction, or the ability to generalize from non-identical experiences to form concepts or classes such as *cars, fruit, animals*.

Children who have experienced early language deprivation are often

Elementary English, 43:129–133, February, 1966. Reprinted with the permission of the National Council of Teachers of English and F. Elizabeth Metz.

baffled by a standardized measure of vocabulary such as the Peabody Picture Vocabulary Test.

The Detroit Great Cities School Improvement Program in Language Arts (7) used a sound approach to planning vocabulary growth by first assessing the actual spoken language vocabularies of culturally deprived children who had just finished kindergarten.

Shaw (6), in discussing the language problems of culturally disadvantaged children, states, "We have built our aptitude and intelligence tests so that reading and vocabulary count very heavily, and have found them valid as predictors of academic success."

It has long been the writer's opinion that group tests of intelligence measure the young child's language deprivation. Analysis was made of the oral vocabulary required to complete successfully five different group tests of intelligence. In one, the child must understand fourteen geometric terms to comprehend the teacher's oral directions. Language-deprived children often lack the concepts of such terms; for example, *pointed, oval-shaped, opening* (noun), or *partly curved.* This same test includes more than twenty directional words and phrases, among which are *toward the left, opposite from, the next after,* and *exactly under.* How, when we know such tests ?re valid as predictors of academic success, can we fail to teach the language-deprived child this vocabulary?

Most group tests of intelligence include tasks called *non-verbal* which involve ability in abstraction or classification. The task may involve the selection of an object or design from a series because it is *different* or *not like the others.* It may require the selection of two items from a series because they are related as are no other items in the series. Such tasks involve the ability to relate or isolate items on the basis of multiple determinants. Choice must sometimes be made on the basis of *use*; for example, isolating an *eraser* from a series of *tools for writing.* In other tasks the choice might be determined by *direction,* up or down or left and right. *Spatial* factors such as symmetric—asymmetric may be involved. Examples of still other determinants are: spatial-numerical; reality testing; series-patterning. Are these tasks really *non-verbal?* Let us compare the responses of children from adequate language environments with those of language-deprived children. On a relatively simple task such as selecting a *tiger* as different from a *pig,* a *horse,* and a *sheep,* both children will probably succeed. When the first child is told, "Tell why," he can easily explain, "Well, the pig and the sheep and the horse are all farm animals, but the tiger is a jungle animal." Many language-deprived children, on the other hand, will be unable to give a verbal explanation of their thought processes.

One child responded by pointing to each farm animal saying, "Him here," then pointing to the tiger and saying, "Him not here!" Can we doubt that some quality of inner-language is being employed by a child when he performs such so-called *non-verbal* tasks? On more complicated items of a test, the language-deprived child will probably fail the task even without verbalization. Examine the inner-language needed to solve such an item as this:

> Let's see, there are four squares here. Each one is outlined by figures such as triangles, circles, stars, and squares. Two of the large squares use triangles and small squares—the other two use stars and circles . . . no, that won't help find the one that is different. . . . Aha! Three of the large squares have the same small figure in all four corners, with two each of the second kind of small figures filling in each side. The different large square uses two different small figures and has them arranged first one kind and then the other kind, all around the large square!

It might well be contended that language-deprived children should have motivated learning experiences with classification tasks, with the teacher supplying the necessary oral language to show the child how one thinks through language. Children enjoy these tasks when they are removed from a test situation. Call the activity "Look, Think, and Find Time," and they will participate enthusiastically. Many of Dr. Marianne Frostig's materials (4) for improving visual perception could be used for such activity.

Language-deprived children will need continuing special consideration throughout the elementary grades. For example, if a fourth-grade teacher in a slum school wishes to introduce a creative writing project employing verse to express children's reactions to colors, her work will be quite different from that of a teacher in a school with a middle-income population. She will provide much more preparatory time, possibly sharing some of her own responses and bringing examples from literature into the classroom. Even then, the children may not have in their own mental warehouses the vocabulary needed to express their ideas. It may be necessary for the teacher to cover the chalkboards with words such as *sad, joyous, gloomy, cool, a rainy day, like dying,* etc., to give the children the tools with which to create. Some children may say they respond to no colors. The teacher can then use her knowledge of the individual child to ask such questions as, "Let's see, Sam, you are dreaming of the day when you will own a car. What color would you like it to be? Oh! A red one. Why don't you think about why the car's color matters to you. Think of some words to tell how you would feel at the wheel of a new red car."

Teachers use many ingenious ways of motivating vocabulary growth. Better ways for distributing and sharing such methods are needed.

Limitations in the Phonetic Structure of Language

Educators are becoming fully cognizant of the importance of phonic skills in the total language arts instructional program. To be able to spell, for instance, a child must think of written symbols (letters) for the speech sounds he hears. To read, he must think of the sounds of the letters he sees.

It is questionable whether the professional training of elementary school teachers provides sufficient work in the areas of language development, speech improvement, and individual differences in speech and language. Teachers need to be skilled, critical listeners. They should be able to recognize the sound substitutions, omissions, and distortions which children produce. Schools including speech clinicians as part of special staff could provide such information to teachers through an economical amount of in-service training. Speech errors could be related to the particular phonetic charts employed in the reading program to improve teachers' skills. They could then discriminate between speech errors typical for particular dialects, for non-standard English, and for clinical speech defects.

The goal for speech sound articulation should not be absolute uniformity. Regional expressions and dialect often enrich our total language. Change should be a goal, however, when differences lessen the intelligibility of speech or when they are commonly identified as non-standard English. The Norwegian's *dis* for *this* may be enchanting, but the American Negro high school graduate who says *dis, dem,* and *dose* may not get the job he is seeking! The non-standard English of those from the sub-culture of poverty might almost be considered a *second language*. Golden (5) advises, "Speech improvement must be self-improvement. We cannot change the student's patterns for him, but we can bring about awareness of a need for change, aid him in finding ways to make the change, and encourage his efforts at self-improvement."

Limitations in the Syntactic Structure of Language

The use of language is the conveyance of meaning. Clarity of meaning depends upon grammatical structure, which involves inflection, word order, intonation, and word variations which indicate number, time action, and other functions. The best way to learn English grammar is the *Mother's Method,* through which the child with an adequate early language environment gains automatic grammatical responses through audition of the language he hears in the home. This *automaticity* of response is essential. Concepts and symbols will not give usable and meaningful speech and language unless the language processes become automatic. Consider, for example, the ability to form plurals, which ranges from simple addition of *s* (*toy—toys*), to the inflectional change demanded by the addition of *es* (*church—churches*), to the formation of irregular plurals, *man—men, mouse—mice, leaf—leaves,* etc. Ervin's (3) study of structure in children's language indicated that most children had acquired the ability to form plurals before the age of three. Through the writer's experience with language-deprived children, it has become obvious that many children lack this ability at age six or even age eight! The Auditory-Vocal Automatic Test, a sub-test of the Illinois Test of Psycholinguistic Abilities, includes nine items of plural formation. Most slum children form no more than three or four of the plurals correctly. Some creative teacher could easily devise a card game which would make repetition of correct plurals fun for the children.

Another automatic language ability assessed by the Illinois Test of Psycholinguistic Abilities is that of being able to make comparisons by use of the comparative and superlative degrees of adjectives and adverbs. For example, the examiner shows the child a picture of two cakes and says, "This cake looks good. This cake looks even ----------." Few young slum children are able to supply the comparative form *better*. Typical responses are *good, gooderer, gooder*. One eight-year-old Mexican-American child pointed to the first cake, saying, "This one little good,"—then, pointing triumphantly to the other cake, "This one *yes* good!"

One group test of intelligence for second-grade children requires the teacher to use in the oral directions ten terms of superlative degree; for example, *largest, nearest,* and *fewest*.

Some language texts introduce this study of degree as late as sixth grade, even though the children need such oral skills for the first years of formal learning.

Is anything more mercurial than the English verb? All children experience some difficulty with the structural shifts and changes required for proper person, tense, and number. The verbs *to be* and *have* are customarily slaughtered by language-deprived children, since *they was* and *we has* sound right to them. One typical distortion by Negro children from language-deprived homes is, "She don't be here today."

The writer made a study comparing written language of three groups of ten-year-old children last year. The groups were: Negroes from low-income public housing; Spanish-speaking from a low-income area; profoundly deaf Caucasian children in a special oral day class. The Negro children made as many verb errors of number and tense as did the deaf children! Spanish-speaking children were unable to employ clauses for better expression. Negro children did not use progressive verb forms. The writer's observations confirm this problem. When shown action pictures and asked, "What is he doing?" the Negro child will usually respond, "He skatin'," omitting the auxiliary, rather than "He is skating."

It seems evident that language-deprived children need repetitive, structured oral experiences with proper language usage early in their school experience. When a six-year-old girl asks, "I doing good a little?" or a seven-year-old boy says, "You know that River Street? Him live Johnnie" it is time for remediation to achieve correct word order and usage.

Some language-deprived children may have vocabularies just good enough to mask their real language problems. *Naming* is not of much use if a child is unable *to tell something about* the object he has named. Such children need oral experiences with guidance in *telling about things,* so they can ask themselves, *What is it?, What color is it?, What size?, What looks like it?, How is it used?, What is it made of?*

It is important to improve language usage as early as possible in the child's life. A recent study (2) indicates that high school students' awareness of structural relationships in English does not improve significantly after three years of formal study of English grammar! Other evidence supports the hypothesis that early instruction is most effective in changing language usage.

Since language skills and learning ability are so interdependently related, surely our schools have a responsibility to children with limited language. This responsibility involves adequate definition of the problem and commitment to the development of teaching methods that will meet the children's special needs. If the slum child's foundation of language skill can be strengthened through pre-school, kindergarten, and primary programs, he will then be able to compete more successfully during the subsequent years of school. Attention to this one specific symptom of *poverty* is not a total solution. However, as is stated by I. M. Berlin (1), "Beginning to learn academic material is one way of beginning to deal with the real world. The successes in the mastery of subject matter mean a great deal to a sick child's concept of himself."

No special educational techniques can succeed in the wrong *attitudinal climate!* Progress in teaching slum children will depend upon the feelings of the staff of such schools. If children are viewed as *unteachable* or *hopeless from the start,* both teachers and children will find school a place of frustration and discouragement. Successful education of the children of poverty must be viewed as an exciting professional challenge and as a social and economic necessity.

REFERENCES

1. Berlin, I. N., "Unrealities in Teacher Education," *Saturday Review*, December 19, 1964.
2. Davis, O. L., Harold C. Smith, and Norman D. Bowers, "High School Students Awareness of Structural Relationships in English," *The Journal of Educational Research*, 58 (October, 1964), 69–71.
3. Ervin, S. M., "Structure in Children's Language," paper presented at International Congress of Psychology, Washington, D.C., 1963.
4. Frostig, Marianne, and David Horne, *The Frostig Program for the Development of Visual Perception.* Chicago: Follett Publishing Company.
5. Golden, Ruth I., *Improving Patterns of Language Usage.* Detroit: Wayne State University Press, p. 5.
6. Shaw, A. B., "Slums and School People," an editorial, *The School Administrator*, 22 (December, 1964).
7. Wachner, Clarence W., "Detroit Great Cities School Improvement Program in Language Arts," paper presented at Annual Meeting of National Council of Teachers of English, (November, 1963).

GROWTH AND ITS RELATIONSHIP TO LEARNING AND TEACHING

• In the past few years, many publications favoring various types of social planning have appeared in the professional literature. The central idea is, as Bruner indicates, that man is sufficiently developed to become an active agent in planning the future of his kind or in managing his own evolution, at least as far as consciously influencing causal aspects of his social and physical environments is concerned. It is significant that this point of view has been advanced by representatives from several disciplines. For example, Dobzhansky,[1] from the viewpoint of a biologist, and Harrington,[2] as a sociologist, strongly advocate that the future no longer be left to chance but that available knowledge and talent be used to influence what will happen.

As a matter of fact, schools traditionally have been the principal societal agents responsible for transmitting the culture. The question of whether educators should mold or alter cultural patterns apparently has already been decided by society's insistence that the educational policy-making function remain under lay and voter control. This is not to say, however, that taking

[1] Theodosius Dobzhansky, *Mankind Evolving* (New Haven: Yale University Press, 1962), pp. 345–348.

[2] Michael Harrington, *The Accidental Century* (New York: The Macmillan Company, 1965), 322 pp.

a part in determining the future of its students, and through them the society, is not the school's job, or that educators should not select from the culture those elements that should be transmitted. It is our opinion that many of the factors that cause youngsters to fail in, or drop out of, school exist outside the school as a result of family and community conditions. If schools are to be maximally effective, they will have to find ways to exert more and more influence to ameliorate these conditions.

The protagonists of social planning do not maintain that society be controlled by psychologists, biologists, or social scientists or that any individual's life be ordered and regulated. Rather they would enlist the cooperation and knowledge of many disciplines in dealing with causal and inhibiting societal factors, so that people can be free to grow and to achieve maximum development.

The editors feel that this is not an issue pertinent only to the disadvantaged or culturally deprived but that almost all individuals have much more potential than they are able to use and apply. Only a fraction of the capacity of the human brain is utilized by most people, and physical feats once thought to be impossible are now quite common in track and field meets. The question of what holds people back and what prevents their becoming as much as they could be is worthy of our best investigation. If a man has the right to life, he also has the right to live completely and to his fullest capacity. Yet, as Bruce indicates, there are many things done in the school that produce growth in the direction of alienation.

We believe that Bruner's article was almost made to order for this section because it so effectively relates learning and teaching to the ongoing processes of educational growth, including personality change. Elsewhere[3] we have described the nature of man much as Bruner has—as a tool-using, verbal, social creature who enjoys the process of growth and learning. Think of this, and of other aspects of Bruner's presentation, in terms of your role as a teacher. The article says to us that curricular content must be flexible, changing, ever new, necessarily contemporary, but that there is a structure that is necessary, logical, and definable. It says that the job of the teacher is to teach pupils how to learn and that some of the things we teach are more important than others; *e.g., it is more important to know what man might be than to know what he has been*—a message reiterated by Bruce. Finally, it says teachers cannot cease to grow, because as we make structure and process clear to pupils we make things clear and comprehensible to ourselves.

[3] H. W. Bernard and D. W. Fullmer, *Foundations of Guidance: A Basic Text* (Cleveland: The World Publishing Company, 1967), Chap. 2.

Bruner and Bruce advance or imply ideas concerning causal factors and suggestions for dealing with them. As the reader progresses through the remaining selections in these readings, we suggest that he actively involve himself in searching for answers to these growth questions: What are the limits of my own effectiveness? Of the effectiveness of my pupils? To what degree are the limits imposed by physical environment as contrasted to personal outlook?

JEROME S. BRUNER
Professor of Psychology, Harvard University

18 · EDUCATION AS
SOCIAL INVENTION

● I shall take it as self-
evident that each generation must define afresh the nature, direction, and
aims of education to assure such freedom and rationality as can be attained
for a future generation. For there are changes both in circumstances and
in knowledge that impose constraints on and give opportunities to the
teacher in each succeeding generation. It is in this sense that education is
in constant process of invention. I should like particularly to comment
upon four changes in our own time that require consideration in thinking
about education.

The first of these derives from our increasing understanding of man as
a species. As one reads the enormously rich reports of the last decade or
two, it is plain that there has been a revolution that forces us to reconsider
what it is we do when we occupy man's long growing period in certain
ways now familiar as "schooling."

A second basis for redefining education is the increase in our understanding of the nature of individual mental growth. There have been
profound reorientations in developmental theory in the last generation,
changes that have been hastened by studies of normal and pathological
growth, by analyses of the effects of different types of early environments,
by studies of the development of language and its impact on thought. All
of this work has forced us to reconsider the role of man's symbolic
operations.

Third, there is reason to believe that we have come to understand the
process of education somewhat more clearly than before. This has been a

Reprinted by permission of the publishers from Jerome S. Bruner, *Toward a Theory of Instruction*, Cambridge, Mass.: Belknap Press of Harvard University Press, Copyright © 1966 by President and Fellows of Harvard College.

decade of intense educational experiment involving many of the finest minds of our generation. It has given me pause to see in what measure an eight-year-old can be led to grasp what a poem is, or come to a conception of the conservation of momentum, or arrive slowly but surely at the powerful generality of a quadratic function as a set of sets in which the elements in each set are the same as the number of sets.

Finally, and most obviously, the rate of change in the society in which we live forces us to redefine how we shall educate a new generation. John Dewey's *My Pedagogic Creed,* a movingly concerned document, rests principally upon reflections of the author prior to the first Great War—a yearningly long time ago.

I shall consider each of these matters; but before I do, I must confess some of my own doubts. It is reasonably plain to me, as a psychologist, that however able psychologists may be, it is not their function to decide upon educational goals any more than the ablest general decides whether a nation should or should not be at war. Whatever I know about policy-making reinforces the conviction that technicians and scientists often lack the kind of follow-up commitment that is the requisite of wise social policy. I cannot work up much enthusiasm for philosopher kings, psychologist kings, doctor kings, or even mixed-committee kings. The political process—and decisions about the aims of education must work their way through that process—is slow, perhaps, but is committed to the patient pursuit of the possible.

Yet it is also clear that generals do in fact have a strong influence on the politics of war and peace and that scientists have had and will have a powerful influence on our defense and other policies. What is not so clear is the distinction between ends and means, between goals and their implementation. And perhaps it is just as well, for there is an intuitive familiarity that generals have with what is possible and what is not possible in war and in containing its threat, and there is a certain familiarity that psychologists have with how one can get somebody to learn or to pay attention or to stay free of anxiety. While these are not ends in the strict sense, they shape our ends in educational policy as in defense policy. It is, if you will, the psychologist's lively sense of what is possible that can make him a powerful force. If he fails to fill his role as a diviner and delineator of the possible, then he does not serve the society wisely. If he confuses his function and narrows his vision of the possible to what he counts as desirable, then we shall all be the poorer. He can and must provide the full range of alternatives to challenge the society to choice. And now back to the main theme.

How evaluate education in the light of our newly gained knowledge of man as a species? Let me begin by proposing a view that might best be called evolutionary instrumentalism. Man's use of mind is dependent upon his ability to develop and use "tools" or "instruments" or "technologies" that make it possible for him to express and amplify his powers. His very evolution as a species speaks to this point. It was consequent upon the development of bipedalism and the use of spontaneous pebble tools that man's brain and particularly his cortex developed. It was not a large-brained hominid that developed the technical-social life of the human; rather it was the tool-using, cooperative pattern that gradually changed man's morphology by favoring the survival of those who could link themselves with tool systems and disfavoring those who tried to go it on big jaws, heavy dentition, or superior weight. What evolved as a human nervous system was something, then, that required outside devices for expressing its potential. It was a swift progress. The first primitive primates appeared five million years ago and man reached his present morphology and brain size about half a million years ago—with the major development of higher hominid to tool-user occupying probably less than half a million of the years between. From then on, all major changes in the species were, in Weston La Barre's startling phrase, by prosthetic devices,[1] by man's learning how to link himself to amplifiers of his muscles, of his senses, and of his powers of ratiocination.

The British biologist Peter Medawar remarks that it is likely that at about this same point in human history human culture became sufficiently elaborated for evolution to become Lamarckian and reversible rather than Darwinian and irreversible.[2] It is a figure of speech, of course, but Medawar's point is well taken: what is transmitted by the culture is indeed a pool of acquired characteristics, a pool that can get lost just as surely as the Easter Islanders, the Incas, and the Mayans lost whatever skills made it possible for them to leave such splendid ruins to disabled descendants whose genes were probably not one whit changed.

I know that the terms "tool" and "technology" and even "instrument" offend when one speaks of man as dependent upon them for the realization of his humanity. For these words denote "hardware," and it is mostly "software" that I have in mind—skills that are tools. Language is perhaps the ideal example of one such powerful technology, with its power not

[1] Weston La Barre, *The Human Animal* (Chicago: University of Chicago Press, 1954).

[2] Peter Medawar, "Onwards from Spencer: Evolution and Evolutionism," *Encounter* 21(3):35–43 (September 1963).

only for communication but for encoding "reality," for representing matters remote as well as immediate, and for doing all these things according to rules that permit us both to represent "reality" and to transform it by conventional yet appropriate rules. All of this depends on the external resources of a grammar, a lexicon, and (likely as not) a supporting cast of speakers constituting the linguistic community.

Language happens to be a tool of the most general sort, in the sense that it provides direction and amplification for the way we use our muscular apparatus, our senses, and our powers of reflection. But each of these domains also has its skills that are expressed through various kinds of tool-using. There are time- and strength-saving skills for using our muscles, and they are built into the tools we devise for them. There are attention-saving skills in perception that are imparted and then become the basis for understanding the icons we construct for representing things by drawing, diagram, and design. And there are, finally and most importantly, strain-reducing heuristics to help us figure out things—how to cancel out nuisance parameters, how to use our heads and save our heels, how to make quick but decent approximations, and so on.

Many of these skills are taught in the subtle interaction of parent and child—as in the case of primary linguistic skills. And, as in the case of language learning, where the pedagogy is highly unselfconscious, it is probably true that most of the primitive skills of manipulating and looking and attending are also taught in this way. It is when the society goes beyond these relatively primitive techniques that the less spontaneous instruction of school must be relied upon. At this point the culture necessarily comes to rely upon its formal education as a means of providing skills. And insofar as there has been any innovation in tools or tool-using (taking these expressions in the broadest sense), the educational system is the sole means of dissemination—the sole agent of evolution, if you will.

Consider now our understanding of the nature of human ontogenetic development. Several important conclusions stand out. None of them, so far as I know, have been seriously considered in defining the aims and conduct of education.

The first is that mental growth is not a gradual accretion, either of associations or of stimulus-response connections or of means-end readinesses or of anything else. It appears to be much more like a staircase with rather sharp risers, more a matter of spurts and rests. The spurts ahead in growth seem to be touched off when certain capacities begin to develop. And some capacities must be matured and nurtured before others can be called into being. The sequence of their appearance is highly constrained. But these steps or stages or spurts or whatever you may choose to call them are *not* very clearly linked to age: some environments can slow the sequence down or bring it to a halt, others move it along faster. In the main, one can characterize these constrained sequences as a series of prerequisites. It is not until the child can hold in mind two features of a display at once, for example, that he can deal with their relationship, as in a ratio.

The steps or stages have been variously described by a variety of investigators working in centers as various as Geneva, Moscow, Paris, London, Montreal, Chicago, and Cambridge, but they seem to have an interesting likeness, even though the proposed dynamism varies. The first stages are relatively manipulative, marked by highly unstable and single-track attention. Knowing is principally knowing how to do, and there is minimum reflection. There follows a period of more reflective functioning in which the young human being is capable of an internal representation, by representative images, of greater chunks of the environment. The high point in this stage is between five and seven. Finally, something very special happens around adolescence, when language becomes increasingly important as a medium of thought. It is evidenced by an ability to consider propositions rather than objects; concepts become more exclusively hierarchal in structure; alternative possibilities can be handled in a combinatorial fashion. There is considerable doubt whether these things have anything directly to do with the onset of physiological adolescence—for there are equally sharp cognitive turning points at the onset of language and at the age five-to-seven turning point without much discernible assist from hormonal tides. And hormonal adolescents in technically less mature societies do not enter this stage.

What comes out of this picture, rough though I have sketched it, is a view of human beings who have developed three parallel systems for processing information and for representing it—one through manipulation and action, one through perceptual organization and imagery, and one through symbolic apparatus. It is not that these are "stages" in any sense; they are rather emphases in development. You must get the perceptual field organized around your own person as center before you can impose other, less egocentric axes upon it, for example. In the end, the mature organism seems to have gone through a process of elaborating three systems of skills that correspond to the three major tool systems to which he must link himself for full expression of his capacities—tools for the hand, for the distance receptors, and for the process of reflection.

It is not surprising in the light of this that early opportunities for development have loomed so large in our recent understanding of human mental growth. The importance of early experience is only dimly sensed today. The evidence from animal studies indicates that virtually irreversible deficits can be produced in mammals by depriving them of opportunities that challenge their nascent capacities. In the last few years there have been reports showing the crippling effect of deprived human environments, as well as indications that "replacement therapies" can be of considerable success, even at an age on the edge of adolescence. The principal deficits appear to be linguistic in the broadest sense—the lack of opportunity to share in dialogue, to have occasion for paraphrase, to internalize speech as a vehicle of thought. None of these matters are well understood, save that the principle discussed earlier seems to be operative, that, unless certain basic skills are mastered, later, more elaborated ones become increasingly out of reach. It is in the light of this fact that we can understand the increasing difference of intelligence with age between such culturally deprived groups as rural Southern Negroes and more culturally privileged whites. In time, and with sufficient failure, the gap is reinforced to irreversibility by a sense of defeat.

What has been learned about the educational process that may give guidance to our task of redefinition? Very little that is certain, but some extremely interesting impressions that can possibly be converted into testable hypotheses.

The "curriculum revolution" has made it plain even after only a decade that the idea of "readiness" is a mischievous half-truth. It is a half-truth largely because it turns out that one *teaches* readiness or provides opportunities for its nurture, one does not simply wait for it. Readiness, in these terms, consists of mastery of those simpler skills that permit one to reach higher skills. Readiness for Euclidian geometry can be gained by teaching intuitive geometry or by giving children an opportunity to build increasingly elaborate constructions with polygons. Or, to take the aim of the new, "second-generation" mathematics project,[3] if you wish to teach the calculus in the eighth grade, then begin it in the first grade by teaching the kinds of ideas and skills necessary for its mastery later. Mathematics is no exception to the general rule, though admittedly it is the most easily understood from the point of view of what must be clear before something else can be grasped. Since most subjects can be translated into forms that place emphasis upon doing, or upon the development of appropriate imagery,

[3] See the report of the Cambridge Conference on School Mathematics, *Goals for School Mathematics* (Boston: Houghton Mifflin, 1963).

or upon symbolic-verbal encoding, it is often possible to render the end result to be achieved in a simpler, more manageable form so that the child can move more easily and deeply to full mastery.

The second thing that emerges from pedagogical experiments of the last decade is that cognitive or intellectual mastery is rewarding. It is particularly so when the learner recognizes the cumulative power of learning, that learning one thing permits him to go on to something that before was out of reach, and so on toward such perfection as one may reach. It is a truth that every good athletic coach since the Greek Olympics has known. Teachers also gain pleasure when a student learns to recognize his own progress well enough so that he can take over as his own source of reward and punishment.

A third result of contemporary exploration in teaching is the conclusion that educational experiment, in the main, has been conducted and is being conducted in the dark—without feedback in usable form. The substitute for light (or usable feedback) is evaluation after the job has been completed. After the working party has been scattered, the evaluators enter. By then, it is so late in the day that only patching can be done. Indeed, such is the latitude in the choice of criteria for evaluation that something nice can usually be said about practically any course or curriculum. It would seem much more sensible to put evaluation into the picture *before and during* curriculum construction, as a form of intelligence operation to help the curriculum maker in his choice of material, in his approach, in his manner of setting tasks for the learner.

Finally, one is struck by the absence of a theory of instruction as a guide to pedagogy—a prescriptive theory on how to proceed in order to achieve various results, a theory that is neutral with respect to ends but exhaustive with respect to means. It is interesting that there is a lack of an integrating theory in pedagogy, that in its place there is principally a body of maxims.

As our technology grows increasingly complex in both machinery and human organization, the role of the school becomes more central in the society, not simply as an agent of socialization, but as a transmitter of basic skills. To this we turn next as our final basis for redefining education—the changing society.

In recent years I have wondered, particularly in connection with work in West Africa, why societies are not more mindful of the role of education in shaping their futures. Why in Africa, for example, is the short-term political allure of universal primary education given priority over training a corps of administrators, teachers, and technicians? In many cases, the second is financially precluded by the first, and the long-run result may prove a terrible time bomb as semiliterate youths flock into the new urban Africa with no marketable skills, their familial and tribal boats burned, and no properly trained corps of teachers and civil servants to maintain stability or to teach the untrained.

That is what set me brooding, and while I have no answer to the African problem, I do have some thoughts about our own. They crystallized while reading an essay by the distinguished Italian architect-designer Pier Luigi Nervi.[4] Nervi describes the loss in freedom of the architect-designer in an age of technological maturity. You can build a road or a path in any meandering shape you wish, provided the only users are men on foot, or on horse, or in wagons, or in slow cars. But the moment the speed of the vehicle passes a certain critical point, fantasy is constrained and you must conform to the idea of a containing arc. A car at seventy cannot turn on a fanciful curlicue.

There was a great deal of public soul-searching at the time of Sputnik as to whether our educational system was adequate to the task ahead. In fact, much new curriculum reform had started before then—out of a sense of the frightening gap between expert knowledge of our technology and public knowledge. I rather suspect that there will never again be such a period of careless or ritualistic regard for public education—but, then, universal public education as a working concept is not yet a century old!

It may well be the case that not only are we entering a period of technological maturity in which education will require constant redefinition, but that the period ahead may involve such a rapid rate of change in specific technology that narrow skills will become obsolete within a reasonably short time after their acquisition. Indeed, perhaps one of the defining properties of a highly matured technology is that there exists a lively likelihood of major technological change within the compass of a single generation—just as ours has seen several such major changes.

I entertained myself and some young students with whom I was working during the summer of 1964 on a social-studies curriculum by formulating Bruner's Rule—critical changes related to the order of magnitude in years away. I used this as an extension of the square law for the retinal angle— that the size of the retinal image is the reciprocal of the square of the distance of an object from the eye. Therefore, the further away a period of time, the longer its duration in order to be discerned! And so:

[4] Pier Luigi Nervi, "Is Architecture Moving Toward Forms and Characteristics Which Are Unchangeable?" in Gyorgy Kepes, ed., *Structure in Art and Science* (New York: Braziller, 1965).

5×10^9	5,000,000,000	Birth of Earth
5×10^8	500,000,000	Vertebrates
5×10^7	50,000,000	Mammals
5×10^6	5,000,000	Primates
5×10^5	500,000	Present man
5×10^4	50,000	Great glacial migrations
5×10^3	5,000	Recorded history
5×10^2	500	Printing
5×10^1	50	Radio / mass education
5×10^0	5	Artificial intelligence

What I learned from my pupils was their conclusion that things were coming thick and fast. Life probably started about 2.5×10^9, so that half the history of the earth was lifeless. Some 99.999 percent of the earth's life has been manless, and from there on out the record is impressive and awesome. It would seem, indeed, as if the principal thing about tools and techniques is that they beget other more advanced ones at ever-increasing speed. And as the technology matures in this way, education in its very nature takes on an increasing role by providing the skills needed to manage and control the expanding enterprise.

The first response of educational systems under such acceleration is to produce technicians and engineers and scientists as needed, but it is doubtful whether such a priority produces what is required to manage the enterprise. For no specific science or technology provides a metalanguage in terms of which to think about a society, its technology, its science, and the constant changes that these undergo with innovation. Could an automotive engineer have foreseen the death of small-town America with the advent of the automobile? He would have been so wedded to his task of making better and better automobiles that it would never have occurred to him to consider the town, the footpath, leisure, or local loyalty. Somehow, if change is to be managed, it requires men with skills in sensing continuity and opportunity for continuity. This is a matter to which we shall return shortly.

What may we conclude from all this? It seems to me that four general policies follow from the issues that we have passed in review.

The first has to do with what is taught. It would seem, from our consideration of man's evolution, that principal emphasis in education should be placed upon skills—skills in handling, in seeing and imaging, and in symbolic operations, particularly as these relate to the technologies that have made them so powerful in their human expression.

It is hard to spell out in specific terms what such an emphasis upon skills entails, but some examples might provide a concrete basis for criticism. With respect, first, to the education of the perceptual-imaginal capacities, I can suggest at least one direction to travel. It is in the training of subtle spatial imagery. I have recently been struck by the increased visual power and subtlety of students exposed to courses in visual design—all differently conceived and with different objectives in view: one for undergraduates given by I. A. Richards at Harvard, another for teachers by Bartlett Hayes at Andover, and a third for city planners given by Gyorgy Kepes and Kevin Lynch at M.I.T. All of them produced what seemed to me like fresh discrimination in viewing the altered environment of urban America; all provided the students with new models in terms of which to analyze and sort their surroundings. My colleagues Gerald Holton and Edward Purcell have been experimenting with instruction in visual pattern as a mode of increasing the visualizing subtlety of concentrators in physics—visual subtlety and capacity to represent events visually and nonmetrically. I do not think that we have begun to scratch the surface of training in visualization—whether related to the arts, to science, or simply to the pleasures of viewing our environments more richly. Let me note in passing, by the way, that Maria Montessori, that strange blend of the mystic and the pragmatist, was groping toward some such conception as this.

At the level of symbolic operation, I think the work of Martin Deutsch with underprivileged children provides an interesting case in point—a conscious effort to lead children to verbal skills, to a sense of paraphrase and exchange.[5] It surely should not be limited, such an effort, to the underprivileged. The new mathematics curricula illustrate how much can be done in training symbolic skills.

This brings us immediately to a second conclusion. It relates literally to the meaning of the word *curriculum*, a word that derives from a course to be run. It is perhaps a wrong word. A curriculum should involve the mastery of skills that in turn lead to the mastery of still more powerful ones, the establishment of self-reward sequences. It is clear that this can be done in mathematics and science. But it is also the case that reading simpler poetry brings more complex poetry into reach, or that reading a poem once makes a second reading more rewarding. The reward of deeper understanding is a more robust lure to effort than we have yet realized.

A corollary of this conclusion (one I have urged before) is that there is

[5] Martin Deutsch, "The Disadvantaged Child and the Learning Process: Some Social Psychological and Developmental Considerations," in A. Harry Passow, ed., *Education in Depressed Areas* (New York: Teachers College Press, 1963).

an appropriate version of any skill or knowledge that may be imparted at whatever age one wishes to begin teaching—however preparatory the version may be. The choice of the earlier version is based upon what it is one is hoping to cumulate. The deepening and enrichment of this earlier understanding is again a source of reward for intellectual labors.

The third conclusion relates to change. If there is any way of adjusting to change, it must include, as we have noted, the development of a metalanguage and "metaskills" for dealing with continuity in change. What these might be is, of course, a moot point, but not completely so by any means. Mathematics is surely the most general metalanguage we have developed, and it provides the forms and patterns in terms of which regularities in nature are comprehended. I find myself forced to the conclusion that our survival may one day depend upon achieving a requisite mathematical literacy for rendering the seeming shocks of change into something that is continuous and cumulative. But, by the same token, there is a second discipline that deals with the search for likeness beneath the surface of diversity and change. It is, of course, the discipline of poetry, the vehicle for searching out unsuspected kinship.

A further speculation about preparation for change is that we are bound to move toward instruction in the sciences of behavior and away from the study of history. Recorded history is only about five thousand years old, as we saw. Most of what we teach is within the last few centuries, for the records before that are minimal while the records after are relatively rich. But just suppose that the richness of record increases as a function of our ability to develop systems for storing and retrieving information. A thousand years from now we will be swamped. One would surely not dwell then with such loving care over the details of Brumaire or the Long Parliament or the Louisiana Purchase. These are the furbelows of documentary short supply. But there is a more compelling reason to shift away from history toward the social or behavioral sciences.

It has to do with the need for studying the possible rather than the achieved—a necessary step if we are to adapt to change. It is the behavioral sciences and their generality with respect to variations in the human condition that must be central to our presentation of man, not the particularities of his history. This is not to say that we should give up study of the past, but rather that we should pursue such study with a different end in view—the end of developing style. For the development of style, be it style of writing or loving or dancing or eating, requires a sense of contrast and concreteness, and this we do not find in the behavioral sciences.

Finally, it is plain that if we are to evolve freely as a species by the use of the instrument of education, then we shall have to bring far greater resources to bear in designing our educational system. For one thing, if we are to respond to accelerated change, then we shall have to reduce turn-around time in the system. To do this requires greater participation on the part of those at the frontiers of learning. A distinguished mathematician and teacher, John Kemeny, did a survey of high-school mathematics teaching a decade ago and found no mathematics newer than a hundred years old being taught! That has been remedied somewhat in the decade since, but the work has hardly begun.

Another resource that must be brought to bear is modern psychology. Something happened to educational psychology a few decades ago that brought it to the low status it now enjoys. The circumstances need not concern us save in one respect. Part of the failure of educational psychology was its failure to grasp the full scope of its mission. It has too readily assumed that its central task was the application of personality theory or of group dynamics or whatnot. In fact, none of these efforts produced a major contribution to educational practice largely because the task was not really one of application in any obvious sense, but of formulation. Learning theory, for example, is distilled from descriptions of behavior in situations where the environment has been arranged either for the convenience of observing learning behavior or out of a theoretical interest in some special aspect of learning—reinforcement, cue distinctiveness, or whatever. But a theory of instruction, which must be at the heart of educational psychology, is principally concerned with how to arrange environments to optimize learning according to various criteria—to optimize transfer or retrievability of information, for example. Psychologists must re-enter the field of education in order to contribute to man's further evolution, an evolution that now proceeds through social invention. For it is psychology more than any other discipline that has the tools for exploring the limits of man's perfectibility. By doing so, it can, I think, have its major social impact by keeping lively the society's full sense of what is possible.

Aside from that, it becomes necessary for the various fields of learning to assess the manner in which they contribute to the amplification of mind—the way of doing or experiencing or ratiocinating that is integral to them and that should be part of the way of mind of an educated member of the culture. There are too many particulars to teach and to master. If we are to do justice to our evolution, we shall need, as never before, a way of transmitting the crucial ideas and skills, the acquired characteristics that express and amplify man's powers. We may be sure that the task will demand our highest talents. I would be content if we began, all of us, by recognizing that this is our task as learned men and scientists, that discovering how to make something comprehensible to the young is only a continuation of making something comprehensible to ourselves in the first place—that understanding and aiding others to understand are both of a piece.

psychology and humanistic psychology, leaving out psychoanalysis, which tends to be too clinically oriented to have much appeal to educators.

Scientific psychology already has a head start in its appeal to some educators because so much of its concern is and has been with the psychology of learning—the area in which the schools are primarily interested. Historically this branch has had much to say about school learning, and much of educational psychology makes use of principles developed there. Today, programmed instruction (teaching machines) is the most recent example of application of these principles. *If* you know what you want to teach, this branch of psychology has means for investigating the most efficient means for getting it taught.

The problem lies with the *"if"* in the preceding statement. This movement in psychology is of no help to an educational profession without a philosophy. In fact, I see it as being detrimental to the extent that technology is developed without due consideration given to the content which is to be utilized by the technology. Accepting scientific psychology does not solve education's problem of a commitment to a philosophy. (It is one thing for scientific psychology to embrace logical positivism for its philosophical support, but this is no answer to education's dilemma.)

Humanism

My own preference and commitment is to the humanistic movement in psychology. Unlike scientific psychology, this school does not beg the question of values. Implicit in their formulations is the basic assumption of the inherent "goodness" of human nature. In fact, for some, "goodness" is defined as that which is basically natural. Development of man's basic human potential becomes the goal and purpose of this movement. The emphasis and focus are not on what an individual has been but on what he is and can become. Thus it is a positive, forward looking, progressive philosophy.

Also basic to this school of thought is the assumption of man's inherent capabilities of being rational and self-determining. Thus the movement (unlike the two other forces in psychology) is consistent and compatible with our democratic heritage and our cultural ideal. Focus here is on the uniqueness and integrity of the individual deemphasizing the understanding of man in terms of norms or averages. "Nomothetic" science, whereby populations of individuals are studied segmentally and described statistically, is replaced by "idiographic" science, whereby individuals are studied as integrated units in their own right, and reported descriptively and dynamically. *Individuality* is stressed over the principle of individual differences.

For education this new movement in psychology offers a challenge as well as an alternative to its present state of alienation. (Some in education have recognized this challenge, as evidenced by the 1962 Yearbook of the Association for Supervision and Curriculum Development entitled *Perceiving, Behaving, Becoming.*) Actually, this psychology provides a framework in which much of what is already substantiated as good, effective educational practice can logically fit. Humanistic psychology provides a rationale for child-centered, individual-centered education. It lends itself beautifully to the recent emphasis on creativity. Its broad goals of self-actualization (self-fulfillment, self-realization) encourage breadth as well as depth of the curriculum—cognitive development in all subject and skill areas as well as conative, emotional development of the person as a dynamic, integrated human being.

Rather than grading practice being discouraging and defeating as it presently is for many (because of the unrealistic practice of using a single, normative standard whereby success is not attainable by all), under humanistic principles, the evaluation process can become encouraging and positive since progress would be noted in terms of each student's potential. This suggestion may be considered too idealistic for many to accept; on the other hand, convincing evidence is mounting from many sources in psychology on the importance of success over failure experiences (positive over negative reinforcement) for effective learning situations.

From the standpoint of curriculum, all subject or skill areas can find their place within the purview of humanistic psychology and philosophy. Emphasis shifts, however, from absolute standards of excellence to excellence according to each student's potential in that subject area. Emphasis also shifts from a common standard curriculum for all to tailor-made curricula to meet unique needs and talents of individual students. (The present experimentation with multi-grade classes, flexible scheduling, etc., would find a philosophical home here.) Instruction thus becomes freed from the chains of evaluation and curriculum as they presently exist (based on single and absolute standards) to become indeed individualized and thus more realistically consistent with what psychology has shown to be effective.

Under this philosophy, guidance would have a prominent function and one compatible with the entire educational program instead of supplementary to it as it is now. The concern of guidance for the promotion of and the provision for the individuality of each student would become central to the educational establishment.

Indeed, if education could identify itself (even in part) with this humanistic movement, many of its current problems, though not all, would be solved, would be set on a course toward solution. There would be a philosophical base for experimentation, for making curricular and instructional decisions, for meeting the public with a sound, challenging program, for reacting to unfounded attacks, for developing a dedicated, creative leadership.

THE NATURE AND MEASUREMENT OF INDIVIDUAL DIFFERENCES

• It is generally accepted that no two individuals are exactly alike. Not even identical twins with the same hereditary endowment have precisely identical environments. Hence, they never turn out to be carbon copies. The wide range of possible genetic backgrounds, to say nothing of the influences of differing environments, serves to account for these differences. On this subject, Hurlock[1] emphasizes that there is a tremendous variety of possible hereditary combinations and that these occur entirely by chance. For example, in one ejaculation of seminal fluid there can be as many as 200,000,000 sperm, any one of which can fertilize the ovum and each of which carries a different genetic blueprint. It has been estimated that at the moment of fertilization 16,777,216 different combinations of chromosomes are possible and that the particular arrangement that occurs as a result of the merging of the nuclei of the maternal and paternal germ cells is also a matter of chance. When these possibilities are considered, it is easy to account for our concern with individual differences and to see why entire courses on this subject are required of psychology majors.

One of the "hot" issues in school practices today relates to the uses and misuses of intelligence tests. Reger's article is one which deals so tersely

[1] Elizabeth B. Hurlock, *Child Development*, 4th ed. (New York: McGraw-Hill Book Company, 1964), pp. 39, 40.

with some of the prominent dilemmas that the reader thinks, "I wish I had written that."

An explanation of terms used in discussing tests will help the reader understand this and related articles. *Validity* relates to the degree to which an item or test measures what it is supposed to measure. If for instance, the level of a test score depends on reading or school training, then it may be a more valid measure of reading or school achievement than of intelligence. *Reliability* refers to the consistency with which a test measures what it is supposed to measure; *i.e.,* repeated measures of the same subject with the same instrument should result in substantially the same score. And thanks to Reger for stating that there is no such thing as an IQ test. We have instruments that assess intelligence and express the score through an IQ, but we are not testing the IQ.

Reger has also stated some facts of life: A test is not "unfair" if the results show that a child has not had the advantage of having learned some of the things that condition his success in school. The opportunities may be unfair, but is the test unfair when it assesses the results of those opportunities? The reader might well come back to Reger's Myth #5 after he has read about the role of motivation in establishing levels of aspiration and in determining the extent to which pupils will use the intellectual potential they do have—however acquired and however developed.

Occasionally there is a book or article that summarizes significant and historically valuable data so well that one feels he is meeting old friends again. Such is the article by Dr. Hunt. The authors and researches he cites will provide acquaintance with key people and ideas that will be encountered again and again. One of the editors has said elsewhere[2] that psychological tests are valuable indicators or approximations (not necessarily measures) of the present status of the individual. Hunt seems to be saying something quite similar when he cites low correlations between tests given at widely separated intervals. His conclusions regarding what can be done to stimulate early intellectual development are in agreement with the postulations of many others. We may see herein some of the future development of education. The ideas presented by Hunt on motivation, deprivation, verbal behavior, early experiences, and other factors related to developing intelligence are key ideas with which the reader should be familiar.

Much of the use to which tests have been put is of a negative nature; *i.e.,* causing teachers to limit a pupil's experience or lowering the pupil's self-esteem. Some of the causes of this are:

1. Tests have been used to label, to categorize, and to evaluate, rather

[2] Harold W. Bernard, *Psychology of Learning and Teaching,* 2nd ed. (New York: McGraw-Hill Book Company, 1965), p. 197.

than to delineate the position or the extent of the development of the person tested. An upper limit has been placed on the youngster in the minds of those who know the test results. We do know that there is a tendency to force people to conform to expectations and a tendency for them to yield to such pressure. When tests are used positively, the results are viewed merely as an indication of the person's position when the test was given and as a starting point for improving that position. The attitude is that testing is best used to establish a lower rather than an upper limit.

2. The intelligence quotient, or IQ, has been equated with intellectual ability. This has been seen as innate and unchanging. Actually the IQ is no more than an inference drawn from a sampling of behavior. Because of the constancy and consistency of human actions, predictions can be made from it. It must be remembered, however, that at the same time the IQ is considered as a measure of intelligence, it also must be considered as a measure of all of the inhibiting factors acting upon the individual at the time that the test was administered.

3. Decisions influencing a youngster's future too often are made on the basis of incomplete data. No one test score is ever valid or reliable enough to justify this. A series of corroborating scores and observations is essential before any decision can be made, particularly if it is one that will deny an educational opportunity to the youngster.

4. Similar IQ's have been thought to indicate similar levels of academic ability, and youngsters have been grouped together in the expectation that they are equally capable and will progress at comparable rates. This not only is erroneous, but it sometimes leads to teacher attitudes that discourage youngsters. In the first place, the IQ is derived from the number of answers accepted as correct or scorable on the test. Obviously, a number of persons could miss the same number of, but different, questions, come out with identical IQ's, and present as many different patterns of intellectual functioning as there were subjects tested. In the second place, innate intellectual ability is only one of many factors that influence test performance. The emotional state of the subject, his habitual approach to problems, his motivation and drive to accomplish, the expertise of the examiner, and even the state of subject's digestive processes are only a few of the many variables that may influence test performance.

A rule of thumb for teachers and other school personnel to follow regarding the use of all types of psychological tests and measurements is: "If you cannot describe clearly the manner in which test data will facilitate a youngster's growth and development, do not give the test or use the results."

ROGER REGER

Director, Special Educational Services, Board of Cooperative Educational Services, Buffalo, New York

20 · MYTHS ABOUT INTELLIGENCE

● School psychologists are faced with a continuously growing body of folklore about intelligence and intelligence tests. This problem is not endemic to school psychology, but school psychologists are in the unique position of being the most vulnerable to this folklore and at the same time in a position to begin culling myth from fact.

The over-all problem presented by this folklore will not be an easy one to resolve. Much of the folklore is so steeped in tradition that its very longevity can be used as an emotionally-laden argument for its fancied verity. Similarly, the widespread—even universal—acceptance of these fictions as fact makes their recognition most difficult.

"Basic" Myths

Probably the most effective preservative of myths about intelligence and intelligence tests are the pseudo-arguments that purport to challenge certain of these myths, when in fact they result in a strengthening of the over-all illusion.

MYTH #1: RELIABILITY AS VALIDITY

One of these pseudo-arguments is presented in the form of questions about the *validity* of intelligence tests (e.g., "How do we know that an intelligence test measures what it is supposed to measure?"). These ques-

Psychology in the Schools, 3:39–44, January, 1966. Used by permission of the author and *Psychology in the Schools*.

tions invariably are appropriate and in need of investigation. But just as invariably the questions are answered in terms of *reliability* rather than validity (Cattell, 1964).

At a less sophisticated level, questions related to such matters as "the constancy of the IQ," more obviously matters of reliability, sometimes are discussed as if validity were the issue being considered. As Cureton (1950) suggests, using a measure to predict itself is hardly a test of validity.

Hagen (1963) notes that in spite of existing weaknesses, intelligence tests are the best available predictors of academic success. However, she then illustrates the weaknesses of intelligence tests by comparing them with the unreliability of bathroom scales and dressmakers' measurements. Neel (1964) similarly presents questions relating to validity and then discusses these questions in terms of reliability.

Intelligence tests today are, in fact, tacitly assumed to be self-validating (though sometimes unreliable!). Scores from a test that measures intelligence are assumed to be as self-evident (i.e., valid) as "scores" obtained from a yardstick that measures height. A child is placed at a "level" of intellectual ability that allows a comparison to be made with his age peers, just as he is placed at a "level" of height that allows similar age-peer comparisons. Nevertheless, this analogy is inappropriate. Yardsticks (and bathroom scales) are direct measures. Intelligence tests, on the other hand, do not directly measure "intelligence," but *infer* that intelligence is somehow indirectly being measured (Benton, 1964; Rawlings, 1963, p. 361).

Validity remains an essential but largely ignored feature of intelligence tests. Confusing reliability with validity is a fertile source of folklore.

MYTH #2: DESCRIPTION AS EXPLANATION

Gallagher (1964) states that "Intelligence tests have served in three rather distinct capacities: (a) prediction, (b) classification, and (c) diagnosis" (p. 499). Gallagher and Moss (1963) earlier had discussed this in more detail. However, it seems that ultimately classification and diagnosis are based on predictions. As Thorndike (1964) observes, "Decisions imply predictions" (p. 104). In this intricate area lies the source of another rich spring of folklore.

Mythology abounds from failure to recognize that intelligence tests are predictive devices, and nothing more. Astin (1964) states that "In developing a test which is to be used primarily in an applied setting, investigators frequently construct, 'standardize,' and market the test first, and look around for criteria against which to 'validate' it afterward. It is an understatement to say that this practice is an anachronism" (p. 814).

The contents of intelligence tests are necessarily derived from the core of social and cultural knowledge, and it is this same core from which the school curriculum is derived. Thus, in a very significant sense, intelligence tests measure school-related knowledge. Indeed, Hagen (1963) acknowledges that "many people feel that 'general intelligence' is a misnomer for this test—that 'scholastic aptitude' would be a more precise term" (p. 6).

It is understandable that minority and/or "culturally deprived" groups typically score low on intelligence tests (Kennedy, Van de Riet, & White, 1963; Neel, 1964). In this case it is irrelevant to focus on the tests as being "unfair," because the *predictions* that can be derived from the tests are only reflecting an actual condition and are in themselves justifiable (McNemar, 1964). Intelligence tests are unfair only when they are inappropriately used for direct classification and diagnosis. It is unfair, at any time, to deny any school age child educational opportunities because he happens to score low on an intelligence test.

Consider the low-performing child referred to a school psychologist. It is found that the child scores low on a measure of school-related knowledge. This legitimately allows the school psychologist to state the prediction that the child's performance in school will be poor for some *unknown* length of time. It is of questionable appropriateness for the school psychologist to state that the low-scoring child is mentally retarded, and that his mental retardation in turn *explains* why he probably will have difficulty with school work (Staats & Staats, 1963). The thinking in that case becomes circular: a child's performance is poor; therefore, he is mentally retarded; therefore, his mental retardation explains his poor performance. Description is used as if explanation and prediction were being invoked[1] (Ellis, 1963).

"Secondary" Myths

Following are capsule outlines of other myths, some of which derive from the two major sources suggested so far: confusion between validity and reliability, and circular descriptive thinking used as explanation and prediction.

MYTH #3: THE IQ AS A BODILY ORGAN

A child does not "have" an IQ; an IQ is only a measuring device. The assumption that the test measures something inside the child (his IQ)

---

[1] There are educational implications involved in thinking, not of "mental" retardation, but of predicted *educational retardation*. See "The Concept of Educational Handicap" in Reger (1965), and "Special Education and the Concept of Educational Handicap," Reger (Unpublished manuscript).

is frankly ridiculous. However, belief that the IQ is a real internal characteristic is fairly common. Even such an illustrious figure as E. A. Doll (1964), in discussing the relative merits of mental age versus IQ, has made the curious statement that "we learn with our mental ages rather than our IQ's" (p. 39).

Because children do not possess a mysterious internal organ called "a real IQ," it is useless to pursue this phantom with relentless testing, as it will invariably escape.

MYTH #4: IQ FUNCTIONING

The idea of "depressed" intelligence, sometimes leading to the anomalous "diagnosis" of pseudofeeblemindedness (Arthur, 1947; Cantor, 1955), is depressing. Such an idea carries the assumption that there is such a thing as "a real IQ," or a static but "covered" level of intelligence (perhaps covered with a pseudogeological "emotional overlay").

According to such an assumption it follows that intelligence tests often fail to ferret out this real IQ, and *only* for this reason are often said to be "inaccurate." Therefore, it is asserted that a determination from "other factors" must help in the diagnosis of mental retardation, a subjective process which sometimes is suggested as being outside the competence of test-bound psychologists (Hirning, 1964).

MYTH #5: PREDICTING versus DETERMINING PERFORMANCE

Such phrases as "working up to the IQ," or "the functioning IQ level," contain the explicit assumption that not only should intelligence test performance *predict* school performance, it should *determine* school performance. This myth is the source of the "overachievement" notion. Carter (1964), for example, states that "over- and under-achievers are those who achieve more, or less, respectively, than expected in the light of measured intelligence" (p. 175).

The determination of performance undoubtedly has an interaction effect on predictions. Babbott and Grant (1964), and Edwards and Kirby (1964), for example, studied the usefulness of IQ scores in "predicting" academic success. They computed correlations between IQ scores and grades or achievement scores in several areas, using data obtained from records of past events. These typical studies leave unanswered the question of whether or not IQ scores in fact partially determined the grades or achievement expectations presented to the students by the teachers.

MYTH #6: RAISING THE POPULATION IQ

Because intelligence tests are statistical artifacts (Gerberich, 1963), it is meaningless to talk about "increases in IQ" in the population at large. If a test is standardized with a certain mean and standard deviation, and subsequent surveys show that the population actually has a "higher IQ" than the putative mean, this would suggest faulty test construction more than anything else.

The idea that the intelligence of children increases with age, in the sense that individual children who score 105 at one age might score 115 at a later age, which now and then is suggested, is another impossibility simply because of the way in which intelligence tests are statistically designed. This is true not only for recently devised tests, but also for older tests, such as the 1937 Stanford-Binet. If it were found, for example, that children knew "twice as much" at age ten as they did at age eight, individual children who scored 100 on a test at age eight would still score 100 at age ten because, even though they have become "smarter," so have their peers with whom they are being compared.

Many feel that the use of "mental age" on older tests gets around this problem but they have only concretized the mental age *concept* and assume that it, too, like the IQ, is a characteristic of children rather than of measuring devices. Again, children do not "have" a mental age any more than they "have" an IQ. If there are changes in the mental age scores of same-age groups of children over the years it is extremely difficult to determine the reasons for these changes. It is possible, for example, that many of the items in the 1937 Stanford-Binet have been incorporated into the school curriculum of today. While this should be reflected currently in higher scores than we obtained 15 years ago, particularly among younger and brighter children (as found, in fact, by Lindholm, 1964), it is pointless to assert that this is a reflection of a higher general level of population intelligence.

MYTH #7: LOW PERFORMANCE AS SUBHUMAN

Finally, the terms used to refer to low-performing children are sad reflections on the sophistication of the professions.

Consider the following sordid collection of terms: weakminded, feebleminded, backward, or stupid children; morons, imbeciles, idiots, simpletons, dolts, oafs, blockheads, ignoramuses, vegetables, Mongoloids (and other type-labels), retards, retardates, garden variety retardates, high or low grade retardates, defectives, familials, aments, organics, good organics, dummies, dumbbells, dullards, dodos, subnormals "a sixty-five" (or some other number), untrainables, trainables, TMRs or TMHs, and educables, EMRs, or EMHs.

Most of these are terms of invective, of scorn and disdain. Admittedly, changing words does not necessarily take away an existing stigma. If a group carries a stigma, it will not be long before new words applied to the group (e.g., exceptional, slow learning) take on the aroma of the stigma. But referring to children as if they were livestock or vegetation, or simply numbers, certainly does not help matters.

More importantly, the condescending paternalism with which low-performing children are treated today hardly suggests that sincere efforts are being made to ease the stigma itself. From an educational standpoint, is there really something "wrong" with low-performing children, or rather is there more often something wrong with the educational conditions (including attitudes) provided for such children?

Conclusions

The following conclusions are drawn from this brief examination of folklore about intelligence and intelligence tests:

First, the only legitimate use of intelligence tests is for predictive purposes. Other purported uses depend upon prediction.

Second, it is not justifiable for educational personnel to say that a child is mentally retarded on the basis of results from an intelligence test or from observations of classroom performance. It *is* justifiable to state that a prediction can be made about educational performance on the basis of results from intelligence tests. Thus, educational retardation can be predicted from low performance on intelligence tests.

"Mental retardation" is a noneducationally-relevant conception of a behavioral condition that produces no significant consequences for educational programing; educational retardation, on the other hand, is highly relevant to educational programing with important consequences.

Third, if sense is not substituted for nonsense in the use of intelligence tests, it will become more and more apparent that their use in the schools should be curtailed or eliminated entirely. Continued gross misuse of tests and ignorance about the meaning of test results is leading in this direction.

McNemar (1964) reasonably suggests that "it is high time for the profession to establish a bureau of standards to test the tests instead of coasting down a road that is tinged with some of the trappings of Madison Avenue. Better to have informed control than ignorant, hostile, external control"

(p. 876). Even so, control of test construction and distribution will not control the inappropriate use of tests. There are good tests available today but their misuse often makes them worthless.

Fourth, it is time to begin eliminating the prejudice that exists about low-performing children. Educationally retarded children in the schools do not need "help" (i.e., condescending "understanding" and pity); they need educational opportunities. Teachers who work with educationally retarded children are engaging in challenging work for which they should receive adequate pay and professional satisfactions.

REFERENCES

Arthur, G. Pseudo-feeblemindedness. *American Journal of Mental Deficiency*, 1947, 52, 137–142.

Astin, A. W. Criterion-centered research. *Educational and Psychological Measurements*, 1964, 24, 807–822.

Babbott, E. F., and Grant, C. W. I.Q. as one of several variables in predicting academic success. *The School Counselor*, 1964, 12, 18–21.

Benton, A. L. Psychological evaluation and differential diagonsis. In H. A. Stevens, and R. Heber (Eds.), *Mental retardation.* Chicago: Univer. of Chicago Press, 1964. Pp. 16–56.

Cantor, G. N. On the incurability of mental deficiency. *American Journal of Mental Deficiency*, 1955, 60, 362–365.

Carter, H. D. Over- and under-achievement in reading. *California Journal of Educational Research*, 1964, 15, 175–183.

Cattell, R. B. Validity and reliability; a proposed more basic set of concepts. *Journal of Educational Psychology*, 1964, 55, 1–22.

Cureton, E. E. Validity, reliability and baloney. *Educational and Psychological Measurement*, 1950, 10, 94–96.

Doll, E. A. Mental age versus IQ. *The Pointer*, 1964, 8 (3), 339–40.

Edwards, A. J., and Kirby, M. Elsie. Predictive efficiency of intelligence test scores: intelligence quotients obtained in grade one and achievement test scores obtained in grade three. *Educational and Psychological Measurement*, 1964, 24, 941–946.

Ellis, N. R. (Ed.) Introduction. *Handbook of Mental Deficiency.* New York: McGraw-Hill, 1963. Pp. 1–7.

Gallagher, J. J. Meaningful learning and retention: intrapersonal cognitive variables. *Review of Educational Research*, 1964, 34, 499–512.

Gallagher, J. J., and Moss, J. W. New concepts of intelligence and their effect on exceptional children. *Exceptional Children*, 1963, 30, 1–5.

Gerberich, J. R. The development of educational testing. *Theory into Practice*, 1963, 2, 184–191.

Hagen, Elizabeth. Standardized tests: tyranny or tools? *Teaching and Learning*, 1963. 5–11.

Hirning, L. C. Some experiences in school psychiatry. *Teachers College Record*, 1964, 66, 64–70.

Kennedy, W. A., Van de Riet, V., and White, J. C., Jr. A normative sample of intelligence and achievement of Negro elementary school children in the Southeastern United States. *Monographs of the Society for Research in Child Development*, 1963, Series No. 90, 28, No. 6.

Lindholm, B. W. Changes in conventional and deviation IQ's. *Journal of Educational Psychology*, 1964, 55, 110–113.

McNemar, Q. Lost, our intelligence? Why? *American Psychologist*, 1964, 19, 871–882.

Neel, Ann F. What does IQ mean? *Clinical Pediatrics*, 1964, 3, 374–378.

Rawlings, Grace. Examination and diagnosis. In R. F. Tredgold, and K. Soddy (Eds.), *Textbook of mental deficiency (subnormality)*. Baltimore: Williams & Wilkins, 1963. Pp. 357–409.

Reger, R. *School psychology*. Springfield, Ill.: Charles C Thomas, 1965.

Reger, R. Special education and the concept of educational handicap. Unpublished manuscript.

Staats, A. W., and Staats, Carolyn K. *Complex human behavior: a systematic extension of learning principles*. New York: Holt, Rinehart & Winston, 1963.

Thorndike, R. L. Educational decisions and human assessment. *Teachers College Record*, 1964, 66, 103–112.

J. McVICKER HUNT
Professor of Psychology, University of Illinois

21 · HOW CHILDREN DEVELOP INTELLECTUALLY

• The task of maximizing the intellectual potential of our children has acquired new urgency. Two of the top challenges of our day lie behind this urgency. First, the rapidly expanding role of technology, now taking the form of automation, decreases opportunity for persons of limited competence and skills while it increases opportunity for those competent in the use of written language, in mathematics, and in problem solving. Second, the challenge of eliminating racial discrimination requires not only equality of employment opportunity and social recognition for persons of equal competence, but also an equalization of the opportunity to develop that intellectual capacity and skill upon which competence is based.

During most of the past century anyone who entertained the idea of increasing the intellectual capacity of human beings was regarded as an unrealistic "do-gooder." Individuals, classes, and races were considered to be what they were because either God or their inheritance had made them that way; any attempt to raise the intelligence quotient (IQ) through experience met with contempt. Man's nature has not changed since World War II, but some of our conceptions of his nature have been changing rapidly. These changes make sensible the hope that, with improved understanding of early experience, we might counteract some of the worst effects of cultural deprivation and raise substantially the average level of intellectual capacity. This paper will attempt to show how and why these con-

Children, 11:83–91, May–June, 1964 (a publication of the U.S. Office of Education).

ceptions are changing, and will indicate the implications of these changes for experiments designed to provide corrective early experiences to children and to feed back information on ways of counteracting cultural deprivation.

CHANGING BELIEFS

Fixed Intelligence. The notion of fixed intelligence has roots in Darwin's theory that evolution takes place through the variations in strains and species which enable them to survive to reproduce themselves. Finding in this the implicit assumption that adult characteristics are determined by heredity, Francis Galton, Darwin's younger cousin, reasoned that the improvement of man lies not in education, or euthenics, but in the selection of superior parents for the next generation—in other words, through eugenics. To this end, he founded an anthropometric laboratory to give simple sensory and motor tests (which failed, incidentally, to correlate with the qualities in which he was interested), established a eugenics society, and imparted his beliefs to his student, J. McKeen Cattell, who brought the tests to America.

About the same time G. Stanley Hall, an American who without knowing Darwin became an ardent evolutionist, imparted a similar faith in fixed intelligence to his students, among them such future leaders of the intelligence testing movement as H. H. Goddard, F. Kuhlmann, and Lewis Terman (1). This faith included a belief in the constant intelligence quotient. The IQ, originally conceived by the German psychologist Wilhelm Stern, assumes that the rate of intellectual development can be specified by dividing the average age value of the tests passed (mental age) by the chronological age of the child.

The considerable debate over the constancy of the IQ might have been avoided if the work of the Danish geneticist Johannsen had been as well known in America as that of Gregor Mendel, who discovered the laws of hereditary transmission. Johannsen distinguished the genotype, which can be known only from the ancestry or progeny of an individual, from the phenotype, which can be directly observed and measured. Although the IQ was commonly treated as if it were a genotype (innate capacity), it is in fact a phenotype and, like all phenotypes (height, weight, language spoken), is a product of the genotype and the circumstances with which it has interacted (1).

Johannsen's distinction makes possible the understanding of evidence dissonant with the notion of fixed intelligence. For instance, identical twins (with the same genotype) have been found to show differences in IQ of as much as 24 points when reared apart, and the degree of difference appears to be related to the degree of dissimilarity of the circumstances in which they were reared. Also, several investigators have reported finding substantial improvement in IQ after enrichment of experience, but their critics have attributed this to defects in experimental control.

When results of various longitudinal studies available after World War II showed very low correlation between the preschool IQ and IQ at age 18, the critics responded by questioning the validity of the infant tests, even though Nancy Bayley (2) had actually found high correlations among tests given close together in time. Blaming the tests tended to hide the distinction that should have been made between cross-sectional validity and predictive validity: What a child does in the testing situation correlates substantially with what he will do in other situations, but attempting to predict what an IQ will be at age 18 from tests given at ages from birth to 4 years, before the schools have provided at least some standardization of circumstances, is like trying to predict how fast a feather will fall in a hurricane.

Predetermined Development. Three views of embryological and psychological development have held sway in the history of thought: preformationism, predeterminism, and interactionism (1). As men gave up preformationism, the view that the organs and features of adulthood are preformed in the seed, they turned to predeterminism, the view that the organs and features of adulthood are hereditarily determined. G. Stanley Hall in emphasizing the concept of recapitulation—that the development of the individual summarizes the evolution of his species—drew the predeterministic moral that each behavior pattern manifest in a child is a natural stage with which no one should interfere. The lifework of Arnold Gesell exemplifies the resulting concern with the typical or average that has shaped child psychology during the past half century.

The theory of predetermined development got support from Coghill's finding that frogs and salamanders develop behaviorally as they mature anatomically, from head-end tailward and from inside out, and from Carmichael's finding that the swimming patterns of frogs and salamanders develop equally well whether inhibited by chloretone in the water or stimulated by vibration. Such findings appeared to generalize to children: The acquisition of such skills as walking, stair climbing, and buttoning cannot be speeded by training or exercise; Hopi children reared on cradleboards learn to walk at the same age as Hopi children reared with arms and legs free (3).

Again, however, there was dissonant evidence. Although Cruze found that chicks kept in the dark decreased their pecking errors during the first 5 days after hatching—a result consonant with predeterminism—he also found that chicks kept in the dark for 20 days failed to improve their pecking. Moreover, studies of rats and dogs, based on the theorizing of Donald Hebb, suggest that the importance of infantile experience increases up the phylogenetic scale (4).

Evidence that such findings may apply to human beings comes from studies by Goldfarb (5) which indicate that institutional rearing (where the environment is relatively restricted and unresponsive) results in lower intelligence, less ability to sustain a task, and more problems in interpersonal relations than foster-home rearing (where the environment provides more varied experiences and responsiveness). Wayne Dennis (6) has found that in a Teheran orphanage, where changes in ongoing stimulation were minimal, 60 percent of the 2-year-olds could not sit alone and 85 percent of the 4-year-olds could not walk alone. Such a finding dramatizes the great effect preverbal experience can have on even the rate of locomotor development. Presumably the effect on intellectual functions would be even greater.

Static Brain Function. In 1900, when C. Lloyd Morgan and E. L. Thorndike were attempting to explain learning in terms of stimulus-response bonds, they used the newly invented telephone as a mechanical model of the brain's operation. Thus they envisioned the brain as a static switchboard through which each stimulus could be connected with a variety of responses, which in turn could become the stimuli for still other responses.

Soon objective stimulus-response methodology produced evidence dissonant with this switchboard model theory, implying some kind of active processes going on between the ears. But it took the programing of electronic computers to clarify the general nature of the requirements for solving logical problems. Newell, Shaw, and Simon (7) describe three major components of these requirements: (a) memories, or information, coded and stored; (b) operations of a logical sort which can act upon the memories; and (c) hierarchically arranged programs of these operations for various purposes. Pribram (8) found a likely place for the brain's equivalents of such components within the intrinsic portions of the cerebrum which have no direct connections with either incoming fibers from the receptors of experience or outgoing fibers to the muscles and glands.

So, the electronic computer supplies a more nearly adequate mechanical model for brain functioning. Thus, experience may be regarded as programing the intrinsic portions of the cerebrum for learning and problem solving, and intellectual capacity at any given time may be conceived as a function of the nature and quality of this programing (1, 9).

As Hebb (4) has pointed out, the portion of the brain directly connected with neither incoming nor outgoing fibers is very small in animals such as frogs and salamanders, whence came most of the evidence supporting the belief in predetermined development. The increasing proportion of the intrinsic portion of the brain in higher animals suggests an anatomic basis for the increasing role of infantile experience in development, as evidenced by the greater effect of rearing on problem solving ability in dogs than in rats (9). Frogs and salamanders have a relatively higher capacity for regeneration than do mammals. This suggests that the chemical factors in the genes may have more complete control in these lower forms than they have further up the phylogenic scale.

Motivation by Need, Pain, and Sex. Our conception of motivation is also undergoing change. Although it has long been said that man does not live by bread alone, most behavioral scientists and physiologists have based their theorizing on the assumption that he does. Freud popularized the statement that "all behavior is motivated." He meant motivated by painful stimulation, homeostatic need, and sexual appetite or by acquired motives based on these; and this concept has generally been shared by physiologists and academic behavioral theorists.

Undoubtedly, painful stimulation and homeostatic need motivate all organisms, as sex motivates all mammalian organisms, but the assertion that all behavior is so motivated implies that organisms become quiescent in the absence of painful stimulation, homeostatic need, and sexual stimulation. Observation stubbornly indicates that they do not: Young animals and children are most likely to play in the absence of such motivation; young rats, cats, dogs, monkeys, chimpanzees, and humans work for nothing more substantial than the opportunity to perceive, manipulate, or explore novel circumstances. This evidence implies that there must be some additional basis for motivation.

Reflex vs. Feedback. A change in our conception of the functional unit of the nervous system from the reflex arc to the feedback loop helps to suggest the nature of this other motivating mechanism. The conception of the reflex arc has its anatomical foundations in the Bell-Magendie law, based on Bell's discovery of separate ventral and dorsal roots of the spinal nerves and on Magendie's discovery that the dorsal roots have sensory or "input" functions while the ventral roots have motor or "output" functions. But the Bell-Magendie law was an overgeneralization, for motor fibers have been discovered within the presumably sensory dorsal roots, and sensory fibers have been discovered within the presumably motor ventral roots.

The most important argument against the reflex as the functional unit of the nervous system comes from the direct evidence of feedback in both sensory input and motor output. The neural activity that results when cats are exposed to a tone is markedly reduced when they are exposed to the sight of mice or the smell of fish, thus dramatizing feedback in sensory input. Feedback in motor output is dramatized by evidence that sensory input from the muscle spindles modulates the rate of motor firing to the muscles, thereby controlling the strength of contraction (9).

Incongruity as Motivation. The feedback loop which constitutes a new conceptual unit of neural function supplies the basis for a new mechanism of motivation. Miller, Galanter, and Pribram (10) have called the feedback loop the Test-Operate-Test-Exit (TOTE) unit. Such a TOTE unit is, in principle, not unlike the room thermostat. The temperature at which the thermostat is set supplies a standard against which the temperature of the room is continually being tested. If the room temperature falls below this standard, the test yields an *incongruity* which starts the furnace to "operate," and it continues to operate until the room temperature has reached this standard. When the test yields *congruity*, the furnace stops operating and the system makes its exit. Similarly, a living organism is free to be otherwise motivated once such a system has made its exit.

Several classes of similarly operating standards can be identified for human beings. One might be described as the "comfort standard" in which incongruity is equivalent to pain. Another consists of those homeostatic standards for hunger (a low of glycogen in the bloodstream) and for thirst (a high level of hydrogen ion concentration within the blood and interstitial fluids). A third class, which stretches the concept of incongruity somewhat, is related to sex.

Other standards derive from the organism's informational interaction with the environment. Thus, a fourth class appears to consist of ongoing inputs, and, just as "one never hears the clock until it has stopped," any change in these ongoing inputs brings attention and excitement. Repeated encounters with such changes of input lead to expectations, which constitute a fifth class of standards. A sixth class consists of plans quite independent of painful stimulation, homeostatic need, or sex. Ideals constitute a seventh class.

There is evidence that incongruity with such standards will instigate action and produce excitement (9). There is also evidence that an optimum of such incongruity exists. Too little produces boredom as it did among McGill students who would remain lying quietly in a room no more than 3 days, although they were paid $20 a day to do so (9). Too much produces fearful emotional stress, as when a baby chimpanzee sees his keeper in a Halloween mask (11), a human infant encounters strangers, or primitive men see an eclipse.

While this optimum of incongruity is still not well understood, it seems to involve the matching of incoming information with standards based on information already coded and stored within the cerebrum (9). Probably only the individual himself can choose a source of input which provides him with an optimum of incongruity. His search for this optimum, however, explains that "growth motivation" which Froebel, the founder of the kindergarten movement, postulated and which John Dewey borrowed; and it may be the basic motivation underlying intellectual growth and the search for knowledge. Such motivation may be characterized as "intrinsic" because it inheres in the organism's informational interaction with the environment.

Emotional vs. *Cognitive Experience.* Another fundamental change is in the importance attributed to early—and especially very early—preverbal experience. Traditionally, very little significance had been attached to preverbal experience. When consciousness was believed to control conduct, infantile experience, typically not remembered, was regarded as having hardly any effect on adult behavior. Moreover, when development was conceived to be predetermined, infantile experience could have little importance. While Freud (12) believed that preverbal experiences were important, he argued that their importance derived from the instinctive impulses arising from painful stimulation, homeostatic need, and especially pleasure striving, which he saw as sexual in nature.

Freud's work spread the belief that early emotional experiences are important while early cognitive experiences are not. It now appears that the opposite may possibly be more nearly true. Objective studies furnish little evidence that the factors important according to Freud's theory of psychosexual development are significant (13, 14). Even the belief that infants are sensitive organisms readily traumatized by painful stimulation or intense homeostatic need has been questioned as the result of studies involving the shocking of nursling rats.

Rats shocked before weaning are found to be less likely than rats left unmolested in the maternal nest to urinate and defecate in, or to hesitate entering, unfamiliar territory, and more likely to be active there. Moreover, as adults, rats shocked before weaning often require stronger shocks to instigate escape activity than do rats left unmolested; they also show less fixative effect from being shocked at the choice-point in a T-maze (15). Evidence that children from low socioeconomic and educational classes, who have frequently known painful stimulation, are less likely to be fearful than middle-class children, who have seldom known painful stimulation, suggests that the findings of these rat studies may apply to human beings (16).

While such observations have contradicted the common conception of the importance of early emotional experience, the experiments stemming from Hebb's theorizing (4) have repeatedly demonstrated the importance of early perceptual and cognitive experience. At earlier phases of development, the variety of circumstances encountered appears to be most important; somewhat later, the responsiveness of the environment to the infant's activities appears to be central; and at a still later phase, the opportunity to understand the causation of mechanical and social relationships seems most significant.

In this connection, a study by Baldwin, Kalhorn, and Breese (17) found that the IQ's of 4- to 7-year-old children tend to increase with time if parental discipline consists of responsive and realistic explanations, but tend to fall if parental discipline consists of nonchalant unresponsiveness or of demands for obedience for its own sake, with painful stimulation as the alternative.

Motor Response and Receptor Input. One more important traditional belief about psychological development which may have to be changed concerns the relative importance of motor response and receptor input for the development of the autonomous central processes which mediate intellectual capacity. A century ago, the "apperceptive mass" conceived by Herbart, a German educational psychologist, was regarded as the product of previous perceptual input; and Froebel and Montessori both stressed sensory training. However, after World War I, the focus of laboratory learning-studies on response, coupled with the notion of brain function as a static switchboard, gradually shifted the emphasis from the perceptual input to the response output. It is hard to make the great importance attributed to the response side jibe with the following findings:

1. Hopi infants reared on cradleboards, where the movements of arms and legs are inhibited during waking hours, learn to walk at the same age as Hopi infants reared with arms and legs free (3).

2. Eighty-five percent of the 4-year-olds in a Teheran orphanage, where variations in auditory and visual input were extremely limited, did not walk alone (6).

Such observations and those of Piaget (18, 19) suggest that the repeated correction of expectations deriving from perceptual impressions and from cognitive accommodations gradually create the central processes mediating the logical operations of thought. Wohlwill (20) and Flavel (21) have assembled evidence which relates the inferential processes of thought to experience and have given this evidence some formal theoretical organization.

COUNTERACTING CULTURAL DEPRIVATION

The intellectual inferiority apparent among so many children of parents of low educational and socioeconomic status, regardless of race, is already evident by the time they begin kindergarten or first grade at age 5 or 6 (22). Such children are apt to have various linguistic liabilities: limited vocabularies, poor articulation, and syntactical deficiencies that are revealed in the tendency to rely on unusually short sentences with faulty grammar (23). They also show perceptual deficiencies in the sense that they recognize fewer objects and situations than do most middle-class children. And perhaps more important, they usually have fewer interests than do the middle-class children who are the pace setters in the schools. Moreover, the objects recognized by and the interests of children typical of the lower class differ from those of children of the middle class. These deficiencies give such children the poor start which so commonly handicaps them ever after in scholastic competition.

So long as it was assumed that intelligence is fixed and development is predetermined, the intellectual inferiority of children from families of low educational and socioeconomic status had to be considered an unalterable consequence of their genes. With the changes in our conception of man's intellectual development, outlined in the foregoing pages, there emerges a hope of combating such inferiority by altering, for part of their waking hours, the conditions under which such children develop. The question is "how?"

Clues from Intrinsic Motivation. A tentative answer, worthy at least of investigative demonstration, is suggested by the existence of a change during the preschool years in the nature of what I have called "intrinsic motivation." An approximation of the character of this change has been supplied by the observations which Piaget made on the development of his three children (18, 19, 24). At least three stages in the development of intrinsic motivation appear. These may be characteristic of an organism's progressive relationship with any new set of circumstances and seem to be stages in infant development only because the child is encountering so many new sets of circumstances during his first 2 or 3 years.

In the first stage the infant is essentially responsive. He is motivated, of course, by painful stimulation, homeostatic need, and, in Freud's sense, by sex. Russian investigators have shown that the orienting response is ready-made at birth in all mammals, including human beings (25). Thus, any changes in the ongoing perceptual input will attract attention and excite the infant. During this phase each of the ready-made sensorimotor organizations—sucking, looking, listening, vocalizing, grasping, and wiggling—changes, by something like Pavlov's conditioning process, to become coordinated with the others. Thus, something heard becomes something to look at, something to look at becomes something to grasp, and something to grasp becomes something to suck. This phase ends with a "landmark of transition" in which the infant, having repeatedly encountered certain patterns of stimulus change, tries actively to retain or regain them (24).

During the second stage the infant manifests interest in, and efforts to retain, something newly recognized as familiar—a repeatedly encountered pattern of change in perceptual input. The infant's intentional effort is familiar to anyone who has jounced a child on his knee and then stopped his jouncing only to find the child making a comparable motion, as if to invite the jouncing adult to continue. Regaining the newly recognized activity commonly brings forth such signs of delight as the smile and the laugh, and continued loss brings signs of distress. The effort to retain the newly recognized may well account for the long hours of hand watching and babbling commonly observed during the child's third, fourth, and fifth months. This second stage ends when, with these repeated encounters, the child becomes bored with the familiar and turns his interest to whatever is novel in familiar situations (24).

The third stage begins with this interest in the novel within a familiar context, which typically becomes noticeable during the last few months of the first year of life. Piaget (18) describes its beginnings with the appearance of throwing, but it probably can be found earlier. While he throws, the child intentionally shifts his attention from the act of throwing to the trajectory of the object that he has thrown.

Interest in the novel is also revealed in the infant's increasing development of new plans through an active, creative process of groping, characterized by C. Lloyd Morgan as "trial-and-error." It also shows in the child's increasing attempts to imitate new vocal patterns and gestures (19, 24).

Interest in the new is the infant's basis for "growth motivation." It has also been found in animals, particularly in an experiment in which rats in a figure-eight maze regularly changed their preference to the more complex loop.

Thus Piaget's (18) aphorism, "the more a child has seen and heard, the more he wants to see and hear," may be explained. The more different visual and auditory changes the child encounters during the first stage, the more of these will he recognize with interest during the second stage. The more he recognizes during the second stage, the more of these will provide novel features to attract him during the third stage.

Effects of Social Environment. Such development prepares the child to go on developing. But continuing development appears to demand a relationship with adults who enable the infant to pursue his locomotor and manipulative intentions and who answer his endless questions of "what's that?", "is it a 'this' or a 'that'?", and "why is it a 'this' or a 'that'?". Without these supports during the second, third, and fourth years of life, a child cannot continue to profit no matter how favorable his circumstances during his first year.

Although we still know far too little about intellectual development to say anything with great confidence, it is unlikely that most infants in families of low socioeconomic status suffer great deprivation during their first year. Since one distinguishing feature of poverty is crowding, it is conceivable that an infant may actually encounter a wider variety of visual and auditory inputs in conditions of poverty than in most middle- or upper-class homes. This should facilitate the intellectual development of the infant during his first year.

During the second year, however, crowded living conditions would probably hamper development. As an infant begins to move under his own power, to manipulate things, and to throw things, he is likely to get in the way of adults who are apt already to be ill-tempered from their own discomforts and frustrations. Such situations are dramatized in Lewis's "The Children of Sanchez," an anthropological study of life in poverty (26). In such an atmosphere, a child's opportunity to carry out the activities required for his locomotor and manipulative development must almost inevitably be sharply curbed.

Moreover, late in his second or early in his third year, after he has developed a number of pseudo-words and achieved the "learning set" that "things have names," the child in a crowded, poverty-stricken family probably meets another obstacle: His questions too seldom bring suitable answers, and too often bring punishment that inhibits further questioning. Moreover, the conditions that originally provided a rich variety of input for the very young infant now supply a paucity of suitable playthings and models for imitation.

The effects of a lower-class environment on a child's development may become even more serious during his fourth and fifth years. Furthermore, the longer these conditions continue, the more likely the effects are to be lasting. Evidence from animal studies supports this: Tadpoles immobilized with chloretone for 8 days are not greatly hampered in the development of their swimming patterns, but immobilization for 13 days leaves their swimming patterns permanently impaired; chicks kept in darkness for as many as 5 days show no apparent defects in their pecking responses, but keeping them in darkness for 8 or more days results in chicks which never learn to peck at all (1).

Possible Counteracting Measures. Such observations suggest that if nursery schools or day-care centers were arranged for culturally deprived children from age 4—or preferably from age 3—until time for school at 5 or 6 some of the worst effects of their rearing might be substantially reduced.

Counteracting cultural deprivation at this stage of development might best be accomplished by giving the child the opportunity to encounter a wide variety of objects, pictures, and appropriate behavioral models, and by giving him social approval for appropriate behavior. The setting should encourage him to indulge his inclinations to scrutinize and manipulate the new objects as long as he is interested and should provide him with appropriate answers to his questions. Such varied experiences would foster the development of representative imagery which could then be the referents for spoken words and later for written language.

Children aged 3 and 4 should have the opportunity to hear people speak who provide syntactical models of standard grammar. The behavioral models would lead gradually to interest in pictures, written words, and books. The objects provided and appropriate answers to the "why" questions would lead to interest in understanding the workings of things and the consequences of social conduct. Thus, the child might gradually overcome most of the typical handicaps of his lower-class rearing by the time he enters grade school.

There is a danger, however, in attempting to prescribe a remedy for cultural deprivation at this stage of knowledge. Any specific prescription of objects, pictures, behavioral models, and forms of social reinforcement may fail to provide that attractive degree of incongruity with the impressions which the toddler of the lower class has already coded and stored in the course of his experience. Moreover, what seem to be appropriate behavioral models may merely produce conflict. Therefore, it may be wise to reexamine the educational contributions of Maria Montessori (27, 28). These have been largely forgotten in America, perhaps because they were until recently too dissonant with the dominant notions of motivation and the importance attributed to motor responses in development.

Montessori's contributions are especially interesting, despite some of the rigid orthodoxy that has crept into present-day Montessori practice, because she based her teaching methods on children's spontaneous interest in learning, that is, on "intrinsic motivation." Moreover, she stressed the importance of teachers' observing children to discover what things would most interest them and most foster their growth. Further, she stressed the need to train the perceptual processes, or what we would today call the information processes. The coded information stored in culturally deprived children from lower-class backgrounds differs from that stored in children with middle-class backgrounds. This difference makes it dangerous for middle-class teachers to prescribe intuitively on the basis of their own experiences or of their experiences in teaching middle-class youngsters.

Montessori also broke the lockstep in the education of young children. She made no effort to keep them doing the same thing at the same time. Rather, each child was free to examine and work with whatever happened to interest him, for as long as he liked. It is commonly believed that the activity of preschoolers must be changed every 10 or 15 minutes or the children become bored. But Dorothy Canfield Fisher (29) the novelist, who spent the winter of 1910–11 at Montessori's Casa de Bambini in Rome, observed that 3-year-olds there commonly remained engrossed in such mundane activities as buttoning and unbuttoning for 2 hours or more at a time. In such a setting the child has an opportunity to find those particular circumstances which match his own particular phase of development and which provide the proper degree of incongruity for intrinsic motivation. This may well have the corollary advantage of making learning fun and the school setting interesting and attractive.

Montessori also included children from 3 to 6 years old in the same group. In view of the changes that occur in intellectual development, this has the advantage of providing younger children with a variety of novel models for imitation while supplying older children with an opportunity to teach, an activity which provides many of its own rewards.

Conclusions

At this stage of history and knowledge, no one can blueprint a program of preschool enrichment that will with certainty be an effective antidote for the cultural deprivation of children. On the other hand, the revolutionary changes taking place in the traditional beliefs about the development of human capacity and motivation make it sensible to hope that a program of preschool enrichment may ultimately be made effective. The task calls for creative innovations and careful evaluative studies of their effectiveness.

Discoveries of effective innovations will contribute also to the general theory of intellectual development and become significant for the rearing and education of all children. Effective innovations will also help to minimize those racial differences in school achievement which derive from cultural deprivation and so help to remove one stubborn obstacle in the way of racial integration.

Although it is likely that no society has ever made the most of the intellectual potential of its members, the increasing role of technology in our culture demands that we do better than others ever have. To do so we must become more concerned with intellectual development during the preschool years and especially with the effects of cultural deprivation.

REFERENCES

1. Hunt, J. McV. Intelligence and experience. Ronald Press Co., New York. 1961.
2. Bayley, Nancy. Mental growth in young children. *In* Thirty-ninth yearbook of the National Society for the Study of Education, part II. Public School Publishing Co., Bloomington, Ill. 1940.
3. Dennis, W., Dennis, Marsena G. The effect of cradling practice upon the onset of walking in Hopi children. *Journal of Genetic Psychology*, vol. 56, 1940.
4. Hebb, D. O. The organization of behavior. John Wiley & Sons, New York. 1949.
5. Goldfarb, W. The effects of early institutional care on adolescent personality. *Journal of Experimental Education*, vol. 12, 1953.
6. Dennis, W. Causes of retardation among institutional children: Iran. *Journal of Genetic Psychology*, vol. 96, 1960.
7. Newell, A., Shaw, J. C., Simon, H. A. Elements of a theory of human problem-solving. *Psychological Review*, vol. 65, 1958.

8. Pribram, K. H. A review of theory in physiological psychology. *Annual Review of Psychology*, vol. 11, 1960.

9. Hunt, J. McV. Motivation inherent in information processing and action. *In* Motivation and social interaction: cognitive determinants. (O. J. Harvey, ed.) Ronald Press Co., New York, 1963.

10. Miller, G. A., Galanter, E., Pribram, K. H. Plans and the structure of behavior. Henry Holt & Co., New York. 1960.

11. Hebb, D. O. On the nature of fear. *Psychological Review*, vol. 53, 1946.

12. Freud, S. Three contributions to the theory of sex. *In* The basic writings of Sigmund Freud. (A. A. Brill, ed.) Modern Library, New York. 1938.

13. Hunt, J. McV. Experimental psychoanalysis. *In* The encyclopedia of psychology. (P. L. Harriman, ed.) Philosophical Library, New York. 1946.

14. Orlansky, H. Infant care and personality. *Psychological Bulletin*, vol. 46, 1949.

15. Salama, A. A., Hunt, J. McV. "Fixation" in the rat as a function of infantile shocking, handling, and gentling. *Journal of Genetic Psychology*, vol. 100, 1964.

16. Holmes, F. B. An experimental study of the fears of young children. *In* Children's fears. (A. T. Jersild, F. B. Holmes.) Child Development Monographs, No. 20, Teachers College, Columbia University, New York. 1935.

17. Baldwin, A. L., Kalhorn, J., Breese, F. H. Patterns of parent behavior. *Psychological Monographs*, vol. 58, 1945.

18. Piaget, J. The origins of intelligence in children (1936). (Translated by Margaret Cook.) International Universities Press, New York. 1952.

19. ———. Play, dreams, and imitation in childhood (1945). (Translation of *La formation du symbole chez l'enfant* by C. Gattegno and F. M. Hodgson.) W. W. Norton & Co., New York. 1951.

20. Wohlwill, J. F. Developmental studies of perception. *Psychological Bulletin*, vol. 57, 1960.

21. Flavel, J. H. The developmental psychology of Jean Piaget. D. Van Nostrand Co., New York. 1963.

22. Kennedy, W. A., et al. A normative sample of intelligence and achievement of Negro elementary school children in the Southeastern United States. *Monographs of the Society for Research in Child Development*, Serial No. 90, vol. 28, 1963.

23. John, Vera P. The intellectual development of slum children. *Merrill-Palmer Quarterly*, vol. 10, 1964.

24. Hunt, J. McV. Piaget's observations as a source of hypotheses concerning motivation. *Merrill-Palmer Quarterly*, vol. 9, 1963.

25. Razran, G. The observable unconscious and the inferable conscious in current Soviet psychophysiology: interoceptive conditioning, semantic conditioning, and the orienting reflex. *Psychological Review*, vol. 68, 1961.

26. Lewis, O. The children of Sanchez. Random House, New York. 1961.

27. Montessori, Maria. The Montessori method (1907). Frederick A. Stokes, New York. 1912.

28. Rambusch, Nancy McC. Learning how to learn: an American approach to Montessori. Helicon Press, Baltimore, Md. 1962.

29. Fisher, Dorothy Canfield. A Montessori mother. Henry Holt & Co., New York. 1912.

THE NATURE AND NURTURE OF INTELLIGENCE

• Although only one se-
lection was made for this section, it is of such nature that the reader may
discover new ideas, concepts, and associations for developing his own frame
of reference in any one of a number of spaced rereadings. We wish to call
the reader's attention to, and comment on, some of the salient ideas that
our point of view helped to identify and to make meaningful for us.

The first of these is Bruner's idea of the interdependence of mind, or
intelligence, and culture. It is not our purpose to engage in the old argument: "Does mind create culture or does culture create mind?" but the
recognition that neither can exist by itself and that one can be influenced
by changes in the other is important. Perhaps if pedagogy is to be, as
Bruner terms it, "the psychology of assisted growth," educators will have
to become students of sociology and the other behavioral sciences as well as
applied psychologists.

The second idea which impresses us is the concept of amplification
systems as furnished by the culture in which the individual develops. We
see these as tools which serve to increase the influence and impact which the
individual can make as a member of that culture. An example will show
how this works. Consider the amplification of power which a bulldozer
operator can bring to bear, and consider that neither the operator nor the
machine could do this without the other. Also consider that neither would
exist or function in a power-exerting capacity without both the educating
and manufacturing aspects of the culture. This is true in almost all instances

where the brain and intelligence of a man is teamed with the facility and power of a computer or a mechanical device.

With the increasing emphasis on technology and automation, the physical-skill requirements of the amplification systems provided by the culture are continually decreasing while the intellectual demands are coming to far exceed the supply that present educational systems and methods are able to furnish. We appear to have been more successful in developing power and capacity for getting things done than we have in effectively applying this power; *i.e.,* we probably have more amplification systems available in the culture than most of us have learned how to use.

Despite a good deal of speculation, definitions and descriptions of intelligence generally have met with as much disagreement as accord among psychologists. While most psychologists believe intelligence to be many-faceted, they by no means agree on the manner in which the various facets are related, organized, and described. They differ, for example, with respect to the number of components that can be identified as representing the totality of intelligence, and they differ according to the way in which they describe the arrangement of these components. Some see each factor of intelligence as possessing a certain amount of a general or "G" factor and describe this as a sort of unifying or integrating component that all factors have in common. Others do not view the various factors as necessarily related; they describe them without reference to a central or integrating component.

Because the nature, scope, and composition of intelligence is, at best, only partly understood, it has been equally difficult to define as to describe. While intelligence is rather facetiously referred to as "what intelligence tests test" by some and given more lengthy and detailed definitions by others, those who define it merely as "coping behavior" may have as adequate a point of view as any. At least a part of the difficulty of definition lies in the dynamic nature of the concept. There appears to be a tendency to confuse intelligence with amounts of knowledge and information and to overlook the fact that it is only as these are applied in problem situations that intelligence or "coping behavior" really becomes manifest. The heavy emphasis upon the acquisition of knowledge in schools probably is made from this frame of reference. It is the opinion of the editors that the external imposition of information just to increase what is known is much different from the internal need to seek and formulate ideas in order to cope more effectively with environmental situations. Although both are necessary, we are quite certain that the application of information to the learning of new things and new ways of coping is more indicative of intelligence than the ability to function as a repository of knowledge.

At the same time that technology has been engaged in an exponential increase of the amplification systems available to men, it has placed a premium upon individuals who know how to apply this power. Computers do not solve problems without someone who knows the process of programing data into questions. This, of course, does not come without some knowledge of how the answers can be applied. While a large part of the information stored in the computer is unnecessary to its operator, his knowledge of how to work the computer is not.

In their preoccupation with knowledge and information, schools appear to be providing a culture in which some of the facets of intelligence are developed to a greater degree than others. Perhaps schools need to become more concerned with helping students learn how to find out than with helping them pile up more bits of unapplied information. Neither power nor knowledge is of much value if the way to apply it is poorly understood.

JEROME S. BRUNER
Center for Cognitive Studies, Harvard University

22 · THE GROWTH OF MIND[1]

• These past several
years, I have had the painful pleasure—and it has been both—of exploring
two aspects of the cognitive processes that were new to me. One was
cognitive development, the other pedagogy. I knew, as we all know, that
the two were closely related, and it was my naive hope that, betimes, the
relation would come clear to me. Indeed, 2 years ago when I first knew
that in early September 1965 I would be standing here, delivering this
lecture, I said to myself that I would use the occasion to set forth to my
colleagues what I had been able to find out about this vexed subject, the
relation of pedagogy and development. It seemed obvious then that in 2
years one could get to the heart of the matter.

The 2 years have gone by. I have had the privilege of addressing this
distinguished audience (Bruner, 1964) on some of our findings concerning
the development of cognitive processes in children, and I have similarly set
forth what I hope are not entirely unreasonable ideas about pedagogy
(Bruner, in press). I am still in a very deep quandary concerning the relation of these two enterprises. The heart of the matter still eludes me, but
I shall stand by my resolve. I begin on this autobiographical note so that
you may know in advance why this evening is more an exercise in conjecture than a cataloguing of solid conclusions.

What is most unique about man is that his growth as an individual
depends upon the history of his species—not upon a history reflected in
genes and chromosomes but, rather, reflected in a culture external to man's

American Psychologist, 20:1007–1017, 1965. Copyright © 1965 by the American
Psychological Association, and reproduced by permission.

[1] Address of the President to the Seventy-Third Annual Convention of the
American Psychological Association, Chicago, September 4, 1965.

tissue and wider in scope than is embodied in any one man's competency. Perforce, then, the growth of mind is always growth assisted from the outside. And since a culture, particularly an advanced one, transcends the bounds of individual competence, the limits for individual growth are by definition greater than what any single person has previously attained. For the limits of growth depend on how a culture assists the individual to use such intellectual potential as he may possess. It seems highly unlikely—either empirically or canonically—that we have any realistic sense of the furthest reach of such assistance to growth.

The evidence today is that the full evolution of intelligence came as a result of bipedalism and tool using. The large human brain gradually evolved as a sequel to the first use of pebble tools by early near-man. To condense the story, a near-man, or hominid, with a slightly superior brain, using a pebble tool, could make out better in the niche provided by nature than a near-man who depended not on tools but on sheer strength and formidable jaws. Natural selection favored the primitive tool user. In time, thanks to his better chance of surviving and breeding, he became more so: The ones who survived had larger brains, smaller jaws, less ferocious teeth. In place of belligerent anatomy, they developed tools and a brain that made it possible to use them. Human evolution thereafter became less a matter of having appropriate fangs or claws and more one of using and later fashioning tools to express the powers of the larger brain that was also emerging. Without tools the brain was of little use, no matter how many hundred cubic centimeters of it there might be. Let it also be said that without the original programmatic capacity for fitting tools into a sequence of acts, early hominids would never have started the epigenetic progress that brought them to their present state. And as human groups stabilized, tools became more complex and "shaped to pattern," so that it was no longer a matter of reinventing tools in order to survive, but rather of mastering the skills necessary for using them. In short, after a certain point in human evolution, the only means whereby man could fill his evolutionary niche was through the cultural transmission of the skills necessary for the use of priorly invented techniques, implements, and devices.

Two crucial parallel developments seem also to have occurred. As hominids became increasingly bipedal, with the freed hands necessary for using spontaneous pebble tools, selection also favored those with a heavier pelvic bony structure that could sustain the impacting strain of bipedal locomotion. The added strength came, of course, from a gradual closing down of the birth canal. There is an obstetrical paradox here: a creature with an increasingly larger brain but with a smaller and smaller birth canal to get through. The resolution seems to have been achieved through the immaturity of the human neonate, particularly cerebral immaturity that assures not only a smaller head, but also a longer period of transmitting the necessary skills required by human culture. During this same period, human language must have emerged, giving man not only a new and powerful way of representing reality but also increasing his power to assist the mental growth of the young to a degree beyond anything before seen in nature.

It is impossible, of course, to reconstruct the evolution in techniques of instruction in the shadow zone between hominids and man. I have tried to compensate by observing contemporary analogues of earlier forms, knowing full well that the pursuit of analogy can be dangerously misleading. I have spent many hours observing uncut films of the behavior of free-ranging baboons, films shot in East Africa by my colleague Irven DeVore with a very generous footage devoted to infants and juveniles. I have also had access to the unedited film archives of a hunting-gathering people living under roughly analogous ecological conditions, the !Kung Bushman of the Kalahari, recorded by Laurance and Lorna Marshall, brilliantly aided by their son John and daughter Elizabeth.[2] I have also worked directly but informally with the Wolof of Senegal, observing children in the bush and in French-style schools. Even more valuable than my own informal observations in Senegal were the systematic experiments carried out later by my colleague, Patricia Marks Greenfield (in press).

Let me describe very briefly some salient differences in the free learning patterns of immature baboons and among !Kung children. Baboons have a highly developed social life in their troops, with well-organized and stable dominance patterns. They live within a territory, protecting themselves from predators by joint action of the strongly built, adult males. It is striking that the behavior of baboon juveniles is shaped principally by play with their peer group, play that provides opportunity for the spontaneous expression and practice of the component acts that, in maturity, will be orchestrated into either the behavior of the dominant male or of the infant-protective female. All this seems to be accomplished with little participation by any mature animals in the play of the juveniles. We know from the important experiments of Harlow and his colleagues (Harlow & Harlow, 1962) how devastating a disruption in development can be pro-

[2] I am greatly indebted to Irven DeVore and Educational Services Incorporated for the opportunity to view his films of free-ranging baboons, and to Laurance and Lorna Marshall for the opportunity to examine their incomparable archives. DeVore and the Marshalls have been generous in their counsel as well.

duced in subhuman primates by interfering with their opportunity for peer-group play and social interaction.

Among hunting-gathering humans, on the other hand, there is *constant* interaction between adult and child, or adult and adolescent, or adolescent and child. !Kung adults and children play and dance together, sit together, participate in minor hunting together, join in song and story telling together. At very frequent intervals, moreover, children are party to rituals presided over by adults—minor, as in the first haircutting, or major, as when a boy kills his first Kudu buck and goes through the proud but painful process of scarification. Children, besides, are constantly playing imitatively with the rituals, implements, tools, and weapons of the adult world. Young juvenile baboons, on the other hand, virtually never play with things or imitate directly large and significant sequences of adult behavior.

Note, though, that in tens of thousands of feet of !Kung film, one virtually never sees an instance of "teaching" taking place outside the situation where the behavior to be learned is relevant. Nobody "teaches" in our prepared sense of the word. There is nothing like school, nothing like lessons. Indeed, among the !Kung children there is very little "telling." Most of what we would call instruction is through showing. And there is no "practice" or "drill" as such save in the form of play modeled directly on adult models—play hunting, play bossing, play exchanging, play baby tending, play house making. In the end, every man in the culture knows nearly all there is to know about how to get on with life as a man, and every woman as a woman—the skills, the rituals and myths, the obligations and rights.

The change in the instruction of children in more complex societies is twofold. First of all, there is knowledge and skill in the culture far in excess of what any one individual knows. And so, increasingly, there develops an economical technique of instructing the young based heavily on *telling* out of context rather than *showing* in context. In literate societies, the practice becomes institutionalized in the school or the "teacher." Both promote this necessarily abstract way of instructing the young. The result of "teaching the culture" can, at its worst, lead to the ritual, rote nonsense that has led a generation of critics from Max Wertheimer (1945) to Mary Alice White (undated) of Teachers College to despair. For in the detached school, what is imparted often has little to do with life as lived in the society except insofar as the demands of school are of a kind that reflect *indirectly* the demands of life in a technical society. But these indirectly imposed demands may be the most important feature of the detached school. For school is a sharp departure from indigenous practice. It takes learning, as we have noted, out of the context of immediate action just by dint of putting it into a school. This very extirpation makes learning become an act in itself, freed from the immediate ends of action, preparing the learner for the chain of reckoning remote from payoff that is needed for the formulation of complex ideas. At the same time, the school (if successful) frees the child from the pace setting of the round of daily activity. If the school succeeds in avoiding a pace-setting round of its own, it may be one of the great agents for promoting reflectiveness. Moreover, in school, one must "follow the lesson" which means one must learn to follow either the abstraction of written speech—abstract in the sense that it is divorced from the concrete situation to which the speech might originally have been related— or the abstraction of language delivered orally but out of the context of an ongoing action. Both of these are highly abstract uses of language.

It is no wonder, then, that many recent studies report large differences between "primitive" children who are in schools and their brothers who are not: differences in perception, abstraction, time perspective, and so on. I need only cite the work of Biesheuvel (1949) in South Africa, Gay and Cole (undated) in Liberia, Greenfield (in press) in Senegal, Maccoby and Modiano (in press) in rural Mexico, Reich (in press) among Alaskan Eskimos.

What a culture does to assist the development of the powers of mind of its members is, in effect, to provide amplification systems to which human beings, equipped with appropriate skills, can link themselves. There are, first, the amplifiers of action—hammers, levers, digging sticks, wheels— but more important, the programs of action into which such implements can be substituted. Second, there are amplifiers of the senses, ways of looking and noticing that can take advantage of devices ranging from smoke signals and hailers to diagrams and pictures that stop the action or microscopes that enlarge it. Finally and most powerfully, there are amplifiers of the thought processes, ways of thinking that employ language and formation of explanation, and later use such languages as mathematics and logic and even find automatic servants to crank out the consequences. A culture is, then, a deviser, a repository, and a transmitter of amplification systems and of the devices that fit into such systems. We know very little in a deep sense about the transmission function, how people are trained to get the most from their potential by use of a culture's resources.

But it is reasonably clear that there is a major difference between the mode of transmission in a technical society, with its schools, and an indigenous one, where cultural transmission is in the context of action. It is not just that an indigenous society, when its action pattern becomes disrupted, falls apart—at a most terrifying rate—as in uncontrolled urbanization in some parts of Africa. Rather, it is that the institution of a school serves to convert knowledge and skill into more symbolical, more abstract, more verbal form. It is this process of transmission—admittedly very new in human history—that is so poorly understood and to which, finally, we shall return.

There are certain obvious specifications that can be stated about how a society must proceed in order to equip its young. It must convert what is to be known—whether a skill or a belief system or a connected body of knowledge—into a form capable of being mastered by a beginner. The more we know of the process of growth, the better we shall be at such conversion. The failure of modern man to understand mathematics and science may be less a matter of stunted abilities than our failure to understand how to teach such subjects. Second, given the limited amount of time available for learning, there must be a due regard for saving the learner from needless learning. There must be some emphasis placed on economy and transfer and the learning of general rules. All societies must (and virtually all do) distinguish those who are clever from those who are stupid—though few of them generalize this trait across all activities. Cleverness in a particular activity almost universally connotes strategy, economy, heuristics, highly generalized skills. A society must also place emphasis upon how one derives a course of action from what one has learned. Indeed, in an indigenous society, it is almost impossible to separate what one does from what one knows. More advanced societies often have not found a way of dealing with the separation of knowledge and action—probably a result of the emphasis they place upon "telling" in their instruction. All societies must maintain interest among the young in the learning process, a minor problem when learning is in the context of life and action, but harder when it becomes more abstracted. And finally, and perhaps most obviously, a society must assure that its necessary skills and procedures remain intact from one generation to the next—which does not always happen, as witnessed by Easter Islanders, Incas, Aztecs, and Mayas.[3]

Unfortunately, psychology has not concerned itself much with any of

[3] I have purposely left out of the discussion the problems of impulse regulation and socialization of motives, topics that have received extended treatment in the voluminous literature on culture and personality. The omission is dictated by emphasis rather than evaluation. Obviously, the shaping of character by culture is of great importance for an understanding of our topic as it bears, for example, upon culture-instilled attitudes toward the uses of mind. Since our emphasis is upon human potential and its amplification by culturally patterned instrumental skills, we mention the problem of character formation in passing and in recognition of its importance in a complete treatment of the issues under discussion.

these five requisites of cultural transmission—or at least not much with four of them. We have too easily assumed that learning is learning is learning—that the early version of what was taught did not matter much, one thing being much like another and reducible to a pattern of association, to stimulus-response connections, or to our favorite molecular componentry. We denied there was a problem of development beyond the quantitative one of providing more experience, and with the denial, closed our eyes to the pedagogical problem of how to represent knowledge, how to sequence it, how to embody it in a form appropriate to young learners. We expended more passion on the part-whole controversy than on what whole or what part of it was to be presented first. I should except Piaget (1954) Köhler (1940), and Vygotsky (1962) from these complaints—all until recently unheeded voices.

Our neglect of the economy of learning stems, ironically, from the heritage of Ebbinghaus (1913), who was vastly interested in savings. Our nonsense syllables, our random mazes failed to take into account how we reduce complexity and strangeness to simplicity and the familiar, how we convert what we have learned into rules and procedures, how, to use Bartlett's (1932) term of over 30 years ago, we turn around on our own schemata to reorganize what we have mastered into more manageable form.

Nor have we taken naturally to the issue of knowledge and action. Its apparent mentalism has repelled us. Tolman (1951), who bravely made the distinction, was accused of leaving his organisms wrapt in thought. But he recognized the problem and if he insisted on the idea that knowledge might be organized in cognitive maps, it was in recognition (as a great functionalist) that organisms go somewhere on the basis of what they have learned. I believe we are getting closer to the problem of how knowledge affects action and vice versa, and offer in testimony of my conviction the provocative book by Miller, Galanter, and Pribram (1960), *Plans and the Structure of Behavior*.

Where the maintenance of the learner's interest is concerned, I remind you of what my colleague Gordon Allport (1946) has long warned. We have been so concerned with the model of driven behavior, with drive reduction and the *vis a tergo* that, again, until recently, we have tended to overlook the question of what keeps learners interested in the activity of learning, in the achievement of competence beyond bare necessity and first payoff. The work of R. W. White (1959) on effectance motivation, of Harlow and his colleagues (Butler, 1954; Harlow, 1953) on curiosity, and of Heider (1958) and Festinger (1962) on consistency begins to redress the balance. But it is only a beginning.

The invention of antidegradation devices, guarantors that skill and knowledge will be maintained intact, is an exception to our oversight. We psychologists have been up to our ears in it. Our special contribution is the achievement test. But the achievement test has, in the main, reflected the timidity of the educational enterprise as a whole. I believe we know how to determine, though we have not yet devised tests to determine, how pupils use what they learn to think with later in life—for there is the real issue.

I have tried to examine briefly what a culture must do in passing on its amplifying skills and knowledge to a new generation and, even more briefly, how we as psychologists have dealt or failed to deal with the problems. I think the situation is fast changing—with a sharp increase in interest in the conversion problem, the problems of economy of learning, the nature of interest, the relation of knowledge and action. We are, I believe, at a major turning point where psychology will once again concern itself with the design of methods of assisting cognitive growth, be it through the invention of a rational technology of toys, of ways of enriching the environment of the crib and nursery, of organizing the activity of a school, or of devising a curriculum whereby we transmit an organized body of knowledge and skill to a new generation to amplify their powers of mind.

I commented earlier that there was strikingly little knowledge available about the "third way" of training the skills of the young: the first being the play practice of component skills in prehuman primates, the second the teaching-in-context of indigenous societies, and the third being the abstracted, detached method of the school.

Let me now become highly specific. Let me consider a particular course of study, one given in a school, one we are ourselves constructing, trying out, and in a highly qualitative way, evaluating. It is for schools of the kind that exist in Western culture. The experience we have had with this effort, now in its third year, may serve to highlight the kinds of problems and conjectures one encounters in studying how to assist the growth of intellect in this "third way."

There is a dilemma in describing a course of study. One begins by setting forth the intellectual substance of what is to be taught. Yet if such a recounting tempts one to "get across" the subject, the ingredient of pedagogy is in jeopardy. For only in a trivial sense is a course designed to "get something across," merely to impart information. There are better means to that end than teaching. Unless the learner develops his skills, disciplines his taste, deepens his view of the world, the "something" that is got across is hardly worth the effort of transmission.

The more "elementary" a course and the younger its students, the more serious must be its pedagogical aim of forming the intellectual powers of those whom it serves. It is as important to justify a good mathematics course by the intellectual discipline it provides or the honesty it promotes as by the mathematics it transmits. Indeed, neither can be accomplished without the other. The content of this particular course is man: his nature as a species, the forces that shaped and continue to shape his humanity. Three questions recur throughout:

What is human about human beings?
How did they get that way?
How can they be made more so?

In pursuit of our questions we explore five matters, each closely associated with the evolution of man as a species, each defining at once the distinctiveness of man and his potentiality for further evolution. The five great humanizing forces are, of course, tool making, language, social organization, the management of man's prolonged childhood, and man's urge to explain. It has been our first lesson in teaching that no pupil, however eager, can appreciate the relevance of, say, tool making or language in human evolution without first grasping the fundamental concept of a tool or what a language is. These are not self-evident matters, even to the expert. So we are involved in teaching not only the role of tools or language in the emergence of man, but, as a necessary precondition for doing so, setting forth the fundamentals of linguistics or the theory of tools. And it is as often the case as not that (as in the case of the "theory of tools") we must solve a formidable intellectual problem ourselves in order to be able to help our pupils do the same. I should have said at the outset that the "we" I employ in this context is no editorial fiction, but rather a group of anthropologists, zoologists, linguists, theoretical engineers, artists, designers, camera crews, teachers, children, and psychologists. The project is being carried out under my direction at Educational Services, Incorporated, with grants from the National Science Foundation and the Ford Foundation.

While one readily singles out five sources of man's humanization, under no circumstances can they be put into airtight compartments. Human kinship is distinctively different from primate mating patterns precisely because it is classificatory and rests on man's ability to use language. Or, if you will, tool use enhances the division of labor in a society which in turn affects kinship. So while each domain can be treated as a separate set of ideas, their teaching must make it possible for the children to have a sense of their interaction. We have leaned heavily on the use of contrast, highly controlled contrast, to help children achieve detachment from the all too familiar matrix of social life: the contrasts of man versus higher primates, man versus prehistoric man, contemporary technological man versus "primitive" man, and man versus child. The primates are principally baboons, the prehistoric materials mostly from the Olduvai Gorge and Les Eyzies, the "primitive" peoples mostly the Netsilik Eskimos of Pelly Bay and the !Kung Bushmen. The materials, collected for our purposes, are on film, in story, in ethnography, in pictures and drawings, and principally in ideas embodied in exercises.

We have high aspirations. We hope to achieve five goals:

1. To give our pupils respect for and confidence in the powers of their own minds

2. To give them respect, moreover, for the powers of thought concerning the human condition, man's plight, and his social life

3. To provide them with a set of workable models that make it simpler to analyze the nature of the social world in which they live and the condition in which man finds himself

4. To impart a sense of respect for the capacities and plight of man as a species, for his origins, for his potential, for his humanity

5. To leave the student with a sense of the unfinished business of man's evolution.

One last word about the course of study that has to do with the quality of the ideas, materials, and artistry—a matter that is at once technological and intellectual. We have felt that the making of such a curriculum deserved the best talent and technique available in the world. Whether artist, ethnographer, film maker, poet, teacher—nobody we have asked has refused us. We are obviously going to suffer in testing a Hawthorne effect of some magnitude. But then, perhaps it is as well to live in a permanent state of revolution.

Let me now try to describe some of the major problems one encounters in trying to construct a course of study. I shall not try to translate the problems into refined theoretical form, for they do not as yet merit such translation. They are more difficulties than problems. I choose them, because they are vividly typical of what one encounters in such enterprises. The course is designed for 10-year-olds in the fifth grade of elementary school, but we have been trying it out as well on the fourth and sixth grades better to bracket our difficulties.

One special point about these difficulties. They are born of trying to achieve an objective and are as much policy bound as theory bound. It is like the difference between building an economic theory about monopolistic practices and constructing policies for controlling monopoly. Let me remind you that modern economic theory has been reformulated, refined, and revived by having a season in policy. I am convinced that the psychology of assisted growth, i.e., pedagogy, will have to be forged in the policy crucible of curriculum making before it can reach its full descriptive power as theory. Economics was first through the cycle from theory to policy to theory to policy; it is happening now to psychology, anthropology, and sociology.

Now on to the difficulties. The first is what might be called *the psychology of a subject matter.* A learned discipline can be conceived as a way of thinking about certain phenomena. Mathematics is one way of thinking about order without reference to what is being ordered. The behavioral sciences provide one or perhaps several ways of thinking about man and his society—about regularities, origins, causes, effects. They are probably special (and suspect) because they permit man to look at himself from a perspective that is outside his own skin and beyond his own preferences—at least for a while.

Underlying a discipline's "way of thought," there is a set of connected, varyingly implicit, generative propositions. In physics and mathematics, most of the underlying generative propositions like the conservation theorems, or the axioms of geometry, or the associative, distributive, and commutative rules of analysis are by now very explicit indeed. In the behavioral sciences we must be content with more implicitness. We traffic in inductive propositions: e.g., the different activities of a society are interconnected such that if you know something about the technological response of a society to an environment, you will be able to make some shrewd guesses about its myths or about the things it values, etc. We use the device of a significant contrast as in linguistics as when we describe the territoriality of a baboon troop in order to help us recognize the system of reciprocal exchange of a human group, the former somehow provoking awareness of the latter.

There is nothing more central to a discipline than its way of thinking. There is nothing more important in its teaching than to provide the child the earliest opportunity to learn that way of thinking—the forms of connection, the attitudes, hopes, jokes, and frustrations that go with it. In a word, the best introduction to a subject is the subject itself. At the very first breath, the young learner should, we think, be given the chance to solve problems, to conjecture, to quarrel as these are done at the heart of the discipline. But, you will ask, how can this be arranged?

Here again the problem of conversion. There exist ways of thinking characteristic of different stages of development. We are acquainted with Inhelder and Piaget's (1958) account of the transition from preoperational, through concrete operational, to propositional thought in the years from preschool through, say, high school. If you have an eventual pedagogical objective in mind, you can translate the way of thought of a discipline into its Piagetian (or other) equivalent appropriate to a given level of development and take the child onward from there. The Cambridge Mathematics Project of Educational Services, Incorporated, argues that if the child is to master the calculus early in his high school years, he should start work early with the idea of limits, the earliest work being manipulative, later going on to images and diagrams, and finally moving on to the more abstract notation needed for delineating the more precise idea of limits.

In "Man: A Course of Study," (Bruner, 1965) there are also versions of the subject appropriate to a particular age that can at a later age be given a more powerful rendering. We have tried to choose topics with this in mind: The analysis of kinship that begins with children using sticks and blocks and colors and whatnot to represent their own families, goes on to the conventional kinship diagrams by a meandering but, as you can imagine, interesting path, and then can move on to more formal and powerful componential analysis. So, too, with myth. We begin with the excitement of a powerful myth (like the Netsilik Nuliajik myth), then have the children construct some myths of their own, then examine what a set of Netsilik myths have in common, which takes us finally to Lévi-Strauss's (1963) analysis of contrastive features in myth construction. A variorum text of a myth or corpus of myths put together by sixth graders can be quite an extraordinary document.

This approach to the psychology of a learned discipline turns out to illuminate another problem raised earlier: the maintenance of interest. There is, in this approach, a reward in understanding that grows from the subject matter itself. It is easier to engineer this satisfaction in mathematics, for understanding is so utter in a formal discipline—a balance beam balances or it does not; therefore there is an equality or there is not. In the behavioral sciences the payoff in understanding cannot be so obviously and startlingly self-revealing. Yet, one can design exercises in the understanding of man, too—as when children figure out the ways in which, given limits of ecology, skills, and materials, Bushmen hunt different animals, and then compare their predictions with the real thing on film.

Consider now a second problem: *how to stimulate thought in the setting of a school.* We know from experimental studies like those of Bloom and Broder (1950), and of Goodnow and Pettigrew (1955), that there is a striking difference in the acts of a person who thinks that the task before him represents a problem to be solved rather than being controlled by random forces. School is a particular subculture where these matters are concerned. By school age, children have come to expect quite arbitrary and, from their point of view, meaningless demands to be made upon them by adults—the result, most likely, of the fact that adults often fail to recognize the task of conversion necessary to make their questions have some intrinsic significance for the child. Children, of course, will try to solve problems if they recognize them as such. But they are not often either predisposed to or skillful in problem finding, in recognizing the hidden conjectural feature in tasks set them. But we know now that children in school can quite quickly be led to such problem finding by encouragement and instruction.

The need for this instruction and encouragement and its relatively swift success relates, I suspect, to what psychoanalysts refer to as the guilt-ridden oversuppression of primary process and its public replacement by secondary process. Children, like adults, need reassurance that it is all right to entertain and express highly subjective ideas, to treat a task as a problem where you *invent* an answer rather than *finding* one out there in the book or on the blackboard. With children in elementary school, there is often a need to devise emotionally vivid special games, story-making episodes, or construction projects to reestablish in the child's mind his right not only to have his own private ideas but to express them in the public setting of a classroom.

But there is another, perhaps more serious difficulty: the interference of intrinsic problem solving by extrinsic. Young children in school expend extraordinary time and effort figuring out what it is that the teacher wants—and usually coming to the conclusion that she or he wants tidiness or remembering or to do things at a certain time in a certain way. This I refer to as extrinsic problem solving. There is a great deal of it in school.

There are several quite straightforward ways of stimulating problem solving. One is to train teachers to want it and that will come in time. But teachers can be encouraged to like it, interestingly enough, by providing them and their children with materials and lessons that *permit* legitimate problem solving and permit the teacher to recognize it. For exercises with such materials create an atmosphere by treating things as instances of what *might* have occurred rather than simply as what did occur. Let me illustrate by a concrete instance. A fifth-grade class was working on the organization of a baboon troop—on this particular day, specifically on how they might protect against predators. They saw a brief sequence of film in which six or seven adult males go forward to intimidate and hold off three cheetahs. The teacher asked what the baboons had done to keep the cheetahs off, and there ensued a lively discussion of how the dominant adult males, by showing their formidable mouthful of teeth and making threatening gestures had turned the trick. A boy raised a tentative hand and asked whether cheetahs always attacked together. Yes, though a single cheetah sometimes followed behind a moving troop and picked off an older, weakened straggler or an unwary, straying juvenile. "Well, what if there were four cheetahs and two of them attacked from behind and two from in front. What would the baboons do then?" The question could have been answered empirically— and the inquiry ended. Cheetahs *do not* attack that way, and so we do not know what baboons *might* do. Fortunately, it was not. For the question opens up the deep issues of what might be and why it is not. Is there a necessary relation between predators and prey that share a common ecological niche? Must their encounters have a "sporting chance" outcome? It is such conjecture, in this case quite unanswerable, that produces rational, self-consciously problem-finding behavior so crucial to the growth of intellectual power. Given the materials, given some background and encouragement, teachers like it as much as the students.

I should like to turn now to the *personalization of knowledge*. A generation ago, the progressive movement urged that knowledge be related to the child's own experience and brought out of the realm of empty abstractions. A good idea was translated into banalities about the home, then the friendly postman and trashman, then the community, and so on. It is a poor way to compete with the child's own dramas and mysteries. A decade ago, my colleague Clyde Kluckhorn (1949) wrote a prize-winning popular book on anthropology with the entrancing title *Mirror for Man*. In some deep way, there is extraordinary power in "that mirror which other civilizations still hold up to us to recognize and study . . . [the] image of ourselves [Lévi-Strauss, 1965]." The psychological bases of the power are not obvious. Is it as in discrimination learning, where increasing the degree of contrast helps in the learning of a discrimination, or as in studies of concept attainment where a negative instance demonstrably defines the domain of a conceptual rule? Or is it some primitive identification? All these miss one thing that seems to come up frequently in our interviews with the children. It is the experience of discovering kinship and likeness in what at first seemed bizarre, exotic, and even a little repellent.

Consider two examples, both involving film of the Netsilik. In the films, a single nuclear family, Zachary, Marta, and their 4-year-old Alexi, is followed through the year—spring sealing, summer fishing at the stone weir, fall caribou hunting, early winter fishing through the ice, winter at the big ceremonial igloo. Children report that at first the three members of the family look weird and uncouth. In time, they look normal, and eventually, as when Marta finds sticks around which to wrap her braids, the girls speak of how pretty she is. That much is superficial—or so it seems. But consider a second episode.

It has to do with Alexi who, with his father's help, devises a snare and catches a gull. There is a scene in which he stones the gull to death. Our children watched, horror struck. One girl, Kathy, blurted out, "He's not even human, doing that to the seagull." The class was silent. Then another girl, Jennine, said quietly: "He's got to grow up to be a hunter. His mother was smiling when he was doing that." And then an extended discussion about how people have to do things to learn and even do things to learn how to feel appropriately. "What would you do if you had to live there? Would you be as smart about getting along as they are with what they've got?" said one boy, going back to the accusation that Alexi was inhuman to stone the bird.

I am sorry it is so difficult to say it clearly. What I am trying to say is that to personalize knowledge one does not simply link it to the familiar. Rather one makes the familiar an instance of a more general case and thereby produces awareness of it. What the children were learning about was not seagulls and Eskimos, but about their own feelings and preconceptions that, up to then, were too implicit to be recognizable to them.

Consider finally the problem of *self-conscious reflectiveness*. It is an epistemological mystery why traditional education has so often emphasized extensiveness and coverage over intensiveness and depth. We have already commented on the fact that memorizing was usually perceived by children as one of the high-priority tasks but rarely did children sense an emphasis upon ratiocination with a view toward redefining what had been encountered, reshaping it, reordering it. The cultivation of reflectiveness, or whatever you choose to call it, is one of the great problems one faces in devising curriculum. How lead children to discover the powers and pleasures that await the exercise of retrospection?

Let me suggest one answer that has grown from what we have done. It is the use of the "organizing conjecture." We have used three such conjectures—what is human about human beings, how they got that way, how they could become more so. They serve two functions, one of them the very obvious though important one of putting perspective back into the particulars. The second is less obvious and considerably more surprising. The questions often seemed to serve as criteria for determining where they were getting, how well they were understanding, whether anything new was emerging. Recall Kathy's cry: "He's not human, doing that to the seagull." She was hard at work in her rage on the conjecture what makes human beings human.

There, in brief, are four problems that provide some sense of what a psychologist encounters when he takes a hand in assisting the growth of mind in children in the special setting of a school. The problems look quite different from those we encounter in formulating classical developmental theory with the aid of typical laboratory research. They also look very different from those that one would find in an indigenous society, describing how children picked up skills and knowledge and values in the context of action and daily life. We clearly do not have a theory of the school that is sufficient to the task of running schools—just as we have no adequate theory of toys or of readiness building or whatever the jargon is for preparing children to do a better job the next round. It only obscures the issue to urge that some day our classical theories of learning will fill the gap. They show no sign of doing so.

I hope that we shall not allow ourselves to be embarrassed by our present ignorance. It has been a long time since we have looked at what is involved in imparting knowledge through the vehicle of the school—if ever we did look at it squarely. I urge that we delay no longer.

But I am deeply convinced that the psychologist cannot alone construct a theory of how to assist cognitive development and cannot alone learn how to enrich and amplify the powers of a growing human mind. The task belongs to the whole intellectual community: the behavioral scientists and the artists, scientists, and scholars who are the custodians of skill, taste, and knowledge in our culture. Our special task as psychologists is to convert skills and knowledge to forms and exercises that fit growing minds—and it is a task ranging from how to keep children free from anxiety and how to translate physics for the very young child into a set of playground maneuvers that, later, the child can turn around upon and convert into a sense of inertial regularities.

And this in turn leads me to a final conjecture, one that has to do with the organization of our profession, a matter that has concerned me greatly during this past year during which I have had the privilege of serving as your President. Psychology is peculiarly prey to parochialism. Left to our own devices, we tend to construct models of a man who is neither a victim of history, a target of economic forces, or even a working member of a society. I am still struck by Roger Barker's (1963) ironic truism that the best way to predict the behavior of a human being is to know where he is: In a post office he behaves post office, at church he behaves church.

Psychology, and you will forgive me if the image seems a trifle frivolous, thrives on polygamy with her neighbors. Our marriage with the biological sciences has produced a cumulation of ever more powerful knowledge. So, too, our joint undertakings with anthropology and sociology. Joined together with a variety of disciplines, we have made lasting contributions to the health sciences and, I judge, will make even greater contributions now that the emphasis is shifting to the problems of alleviating stress and arranging for a community's mental health. What I find lacking is an alignment that might properly be called the growth sciences. The field of pedagogy is one participant in the growth sciences. Any field of inquiry devoted to assisting the growth of effective human beings, fully empowered with zest, with skill, with knowledge, with taste is surely a candidate for this sodality. My friend Philip Morrison once suggested to his colleagues at Cornell that his department of physics grant a doctorate not only for work in theoretical, experimental, or applied physics, but also for work in pedagogical physics. The limits of the growth sciences remain to be drawn. They surely transcend the behavioral sciences cum pediatrics. It is plain that, if we are to achieve the effectiveness of which we as human beings are capable, there will one day have to be such a field. I hope that we psychologists can earn our way as charter members.

REFERENCES

Allport, G. Effect: A secondary principle of learning. *Psychological Review*, 1946, 53, 335–347.

Barker, R. On the nature of the environment. *Journal of Social Issues*, 1963, 19, 17–38.

Bartlett, F. *Remembering*. Cambridge, England: Cambridge Univer. Press, 1932.

Biesheuvel, S. Psychological tests and their application to non-European peoples. *Yearbook of Education*. London: Evans, 1949. Pp. 87–126.

Bloom, B., and Broder, L. Problem solving processes of college students. *Supplementary Educational Monograph*, No. 73. Chicago: Univer. Chicago Press, 1950.

Bruner, J. The course of cognitive growth. *American Psychologist*, 1964, 19, 1–15.

Bruner, J. Man: A course of study. *Educational Services Inc. Quarterly Report*, 1965, Spring-Summer, 3–13.

Bruner, J. *Toward a theory of instruction.* Cambridge: Harvard Univer. Press, in press.

Butler, R. A. Incentive conditions which influence visual exploration. *Journal of Experimental Psychology,* 1954, 48, 19–23.

Ebbinghaus, H. *Memory: A contribution to experimental psychology.* New York: Teachers College, Columbia University, 1913.

Festinger, L. A theory of cognitive dissonance. Stanford: Stanford Univer. Press, 1962.

Gay, J., and Cole, M. Outline of general report on Kpelle mathematics project. Stanford: Stanford University, Institute for Mathematical Social Studies, undated. (Mimeo)

Goodnow, Jacqueline, and Pettigrew, T. Effect of prior patterns of experience on strategies and learning sets. *Journal of Experimental Psychology,* 1955, 49, 381–389.

Greenfield, Patricia M. Culture and conservation. In J. Bruner, Rose Olver, and Patricia M. Greenfield (Eds.), *Studies in cognitive growth.* New York: Wiley, in press. Ch. 10.

Harlow, H., and Harlow, Margaret. Social deprivation in monkeys. *Scientific American,* 1962, November.

Harlow, H. F. Mice, monkeys, men, and motives. *Psychological Review,* 1953, 60, 23–32.

Heider, F. *The psychology of interpersonal relations.* New York: Wiley, 1958.

Inhelder, Bärbel, and Piaget, J. *The growth of logical thinking.* New York: Basic Books, 1958.

Kluckhorn, C. *Mirror for man.* New York: Whittlesey House, 1949.

Köhler, W. *Dynamics in psychology.* New York: Liveright, 1940.

Lévi-Strauss, C. The structural study of myth. *Structural anthropology.* (Trans. by Claire Jacobson and B. Grundfest Scharpf) New York: Basic Books, 1963. Pp. 206–231.

Lévi-Strauss, C. Anthropology: Its achievements and future. Lecture presented at Bicentennial Celebration, Smithsonian Institution, Washington, D.C., September 1965.

Maccoby, M., and Modiano, Nancy. On culture and equivalence. In J. Bruner, Rose Olver, and Patricia M. Greenfield (Eds.), *Studies in cognitive growth,* New York: Wiley, in press. Ch. 12.

Miller, G., Galanter, E., and Pribram, K. *Plans and the structure of behavior.* New York: Holt, 1960.

Piaget, J. *The construction of reality in the child.* New York: Basic Books, 1954.

Reich, Lee. On culture and grouping. In J. Bruner, Rose Olver, and Patricia M. Greenfield (Eds.), *Studies in cognitive growth.* New York: Wiley, in press. Ch. 13.

Tolman, E. Cognitive maps in rats and men. *Collected papers in psychology.* Berkeley and Los Angeles: Univer. California Press, 1951. Pp. 241–264.

Vygotsky, L. *Thought and language.* (Ed. and trans. by Eugenia Hanfmann and Gertrude Vakar) New York: Wiley, 1962.

Wertheimer, M. *Productive thinking.* New York and London: Harper, 1945.

White, Mary A. The child's world of learning. Teachers College, Columbia University, undated. (Mimeo)

White, R. W. Motivation reconsidered: The concept of competence. *Psychological Review,* 1959, 66, 297–333.

MOTIVATION OF LEARNING

• Why do people act as they do? What is it that causes them to respond in certain ways in some situations and differently in others? If these questions could be answered, human behavior would no longer be an enigma. In the first selection for this section, J. McV. Hunt provides not only a description of the more traditional points of view concerning human motivation but advances other interesting possible interpretations. Because of the article's thoroughness and coverage, the reader who lacks previous experience in this area will find it both necessary and rewarding to peruse it carefully.

Educators must be concerned with motivation for a number of reasons. Teaching without the urge to learn on the part of the student is next to impossible. It can be both stimulating and rewarding for teacher and learner alike when the latter really wants to grow intellectually. As mentioned in preceding sections, the editors view the urge to learn new things and to become increasingly aware and more effective as being intrinsic. They feel quite strongly that motivation to learn is more a matter of removing or dealing with inhibiting factors than it is a matter of providing rewards, reinforcements, and a competitive milieu. It well may be that certain conditions within homes, classrooms, and communities actually force youngsters to limit their awareness, or to learn how not to learn, rather than stimulate their curiosity and their urge to find out. When a person is made to doubt his ability, to feel inadequate, and to question his competence, he tends to exclude, or to ignore, those elements of his environment which he does not feel adequate to handle. Unless a youngster is able to listen and to become involved, no amount of teacher expertise in the presentation of subject matter is likely to result in his learning effectively.

Many of the errors in predicting future behavior and achievement by means of psychological tests and other observations occur because no accurate method of assessing levels of motivation is available. The ability to perform is of no avail unless the individual wants to do so. Often a youngster with only an average IQ achieves far in excess of expectations. We are no more able to determine the reason than we are able to say why those with high IQ's may fail to work to capacity. In either case, we tend to deal with our lack of understanding by saying merely that one tries harder than the other.

It appears to the editors that the self-regarding attitudes of the learner may be the determining factor in the amount of awareness, openness, and flexibility he can permit himself. If this is true, then the valuing and judgmental aspects of the classroom environment, plus the teacher's ability to accept and maintain effective interpersonal relationships, are crucial to both motivation and learning. Perhaps the emotional aspects of learning that will be discussed in the next section should be accorded a far greater importance than the traditional, information-centered view that education has permitted up to this time.

J. McVICKER HUNT

Professor of Psychology, University of Illinois

23 · EXPERIENCE AND THE DEVELOPMENT OF MOTIVATION: SOME REINTERPRETATIONS[1]

• A recent issue of the *Saturday Evening Post* carried a cartoon that some of you may have noted. It depicts a boy entering his house, perhaps from school, where his father is sitting with his paper. The boy appears to be fixing his father with an accusing glare. The punch-line reads, "Somebody goofed. I'm improperly motivated."

This cartoon depicts the vantage point from which I have been examining what we think we know about the relation between experience and motivation. When a child's behavior fails to fit the standards somebody in our society holds for him, it is pretty well agreed among us who are supposed to be experts on human nature that "somebody goofed." And that somebody is usually considered to be a parent.

The question is: what is the proper formula? If one examines the accruing evidence relevant to what has been the dominant conception of the experiential sources of motivation, one can hardly escape the conclusion that this conceptual scheme needs some revisions. If we based our child-

Child Development, 31:489–504, 1960. Copyright © 1960 by The Society for Research in Child Development. Used by permission of The Society and the author.

[1] Earlier versions of this paper were read at the Eleventh Annual Institute in Psychiatry and Neurology of the Veterans Administration Hospital at North Little Rock, Arkansas, 27 February 1959, and at colloquia of the Department of Psychology at Vanderbilt University and of the Department of Psychiatry at the Medical School of Colorado. The paper was prepared in connection with a survey of the implications of the work in behavioral science for child-rearing which has been supported by the Russell Sage Foundation.

rearing entirely on our dominant theory of motivational development, we would probably goof as often and as badly as run-of-the-mill parents.

Today I wish, first, to remind you of three of the most basic and general of the propositions in that theory of motivation which has been dominant for the past 30 to 40 years. These are propositions which, although stated in somewhat varied forms, have been shared by both psychoanalysts and academic behavior theorists. Secondly, I wish to cite evidence which calls these propositions into question, and thirdly, to suggest tentatively three new interpretative principles which appear to me to be congruent with a large number of facts and which have interesting implications.

Our conceptions of motivation have traditionally been concerned with three large questions. (a) Why does an organism or person become active? (b) Why does the organism or person act one way rather than another? and (c) How do you get the organism or person to change his behavior to something conceived to be more desirable or appropriate?

The Dominant Theory

DRIVE

According to our dominant theory, it is claimed, first of all, that "all behavior is motivated," and that the aim or function of every instinct, defense, action, or habit is to reduce or eliminate stimulation or excitation within the nervous system. It is not easy to state when this view was first presented. Signs of it appear in the seventh chapter of Freud's *Interpretation of Dreams* (15) in 1900, and the idea is full-blown in his paper entitled *Instincts and Their Vicissitudes* (17) in 1915. The idea also appears in Woodworth's *Dynamic Psychology* (68), published in 1918, where the term *drive* was first introduced into the glossary of American psychology. The idea was full-blown in Dashiell's *Fundamentals of Objective Psychology* (11) in 1928.

Although Freud (17) believed that the source of motivation lay outside the domain of psychology in physiology, American psychologists, untroubled by such limits to their domain, have gone on to answer the first question concerning what motivates organisms to become active by saying that they are *driven*. Organisms have been conceived to be driven, first, by those so-called primary, inner stimuli which arise from homeostatic imbalances or needs. With no shame whatsoever, psychologists have long cited the evidence from the work of such physiologists as Claude Bernard (5) and his successors, and especially of Walter B. Cannon (10), and also of the psychologist Curt Richter (59) to document this answer. Organisms are driven, second, by various forms of intense and painful external stimulation. It has been assumed that these two forms of stimulation arouse an inner state of excitement which has usually been called *drive*.

It is also assumed, as the proposition that "all behavior is motivated" implies, that the organism would be inactive unless driven by either inner or outer stimuli. Freud (17) has been highly explicit about this assumption, and the assumption lies implicitly behind the notion of conditioned or learned drive in behavior theory and behind the traumatic notion of anxiety in psychoanalysis. It is sometimes obvious, of course, that animals and people are sometimes active when it is hard to see how either homeostatic drive or painful external stimulation could be operative. It is then assumed that some of the weak, innocuous stimuli present must have been associated in the past with either painful stimuli or homeostatic needs. In such a way the weak stimuli which are present must have acquired the capacity to arouse the drive, often now called anxiety by psychologists as well as psychoanalysts, and it is such acquired or conditioned drive that is conceived to activate the organism.

Such conditioned drive or anxiety has been well demonstrated in the laboratory. Before World War II, Miller (45, 46) at Yale showed that rats which had been repeatedly shocked in a white box would, when later returned to the white box, make an effort to escape. Moreover, in the course of these efforts, they could be got to learn new skills such as that of turning a wheel to open a door. Rats which had not been shocked in the white box made no such efforts to escape. In another demonstration Solomon and Wynne (64) have shown that dogs which have experienced a tone or a buzzer paired a few times with a subtetanizing shock will run away from that tone or buzzer for hundreds of trials, with the average reaction time of starting continuing to decrease through 600 such trials. In my own work (31) rats fed irregularly in infancy ate more and sometimes (32) hoarded more than their litter-mate controls in adulthood after a period without food. Here, as I conceived it, the cues of hunger were conditioned to intense hunger excitement during the infantile experience. In adulthood the conditioned hunger drive facilitated the rate of eating and, sometimes, hoarding.

Such work has demonstrated that this notion of conditioned drive or anxiety, which goes back to the work of Bekhterev (2) and Watson and Raynor (67), has a solid basis in reality. But in what has been the dominant theory of motivation, as epitomized by Freud's (18) later traumatic theory of anxiety and by the Hull (30) and Dollard-Miller (13, 47) theory of acquired drives, conditioning is conceived to be the only way in which an organism can become fearful of innocuous stimuli.

HABIT

Habit has been the answer to the second question concerned with why an animal or person acts one way rather than another. The organism is controlled by the habits which have served to reduce drive in the past when that organism was in the presence of the inner and outer drive stimuli and the cue stimuli impinging upon him at any given now. Under the term *habit*, I am including psychoanalytic modes, which have supposedly been fixated during infancy in the course of either too much gratification or too much frustration, and I am including also ego-defenses, or anxiety equivalents, and cathexes, as well as the instrumental responses and traits commonly investigated in psychological laboratories.

Changing behavior has been conceived to be a matter of motivating the organism with either punishment or homeostatic need to make the desired behavior which can then be reinforced by arranging for it to reduce the drive aroused by the punishment or the need. Although the conditions and conceptions of psychotherapy in the clinic differ considerably from the conditions and conceptions of the behavior theorist investigating learning in laboratory animals, in either case it is conceived that motivation is a necessity, and motivation means changing the emotional or drive conditions which are quite extrinsic to either the instrumental behavior or the cognitive, informational processes concerned.

This dominant theory has been a conceptual edifice of large dimensions and of considerable detail. It has provided a plausible account of both personality development and social motives. The experimental facts of homeostasis and of conditioned drive and fear are sound. Nevertheless, it has become more and more evident in the past 10 years that some of the basic assumptions of this dominant theoretical scheme and some of the explanatory extrapolations contradict facts and call for reinterpretation.

Reinterpretations

IS ALL BEHAVIOR MOTIVATED?

The first of the assumptions to be called into question is the one that *all behavior is motivated* and that *organisms become inactive unless stimulated* by homeostatic need or painful stimulation or conditional stimuli for these. A large variety of observations contradict this assumption and imply spontaneous molar activity. Beach (1) has reviewed the observations of play in the young to show that playful activities are most likely to occur when either young animals or children are homeostatically satisfied and also comfortably warm. The very occurrence of either homeostatic need or strong external stimulation stops play and turns the young animal or child to activities calculated to relieve such stimulation. Berlyne (3, 4) has shown that well-fed and -watered rats will explore areas new to them if given only the opportunity. Montgomery (49), moreover, has shown that hunger and thirst tend to limit the exploratory behavior of rats rather than facilitate it, and Montgomery and Monkman (50), as well as others, have shown that conditioned fear inhibits exploration. Harlow, Harlow, and Meyer (23) have demonstrated that well-fed monkeys will learn to unassemble a three-device puzzle with no other drive and "no other reward than the privilege of unassembling it." In another study Harlow (20) found two well-fed and well-watered monkeys worked repeatedly at unassembling a six-device puzzle for 10 continuous hours, and they were still showing what he characterized as enthusiasm for their work on the tenth hour of testing. From his observations of the human child, moreover, Piaget (55) remarks repeatedly on the enthusiastic and repeated performance of such emerging skills as the release of a toy, sitting up, standing, etc.

Such evidences of spontaneous behavior, which is unmotivated in the traditional sense, have led to the naming of such new motives as a curiosity drive by Berlyne (4), an exploratory drive by Montgomery (48), an extero-ceptive and curiosity drives by Harlow (21). I would like to object that merely naming such drives explains nothing. If we continue, we shall be revisiting McDougall's (44) practice of postulating a separate drive for almost every variety of activities. Let us stop with noting that such observations do contradict our assumption that organisms will become inactive unless driven by homeostatic needs and painful stimuli and give up this ancient Greek notion that living matter is inert substance to which motion must be imparted by extrinsic forces. We can then embrace the thermo-dynamic conception of living things as open systems of energy exchange which exhibit activity intrinsically and upon which stimuli have a modu-lating effect, but not an initiating effect.

This notion of activity being intrinsic in living tissue is receiving support from studies of organ systems as well as studies of molar organisms. The EEG, for example, shows that brain cells are continuously active (33, 58). In sleep the slow waves of large amplitude are taken to imply that large numbers of cells are firing synchronously, and the effect of waking and stimulation and exciting the brain-stem reticular formation is to asyn-chronize this firing which shows in rapid waves of low magnitude (42).

Granit (19) points out that the spontaneous firing of retinal cells increases with dark adaptation and thereby functions to prevent the deafferentization of visual context with darkness. Twenty years ago, this spontaneous firing was considered, at worst, to be due to some failure of experimental control, or at best, noise in the channel of information. Recently, the Laceys (36) have found spontaneous fluctuations of sudomotor activity and cardiac activity which they also see as functioning in the control of the organism's relations with its environment. Especially intriguing is their notion that the carotid sinus mechanism functions as a feedback loop which participates in the directing of attention inward or outward by inhibiting or facilitating receptor inputs. But the point of mentioning these evidences of spontaneous activities of organ systems here is merely to help inter for good the notion that activity of living systems requires homeostatic need or painful external stimulation and to foster the idea that to live means to be active in some degree.

REINFORCEMENT

This idea of activity being intrinsic in living organisms has implications for our conception of reinforcement. It makes it unnecessary to see all activity as a matter of either reducing or avoiding stimulation which is implied in the assumption that organisms become inactive unless stimulated. This is a second fundamental assumption of the dominant theory which has been shared by psychoanalysts and behavior theorists alike.

On the one hand, there is still a place for drive reduction. It is clear that under conditions of homeostatic need and painful stimulation, and perhaps under circumstances when the conditions of stimulation are changing with too great rapidity, both animals and persons learn techniques and strategies leading to gratification or reduction in external stimulation. The evidence that led Thorndike to formulate the "law of effect" is as convincing as ever. Moreover, in association with reductions of homeostatic need, animals and men may also learn cathexes or emotional attachments. The facts referred to are those highly familiar in secondary reinforcement (30, 54).

On the other hand, the facts implying that organisms show spontaneous molar activity also imply that, when animals and human beings have been living under conditions of low and unchanging stimulation for a time, increases of stimulation become reinforcing. Butler has shown that rhesus monkeys will learn quite complex discriminations with the only reward being a peek through a glass window (7) at the things in the next room or a few seconds of auditory experience (8). Berlyne (3) has shown that, the greater the variety of stimulation in an area which rats are permitted to explore, the longer they continue their explorations.

Especially important in this connection are the studies of human behavior under conditions of minimal variation in stimulation. I refer to the studies of perceptual isolation by Bexton, Heron, and Scott (6) at McGill and also the work of Lilly (41). At McGill, college students were paid 20 dollars a day to do nothing. They lay for 24 hours a day on a comfortable bed. The temperature was optimal and constant. Eyes, ears, and hands were shielded to minimize stimulus variation. Few subjects could endure more than two or three days of such conditions. They developed a desire for variation which was almost overwhelming.

While interpreting such facts in terms of a multiple set of drives for curiosity, exploration, or stimulation will get us only to a redescription of them, Hebb's (26) notion of an optimal level of activation—and, I would like to add, stimulus variation below which *increases* are reinforcing and above which *decreases* are reinforcing—is an integrative conception of fair magnitude. Moreover, the drive-reduction principle of reinforcement may be seen to be but half of this more general curvilinear principle.

But this is probably not the whole story. It looks as if there were natively both positive and negative forms of exciting stimulation. Sheffield, Roby, and Campbell (61) have argued that the reinforcing effect of eating is not a matter of reduction of the hunger drive but rather a matter of the positive value of the consummatory act of eating. Moreover, Sheffield, Wulff, and Backer (62) have shown that male rats will learn mazes to get to females in heat even when they are allowed only intromission but not allowed to continue coitus to the point of drive-reducing ejaculation. From the fact that Davis (12) and his collaborators at Indiana have shown that showing pictures of nude women to college males increases excitement as shown by increased palmar conductance and the arrest of EEG-alpha, it is clear that such stimulation is exciting rather than excitement-reducing. Young (69) has long emphasized the importance of the hedonic quality of experience for reinforcement, and he has shown that speed of running in rat subjects increases with the concentration of sucrose in the incentive drink.

The suggestion that the two forms of excitation, one positive and one negative, are built into organisms comes also from the work of Olds and Milner (53). Electrical stimulation of the septal area is positively reinforcing, but electrical stimulation of the brain-stem reticular formation is negatively reinforcing. Perhaps, it is not without significance that the septal area is part of the old olfactory brain which has been considered to have an especially important part in the mediation of sexual and consummatory behavior in mammals. At any rate, it looks as though certain types of stimulation may be positively reinforcing even though they be intense and exciting. This may mean that the curvilinear principle may be limited in its domain to strong stimulation via the exteroceptors when homeostatic needs are minimized.

The suggestion of innate, positive, and negative exteroceptive stimulation comes secondly from recent work by Harlow (22). It has been customary to see an infant's cathexis or love for its mother developing as secondary reinforcement largely out of its feeding experiences. Freud (16), of course, contended that the pleasure from stimulation of the oral erogenous zone furnished the experiential basis for both pleasure-sucking and maternal attachment, a contention which contradicted his most definitive formulations of drive theory (17). The fact that an infant must suck for its nourishment, according to libido theory (16, p. 587), merely guaranteed discovery of the pleasures of oral stimulation. Behavior theorists have seen both sucking and love of mother as forms of secondary reinforcement deriving from the fact that the child satisfies its hunger by means of sucking the mother's breasts (51, pp. 137ff.). Harlow (22), however, has recently compared the degree of attachment of young monkeys to a wire mother-surrogate on which they nursed at a bottle with attachment to a padded and cloth-covered mother-surrogate on which they received nothing but the feel of the soft-ness. In terms of the amount of time spent on each of the two mother-surrogates, the monkeys showed more than 10 times the attachment to the soft-padded surrogate as to the wire surrogate. When various fear-evoking stimuli were presented to the baby monkeys in their cages, it was to the padded and cloth-covered surrogate that the frightened, infant monkey turned, not to the wire surrogate on which it had been nursed. Harlow argues from these findings that it is the sensory quality of softness which gives the reinforcement. His study suggests, moreover, that it is important to investigate the capacity for various kinds of stimuli for positive and negative reinforcement in the very young. Pratt (57) cites a monograph by Canestrini (9) on the sensory life of the newborn for an observation that certain stimuli are associated with decreases in the rate of the heart rate, and are therefore pleasant, while others are associated with increases in heart rate and are unpleasant.[2] In view of the finding by Davis (12)

---

[2] An examination of Canestrini's (9) monograph shows that Pratt was mistaken in stating that Canestrini remarked upon decreases in heart rate being associated with pleasure, but some of his published kymograph records do indicate decreases in heart rate. It may well be that heart rate could serve as an indicator of the emotional value of various sensory inputs, and these might be tested for their reinforcement values. I am indebted to Dr. William Gerler for reading this mono-graph carefully to check my own impressions of Canestrini's text.

and his collaborators that seeing a picture of a nude female results in reduction in the heart rate of male college students, it is possible that this physiological indicator may provide a technique for determining the direction of the reinforcing effect of stimuli in the newborn. At any rate, what is suggested is that McDougall's (44) old notion of natively positive and negative values for receptors inputs be re-examined.

CONDITIONED FEAR AND ANXIETY

The third assumption that I wish to examine in the light of empirical evidence is the notion that fear and anxiety are *always* inculcated as a consequence of traumatic experiences of helplessness in the face of homeostatic need or painful external stimulation. Note that I am not denying that such conditioned fears do exist. I am only questioning the word *always* . . . are always inculcated as a consequence of traumatic experiences.

The first relevant studies go way back to the 1920's. Harold and Mary Cover Jones (34) attempted to test the claims of Watson (66) and Watson and Raynor (67) concerning conditioned fears. They exposed their subjects of various ages, ranging from early infancy to adult, to a large but sluggish and harmless bull-snake. Fear of the snake was exceedingly common among adults, teenagers, and latency-age children, but it was absent in children below three years of age. It began to appear among children older than three and was typical of children six and older. From the fact that the fear appeared at a younger age in those of higher intelligence than those of lower intelligence, the Joneses argued that fear of snakes is a response which comes automatically into the developing child's repertoire through maturation. This remains as an alternative hypothesis to that of conditioned fear.

A study by Frances Holmes (29), which is seldom cited, calls both of these interpretations into question. Holmes compared the fearfulness of the children of lower-class background, who were attending a day nursery, with the fearfulness of children of upper-class background, who were attending a private nursery school. She got her fear scores by indicating that the child could get some attractive toys with which to play by going into the dark room adjacent to the examining room, or by taking them off a chair situated beside that of a strange woman dressed in a large floppy black hat and a long gray coat, or by climbing along a plank some three feet off the floor. If the child started immediately for the toys, he got a score of one for that item. If he hesitated but ultimately went ahead on his own, he got a score of two. If he would go only if accompanied by the examiner, the score was three. If he refused to go at all, the score was four. There were seven such situations. The results show that the fear scores of the lower-class children average only about half the size of those for the upper-class children, and the fear scores for boys were lower than those for girls. Yet it would be the lower-class children who had experienced the more homeostatic need and painfully rough treatment than the upper-class children, and the boys had probably experienced more painful experiences than the little girls. That intelligence is not the factor is shown by the fact that the fear scores showed a correlation of only about $+ .2$ with mental age, and the differences were still significant when intelligence was partialed out. Something besides either conditioned fear or the correlation between fear and intelligence is required to make these results comprehensible.

Recently evidence even more contradictory to the notion of conditioned fears has been coming from the work of Seymour Levine. Levine, Chevalier, and Korchin (40) have compared the adult behavior of rats shocked and rats petted daily from birth to their 20th day with the adult behavior of rats left continuously in their nests with their mothers. When he started this work, Levine expected to find that the shocked animals would show traumatic effects of their shock experiences in heightened emotionality and damaged capacity to learn adaptive responses. On the contrary, the shocked animals, along with the handled animals, gained weight faster than those left in the nest (37, 38, 39, 40). Byron Lindholm, working with the writer, has repeated and confirmed this finding. Moreover, Levine's shocked and handled animals both showed less emotionality than those left continuously in the nest with their mothers, i.e., less emotionality in the sense that they defecated and urinated less frequently when placed in a strange situation. Finally, the shocked and handled animals, which have appeared alike in all of these experiments, learned an avoidance response more rapidly and drank more readily after 18 hours without water than did the rats left in the nest with their mother.

Clearly these results on both human children and rats imply that fear and anxiety must sometimes have some other basis than that of being associated with painful stimulation. As many of you know, Hebb (24, 25) has formulated a radically different explanation of fear which may be termed either an incongruity or a dissonance theory.

The facts which suggested Hebb's conception came largely from observing chimpanzees being raised under controlled conditions at the Yerkes Laboratory. Fear, defined as withdrawal behavior in response to the appearance of some object, does not appear in young chimpanzees until they are approximately four months old. Then, the objects feared are familiar objects in unfamiliar guise. Fear of strangers is an example. This appears spontaneously to the first stranger seen, so it cannot be based on associating strangers with painful stimulation. Fear of strangers does not appear in chimpanzees—or in children, I might add—who have always been exposed to a large number of persons. While the avoidance response is unlearned, the familiar, expected aspects of objects must be learned. The young animal must have established as residues of his experience cortical firing patterns (or cognitive structures—whichever term you like) from which new receptor inputs can be incongruous. Consider the kinds of objects regularly feared. They are, for instance, the familiar keeper or experimenter in strange clothes, the experimenter in a Hallowe'en mask, a plaster cast of a chimpanzee head (which lacks, of course, the familiarly attached body), an anesthetized chimpanzee infant (from which the familiar patterns of motion are absent). On the other hand, objects which have never entered into the young chimpanzee's life may be strange without evoking withdrawal. In other words, the feared object is one which excites receptors in a fashion which is incongruous with the central, sequential pattern of neural firing which has accrued as a residue of the chimpanzee or human infant's past experience. Until the central pattern has been learned, incongruous stimulation is impossible.

Such a conception can well account for Holmes' findings that lower-class children are less fearful than higher-class children and that boys are less fearful than girls even though both lower-class children and boys of nursery school age are likely to have had the wider experience with the sorts of situations used by Holmes to evoke fear. It may well be that being shocked and handled provides a variety of experience which leaves the rat pups which have been subjected to it less disturbed by such things as open fields and 18 hours without water, but these effects may ultimately be found to be a matter of still another mechanism. It is too early to say.

Taking seriously this incongruity-dissonance conception of the genesis of fear leads to interesting reinterpretations of a great many of the motivational phenomena of child development. Consider these few. In considering separation anxiety, the incongruity principle makes it unnecessary to puzzle about how the absence of mother could be the conditional stimulus for the traumatizing and helpless distress that has been supposed to have occurred in her absence. In considering fear of the dark, it also becomes unnecessary to puzzle about how the absence of light stimulation could so widely have been associated with painful stimulation. Multiple mothering need not be seen as a traumatizing experience in the light of this conception, but rather as an inoculation against social shyness and fear. The timidity of the over-protected child and the social shyness of the rural mountain people get an explanation which has been difficult in terms of the theory of conditioned fear.

Motivation in Terms of the Incongruity-Dissonance Principle

This introduction of the incongruity-dissonance principle concludes the three reinterpretations I wish to present today, but I do wish to call your attention to the pervasive character of this incongruity-dissonance principle. It appears to have great explanation power which figures, in one guise or another, in several systematic theories, besides that of Hebb, all of which have been characterized as nondynamic.

Hebb's (25) theorizing is physiological, at least in a verbal sense, in that he conceives the residues of past inputs to be stored in semiautonomous, reverberating cerebral circuits which he terms *cell assemblies*. These cell assemblies are the neural analogue of concepts, and they get sequentially integrated into what he calls *phase sequences*. The sequential organization in time provides for the subjective phenomenon of expectation. When markedly incongruous receptor inputs disrupt this sequential organization, behavior is changed and the process is felt as unpleasant emotion. Slight degrees of incongruity, which can readily be accommodated, lend interest and may provide attractive problems, but the larger ones are repelling and perhaps even devastating.

Piaget (55, 56) utilizes very much the same incongruity notion to account for the development of intelligence and concepts in human children. In his system, the child comes at birth with certain sensory-motor coordinations which he terms *schemata*. Variation in stimulus situations call for adaptive *accommodations* or changes in these schemata, which changes are *assimilated* or stored as residues. Piaget also finds limited incongruities between central schemata and receptor inputs to be interesting and facilitative of growth, but incongruities which extend beyond the child's capacity for accommodation instigate withdrawal or fear and even terror. In Piaget's theory the child's gestalt-like conceptions of reality (space, time, and number) are schemata which develop through a continuous process of accommodations and assimilations and become fixed or static only when the child's schemata come to correspond so well with reality that no further accommodations are required. Here agreement among people is dictated by reality.

Helson (27, 28) has called the residues of immediate past experience in the typical psychophysical experiment an *adaptation level*. Both he and McClelland (43) have seen affective arousal to be a matter of the size of the discrepancy between receptor inputs and the adaptation level. Small discrepancies may be attractively pleasant, large ones repellingly unpleasant. As an example, some of you will readily recall having experienced the affective startle that comes when you have been set to pick up what you thought was a full pail, only to find it empty.

Festinger (14) has recently written a book entitled *A Theory of Cognitive Dissonance* in which he shows that a discrepancy between belief about a situation and perception of that situation acts like a drive. The subject acts to reduce the *dissonance* by either withdrawing from the incredible situation or by changing his beliefs, and, not incidentally, he finds the dissonance highly unpleasant.

Rogers (60) has described the basis for anxiety as discrepancy between the "phenomenological field" and the perceived reality as represented by his two circles. Rogers' phenomenological field, however, is not the perceptually-given phenomenal field of such German phenomenologists as Delthei and Husserl. It is rather the inferred storehouse of past experience and represented in the present by expectations, aspirations, self-concept, and the like. Thus, his conceptual scheme appears to fall within the domain of the incongruity-dissonance principle.

Kelly's (35) *Psychology of Personal Constructs* also makes central use of this principle. The term *personal constructs* refers to the ways in which individuals construe and anticipate events. These each person derives from the way in which he has experienced such events in the past. When a person's constructions fail to predict events, this is disturbing, even anxiety-producing, and it motivates some kind of change, but the change may take place in defenses against such change of constructs or in avoiding such events, or in the constructs themselves.

Perhaps, it is worth noting in closing that this incongruity-dissonance principle makes both motivation and reinforcement intrinsic to the organism's relations with its environment, intrinsic, if you will, to the organism's information-processing. It is as if the organism operated like an error-actuated, feedback system where the error is derived from discrepancy between receptor-inputs of the present and the residues of past experience which serve as the basis for anticipating the future. The dominant view of the past half century has seen both motivation and reinforcement as extrinsic to the information-processing. This has put a tremendous burden of responsibility for the management of affective motivation on parents, teachers, and all those in positions of authority and control. Visions of man completely controlled, as exemplified by George Orwell's *1984*, are conceivable only by assuming that the extrinsic motivating forces of homeostatic need and painful stimulation are completely dominant. In this light the terror of the baby chimp at seeing his keeper in a Hallowe'en mask and the irritation of the believer when his beliefs are disconfirmed are perhaps symbols of hope. They may justify Abraham Lincoln's well-known dictum that "you can fool some of the people all the time, and all the people some of the time, but you cannot fool all the people all the time."

To return to the cartoon of the lad who was improperly motivated: Perhaps, the task of developing proper motivation is best seen, at least in nutshell form, as limiting the manipulation of extrinsic factors to that minimum of keeping homeostatic need and exteroceptive drive low, in favor of facilitating basic information-processing to maximize accurate anticipation of reality.

REFERENCES

1. Beach, F. A. Current concepts of play in animals. *Amer. Naturalist*, 1945, 79, 523–541.

2. Bekhterev, V. M. *La psychologie objective.* (Translated by N. Kostyleff) Paris: Alcan, 1913.

3. Berlyne, D. E. Novelty and curiosity as determinants of exploratory behavior. *Brit. J. Psychol.*, 1950, 41, 68–80.

4. Berlyne, D. E. The arousal and satiation of perceptual curiosity in the rat. *J. comp. physiol. Psychol.*, 1955, 48, 238–246.

5. Bernard, C. *Leçons sur les propriétés physiologiques et les altérations pathologiques des liquides de l'organisme.* Paris: Ballière, 1859. 2 vols.

6. Bexton, W. H., Heron, W., and Scott, T. H. Effects of decreased variation in the sensory environment. *Canad. J. Psychol.*, 1954, 8, 70–76.

7. Butler, R. A. Discrimination learning by rhesus monkeys to visual exploration motivation. *J. comp. physiol. Psychol.*, 1953, 46, 95–98.

8. Butler, R. A. Discrimination learning by rhesus monkeys to auditory incentives. *J. comp. physiol. Psychol.*, 1957, 50, 239–241.

9. Canestrini, S. Über das Sinnesleben des Neugebornen. [Alzheimer, A., and Lewandowsky, M. (Eds.)] *Monogr. Gesamt. Neurol. Psychiat.* (Heft 5). Berlin: Springer, 1913.

10. Cannon, W. B. *Bodily changes in pain, hunger, fear, and rage.* New York: Appleton-Century, 1915.

11. Dashiell, J. *Fundamentals of objective psychology.* Boston: Houghton Mifflin, 1928.

12. Davis, R. C., and Buchwald, A. M. An exploration of somatic response patterns: stimulus and sex differences. *J. comp. physiol. Psychol.*, 1957, 50, 44–52.

13. Dollard, J., and Miller, N. E. *Personality and psychotherapy.* New York: McGraw-Hill, 1950.

14. Festinger, L. *A theory of cognitive dissonance.* Evanston, Ill.: Row, Peterson, 1957.

15. Freud, S. The interpretation of dreams (1900). In *The basic writings of Sigmund Freud.* (Translated by A. A. Brill) New York: Modern Library, 1938. Pp. 179–548.

16. Freud, S. Three contributions to the theory of sex (1905). In *The basic writings of Sigmund Freud.* (Translated by A. A. Brill) New York: Modern Library, 1938. Pp. 553–629.

17. Freud, S. Instincts and their vicissitudes (1915). In *Collected papers,* Vol. IV. London: Hogarth, 1950. Pp. 60–83.

18. Freud, S. *Inhibition, symptom and anxiety* (1926). (Translated by H. A. Bunker as *The problem of anxiety.*) New York: Norton, 1936.

19. Granit, R. *Receptors and sensory perception.* New Haven: Yale Univer. Press, 1955.

20. Harlow, H. F. Learning and satiation of response in intrinsically motivated complex puzzle performance by monkeys. *J. comp. physiol. Psychol.,* 1950, 43, 289–294.

21. Harlow, H. F. Motivation as a factor in the acquisition of new responses. In *Current theory and research in motivation: a symposium.* Lincoln: Univer. of Nebraska Press, 1953. Pp. 24–49.

22. Harlow, H. F. The nature of love. *Amer. Psychologist,* 1958, 13, 673–685.

23. Harlow, H. F., Harlow, M. K., and Meyer, D. R. Learning motivated by a manipulation drive. *J. exp. Psychol.,* 1950, 40, 228–234.

24. Hebb, D. O. On the nature of fear. *Psychol. Rev.,* 1946, 53, 259–276.

25. Hebb, D. O. *The organization of behavior.* New York: Wiley, 1949.

26. Hebb, D. O. Drives and the CNS (conceptual nervous system). *Psychol. Rev.,* 1955, 62, 243–254.

27. Helson, H. Adaptation-level as frame of reference for prediction of psychophysical data. *Amer. J. Psychol.,* 1947, 60, 1–29.

28. Helson, H. Adaptation-level as a basis for a quantitative theory of frames of reference. *Psychol. Rev.,* 1948, 55, 297–313.

29. Holmes, Frances B. An experimental study of the fears of young children. In A. T. Jersild and Frances B. Holmes, Children's fears. *Child Develpm. Monogr.,* 1935, 20, 167–296.

30. Hull, C. L. *Principles of behavior.* New York: Appleton-Century, 1943.

31. Hunt, J. McV. The effects of infant feeding-frustration upon adult hoarding in the albino rat. *J. abnorm. soc. Psychol.,* 1941, 36, 338–360.

32. Hunt, J. McV., Schlosberg, H., Solomon, R. L., and Stellar, E. Studies on the effects of infantile experience on adult behavior in rats. I. Effects of infantile feeding frustration on adult hoarding. *J. comp. physiol. Psychol.,* 1947, 40, 291–304.

33. Jasper, H. H. Electrical signs of cortical activity. *Psychol. Bull.,* 1937, 34, 411–481.

34. Jones, H. E., and Jones, Mary C. A study of fear. *Child Educ.,* 1928, 5, 136–143.

35. Kelly, G. A. *The psychology of personal constructs*. New York: Norton, 1955.

36. Lacey, J. I., and Lacey, Beatrice C. The relationship of resting autonomic activity to motor impulsivity. In *The brain and human behavior*. Baltimore: Williams & Wilkins, 1958. Pp. 144–209.

37. Levine, S. Infantile experience and consummatory behavior in adulthood. *J. comp. physiol. Psychol.*, 1957, 50, 609–612.

38. Levine, S. Infantile experience and resistance to physical stress. *Science.* 1957, 126, 405.

39. Levine, S. Noxious stimulation in infant and adult rats and consummatory behavior. *J. comp. physiol. Psychol.*, 1958, 51, 230–233.

40. Levine, S., Chevalier, J. A., and Korchin, S. J. The effects of shock and handling in infancy on later avoidance learning. *J. Pers.*, 1956, 24, 475–493.

41. Lilly, J. C. Mental effects of reduction of ordinary levels of physical stimuli on intact, healthy persons. *Psychiat. Res. Rep.*, 1956, No. 5, 1–9.

42. Lindsley, D. B. Psychophysiology and motivation. In M. R. Jones (Ed.), *Nebraska symposium on motivation.* Lincoln: Univer. of Nebraska Press, 1957. Pp. 44–105.

43. McClelland, D. C., Atkinson, J. W., Clark, R. A., and Lowell, E. L. *The achievement motive.* New York: Appleton-Century-Crofts, 1953.

44. McDougall, W. *An introduction to social psychology.* Boston: Luce, 1915.

45. Miller, N. E. An experimental investigation of acquired drives. *Psychol. Bull.*, 1941, 38, 534–535.

46. Miller, N. E. Studies of fear as an acquirable drive: I. Fear as motivation and fear-reduction as reinforcement in the learning of new responses. *J. exp. Psychol.*, 1948, 38, 89–101.

47. Miller, N. E., and Dollard, J. *Social learning and imitation.* New Haven: Yale Univer. Press, 1941.

48. Montgomery, K. C. The relation between exploratory behavior and spontaneous alternation in the white rat. *J. comp. physiol. Psychol.*, 1951, 44, 582–589.

49. Montgomery, K. C. The effect of the hunger and thirst drives upon exploratory behavior. *J. comp. physiol. Psychol.*, 1953, 46, 315–319.

50. Montgomery, K. C., and Monkman, J. A. The relation between fear and exploratory behavior. *J. comp. physiol. Psychol.*, 1955, 48, 132–136.

51. Mussen, P. H., and Conger, J. J. *Child development and personality.* New York: Harper, 1956.

52. Olds, J. Physiological mechanisms of reward. In M. R. Jones (Ed.), *Nebraska symposium on motivation.* Lincoln: Univer. of Nebraska Press, 1955. Pp. 73–139.

53. Olds, J., and Milner, P. Positive reinforcement produced by electrical stimulation of septal area and other regions of the rat brain. *J. comp. physiol. Psychol.*, 1954, 47, 419–427.

54. Pavlov, I. P. *Conditioned reflexes.* (Translated by G. V. Anrep) Oxford: Oxford Univer. Press, 1927.

55. Piaget, J. *The origins of intelligence in children.* New York: International Universities Press, 1952.

56. Piaget, J. *The construction of reality in the child.* (Translated by Margaret Cook) New York: Basic Books, 1954.

57. Pratt, K. C. The neonate. In L. Carmichael (Ed.), *Manual of child psychology.* (2nd Ed.) New York: Wiley, 1954. Pp. 215–291.

58. Prosser, C. L. Action potentials in the nervous system of the crayfish: I. Spontaneous impulses. *J. cell. comp. Physiol.*, 1934, 4, 185–209.

59. Richter, C. P. Animal behavior and internal drives. *Quart. Rev. Biol.*, 1927, 2, 307–343.

60. Rogers, C. R. *Client-centered therapy.* Boston: Houghton Mifflin, 1951.

61. Sheffield, F. D., Roby, T. B., and Campbell, B. A. Drive reduction versus consummatory behavior as determinants of reinforcement. *J. comp. physiol. Psychol.*, 1954, 47, 349–355.

62. Sheffield, F. D., Wulff, J. J., and Backer, R. Reward value of copulation without sex drive reduction. *J. comp. physiol. Psychol.*, 1951, 44, 3–8.

63. Solomon, R. L., and Brush, Elinor S. Experimentally derived conceptions of anxiety and aversion. In M. R. Jones (Ed.), *Nebraska symposium on motivation.* Lincoln: Univer. of Nebraska Press, 1956. Pp. 212–305.

64. Solomon, R. L., and Wynne, L. C. Traumatic avoidance learning: acquisition in normal dogs. *Psychol. Monogr.*, 1953, 67, No. 4 (Whole No. 354).

65. Thorndike, E. L. *Educational psychology.* (Vol. I, *The original nature of man*; Vol. II, *The psychology of learning.*) New York: Teachers Coll., 1913.

66. Watson, J. B. *Psychological care of the infant and child.* New York: Norton, 1928.

67. Watson, J. B., and Raynor, Rosalie. Conditional reactions. *J. exp. Psychol.*, 1920, 3, 1–4.

68. Woodworth, R. S. *Dynamic psychology.* New York: Columbia Univer. Press, 1918.

69. Young, P. T. The role of hedonic processes in motivation. In M. R. Jones (Ed.), *Nebraska symposium on motivation.* Lincoln: Univer. of Nebraska Press, 1955. Pp. 193–237.

ELIZABETH ANN LIDDLE
Professor of Education, Wheelock College

24 · PRESSURES ON THE YOUNG CHILD

● Every young child living in any period of time has had to meet and deal with the pressures in his environment. Growth in any human being relies on the ability of the person to find solutions to his problems and to move forward in becoming an increasingly mature person.

Growth requires conflict. Without conflict life would be dull and static. The young child of every environment has the drive and the inner strength to grow. Our recent experiences with the young child of poverty provide an excellent illustration of the ability of children to want to learn even though the child may come from a family in adverse circumstances. One of the great joys of working with the three-, four- or five-year-old is that he is an aggressive learner and thus grower. He constantly seeks and strives for growth and thus meets conflict.

> Everyone engaged in child rearing needs to recognize the fact that conflict carries constructive possibilities. To deny this proposition is probably to deny that children can be educated.[1]

The Young Child's World

If growth requires conflicts, why then are we so concerned with the pressures upon today's young child? What is there about his world that makes pressures a topic discussed in most journals? How much stress and

Educational Leadership, 23:113–116, November, 1965. Reprinted by permission of *Educational Leadership*.

[1] Willard W. Hartup. "Early Pressures in Child Development." *Young Children*. May 1965. p. 282.

conflict can he undertake and still maintain his equilibrium? Which pressures are realistic and positive and which are limiting and negative? How can we help our young children further develop their inner strengths so they are able to cope[2] with their world?

There is general disagreement and also lack of agreed-upon knowledge on how much pressure should be applied to children. It is undisputed, however, that the young child is living in a fast paced, rapidly changing, increasingly complex and uncertain world. This world is reflected in our children. It is not uncommon to find the four-year-old taking tranquilizers, attending sessions with a psychiatrist and talking about "when I go to college."

The rapidly increasing number of emotionally disturbed young children suggests that the child's world is becoming more and more anxiety-laden; yet this may also suggest that we are becoming better able to diagnose disturbances. However, the adult world must be made aware of the undue pressures being pushed on children.[3] Overprotection brings on its own conflicts and is not the answer to helping children face their world. The security found in a home with loving parents and realistic demands provides some of the foundation needed for coping.

The changing family itself brings new conflicts in living. David, who is just five years old and has been to nursery school for two years, lives with his working mother and two younger siblings in a high-rise apartment. He has moved twice. He goes to school with 35 other five-year-old children in kindergarten. He has to take the elevator 10 floors to get down to the cement playground.

David has flown in a jet, watched the astronauts blast-off into space, seen many beautiful books, and above all has the love and respect of his parent. Already David has learned he is a worthy person. He can meet the many stresses in his life because he knows the limits and recognizes his strengths. David is not an atypical five-year-old in 1965. His life is like many others but he has the extra important ingredient of having an unusually knowing and thoughtful parent. Many other children living under these circumstances may not be as fortunate as David.

Judy is an overprivileged suburban child who is loved by her parents but who is caught up in the pressures of status and rush toward early learning.

---

[2] Coping: ". . . the process of developing ways of dealing with new and difficult situations." Lois Barclay Murphy. *The Widening World of Childhood*. New York: Basic Books, 1962. p. 6.

[3] Association for Childhood Education International. *Don't Push Me*. Washington, D.C.: the Association, 1960. 40 p.

She too goes to kindergarten but with 25 other five-year-olds. She knows that she is in the slow reading group and this upsets her parents. She has learned that the challenges of school mean defeat in the eyes of the adults she wants to please. Judy is learning fast that failure is an uncomfortable and insurmountable conflict.

Judy, too, is not atypical. Were the demands of reading too much for her at this time? Was the preoccupation of her parents with her success in this area too overwhelming? What had happened in her previous learning to justify her inability to cope with this problem? Was love only given to her on a "pay as you go" basis? How will the many Judys meet future conflicts in learning and living?

Relieving Pressures

Each child in his own way, from his own background of experience will meet pressures with either assurance or defeat. The very experience of attending nursery school or kindergarten can be an expansion of or a limitation upon the child's ability to cope with his environment. Educators in the field of early childhood education believe firmly that the experience of early schooling can be most beneficial to the young child.

There is no doubt that each entrance of each child into nursery school or kindergarten is fraught with pressure. This pressure should be one of significant growth to the child. At the same time, such a pressure can be one of extreme pain and stress. Much has been written on preparing the child for school, yet have we thought deeply of the many pressures that encompass the child as he enters the new environment of school?

> There are the new adults who will make different demands on me. There are more children together in one place than I have experienced before and they are all my age though different. Some are bigger, some a different color, some noisy, some afraid. How do I feel? There are all those toys. Which one should I try out first? There is a book like one I have at home. Mother is leaving and I feel lonely and afraid in this strange place. Everyone lies on the floor for rest. I don't want to rest and where is my bed and my stuffed dog?

Pressures, the new classroom is full of them. Can the child cope and learn and flourish in this environment? The trauma of first experience is always difficult. Life is continually presenting new, first adventures. Each successful previous experience provides the basis for coping with the new. A good school for young children is planned to assist each child in confirming his world and in extending his horizons. It is organized so that each child may move toward progressive, positive self-fulfillment and self-realization. The sensitive, knowledgeable teacher can help each child to meet constructively the pressures in his environment and thus to reach his own maximum growth.

When and What to Teach to Whom

One of the major questions asked by today's adults is "Can the young child learn more?" There is no doubt that the young child is learning rapidly. A brief glance at a kindergarten child brings complete awe at what has been learned in five short years. Yet can this five-year-old learn more? More of what? Do we want him to know more about himself, more about how to learn, more about working with others, or more academics? The latter is emphasized in some schools of thinking. No knowing adult is going to prohibit the child from learning all he can about the subjects of our common schools. At the same time no knowing adult is going to thrust or heap on work for work's sake nor is he going to "water down" the second-grade curriculum.

The rapid changes in the world about us make us re-examine what a child can and should learn. This is a different world than we knew as children or young adults. No one wishes to return to the world of yesterday, but rather to catch up with the world of today so that as leaders of children we may be knowing in how to use the best of all worlds. Perhaps this is part of our confusion. The selection of what is to be taught, to whom and when is a continuing, unsolved pressure on the adults.[4]

The constant dilemma faced by parents and teachers is when to teach what to specific children. It is in this area that we find the greatest disagreements. Reputable persons are writing in periodicals that babies can and want to learn to read, that the typewriter provides an incentive and method of early learning, that the young years are wasted, that America has become a nation of child worshipers, and that early training prevents future failure.

In contrast we read and hear that the early years must provide time for exploration and discovery, that the development of the first five years of life provides the psychological foundation for later learning, that childhood is a time of play which has unchallenged learning potential, that any normal child of two can learn to read but should he, or what else is more important and basic in the learning process in the early years?

[4] Agnes Snyder. "Who? What? When? Where? How? Why?" *Childhood Education*. September 1963. p. 5–10.

The recent explosion of knowledge and the overwhelming amount of knowledge to be learned has put all adults in a panic. The panic is transferred to the child and the pressures mount for all. If we stop and examine the claims at either extreme of the pendulum it becomes apparent that everyone is attempting to help the child meet his world more successfully. Each is attempting to resolve the question of what to learn when. One's basic belief about learning and child growth and development becomes evident. It is my belief that young children *can* learn more but in the milieu of their environment and under the positive pressure of growth, rather than under the limiting pressure of satisfying the adults' needs in a restricted situation.

The young child is interested in a myriad of topics and thus is eager to learn about the world in which he lives. Jets, wheels, animals, age-mates, home, the far away, himself, his family, economy and politics, water, snow and rain, make-believe and now, and on and on. The selection of areas of knowing are unending. It may become necessary to learn to read to satisfy insatiable curiosity and then he will begin to read with adult help. This he will do, not because the adult wanted him to read or because it will build the adult image or ego, but because the child wants to know and is willing to undergo the tasks necessary to read. The adult will not prevent, nor will he demand, but rather he will encourage each child to build on his inner strengths and needs to move toward new steps in learning. This learning will not be accidental but the true outgrowth of the developing mind and experiences of the child nurtured by the knowing adult.

The significant growth that will have its permanent effect on the child must come as the child develops a clear and realistic image of himself as a learner. The role of each adult who lives with children must first and foremost provide the opportunity for children to experience success and support and to meet failure honestly. Each new experience should help the child increase his strength to come to grips with each new situation with openness and security.

Pressures become less threatening as one understands and respects the drive and strengths that each child brings to the conflicts in his challenging world. As each young child moves forth with love and direction his ability to cope with his world in 1965 becomes less overwhelming to him as a person. The healthy child is in the process of becoming and is developing a positive approach to life and learning.

EMOTIONAL ASPECTS OF EDUCATION

• Although it has been generally accepted that the individual acts and behaves in a holistic, integrated fashion and that his intellectual, physical, and emotional functions are interdependent, schools have tended to ignore emotions. As a matter of fact, concern with the emotional condition of the learner is of fairly recent vintage. The seeming lack of concern with the emotional welfare of students may be because its effect upon intellectual effectiveness was not understood and hence posed a threat to school personnel. Despite their inability to deal with the emotional aspects of learning or their traditional emphasis upon the intellectual, schools should continually be reminded that if the intellect were predominant, reason would prevail and students would learn. Kelly's assertion that how a person feels is more important than what he knows undoubtedly has more validity than school people traditionally have realized and admitted.

Alienation is a term more and more frequently seen in the psychological literature. As indicated by Jackson, it denotes a lack of feeling of relationship or identity with others and with self. It is characterized, he says, by the individual's failing to assume responsibility for his own actions and his feeling of indifference to what happens. Although it is a sobering thought that societal and school conditions actually may be responsible for this lack of identity, or "anomie," it is not surprising. The authoritarian, overprotective, and materialistic aspects of families, schools, and communities furnish a good explanation. Adolescents who are not allowed to make decisions, to try things, or to share in planning or producing can hardly be expected to feel a part of these institutions. They hardly can be expected to feel that what they do has any influence on what happens or that anyone who makes so little difference is responsible for others or for himself. Stated more simply: "If you can't do anything, you can be responsible for nothing."

Equally sobering is the realization that the growth and development of individuals is hindered by these conditions. How do those whose activities are rigidly structured, and who are told what, how much, and when to learn and how long to wear their hair and their skirts ever find out how to do things, or to think, for themselves? It seems to us that herein lies a ready and plausible explanation for the acts of violence and hostility performed by some teen-agers. In terms of the so-called frustration-aggression hypothesis which views aggressive and hostile actions as always resulting from frustration, an inhibition of the urge to grow is frustrating, and hostile behavior of some kind should be expected.

In any type of problem behavior, however, it must be emphasized that a description and a diagnosis, no matter how good and how satisfying to the observer, does not eliminate the behavior. It is one thing to recognize and to describe self-defeating ways of acting and quite another thing to remove or to ameliorate those patterns. Jackson's point of view that the "phony" teacher may be one of the causal factors appears worth investigating. It is difficult to know how to take the person who says one thing and does something else. For the alienated and unsure youngsters this sort of ambivalence accentuates rather than minimizes feelings of distrust and estrangement from people. It is doubtful that teachers who have failed to achieve a satisfactory adult role themselves can give this type of student the authenticity and stability he needs. Jersild advocates that the teachers must deal with themselves first to be effective.[1] He feels that until teachers can face and accept what they are, they probably will be unsuccessful in helping youngsters to do so.[2]

We are sure of this: People become what they are largely as a result of the interpersonal relationships they experience. They can change and become more effective when their association with others is such that they are encouraged to do so. The variable that the teacher, or any other person, can best manipulate is himself. We agree with Jersild. This is the best and most satisfying place to start.

[1] Arthur T. Jersild, "The Voice of the Self," *NEA Journal,* 57 (Oct. 1965), 23–5.

[2] Arthur T. Jersild, *When Teachers Face Themselves* (Teachers College, Columbia University: Bureau of Publications, 1955), 169 pp.

There is much concern today about "offbeat" young people—the mob protesters, the black-stockinged girl and the unshorn boy, the glue-sniffers and the LSD experimenters, the delinquents and the culturally disadvantaged. It therefore seems appropriate to select for this section an article that deals with alienation and how it might be dealt with in the classroom. It is so temptingly easy to dismiss evidences of alienation (or other unacceptable behaviors) as being the responsibility of someone else or of some other thing—the doltishness of the person, irresponsible parents, the decadence of society, the profit motive in the economic order. But how do schools, teachers, achievement norms contribute to alienation? Jackson's article affords an opportunity for us to look at ourselves and, instead of blaming other things, to say, "The buck stops here."

PHILIP W. JACKSON
Professor of Educational Psychology, University of Chicago

25. ALIENATION
IN THE CLASSROOM[1]

• Every child experiences
the pain of failure and the joy of success long before he reaches school age,
but his achievements, or lack of them, do not really become official until
he enters the classroom. From then on, however, a public record of his
progress gradually accumulates, and as a student he must learn to adapt to
the continued and pervasive spirit of evaluation that will dominate his
school years. For most, the adaptation is not too difficult. Ideally, they will
experience far more success than failure, and will feel appropriately elated
or depressed depending on the judgment their work receives. But, naturally,
the ideal is not always realized. Many students do less well than they
should and, more important, many—including some of the most able—do
not seem to care, one way or the other, how they are doing. Although the
two forms of difficulty—the academic and the motivational—are interrelated and both are serious, the apathetic student (irrespective of his
achievement status) is a more disturbing example of classroom failure than
is the youngster who is not doing well but who cares deeply about his lack
of progress. The student who is willing but unable to do his work indicates,
most frequently, the breakdown of a particular instructional sequence; but
the student who no longer cares how well he does or who otherwise gives
signs of being dissatisfied with school life, may signal the breakdown of
social identification—a much more serious state of affairs. The remarks
that follow focus chiefly on this second type of classroom failure: the
student who cannot or will not respond appropriately to the values, the

Psychology in the Schools, 2:299–308, 1965. Used by permission.

[1] Revised version of a paper read at the Institute for Administrators of Pupil
Personnel Services, Harvard University, Summer, 1964.

rewards, and the expectations that combine to form the culture of the school.

Our understanding of social and psychological problems has been enhanced in recent years by the development of the concept of alienation. As the term was originally used by social theorists, such as Marx and Weber, alienation referred to the psychological discomfort suffered by the worker in an industrialized society. Cut off from both the means and the ends of production, the industrial worker lost the feeling of pride and commitment that had characterized the earlier craftsman. Labor, which was once a unified and intrinsically satisfying activity, had become fragmented and meaningless. The link between the product and the producer was broken, and with nothing to sell but himself, the worker began to feel curiously adrift in a world that seemed to be fashioned increasingly by and for the desires of others.

That which began as a theoretical description of the worker's plight has since been verified empirically, and as it is used today, the concept of alienation has been broadened to include not only the factory worker, but, to some extent, all who live in today's industrialized urban societies. The estrangement of modern man from himself and from others is viewed by many as the major psychological problem of our time. In the present paper ideas derived from empirical and theoretical studies of alienation will be applied to the examination of classroom problems.

Signs of Alienation in the School

As a group, educators are highly achievement-oriented. And understandably so. Not only have their own academic careers been relatively successful—indicating that typically they have embraced the school's values from the beginning—but, in addition, their professional energies are focused almost exclusively on the promotion of achievement in others. It is hardly surprising, therefore, that many teachers view scholastic success as an all-encompassing good, and have a difficult time understanding people who do not share this basic value. Normally the teacher expects the student to be delighted by high grades and deflated by low ones (as he himself was when he was a student). Even when the rewards and punishments of grades are not operating, the student is thought to be gaining personal satisfaction from the growth of his own ability (as the teacher supposedly did), and, therefore, he is expected to undertake school tasks eagerly. When these expectations are not met, the teacher may become puzzled or annoyed by what he perceives as a complete disregard for an obvious virtue. Yet as the statistics on dropouts and delinquents, and the extensive literature devoted to the topic of classroom boredom indicate, there are many students who do not share the teacher's enthusiasms.

One of the first and most important signs of disturbance in a social unit—and, hence, one of the most reliable indicators of alienation—appears when individuals or sub-groups within the unit hold fundamentally different views of either the value of the rewards dispensed to group members or the conditions under which the rewards are distributed.

It is commonly recognized that there are two major reward systems operating in the classroom: the "intrinsic," which arises naturally from the growth of ability, and the "extrinsic," which comprises the evaluations given by teachers, fellow students, and outsiders. When either of these systems begins to misfire, the danger signals of more serious difficulties have been sounded. As has been suggested, the misfiring may occur in two ways: through the devaluation of the reward system or through its misapplication (either real or fancied).[2]

The student who gets no pleasure from his own progress has devaluated the *intrinsic* reward system. Similarly, the student who doesn't care what the teacher or others think has devaluated the *extrinsic* reward system. If the student is unable to see his own progress (or sees some when there is none) the *intrinsic* reward system is being misapplied. Similarly, if the student deserves praise or punishment from others (or thinks he does) and it is not given, the *extrinsic* reward system is being misapplied.

These two forms of malfunctioning—the devaluation and the misapplication of the school's rewards—are clearly interrelated. Indeed, in many instances there seems to be a causal relationship between the two. Devaluation (in the form of student indifference) is often a reaction to the suspicion of unfairness or illogic in the handling of rewards. The student who thinks he is being treated unfairly and who feels unable to do anything about it learns to remain detached and uninvolved. The possibility of there being this kind of causal link is important because it implies that beneath the student's bland indifference harsher feelings may lurk. These feelings may stem from a basic distrust of the classroom environment in general and of school authorities in particular.

A first step, then, in the diagnosis of alienation is to examine the degree of concordance between the objective and the subjective aspects of evaluation, between what society thinks of a person and what he thinks of himself.

[2] Rewards may also be overvalued and, thus, sought more fervently than some people think they should be. The "money-hungry" adult and the "grade-hungry" student are two examples of such overstriving. These forms of pathological motivation will not be discussed in the present paper.

A lack of agreement in these matters would be interpreted as a serious danger signal. Even when there is a perfect agreement, however, and the reward system appears to be operating flawlessly, the search for symptoms of alienation cannot be abandoned. A second important diagnostic query focuses on the person's perception of the powers that give direction to his life. The important question here is how the individual believes his successes and failures come about. Who is responsible?

Basically, there are two sources of action—the self and the non-self—to which the burden of responsibility can be affixed. In extreme terms, we can believe either we are what we are because of our own actions or because of what others, or fate, or "Lady Luck," did to us. In the first instance, we feel in control of our life, as if we are masters of our own destiny. In the second instance, helpless and victimized, as if our destiny is in the hands of forces over which we have little or no control. The beliefs of most people are commonly somewhere between these two extremes, although one point of view may be more dominant than the other.

The student who does not accept personal responsibility for his achievement status is the educational equivalent of society's alienated man. Both his gains and his losses are a function of what others have done to him. Therefore, he cannot honestly feel pride in his achievements or shame for his failures.

Of the many manifestations of alienation, the one dealing with the assignment of responsibility has received the greatest amount of attention from researchers. An example of how this psychological condition is translated into empirical terms and used in studies of children is contained in an investigation by Crandall, Katkovsky, and Preston (1962). These researchers studied a group of forty primary-grade children for whom they constructed a special test, called the Children's Intellectual Achievement Responsibility Questionnaire (abbreviated by the letters IAR). This questionnaire was designed to assess the degree to which the children believed their successes and failures to be the results of their own efforts or to be caused by what others did. The questionnaire contains descriptions of several common experiences of grade school children—some involving success and praise, others involving failure and criticism—and asks the child to tell whether these experiences, when they happen to him, are usually the result of what he does or of what others do. An example of a success item is: "Suppose you did better than usual in a subject at school. Would it probably happen (a) because you tried harder or (b) because someone helped you?" The following is a failure item: "When you make a mistake on a school assignment, is it usually (a) because the assignment the teacher gave was a particularly hard one or (b) because you were careless?" A high self-responsibility score is obtained by choosing the alternatives that imply the acceptance of personal blame or credit for failure or success.

Scores on the IAR were essentially unrelated to achievement behavior for girls, but not for boys. Indeed, the correlations between IAR scores and achievement were positive consistently for boys and were higher than similar statistics obtained with other predictor variables, including measures of need for achievement and general manifest anxiety.

An investigation of a similar phenomenon was conducted by Battle and Rotter (1963) who administered a newly designed projective test of internal-external control to a group of sixth- and eighth-grade students. The test consists of 29 cartoon items about which subjects are questioned concerning the assignment of responsibility for the conditions depicted (e.g., Why is she always hurting herself? Why is her mother always hollering at her?). The most important finding to come out of this study was that differences in attitudes toward internal and external control were related to social class and ethnic group. Lower-class Negroes were significantly more external than were middle-class Negroes or whites. Middle-class children, in general, were significantly more internal than were lower-class children.

A recent study by Bialer (1961) provides a third illustration of how the assignment of personal responsibility is used as a variable in research on children. Bialer developed a scale consisting of 23 questions of the following sort: "Do you really believe a kid can be whatever he wants to be?" "When nice things happen to you, is it only good luck?" "Do you often feel you get punished when you don't deserve it?" He administered this question- naire, together with other tests, to a combined group of 89 mentally retarded and normal children selected from special classes and from regular elemen- tary classrooms of a public school system. The tendency to perceive events as being under internal control (the opposite of being alienated) increased with age and was positively related, in particular, to the mental age of children. Bialer suggests that in the early stages of development there is no conception of the relationship between the outcome of events and one's own behavior. Consequently, he argues, young children, as a group, tend to view all of their experiences as being controlled by the whims or fancies of fate, other people, and other external forces. Young children tend, then, to perceive events hedonistically, as merely pleasant or unpleasant, with- out considering whether or not their own actions might have contributed to the outcome.

The brief descriptions of these three studies give a general impression of how the concept of alienation is being used in studies of children. They also highlight the major findings with respect to the assignment of personal responsibility. They indicate that the tendency to perceive success and failure as being bestowed by outside forces (a) is more characteristic of those who fail in school than of those who succeed; (b) is likely to occur more frequently among lower-class than among middle-class children; (c) is associated with other types of psychological disability, such as anxiety; and (d) is particularly evident in very young and mentally immature persons.

A logical reaction to a life over which one has little control would be to withdraw or to become resigned to the inevitable. It would seem, then, that an attitude of indifference might flow as naturally from the denial of personal responsibility as from the perception of injustice in the distribution of life's rewards. This indifference—which students sometimes describe as "playing it cool"—is the most important single indicator of alienation in the classroom. Underlying it are likely to be found feelings of being mistreated or manipulated by school officials.

The Pervasiveness of Alienation

Only the surface manifestations of alienation have been treated thus far. To probe more deeply requires a consideration of how the syndrome of alienation may permeate many areas of behavior. Also, to this point, alienation has been described more as an individual psychological ailment, than as a shared mode of adaptation to some of the harsher features of social reality. In the comments that follow, the adaptive aspects of this behavioral strategy will be emphasized.

Social theory and research of the last few decades emphatically warns us not to assume that the alienated person is sick, and society well. Indeed, many social analysts believe that the opposite is true. This being so, when the sign of alienation appears in a student it is imperative to determine to what extent the symptoms arise from a unique personal history, and to what extent they stem from the reality of present school and home conditions. Sometimes, for example, the reward system of the school does operate illogically, and sometimes teachers do exert so much control that their students no longer have a feeling of personal power. When these conditions hold it is not surprising to find indifference or apathy in the classroom. Also, many children live in homes and neighborhoods in which there is little or no support for academic values. Small wonder that such students have difficulty working up more than lukewarm enthusiasm over the tasks and the rewards of school life. The badly functioning school and the unsupportive home environment are part of the everyday experience of many children. For these youngsters the syndrome of alienation is more understandable and the steps that might be taken to eliminate it are more obvious than is true for students who do not suffer from such immediate environmental disadvantages.

As he confronts an indifferent student, then, the teacher or counselor must ask whether the signs of motivational withdrawal are situationally confined or whether they pervasively color the student's view of the world. There is a difference between the student who is apathetic during his hours in the classroom, but engrossed in other contexts, and the one who is as indifferent to life outside the classroom as he is to life inside.

Two major difficulties, however, are connected with attempts to determine whether or not alienated behavior is situationally confined. The first arises from the fact that even when the behavior seems to occur only within clearly specified limits—such as a classroom—the question of how much the present situation contributes to the student's attitude is still to be answered. Although our typical reaction might be to place blame for the condition on the immediate setting, the student's present attitudes may be almost exclusively the result of his previous experience. Consider the high school student whose poor attention in mathematics classes stems from bad experiences with arithmetic instruction during his grade school years.

A second difficulty involved in fixing the limits of alienation derives from the fact that the disorder tends to spill over from one area of behavior to another. A major assumption underlying much of the theoretical writing is that when alienation arises in connection with the performance of a person's major social roles—such as worker, or mother, or soldier—it tends to spread to the performance of other roles as well. The alienation of the factory worker, arising out of conditions of the assembly line and mass production, shows up in his home life and his leisure hours as well as in his behavior on the job. In other words, alienation, even when situationally aroused, is not like a set of dirty coveralls that can be left behind when the whistle blows. Rather, it is an enduring perceptual set, which, if unchecked, may be expected to affect larger and larger portions of a person's life. Therefore, when students are identified whose total world view seems to be described appropriately as "alienated" it is unreasonable to assume that the source of this alienation is as diffuse as the symptom itself, although it might be quite difficult to identify the specific area of experience that served as the origin of the general ailment.

One way, then, of thinking about the degree or seriousness of a person's feeling of alienation is to consider the spread of the feeling in time and space; to ask, in effect, in how many different settings does he feel like this, or how many of his waking hours are tainted by these feelings? Another way is to consider the social or psychological depth, so to speak, at which the feeling seems to operate. In this regard, a helpful set of distinctions is suggested by Scott (1964), who argues that the condition of alienation may stem from four major "social sources." In order of increasing seriousness, these are: facilities, roles, norms, and values.

At the most rudimentary level, alienation consists of being unable to control facilities. Among the working class, with whom it was first identified, this feeling of powerlessness was created by the fact that the laborer no longer was able to control the speed of production (because of assembly line production) and was heightened as other major decisions concerning the means and ends of production were taken from him. At the second level, that of role, the alienated person no longer feels the need to adhere to the set of expectations society holds for him. Some of the many roles each person is expected to perform carry more status than others and, hence, are felt to be more important. The failure to accept responsibility for these "primary status-carrying roles" is naturally more serious psychologically and sociologically, than is a comparable failure with respect to more peripheral expectations.

Alienation from norms—Scott's third level—is reflected in the refusal to conform to the rules and regulations by which goals are obtained. The condition of being separated from the norms of society has received the label "anomie" from social theorists, notably Durkheim and Merton. The victim of this condition shares the values of most other men, but he cannot or will not use the normal channels for obtaining them. For such a person the usual relationship between means and ends has undergone a radical change. This change often brings with it a distrust of others, for when the means–ends relationship is altered a person can no longer believe that the motives of others are what they seem to be.

The fourth and most serious source of alienation occurs when the individual rejects, or simply fails to develop, a commitment to one or more fundamental values of his society. The person who is alienated in this sense not only rejects the means of his fellows; he rejects the ends as well. In the most extreme case he does not transfer his allegiance to a set of substitute goals but, instead, turns away from all values. When this "devaluation of valuation" begins, the victim of alienation has entered upon the final separation that threatens to cut him off from all others, and, ultimately, from himself.

There are certain important and perhaps obvious resemblances between recurring forms of student behavior and the four types of alienation suggested by Scott. It is dangerous, however, to assume that these signs of difficulty have the same meaning when observed in students as when observed in adults. It may be, for example, that the separation between the world of children and the world of adults creates strains that produce, in turn, signs of a temporary alienation that will disappear by the time the child becomes an adult. It is equally possible, of course, that the greater social dependency of the child may make it more difficult for him than for the adult to turn away from the expectations and values of other people. Consequently, the behavioral indicators of alienation may signify a much more serious condition when observed in young people than when observed in adults. A variant of the latter argument is offered by Bettelheim (1961), who points out that "with the whole pressure of school, parents, educational system, and society at large favoring success in learning, it often takes a great deal more determination on the part of the non-learner to fail than for the good learner to do well in school." The comparison between adult and juvenile forms of alienation requires much more study than it has been given to date and must, therefore, be made with caution. Nonetheless, the resemblances are there and deserve comment.

The student who is separated from the facilities of scholarship (the first level of alienation in Scott's conceptual scheme) is the one who does not know how to handle the basic tools of learning. With respect to a particular subject (and possibly to all of his work) he may feel "lost" or "at sea." This student might also be overwhelmed by the amount of work he is expected to do and may despair of ever being able to catch up with his classmates.

The classroom equivalent of the adult's separation from role would be the young person's struggles with the responsibility of being a student. It is generally overlooked that the student role involves much more than the satisfactory performance of specific academic skills. A student is expected to maintain severe restrictions on his physical movement and his speech (even in the most "progressive" classroom!); he is expected to show the proper deference to the teacher and other authorities, while demonstrating, at the same time, his growth in autonomy and independence; he is expected to become intensely absorbed in the subject of the teaching session, but he is also expected to shift his interest and his focus of concern at the sound of a bell. He is expected to compete for the approval of the teacher and other educational rewards, but he is also admonished not to be a "show-off," for the reputation he earns in the classroom has to be lived with on the playground and in the dormitory. Given these varied and, at times, conflicting demands, it is hardly surprising that some people find the role of student difficult to perform.

The goals of the school, broadly considered, have to do with learning how to become a productive member of a particular segment of society. But the school is not alone in contributing to this end. Family, friends, and other formal agencies also play a part, and, depending on the particular group in which a person is seeking acceptance, the school's contribution may be great or small compared with that from other sources. It is possible, in other words, for a person to be highly achievement-oriented (in the general sense), to have an intense desire to learn certain things, and to care very much about his status in the eyes of others, without, at the same time, viewing the school as instrumental in helping him to attain these goals. Such a person may be forced, of course, to be in school and, while there, his condition might best be described as alienation from a set of norms. For him the entire education institution, not just the role of student, is senseless. He may seek the same general goals as his classmates, but he does not perceive the classroom as a place where they may be obtained.

Separation from values, the most serious form of alienation in Scott's view, may show up in the classroom in two ways. First, some students may fail to shift from the value system of children—with its hedonistic orientation—to the value system of adults—with its emphasis on the virtues of responsibility, the control of impulse, and the like. Second, some students may fail to shift from the value system of their family and friends to the value system espoused by the school. The school, in other words, extols the virtues that characterize the mature middle-class adult (or are supposed to). Students who are uninterested or unable to become either mature or middle class might exhibit signs of this fourth form of alienation. Such students need not be openly defiant, although rebellion often springs from this condition; they may, instead, behave as if the "proper" values guided their action, but their lack of commitment rarely escapes the eye of the watchful teacher.

The four levels of alienation suggested by Scott—from facilities to values—do then, seem to be crudely identifiable within the classroom. Also, although much more needs to be known about the relationship between juvenile and adult forms of alienation, the increasing seriousness as the source of the separation moves from facilities to values seems to be as applicable to students as to adults. The task remaining is to consider, even though it can only be at the level of conjecture, some of the steps the school might take to check or reverse the progress of this disorder.

The Treatment of Alienation

First, we must admit that no one really knows what to do about the alienated student. At best we can point to some of the common sources of classroom difficulty that seem to be related logically to the development of alienation and trust that improvement in these areas will have beneficial results. Second, we must recognize that extreme forms of alienation may be too difficult for teachers to handle and may require outside help. The student who is extremely disgruntled with school life may also be disgruntled with life in general, and may need individual therapy if he is to begin to change his perceptions of himself and others.

One of the most badly needed changes in school practice is that of broadening our conventional definition of achievement. At present the assessment of achievement typically involves a normative judgment. That is, the student's work is compared with the achievement of his peers, locally and nationally, rather than with some absolute criterion or with his own previous level of performance. The normative approach is unavoidable in those school subjects were a precise statement of objectives is impossible— and there are many such subjects. But this type of evaluation often puts the student at the mercy of his classmates. If, on the one hand, he is "lucky" enough to have fellow students who do not want to work or who are not too bright, he can emerge successful from the experience. If, on the other hand, he happens to be among brilliant, hard-working students, he emerges looking a bit like a dolt. Either way, the student's evaluation is independent, to some extent, of his own efforts. Like the factory worker, he has little to do with setting the standards by which his work is judged.

If, however, some measure of growth were used or some absolute criteria set, the standards of achievement might not be as capricious as they now must seem to some students. The establishment of specific criteria of achieve- ment is an extremely difficult job. Not enough is known about the structure of most school subjects to set anything but arbitrary standards. The use of gain scores as measures of achievement also presents problems. The inter- pretation of the size of gains, for instance, almost invariably reintroduces the concept of norm. Despite these difficulties, it is likely that any improve- ment in the variety and the logical compellingness of our achievement measures would help to reduce one of the common sources of discontent in the classroom.

Closely related to the goal of improving the assessment of achievement is the goal of clarifying academic expectations and the methods of attaining them. Students not only need to know how far they have come; they also need to know where they are headed, and precisely how to get there. Yet scholastic goals and the best methods of reaching them are anything but clear in many classrooms. The clarification of ends and means does not require necessarily that students have a hand in setting their own goals, although it is probable that in some instances student planning would increase the appeal of educational objectives. In many instructional areas, however, it is doubtful that the students are capable of establishing their own goals or of determining how best to achieve them. Clear goals, regardless of how they are set, would help to reduce some of the uncertainty that likely contributes to the development of student indifference.

Academic standards are not the only expectations that operate in the classroom. In addition, there are the requirements that have to do with performing the role of student, and, as indicated earlier, these requirements are often ambiguous and conflicting. Most of the overt disturbances in the classroom appear to result from failure to meet student role expectations rather than from failure to meet academic standards. Therefore, efforts to clarify the student role or to decrease the internal conflict among the various role expectations would almost certainly make life in the classroom easier and more attractive.

Evidence in support of the benefits of greater clarity in the definition of the student role is presented by Kounin and Gump (1958), who conducted an observational study of kindergartens. They found that when teachers made their expectations clear, defined rules precisely, and suggested positive actions the misbehaving child might take, the incidence of unruly behavior diminished. Even when it occurred under these conditions, the misbehavior did not seem to have a negative effect on the rest of the children.

The student is not alone, of course, in his discomfort. The role of the teacher contains its own peculiar stresses, which serve indirectly as an additional source of classroom difficulty. Because teaching is a moral enterprise, the teacher often is encouraged to maintain a public image that is more virtuous, more omniscient, and more altruistic than is humanly possible. When students perceive the discrepancy between what the teacher professes to be and what he truly is, they are likely to charge the teacher with being "a phony." It is not difficult to understand why the student who perceives the teacher as being a bit of a fraud might feel disillusioned and might have some difficulty remaining involved in his role. In modern fiction many of the characters of J. D. Salinger—Holden Caulfield and Franny Glass, in particular—reflect the disillusionment and disgust (harbingers of alienation) that accompany the perception of the "phony" teacher.

Contradictions between preaching and practicing are not new, and teachers are surely not the only offenders. Furthermore, in many instances the charge of phonyness is a bit too severe. As long as people strive to better themselves, a gap of some kind will exist between the real and the ideal. Failure to live constantly in accord with the ideal hardly provides grounds for applying the label "phony." Nonetheless, when students behave as if they believe such a label is appropriate, teachers must be alert enough to recognize this major sign of difficulty and to take steps to remedy it.

The classic educational solution for dealing with chronically failing students is to shower them with "success experiences." The engineering of success is certainly an important remedial strategy, but it is not the all-purpose palliative some educators believe it to be. First, if it is to be effective, the success must be in an area that is significant to the student. Success in building a doorstop or in winning a footrace is not very likely to ease the pain of failing to learn how to read, no matter how much we might believe in the benefits of compensation. The student cannot, in other words, make up for important failures by experiencing trivial successes. Second, success, if it is to have its expected therapeutic impact, must not only be perceived by the student as important, it must also be seen as resulting directly from something the student does. Success may be pre-planned, but it must not be rigged. Educational hand-outs are of doubtful value to the alienated student.

In summary, the prevention and remediation of alienation involves first and foremost the clarification of the school environment. Students need to have a clearer picture of how they are doing, they need to understand the school's expectations and they need to be shown exactly how those expectations can be fulfilled. They need help in resolving the ambiguities of the student role and they need to be surrounded by teachers and administrators who are unequivocal in the perception of their own adult roles.

Finally, a repeated word of caution. Despite the similarities that have been discussed here, the alienated student and the alienated adult are really two distinct phenomena. It would be a mistake, therefore, to exaggerate the prognostic significance of signs of alienation in young people; to imagine, for example, that every indifferent student will become an indifferent adult. Fortunately, many of our least promising students turn out to be models of self-fulfillment when they mature. Not all, however, overcome the stresses of their student days, and others show no signs of difficulty until many years after they have left the classroom. Consequently, although we should not become prophets of despair each time we encounter a student who is less enthusiastic about schooling than we are, neither should we ignore early signs of danger that might erupt into a serious form of classroom failure.

REFERENCES

Battle, Esther S., and Rotter, J. B. Children's feelings of personal control as related to social class and ethnic group. *Journal of Personality*, 1963, 31, 482–490.

Bettelheim, B. The decision to fail. *School Review*, 1961, 69, 377–412.

Bialer, I. Conceptualization of success and failure in mentally retarded and normal children. *Journal of Personality*, 1961, 29, 303–320.

Crandall, V. J., Katkovsky, W., and Preston, Anne. Motivational and ability determinants of young children's intellectual achievement behaviors. *Child Development*, 1962, 33, 643–661.

Kounin, J., and Gump, P. The ripple effect in discipline. *Elementary School Journal*, 1958, 59, 158–162.

Scott, M. B. The social sources of alienation. In I. F. Horowitz (Ed.) *The new sociology: essays in honor of C. Wright Mills.* Oxford Univer. Press, 1964. Pp. 239–252.

EARL C. KELLEY
Professor of Secondary Education, Wayne State University

26 · THE PLACE
OF AFFECTIVE
LEARNING

• I was pleased to be invited to write this editorial because the topic for this month is of the utmost importance. It could well come about that this is one of the most important issues in the history of this publication.

The reason for this statement is that it has now become abundantly clear, from research and from reason, that *how a person feels is more important than what he knows.* This seems true because how one feels controls behavior, while what one knows does not. What one knows is used in behavior, to be sure, but the way it is used depends upon positive or negative feelings. It is possible to be a saint or a demon with similar knowledge. History furnishes ample illustrations of knowledge being put to evil uses. The Nazis who slaughtered six million innocent people knew too much but felt too little.

We in education are slowly waking up to the fact that feelings are really important. This can be seen in educational literature. There is much discussion of the self-concept, the self-image, and of the fact that if one thinks too little of himself he becomes immobile and unable to learn. In fact, the person who has come to hate himself and others does not take in much subject matter.

All of this causes us to take another look at subject matter and its uses. None of the above is to imply that what one knows is not important. One's

Educational Leadership, 22:455–457, April, 1965. Reprinted with permission of the Association for Supervision and Curriculum Development and Earl C. Kelley. Copyright © 1965 by the Association for Supervision and Curriculum Development.

proper subject matter is the universe around him, and without some comprehension of that universe and his relation to it, he could not know how to deal with it, no matter how he felt.

Subject matter and feeling are so closely intertwined that they can no longer be considered a duality. Everyone who learns something has some feeling about it, and so, as in so many other areas, they are inseparable. No matter what we do, affective learning goes on anyway. When this affective learning is positive, the learner becomes constructive in his behavior.

We need to reconsider our ideas and attitudes toward subject matter itself. It has long been considered an end in itself. If the learner came through in possession of a large store of subject matter, we have said he is "good." If the subject matter was something the learner could not or would not store, and be able to prove that he had stored it, he has been considered "bad," or at least a failure.

We ought to be able to reconsider the role of subject matter in the education of our young without being accused of not valuing subject matter. It is not a question of reducing the importance of what is learned, but of seeing the relationship between accumulated information and the unique learner. I have on occasion been charged with not wanting learners to learn anything, but only to feel good. This is not true. One of my basic criticisms of the traditional school is that those in attendance do not learn nearly enough. We have reared a generation of people who have been schooled but not educated.

The main reason for this outcome is that with our rigorous subject matter approach we have closed personalities when we should have been opening them. We have used fear and anxiety as motivating devices, and this has repelled the learner when we should have been attracting him. When the learner has not, because of these destructive feelings, learned what we adults purpose him to learn, we have had to resort to coercion of one form or another. Coercion sets in motion a whole cycle of negative affects, often resulting in open hostility and rejection on the part of both learner and teacher. Many such learners are then headed toward the human scrap-heap—the rejects known as dropouts, the educationally disinherited, who in most cases will be unable to cope with the society of the future. It is from this human scrap-heap that most of our delinquent and mentally ill are drawn.

The basic error in most of our curriculum work is that we start with the materials, which are the tools of education, not the product. We choose our tools first, and then look around to see what we are going to do with them. These materials are usually chosen without regard to the individual differences among the learners, often without regard to the culture of the community where the school is located. Curriculum building is the only operation I know about where the tool is chosen before what is to be built is known or decided upon.

We have for so long chosen the curriculum with little regard for the feelings of the learner that we are of course unskilled in planning curriculum with affect in mind. When new understandings show us that how a person feels is more important than what he knows, our old assumptions and procedures will no longer suffice. We are faced with a requirement to learn new methods of using materials. If we had spent as much time in considering the feelings of the learner as we have in choosing and presenting information, we would by now know how to go about it.

We cannot say that, although planning curriculum with affective learning in mind is a clear necessity, we do not know how to do it, and so we will continue to ignore it. Since such planning is a requirement, we will have to learn how to do it, just as any other workman must do when his past methods have become obsolete.

Getting Started

I cannot of course tell others how to do this. Each school system and each individual teacher must solve this problem in his own way, taking into account his own resources, the nature of his unique learners and the community in which he works. I can, however, make a few general suggestions, which may provide a way of getting started.

Many schools have committees which work on curriculum. Every school needs some organization of this sort. A school cannot in these changing times continue to operate well without somebody examining what is being done, and what ought to be done in the light of new evidence and new conditions. Even in a factory someone has to spend some of his time in planning.

I would like to see such a committee not address itself to the material first, since this had been done many times. I would like the committee members to ask themselves a new set of questions.

How can we secure commitment to the learning task on the part of our learners? *Educational Leadership* had a whole issue on commitment recently, and some articles on the topic even splashed over into another issue. I know of no way to get anybody committed to any task anywhere without consultation and some choice. This raises another question.

What are the ways of bringing about consultation and some choice with the learner? In other words, how go about teacher-pupil planning, so that what is to be done makes some sense to the learner? There is a rich supply of literature in this field.

How can we take advantage of the learner's uniqueness, rather than considering it a handicap?

How can we give the academically gifted a chance to use his ability without depriving him of many of his peers? In our own form of segregation, the gifted are actually deprived.

How can we make available to the learner his proper subject matter, which is not alone held in a book but consists of the whole world around him?

What shall we do about marks? Do they on the whole bring about more negative than positive feeling?

What are our devices for rejection, and how may they be reduced?

These are only a few of the questions which might be raised. Any committee sensitive to the feelings of learners will find more. Eventually, after all of these questions are effectively dealt with, the committee will finally come to this one: What materials shall we use, and how shall we use them?

I have a strong belief that every learner should feel better, more able to cope with unknown vicissitudes, more courageous at the end of a class than he did at the opening. If he feels worse, less able and less courageous, then the class has damaged him, rather than helped him. If this is oft repeated then he is on his way to the human scrap-heap.

I further strongly believe that if a teacher behaves in such a way as to open selves, open personalities, and then has something around for people to learn, they will learn. And this learning will be greater in quantity and in usefulness than would be the case if learners are driven to close themselves. We cannot open selves and render them receptive if we start our classes with threats.

The future must appear promising, not threatening, if learners are to come toward the teacher rather than retreat from him. The learner must have confidence in the teacher, feel that there is no double-cross in prospect, before he can open up. This confidence is not conveyed alone by what we say but mostly by our behavior.

PERSONALITY
AND ITS
DEVELOPMENT

• Probably no other facet of psychology is so varied, so interesting, and so open to theorizing and speculation as the area of personality. Because the subject has been approached from many rather divergent, but also plausible, points of view, students are often inclined to favor first one theory and then another as the focus of their study shifts. They are apt to emerge somewhat confused at the end of the course with few really definite convictions about human behavior. For the reader who is interested in exploring further we recommend:

1. Bischof, Ledford J. *Interpreting Personality Theories.* New York: Harper & Row, 1964.
2. Chaplin, J. P., and T. S. Krawiec. *Systems and Theories of Psychology.* New York: Holt, Rinehart & Winston, 1960.
3. Hall, Calvin S., and Gardner Lindzey. *Theories of Personality.* New York: John Wiley & Sons, Inc., 1957.

Carl Rogers is one of those who have developed a theory of personality. He is typical in the respect that his ideas are based upon work with, and observation of, people. That is, his is a clinical approach. Somewhat more than others, however, Rogers has been concerned with the validation of his concepts. He has formulated and then applied and tested for effectiveness in practice. It is significant in this respect that four of the six conditions which he set for constructive personality change were applied to the therapist rather than to his client.

Lest the reader wonder at this point concerning the pertinence to teachers of such things as personality change and psychotherapy, it probably is appropriate to acquaint him with the similarity between the work of the therapist and the work of the teacher. The therapist is trying to effect personality change through the learning of new attitudes and ways of doing things. Although the methods he employs differ from those of the conventional educator, it may be that the psychological climate he considers necessary for successful therapy and the conditions he strives to maintain so that positive personality changes can take place also will act to facilitate classroom learning. Both psychotherapy and teaching have as an objective the development of more effective individuals.

It is our position that it is more desirable to provide for, and acquaint people with, the processes of positive growth and change through good teaching and education than it is to attempt to reverse negative and self-defeating patterns through psychotherapy and re-education; an ounce of prevention is better than a pound of cure. A teacher who cannot provide the type of instructional milieu in which this can happen has been inadequately prepared to really educate youngsters.

Mussen and Jones's contention that physically retarded adolescent boys are more likely to be personally and socially maladjusted than their physically more mature peers is important to teachers who need to understand this stage of development better. It probably is true that patterns of leadership and status are dependent upon early pubescence and the spurt of physical growth and development that usually accompanies this. Ways of being perceived by one's peers and of perceiving oneself that are established at that time probably tend to become habitual and hence to exert a far-reaching effect upon later development. In common with early childhood, early adolescence is believed to constitute a most crucial period for individual development. Teachers who understand this and who understand the emotional insecurity and anxieties experienced by the late developer may be able to prevent a later need for unlearning and relearning through psychotherapy.

CARL R. ROGERS

Western Behavioral Science Institute, La Jolla, California

---

27 · THE NECESSARY AND SUFFICIENT CONDITIONS OF THERAPEUTIC PERSONALITY CHANGE

● For many years I have been engaged in psychotherapy with individuals in distress. In recent years I have found myself increasingly concerned with the process of abstracting from that experience the general principles which appear to be involved in it. I have endeavored to discover any orderliness, any unity which seems to inhere in the subtle, complex tissue of interpersonal relationship in which I have so constantly been immersed in therapeutic work. One of the current products of this concern is an attempt to state, in formal terms, a theory of psychotherapy, of personality, and of interpersonal relationships which will encompass and contain the phenomena of my experience.[1] What I wish to do in this paper is to take one very small segment of that theory, spell it out more completely, and explore its meaning and usefulness.

Journal of Consulting Psychology, 21:95–103, 1957. Copyright © 1957 by the American Psychological Association, and reproduced by permission.

---

[1] This formal statement is entitled "A theory of therapy, personality and interpersonal relationships, as developed in the client-centered framework," by Carl R. Rogers. The manuscript was prepared at the request of the Committee of the American Psychological Association for the Study of the Status and Development of Psychology in the United States. It will be published by McGraw-Hill in one of several volumes being prepared by this committee. Copies of the unpublished manuscript are available from the author to those with special interest in this field.

The Problem

The question to which I wish to address myself is this: Is it possible to state, in terms which are clearly definable and measurable, the psychological conditions which are both necessary and sufficient to bring about constructive personality change? Do we, in other words, know with any precision those elements which are essential if psychotherapeutic change is to ensue?

Before proceeding to the major task let me dispose very briefly of the second portion of the question. What is meant by such phrases as "psychotherapeutic change," "constructive personality change"? This problem also deserves deep and serious consideration, but for the moment let me suggest a common-sense type of meaning upon which we can perhaps agree for purposes of this paper. By these phrases is meant: change in the personality structure of the individual, at both surface and deeper levels, in a direction which clinicians would agree means greater integration, less internal conflict, more energy utilizable for effective living; change in behavior away from behaviors generally regarded as immature and toward behaviors regarded as mature. This brief description may suffice to indicate the kind of change for which we are considering the preconditions. It may also suggest the ways in which this criterion of change may be determined.[2]

The Conditions

As I have considered my own clinical experience and that of my colleagues, together with the pertinent research which is available, I have drawn out several conditions which seem to me to be *necessary* to initiate constructive personality change, and which, taken together, appear to be *sufficient* to inaugurate that process. As I have worked on this problem I have found myself surprised at the simplicity of what has emerged. The statement which follows is not offered with any assurance as to its correctness, but with the expectation that it will have the value of any theory, namely that it states or implies a series of hypotheses which are open to proof or disproof, thereby clarifying and extending our knowledge of the field.

Since I am not, in this paper, trying to achieve suspense, I will state at once, in severely rigorous and summarized terms, the six conditions which I have come to feel are basic to the process of personality change. The meaning of a number of the terms is not immediately evident, but will be clarified in the explanatory sections which follow. It is hoped that this

---

[2] That this is a measurable and determinable criterion has been shown in research already completed. See (7), especially chapters 8, 13, and 17.

brief statement will have much more significance to the reader when he has completed the paper. Without further introduction let me state the basic theoretical position.

For constructive personality change to occur, it is necessary that these conditions exist and continue over a period of time:

1. Two persons are in psychological contact.

2. The first, whom we shall term the client, is in a state of incongruence, being vulnerable or anxious.

3. The second person, whom we shall term the therapist, is congruent or integrated in the relationship.

4. The therapist experiences unconditional positive regard for the client.

5. The therapist experiences an empathic understanding of the client's internal frame of reference and endeavors to communicate this experience to the client.

6. The communication to the client of the therapist's empathic understanding and unconditional positive regard is to a minimal degree achieved.

No other conditions are necessary. If these six conditions exist, and continue over a period of time, this is sufficient. The process of constructive personality change will follow.

A RELATIONSHIP

The first condition specifies that a minimal relationship, a psychological contact, must exist. I am hypothesizing that significant positive personality change does not occur except in a relationship. This is of course an hypothesis, and it may be disproved.

Conditions 2 through 6 define the characteristics of the relationship which are regarded as essential by defining the necessary characteristics of each person in the relationship. All that is intended by this first condition is to specify that the two people are to some degree in contact, that each makes some perceived difference in the experiential field of the other. Probably it is sufficient if each makes some "subceived" difference, even though the individual may not be consciously aware of this impact. Thus it might be difficult to know whether a catatonic patient perceives a therapist's presence as making a difference to him—a difference of any kind—but it is almost certain that at some organic level he does sense this difference.

Except in such a difficult borderline situation as that just mentioned, it would be relatively easy to define this condition in operational terms and thus determine, from a hard-boiled research point of view, whether the condition does, or does not, exist. The simplest method of determination involves simply the awareness of both client and therapist. If each is aware of being in personal or psychological contact with the other, then this condition is met.

This first condition of therapeutic change is such a simple one that perhaps it should be labeled an assumption or a precondition in order to set it apart from those that follow. Without it, however, the remaining items would have no meaning, and that is the reason for including it.

THE STATE OF THE CLIENT

It was specified that it is necessary that the client be "in a state of incongruence, being vulnerable or anxious." What is the meaning of these terms?

Incongruence is a basic construct in the theory we have been developing. It refers to a discrepancy between the actual experience of the organism and the self picture of the individual insofar as it represents that experience. Thus a student may experience, at a total or organismic level, a fear of the university and of examinations which are given on the third floor of a certain building, since these may demonstrate a fundamental inadequacy in him. Since such a fear of his inadequacy is decidedly at odds with his concept of himself, this experience is represented (distortedly) in his awareness as an unreasonable fear of climbing stairs in this building, or any building, and soon an unreasonable fear of crossing the open campus. Thus there is a fundamental discrepancy between the experienced meaning of the situation as it registers in his organism and the symbolic representation of that experience in awareness in such a way that it does not conflict with the picture he has of himself. In this case to admit a fear of inadequacy would contradict the picture he holds of himself; to admit incomprehensible fears does not contradict his self concept.

Another instance would be the mother who develops vague illnesses whenever her only son makes plans to leave home. The actual desire is to hold on to her only source of satisfaction. To perceive this in awareness would be inconsistent with the picture she holds of herself as a good mother. Illness, however, is consistent with her self concept, and the experience is symbolized in this distorted fashion. Thus again there is a basic incongruence between the self as perceived (in this case as an ill mother needing attention) and the actual experience (in this case the desire to hold on to her son).

When the individual has no awareness of such incongruence in himself, then he is merely vulnerable to the possibility of anxiety and disorganization. Some experience might occur so suddenly or so obviously that the incongruence could not be denied. Therefore, the person is vulnerable to such a possibility.

If the individual dimly perceives such an incongruence in himself, then a tension state occurs which is known as anxiety. The incongruence need not be sharply perceived. It is enough that it is subceived—that is, discriminated as threatening to the self without any awareness of the content of that threat. Such anxiety is often seen in therapy as the individual approaches awareness of some element of his experience which is in sharp contradiction to his self concept.

It is not easy to give precise operational definition to this second of the six conditions, yet to some degree this has been achieved. Several research workers have defined the self concept by means of a Q sort by the individual of a list of self-referent items. This gives us an operational picture of the self. The total experiencing of the individual is more difficult to capture. Chodorkoff (2) has defined it as a Q sort made by a clinician who sorts the same self-referent items independently, basing his sorting on the picture he has obtained of the individual from projective tests. His sort thus includes unconscious as well as conscious elements of the individual's experience, thus representing (in an admittedly imperfect way) the totality of the client's experience. The correlation between these two sortings gives a crude operational measure of incongruence between self and experience, low or negative correlation representing of course a high degree of incongruence.

THE THERAPIST'S GENUINENESS IN THE RELATIONSHIP

The third condition is that the therapist should be, within the confines of this relationship, a congruent, genuine, integrated person. It means that within the relationship he is freely and deeply himself, with his actual experience accurately represented by his awareness of himself. It is the opposite of presenting a facade, either knowingly or unknowingly.

It is not necessary (nor is it possible) that the therapist be a paragon who exhibits this degree of integration, of wholeness, in every aspect of his life. It is sufficient that he is accurately himself in this hour of this relationship, that in this basic sense he is what he actually is, in this moment of time.

It should be clear that this includes being himself even in ways which are not regarded as ideal for psychotherapy. His experience may be "I am afraid of this client" or "My attention is so focused on my own problems that I can scarcely listen to him." If the therapist is not denying these feelings to awareness, but is able freely to be them (as well as being his other feelings), then the condition we have stated is met.

It would take us too far afield to consider the puzzling matter as to the degree to which the therapist overtly communicates this reality in himself to the client. Certainly the aim is not for the therapist to express or talk out his own feelings, but primarily that he should not be deceiving the client as to himself. At times he may need to talk out some of his own feelings (either to the client, or to a colleague or supervisor) if they are standing in the way of the two following conditions.

It is not too difficult to suggest an operational definition for this third condition. We resort again to Q technique. If the therapist sorts a series of items relevant to the relationship (using a list similar to the ones developed by Fiedler [3, 4] and Brown [1]), this will give his perception of his experience in the relationship. If several judges who have observed the interview or listened to a recording of it (or observed a sound movie of it) now sort the same items to represent *their* perception of the relationship, this second sorting should catch those elements of the therapist's behavior and inferred attitudes of which he is unaware, as well as those of which he is aware. Thus a high correlation between the therapist's sort and the observer's sort would represent in crude form an operational definition of the therapist's congruence or integration in the relationship; and a low correlation, the opposite.

UNCONDITIONAL POSITIVE REGARD

To the extent that the therapist finds himself experiencing a warm acceptance of each aspect of the client's experience as being a part of that client, he is experiencing unconditional positive regard. This concept has been developed by Standal (8). It means that there are no *conditions* of acceptance, no feeling of "I like you only *if* you are thus and so." It means a "prizing" of the person, as Dewey has used that term. It is at the opposite pole from a selective evaluating attitude—"You are bad in these ways, good in those." It involves as much feeling of acceptance for the client's expression of negative, "bad," painful, fearful, defensive, abnormal feelings as for his expression of "good," positive, mature, confident, social feelings, as much acceptance of ways in which he is inconsistent as of ways in which he is consistent. It means a caring for the client, but not in a possessive way or in such a way as simply to satisfy the therapist's own needs. It means a caring for the client as a *separate* person, with permission to have his own feelings, his own experiences. One client describes the therapist as "fostering my possession of my own experience . . . that [this] is *my* experience and that I am actually having it: thinking what I think, feeling what I feel, wanting what I want, fearing what I fear: no 'ifs,' 'buts,' or 'not reallys.' " This is the type of acceptance which is hypothesized as being necessary if personality change is to occur.

Like the two previous conditions, this fourth condition is a matter of degree,[3] as immediately becomes apparent if we attempt to define it in terms of specific research operations. One such method of giving it definition would be to consider the Q sort for the relationship as described under Condition 3. To the extent that items expressive of unconditional positive regard are sorted as characteristic of the relationship by both the therapist and the observers, unconditional positive regard might be said to exist. Such items might include statements of this order: "I feel no revulsion at anything the client says"; "I feel neither approval nor disapproval of the client and his statements—simply acceptance"; "I feel warmly toward the client— toward his weaknesses and problems as well as his potentialities"; "I am not inclined to pass judgment on what the client tells me"; "I like the client." To the extent that both therapist and observers perceive these items as characteristic, or their opposites as uncharacteristic, Condition 4 might be said to be met.

EMPATHY

The fifth condition is that the therapist is experiencing an accurate, empathic understanding of the client's awareness of his own experience. To sense the client's private world as if it were your own, but without ever losing the "as if" quality—this is empathy, and this seems essential to therapy. To sense the client's anger, fear, or confusion as if it were your own, yet without your own anger, fear, or confusion getting bound up in it, is the condition we are endeavoring to describe. When the client's world is this clear to the therapist, and he moves about in it freely, then he can both communicate his understanding of what is clearly known to the client

[3] The phrase "unconditional positive regard" may be an unfortunate one, since it sounds like an absolute, an all or nothing dispositional concept. It is probably evident from the description that completely unconditional positive regard would never exist except in theory. From a clinical and experiential point of view I believe that the most accurate statement is that the effective therapist experiences unconditional positive regard for the client during many moments of his contact with him, yet from time to time he experiences only a conditional positive regard— and perhaps at times a negative regard, though this is not likely in effective therapy. It is in this sense that unconditional positive regard exists as a matter of degree in any relationship.

and can also voice meanings in the client's experience of which the client is scarcely aware. As one client described this second aspect: "Every now and again, with me in a tangle of thought and feeling, screwed up in a web of mutually divergent lines of movement, with impulses from different parts of me, and me feeling the feeling of its being all too much and suchlike—then whomp, just like a sunbeam thrusting its way through cloud-banks and tangles of foliage to spread a circle of light on a tangle of forest paths, came some comment from you. [It was] clarity, even disentangle-ment, an additional twist to the picture, a putting in place. Then the con-sequence—the sense of moving on, the relaxation. These were sunbeams." That such penetrating empathy is important for therapy is indicated by Fiedler's research (3) in which items such as the following placed high in the description of relationships created by experienced therapists:

> The therapist is well able to understand the patient's feelings.
> The therapist is never in any doubt about what the patient means.
> The therapist s remarks fit in just right with the patient's mood and content.
> The therapist's tone of voice conveys the complete ability to share the patient's feelings.

An operational definition of the therapist's empathy could be provided in different ways. Use might be made of the Q sort described under Condi-tion 3. To the degree that items descriptive of accurate empathy were sorted as characteristic by both the therapist and the observers, this condi-tion would be regarded as existing.

Another way of defining this condition would be for both client and therapist to sort a list of items descriptive of client feelings. Each would sort independently, the task being to represent the feelings which the client had experienced during a just completed interview. If the correlation be-tween client and therapist sortings were high, accurate empathy would be said to exist, a low correlation indicating the opposite conclusion.

Still another way of measuring empathy would be for trained judges to rate the depth and accuracy of the therapist's empathy on the basis of listen-ing to recorded interviews.

THE CLIENT'S PERCEPTION OF THE THERAPIST

The final condition as stated is that the client perceives, to a minimal degree, the acceptance and empathy which the therapist experiences for him. Unless some communication of these attitudes has been achieved, then such attitudes do not exist in the relationship as far as the client is con-cerned, and the therapeutic process could not, by our hypothesis, be initiated.

Since attitudes cannot be directly perceived, it might be somewhat more accurate to state that therapist behaviors and words are perceived by the client as meaning that to some degree the therapist accepts and understands him.

An operational definition of this condition would not be difficult. The client might, after an interview, sort a Q-sort list of items referring to qualities representing the relationship between himself and the therapist. (The same list could be used as for Condition 3.) If several items descriptive of acceptance and empathy are sorted by the client as characteristic of the relationship, then this condition could be regarded as met. In the present state of our knowledge the meaning of "to a minimal degree" would have to be arbitrary.

SOME COMMENTS

Up to this point the effort has been made to present, briefly and factually, the conditions which I have come to regard as essential for psychotherapeutic change. I have not tried to give the theoretical context of these conditions nor to explain what seem to me to be the dynamics of their effectiveness. Such explanatory material will be available, to the reader who is interested, in the document already mentioned (see footnote 1).

I have, however, given at least one means of defining, in operational terms, each of the conditions mentioned. I have done this in order to stress the fact that I am not speaking of vague qualities which ideally should be present if some other vague result is to occur. I am presenting conditions which are crudely measurable even in the present state of our technology, and have suggested specific operations in each instance even though I am sure that more adequate methods of measurement could be devised by a serious investigator.

My purpose has been to stress the notion that in my opinion we are dealing with an if-then phenomenon in which knowledge of the dynamics is not essential to testing the hypotheses. Thus, to illustrate from another field: if one substance, shown by a series of operations to be the substance known as hydrochloric acid, is mixed with another substance, shown by another series of operations to be sodium hydroxide, then salt and water will be products of this mixture. This is true whether one regards the results as due to magic, or whether one explains it in the most adequate terms of modern chemical theory. In the same way it is being postulated here that certain definable conditions precede certain definable changes and that this fact exists independently of our efforts to account for it.

The Resulting Hypotheses

The major value of stating any theory in unequivocal terms is that specific hypotheses may be drawn from it which are capable of proof or disproof. Thus, even if the conditions which have been postulated as necessary and sufficient conditions are more incorrect than correct (which I hope they are not), they could still advance science in this field by providing a base of operations from which fact could be winnowed out from error.

The hypotheses which would follow from the theory given would be of this order:

If these six conditions (as operationally defined) exist, then constructive personality change (as defined) will occur in the client.

If one or more of these conditions is not present, constructive personality change will not occur.

These hypotheses hold in any situation whether it is or is not labeled "psychotherapy."

Only Condition 1 is dichotomous (it either is present or is not), and the remaining five occur in varying degree, each on its continuum. Since this is true, another hypothesis follows, and it is likely that this would be the simplest to test:

If all six conditions are present, then the greater the degree to which Conditions 2 to 6 exist, the more marked will be the constructive personality change in the client.

At the present time the above hypothesis can only be stated in this general form—which implies that all of the conditions have equal weight. Empirical studies will no doubt make possible much more refinement of this hypothesis. It may be, for example, that if anxiety is high in the client, then the other conditions are less important. Or if unconditional positive regard is high (as in a mother's love for her child), then perhaps a modest degree of empathy is sufficient. But at the moment we can only speculate on such possibilities.

Some Implications

SIGNIFICANT OMISSIONS

If there is any startling feature in the formulation which has been given as to the necessary conditions for therapy, it probably lies in the elements which are omitted. In present-day clinical practice, therapists operate as though there were many other conditions in addition to those described, which are essential for psychotherapy. To point this up it may be well to mention a few of the conditions which, after thoughtful consideration of our research and our experience, are not included.

For example, it is *not* stated that these conditions apply to one type of client, and that other conditions are necessary to bring about psychotherapeutic change with other types of client. Probably no idea is so prevalent in clinical work today as that one works with neurotics in one way, with psychotics in another; that certain therapeutic conditions must be provided for compulsives, others for homosexuals, etc. Because of this heavy weight of clinical opinion to the contrary, it is with some "fear and trembling" that I advance the concept that the essential conditions of psychotherapy exist in a single configuration, even though the client or patient may use them very differently.[4]

It is *not* stated that these six conditions are the essential conditions for client-centered therapy, and that other conditions are essential for other types of psychotherapy. I certainly am heavily influenced by my own experience, and that experience has led me to a viewpoint which is termed "client centered." Nevertheless my aim in stating this theory is to state the conditions which apply to *any* situation in which constructive personality change occurs, whether we are thinking of classical psychoanalysis, or any of its modern offshoots, or Adlerian psychotherapy, or any other. It will be obvious then that in my judgment much of what is considered to be essential would not be found, empirically, to be essential. Testing of some of the stated hypotheses would throw light on this perplexing issue. We may of course find that various therapies produce various types of personality change, and that for each psychotherapy a separate set of conditions is necessary. Until and unless this is demonstrated, I am hypothesizing that effective psychotherapy of any sort produces similar changes

---

[4] I cling to this statement of my hypothesis even though it is challenged by a just completed study by Kirtner (5). Kirtner has found, in a group of 26 cases from the Counseling Center at the University of Chicago, that there are sharp differences in the client's mode of approach to the resolution of life difficulties, and that these differences are related to success in psychotherapy. Briefly, the client who sees his problem as involving his relationships, and who feels that he contributes to this problem and wants to change it, is likely to be successful. The client who externalizes his problem, feeling little self-responsibility, is much more likely to be a failure. Thus the implication is that some other conditions need to be provided for psychotherapy with this group. For the present, however, I will stand by my hypothesis as given, until Kirtner's study is confirmed, and until we know an alternative hypothesis to take its place.

in personality and behavior, and that a single set of preconditions is necessary.

It is *not* stated that psychotherapy is a special kind of relationship, different in kind from all others which occur in everyday life. It will be evident instead that for brief moments, at least, many good friendships fulfill the six conditions. Usually this is only momentarily, however, and then empathy falters, the positive regard becomes conditional, or the congruence of the "therapist" friend becomes overlaid by some degree of facade or defensiveness. Thus the therapeutic relationship is seen as a heightening of the constructive qualities which often exist in part in other relationships, and an extension through time of qualities which in other relationships tend at best to be momentary.

It is *not* stated that special intellectual professional knowledge—psychological, psychiatric, medical, or religious—is required of the therapist. Conditions 3, 4, and 5, which apply especially to the therapist, are qualities of experience, not intellectual information. If they are to be acquired, they must in my opinion, be acquired through an experiential training—which may be, but usually is not, a part of professional training. It troubles me to hold such a radical point of view, but I can draw no other conclusion from my experience. Intellectual training and the acquiring of information has, I believe, many valuable results—but becoming a therapist is not one of those results.

It is *not* stated that it is necessary for psychotherapy that the therapist have an accurate psychological diagnosis of the client. Here too it troubles me to hold a viewpoint so at variance with my clinical colleagues. When one thinks of the vast proportion of time spent in any psychological, psychiatric, or mental hygiene center on the exhaustive psychological evaluation of the client or patient, it seems as though this *must* serve a useful purpose insofar as psychotherapy is concerned. Yet the more I have observed therapists, and the more closely I have studied research such as that done by Fiedler and others (4), the more I am forced to the conclusion that such diagnostic knowledge is not essential to psychotherapy.[5] It may even be that its defense as a necessary prelude to psychotherapy is simply a protective alternative to the admission that it is, for the most part, a colossal waste of time. There is only one useful purpose I have been able to observe which relates to psychotherapy. Some therapists cannot feel secure in the relation-

[5] There is no intent here to miantain that diagnostic evaluation is useless. We have ourselves made heavy use of such methods in our research studies of change in personality. It is its usefulness as a precondition to psychotherapy which is questioned.

ship with the client unless they possess such diagnostic knowledge. Without it they feel fearful of him, unable to be empathic, unable to experience unconditional regard, finding it necessary to put up a pretense in the relationship. If they know in *advance* of suicidal impulses they can somehow be more acceptant of them. Thus, for some therapists, the security they perceive in diagnostic information may be a basis for permitting themselves to be integrated in the relationship, and to experience empathy and full acceptance. In these instances a psychological diagnosis would certainly be justified as adding to the comfort and hence the effectiveness of the therapist. But even here it does not appear to be a basic precondition for psychotherapy.[6]

Perhaps I have given enough illustrations to indicate that the conditions I have hypothesized as necessary and sufficient for psychotherapy are striking and unusual primarily by virtue of what they omit. If we were to determine, by a survey of the behaviors of therapists, those hypotheses which they appear to regard as necessary to psychotherapy, the list would be a great deal longer and more complex.

IS THIS THEORETICAL FORMULATION USEFUL?

Aside from the personal satisfaction it gives as a venture in abstraction and generalization, what is the value of a theoretical statement such as has been offered in this paper? I should like to spell out more fully the usefulness which I believe it may have.

In the field of research it may give both direction and impetus to investigation. Since it sees the conditions of constructive personality change as general, it greatly broadens the opportunities for study. Psychotherapy is not the only situation aimed at constructive personality change. Programs of training for leadership in industry and programs of training for military leadership often aim at such change. Educational institutions or programs frequently aim at development of character and personality as well as at intellectual skills. Community agencies aim at personality and behavioral change in delinquents and criminals. Such programs would provide an opportunity for the broad testing of the hypotheses offered. If it is found that constructive personality change occurs in such programs when the

[6] In a facetious moment I have suggested that such therapists might be made equally comfortable by being given the diagnosis of some other individual, not of this patient or client. The fact that the diagnosis proved inaccurate as psychotherapy continued would not be particularly disturbing, because one always expects to find inaccuracies in the diagnosis as one works with the individual.

hypothesized conditions are not fulfilled, then the theory would have to be revised. If however the hypotheses are upheld, then the results, both for the planning of such programs and for our knowledge of human dynamics, would be significant. In the field of psychotherapy itself, the application of consistent hypotheses to the work of various schools of therapists may prove highly profitable. Again the disproof of the hypotheses offered would be as important as their confirmation, either result adding significantly to our knowledge.

For the practice of psychotherapy the theory also offers significant problems for consideration. One of its implications is that the techniques of the various therapies are relatively unimportant except to the extent that they serve as channels for fulfilling one of the conditions. In client-centered therapy, for example, the technique of "reflecting feelings" has been described and commented on (6, pp. 26–36). In terms of the theory here being presented, this technique is by no means an essential condition of therapy. To the extent, however, that it provides a channel by which the therapist communicates a sensitive empathy and an unconditional positive regard, then it may serve as a technical channel by which the essential conditions of therapy are fulfilled. In the same way, the theory I have presented would see no essential value to therapy of such techniques as interpretation of personality dynamics, free association, analysis of dreams, analysis of the transference, hypnosis, interpretation of life style, suggestion, and the like. Each of these techniques may, however, become a channel for communicating the essential conditions which have been formulated. An interpretation may be given in a way which communicates the unconditional positive regard of the therapist. A stream of free association may be listened to in a way which communicates an empathy which the therapist is experiencing. In the handling of the transference an effective therapist often communicates his own wholeness and congruence in the relationship. Similarly for the other techniques. But just as these techniques *may* communicate the elements which are essential for therapy, so any one of them may communicate attitudes and experiences sharply contradictory to the hypothesized conditions of therapy. Feeling may be "reflected" in a way which communicates the therapist's lack of empathy. Interpretations may be rendered in a way which indicates the highly conditional regard of the therapist. Any of the techniques may communicate the fact that the therapist is expressing one attitude at a surface level, and another contradictory attitude which is denied to his own awareness. Thus one value of such a theoretical formulation as we have offered is that it may assist therapists to think more critically about those elements of their experience, attitudes, and behaviors which are essential to psychotherapy, and those which are nonessential or even deleterious to psychotherapy.

Finally, in those programs—educational, correctional, military, or industrial—which aim toward constructive changes in the personality structure and behavior of the individual, this formulation may serve as a very tentative criterion against which to measure the program. Until it is much further tested by research, it cannot be thought of as a valid criterion, but, as in the field of psychotherapy, it may help to stimulate critical analysis and the formulation of alternative conditions and alternative hypotheses.

Summary

Drawing from a larger theoretical context, six conditions are postulated as necessary and sufficient conditions for the initiation of a process of constructive personality change. A brief explanation is given of each condition, and suggestions are made as to how each may be operationally defined for research purposes. The implications of this theory for research, for psychotherapy, and for educational and training programs aimed at constructive personality change, are indicated. It is pointed out that many of the conditions which are commonly regarded as necessary to psychotherapy are, in terms of this theory, nonessential.

REFERENCES

1. Brown, O. H. An investigation of therapeutic relationship in client-centered therapy. Unpublished doctor's dissertation, Univer. of Chicago, 1954.
2. Chodorkoff, B. Self-perception, perceptual defense, and adjustment. *J. abnorm. soc. Psychol.*, 1954, 49, 508–512.
3. Fiedler, F. E. A comparison of therapeutic relationships in psychoanalytic, non-directive and Adlerian therapy. *J. consult. Psychol.*, 1950, 14, 436–445.
4. Fiedler, F. E. Quantitative studies on the role of therapists' feelings toward their patients. In O. H. Mowrer (Ed.), *Psychotherapy: theory and research.* New York: Ronald, 1953.
5. Kirtner, W. L. Success and failure in client-centered therapy as a function of personality variables. Unpublished master's thesis, Univer. of Chicago, 1955.
6. Rogers, C. R. *Client-centered therapy.* Boston: Houghton Mifflin, 1951.
7. Rogers, C. R., and Dymond, Rosalind F. (Eds.) *Psychotherapy and personality change.* Chicago: Univer. of Chicago Press, 1954.
8. Standal, S. The need for positive regard: a contribution to client-centered theory. Unpublished doctor's dissertation, Univer. of Chicago, 1954.

PAUL HENRY MUSSEN
University of California
MARY COVER JONES
University of California

28 · THE BEHAVIOR-INFERRED MOTIVATIONS OF LATE- AND EARLY-MATURING BOYS

● A number of studies indicate that the adolescent's physical status, mediated by the sociopsychological environment, may exert profound and lasting influences on his personality (4, 5, 6). In our culture, physically retarded adolescent boys are in a disadvantageous competitive position in athletic activities and are likely to be regarded and treated as immature by both adults and peers (5). Hence, they are more likely than their physically accelerated peers to be personally and socially maladjusted during adolescence. Analysis of the TAT responses of early- and late-maturing boys about 17 years of age, subjects in the Adolescent Growth Study (2, 3), revealed that significantly more of the latter group had negative self-concepts, profound feelings of rejection by others, strong affiliative needs (especially for heterosexual affiliation), prolonged dependency needs, and rebellious attitudes toward parents. The psychological picture of the physically accelerated boys, on the other hand, seemed to be much more favorable. As a group, they appeared to have acquired more self-confidence, were less dependent and in need of help, and were more capable of playing an adult male role in interpersonal relations. Contrary to what had been predicted, the two groups did not differ in needs for achievement and recognition, and there was some evidence that early-maturers had stronger aggressive needs than late-maturers (6).

The motives reflected in fantasy productions are presumably covert and

Child Development, 29:61–67, 1958. Used by permission of the senior author and The Society for Research in Child Development, Inc.

not readily apparent in ordinary manifest behavior. It has been demonstrated that, in many cases, manifest behavior and fantasy may be independent or even negatively related (7, 8). Hence, inferences about motivation based on the individual's overt behavior may be quite different from those made on the basis of his fantasy productions.

In the present study, we shall examine the *behavior*-inferred ratings of motivation assigned to early- and late-maturing boys. Under Else Frenkel-Brunswik's direction, almost all subjects in the Adolescent Growth Study were rated on nine drives about a year after they had graduated from high school (1). The strength of each drive was inferred from behavior observed in a wide variety of situations. " 'Intuitive' judgments about motivational tendencies were obtained in the form of standardized ratings from a number of judges well acquainted with the adolescents" (1, p. 134).

The nine drives, selected from Murray's list of needs, were briefly described as follows:

1. *Drive for Autonomy. Striving for independence and freedom;* desire to be free from social ties, to shake off influence, coercion, and restraint; relatively little care for conventions and group ideology; tendency to act as one pleases.

2. *Drive for Social Ties, Social Acceptance. Desire to be generally well-liked;* to conform to custom, to join groups, to live sociably, to be accepted by a group in any form, to make contacts.

3. *Drive for Achievement. Desire to attain a high standard of objective accomplishments;* to increase self-regard by successful exercise of talent, to select hard tasks; high aspiration level. (Rating scale starts from "no desire to accomplish something outstanding" and ends with "excessive demands on himself.")

4. *Drive for Recognition. Desire to excite praise and commendation, to demand respect, social approval and prestige, honors and fame.*

5. *Drive for Abasement. Tendency to self-depreciation, self-blame or belittlement;* to submit passively to external forces, to accept injury, blame, criticism, punishment; tendency to become resigned to fate, to admit inferiority and defeat, to confess, to seek punishment and misfortune; masochistic tendency.

6. *Drive for Aggression. Desire to deprive others* by belittling, attacking, ridiculing, depreciating.

7. *Drive for Succorance. Desire for support from outside;* from people, institutions, or supernatural agencies.

8. *Drive for Control (Dominance). Desire to control one's human environment,* by suggestion, by persuasion or command.

9. *Drive for Escape. Tendency to escape all unpleasant situations;* to avoid blame, hardship, etc., to project own failures on others or

on circumstances; to gain immediate pleasure with inability to postpone pleasure; use of fantasy, etc. (1, pp. 141–142).

"The rating scale was used as a means of summarizing what the judges 'privately' think, or what their hypothesis was, about each subject, or what they otherwise would have used only in writing up an interpretative case study of individuals whom they observed over a long period of time" (1, p. 144). "Though ultimately referred to observed behavior, reference to the underlying motivations was established as the result of a complex process of inference utilizing more subtle indirect cues together with gross features of behavior" (1, p. 261).

Since the drive ratings were found to be significantly correlated with many ratings of social responses and personality traits, Frenkel-Brunswik concluded that they "helped to organize the . . . data on overt behavior observed in social situations" (1, p. 261). "One drive variable [may circumscribe] a family of alternative [behavioral] manifestations unrelated to each other. The meaning of the drive concept emerges in terms of families of divergent manifestations held together dynamically or genotypically, though often not phenotypically" (1, p. 262).

In view of the interrelationships discovered, it may be assumed that these drive ratings refer to "a level of personality which stands behind the surface of overtly displayed social techniques" (1, p. 144), but which is probably not generally as remote from behavior as drives reflected in responses to projective tests. Comparison of late- and early-maturers' motivational ratings may, therefore, provide additional information about the factors underlying behavioral differences between the two groups. The objective meanings of these ratings may be derived from examination of the variables significantly correlated with them.

Subjects and Procedure

The 34 subjects of this study, part of a normal sample of 90 boys who were members of the Adolescent Growth Study (2, 3), were drawn from the two extremes of a distribution of rate of physical maturing. Sixteen of them had been among the most consistently accelerated throughout the adolescent period; the other 18 had been among the most consistently retarded.[1]

Three members of the Adolescent Growth Study staff who were well

---

[1] The present sample includes all those subjects among the 19 most consistently accelerated and 19 most consistently retarded boys in the Adolescent Growth Study who were assigned motivational ratings. Twenty-nine of them were also in Jones and Bayley's (5) group and 31 in Mussen and Jones' (6).

acquainted with the subjects over a period of years served as judges. They independently rated each subject on each of the nine drives listed above. In making the ratings, the judges were asked "to forget about manifest behavior and to group the children according to assumed motivation rather than according to similarities of displayed techniques" (1, p. 139).

Each drive was rated on a five-point scale, a rating of one representing the highest degree, a rating of five representing almost complete absence of the drive in question. In the present study, the three judges' ratings on each drive were averaged to obtain the individual's motivational rating.[2]

Results

Frequency distributions of the ratings of all subjects were made for all the drives. Each distribution was then dichotomized at the point which most nearly enabled the placing of half of the 34 subjects above, and half of them below, the dividing point. Subjects having scores above this point were considered *high* in this particular drive; those with scores below this point were considered *low* in it. Chi square tests were used to ascertain whether or not high ratings in certain drives were more characteristic of one group (late- or early-maturers) than of the other.

Table 1 shows the number of late- and early-maturers with high ratings in each of the drives, the chi square values obtained, and the levels of significance.

As the table shows, the two groups were significantly different in two of the nine drives. A greater proportion of late- than of early-maturing boys were rated high in *Drive for Social Ties; Social Acceptance* and *Drive for Aggression.*

While these drives overlap to some extent, they are by no means identical. The correlation between them, based on the entire Adolescent Growth Study male population, was .48 (1). It should be noted, however, that the early- and late-maturing groups did *not* differ significantly in other drives (*Drives for Recognition, Control,* and *Escape*) that were even more highly correlated with *Drive for Aggression* and/or *Drive for Social Ties* in the entire sample of adolescent boys (1).

It is of course possible that the independent (physical status) and dependent (motivational ratings) variables were not completely inde-

---

[2] The interrater agreements on the nine drive ratings assigned to all the subjects of the Adolescent Growth Study are fully reported by Frenkel-Brunswik. The average reliabilities, corrected by means of the Spearman-Brown formula, were between .70 and .80, with the exceptions of those for Autonomy and Succorance which were .55 and .63 respectively (1, p. 100).

Table 1. Number of Early- and Late-Maturers Assigned High Drive Ratings

Drive	Number rated high		Chi square	P
	Early-maturers $(N = 16)$	Late-maturers $(N = 18)$		
1. Autonomy	7	10	.47	ns
2. Social ties	6	13	4.37	.02–.05
3. Achievement . . .	10	9	.53	ns
4. Recognition	7	9	.15	ns
5. Abasement	9	8	.47	ns
6. Aggression	5	12	4.27	.02–.05
7. Succorance	5	9	1.30	ns
8. Control	9	9	.13	ns
9. Escape	9	11	.09	ns

pendent, i.e., that in evaluating underlying drives the judges were influenced by their own impressions of the subject's rate of physical maturation. However, it seems unlikely that this factor had any significant effects, since the judges were specifically instructed to rate "assumed motivations" rather than more superficial characteristics. Moreover, if the judges had been considerably influenced by the subjects' rates of maturation, the two groups might be expected to differ significantly on more than two of the nine drive ratings.

Discussion

The finding that late-maturers appear to have relatively high motivation for social affiliation and social acceptance is entirely consistent with Jones and Bayley's data which showed that observers rated these boys as higher in sociability, social initiative and eagerness (5). Moreover, the TAT protocols of the late-maturers revealed that these boys have strong needs for affiliation, particularly with the opposite sex (6).

On the basis of evidence reported in earlier studies, it has been hypothesized that the late-maturers' emphasis on social activity and their social initiative and participation are largely of an attention-getting, compensatory nature (5, 6). Examination of the overt social behavior and personality trait variables correlated with *Drive for Social Acceptance* lends support to this hypothesis. For example, high ratings in this drive tended to be associated with high ratings in *energy output, interest in opposite sex, social participation, social self-confidence, social stimulus value, popularity, self-assertiveness* (bossiness), *exuberance, orientation toward the opposite sex*[3] (1). These are characteristics which indicate expressiveness, energy, eagerness and sociability, a constellation labelled "overt social activity" by Frenkel-Brunswik. At the same time, however, high *drive for social ties* was associated with many traits considered to be indicative of emotional maladjustment: *attention-seeking, affectation, dependence on approval, excitedness, tenseness, impulsiveness,* and *exploitiveness* (1). Hence, it may be inferred that, while late-maturers often reveal high motivation for social affiliation and a great deal of social activity, their social techniques are often childish and affected. Moreover, their high social drives may be based on general insecurity (reflected in *tenseness* and *impulsiveness*) and basic feelings of dependency (indicated by *dependence on others* and *exploitiveness*). The last conclusion is consistent with the finding that the TAT protocols of late-maturers revealed strong underlying dependency needs (6).

The relatively high aggressive motivation ratings assigned to the late-maturers may also be attributed, at least in part, to their basic insecurities, feelings of rejection, and intense dependency needs. Frenkel-Brunswik's data showed that *Drive for Aggression* had considerably higher correlations with emotionally maladjusted behavior than with "overt social activity." Among the manifestations of the latter, only four (*energy output, interest in opposite sex, social participation,* and *social self-confidence*) were significantly correlated with *Drive for Aggression.* On the other hand, 10 indicators of emotional maladjustment (*attention-seeking, affectation, dependence on approval, excitedness, tenseness, impulsiveness, frequent mood swings, selfishness, irresponsibility,* and *exploitiveness*) were associated with high ratings in aggressive motivation. Apparently, the personal and social maladjustments of the late-maturers are often reflected in overt behavior which trained observers are likely to interpret as stemming from strong underlying aggressive motivations.

This finding is particularly interesting in view of the fact that late-maturers had relatively *low* fantasy (TAT) aggression scores, while the early-maturers had *high* scores in this variable (6). The present data do not enable us to specify the determinants of this discrepancy between behavior-inferred aggressive ratings and TAT aggression scores. Some of it may be due to the middle-class status of most of our subjects. It has been suggested that in this social class cultural prohibitions prevent the overt gratification of aggressive needs and thereby increase their intensity in the

---

[3] The correlations between the drive ratings and social behavior are fully reported in Frenkel-Brunswik's monograph (1, p. 186–7).

individual's fantasies (7, 8). If this is true, it may be hypothesized that the early-maturers, having identified with a mature male role, have incorporated these prohibitions and are less likely to behave aggressively. As a result, they are more likely to express their aggressive motivations in fantasy. On the other hand, the late-maturers, being defiant of authority (6), may not accept the middle-class standards of behavior so readily. Consequently, they may express aggression more freely and overtly and, therefore, may reveal less aggressive motivation in their fantasy productions.

It may be concluded that these group differences in motivational ratings add further support to the general hypothesis that the late-maturing adolescent is more likely to be personally and socially maladjusted than his early-maturing peer. Apparently in our culture, the physically retarded boy is more likely to encounter a sociopsychological environment which may have adverse effects on his personality development. The early-maturer's experiences, on the other hand, seem to be more conducive to good psychological adjustment.

Summary

In this investigation, observers' ratings of 18 late-maturing and 16 early-maturing adolescent boys on nine drives were compared. The results showed that high drives for social acceptance and for aggression are more characteristic of the physically retarded than of the physically accelerated.

The meaning of group differences in these ratings may be clarified by examination of the social behavior and personality correlates of the two drives. These suggest that the late-maturer's high social drives may stem from feelings of insecurity and dependence and are often manifested in childish, affected, attention-getting social techniques. Moreover, high aggressive drives tended to be associated with social behavior and personality characteristics indicative of social and emotional maladjustment. Thus, among the physically retarded, the strength of these drives may be partially attributable to underlying feelings of inadequacy, rejection, and dependence.

In general, the data of this investigation support the findings of earlier studies which showed that, among boys, physical retardation may have adverse effects on personality. Physical acceleration, on the other hand, may be conducive to better social and psychological adjustment.

REFERENCES

1. Frenkel-Brunswik, Else. Motivation and behavior. *Genet. Psychol. Monogr.*, 1942, 26, 121–165.

2. Jones, H. E. Observational methods in the study of individual development. *J. Consult. Psychol.*, 1940, 4, 234–238.

3. Jones, H. E. *Development in Adolescence.* New York: Appleton-Century, 1943.

4. Jones, M. C. The later careers of boys who were early- or late-maturing. *Child Develpm.*, 1957, 28, 113–128.

5. Jones, M. C., and Bayley, N. Physical maturing among boys as related to behavior. *J. Educ. Psychol.*, 1950, 41, 129–148.

6. Mussen, P. H., and Jones, M. C. Self-conceptions, motivations, and interpersonal attitudes of late- and early-maturing boys. *Child Develpm.*, 1957, 28, 243–256.

7. Mussen, P. H., and Naylor, H. K. The relationship between overt and fantasy aggression. *J. Abnorm. Soc. Psychol.*, 1954, 49, 235–240.

8. Sanford, R. N., Adkins, N. M., Miller, R. B., Cobb, E. A., *et al.* Physique, personality, and scholarship: a cooperative study of school children. *Monogr. Soc. Res. Child Develpm.*, 1943, 8, No. 1.

THE CHILD
AS A LEARNER

• Both of the selections included in this section appear to emphasize one very important fact. That is, children learn their behaviors and attitudes from the adults with whom they are in contact. While parents are of primary importance in this respect, the role which teachers play in influencing youngsters is also of tremendous importance. This is of much interest to us (the editors). It is our opinion that teacher-preparing institutions should manifest much more concern about teachers' ineptness in assessing the impact which they make as persons upon their students. The fact that teachers influence youngsters is indisputable; the fact that most of them are unaware of the effect and nature of this influence needs to be remedied. It is almost axiomatic that what a teacher is and what he does is often more important than what he says.

No amount of talking can possibly have much influence if actions and feelings have already disqualified the communication for those who are supposed to listen, attend, and absorb. It is sobering for most people to learn of their inability to hide their feelings from others. The psychological climate of a classroom is often sensed by students with an accuracy that would be astounding to the teacher who played the major part in its generation. Because of this transparency, the basic or causal aspects of teacher attitudes must be of concern to education in general and to teachers specifically.

The maintenance of effective interpersonal relationships is so important to teaching that it can almost be said that good teaching is essentially good teacher-student interaction. The need for communication and the need for respect emphasized by Riessman are facets of this relationship. How teachers see themselves and their students has much to do with it. If they view their role as contributing and not receiving, if they see their position as restricted and static, and if they look upon what they do as a job rather than an opportunity, they will communicate this attitude despite efforts to conceal their feelings. If, on the other hand, they are able to perceive each youngster's uniqueness as an opportunity for a new experience in human relationships, and if they can see themselves as learning and growing along with their students, they will communicate respect and acceptance. In teaching as well as in other types of interpersonal relationships, one must look at himself first to see whether what he is inhibits or promotes what he is trying to accomplish. Perhaps it is too innovative and too threatening to the traditional concept of teaching, but one day soon teachers are going to have to enter the process of "growing and becoming" with their students. They are going to have to learn to use youngsters as sources of feedback on the effectiveness of the relationships they maintain. They are going to have to ask with sincerity and with a lack of defensiveness: "How am I doing and how can I do better?"

MAYA PINES
Free-Lance Writer

29 · HOW THREE-YEAR-OLDS TEACH THEMSELVES TO READ—and LOVE IT

• Sitting alone in a bare cubicle, a little girl of five happily pecks away at a specially designed automated typewriter and composes a poem. A two-and-a-half-year-old teaches herself to read and write by banging the jam-proof keys of a similar "talking typewriter." Along with several dozen other youngsters, they are taking part in a series of experiments which may have loud repercussions and a surprisingly humanistic effect on education as a whole. The project is the brainchild of a Yale sociologist, Dr. Omar Khayyam Moore.

He believes that the years from two to five are the most creative and intellectually active period of our lives. This is when children first acquire speech and begin to classify their environment. Normally they receive no schooling at this time. And certainly they should not be stuffed with rules and facts. But—says Dr. Moore—they are capable of extraordinary feats of inductive reasoning if left to themselves in a properly "responsive" environment. Furthermore, performing such feats may become a habit and lead to a new breed of highly individualistic, highly imaginative human beings far better prepared than their parents to cope with a complex and unpredictable society.

To Professor Moore—himself highly individualistic and imaginative at forty-three—this is the significance of his "Responsive Environments Laboratory." A man of medium height, with close-cropped hair and deep-set expressive eyes, he is now on sabbatical from his associate professor's post

Harper's Magazine, 226 (No. 1356):58–64, May, 1963. Copyright © 1963, by Harper's Magazine, Inc. Reprinted by permission of the author.

at Yale. He spends most of his time at Hamden Hall Country Day School, a small private school near New Haven, Connecticut. In his laboratory, which is supported by the Carnegie Corporation of New York, Hamden Hall's pupils learn to read, write, type, take dictation, and compose their own stories before they enter first grade. To Dr. Moore this accomplishment is just a happy by-product of his extensive research on culture, learning theory, and "human higher-order problem solving" behavior.

The children who come to his Lab spend no more than half an hour a day there. They may stay away if they wish, or leave after only a few minutes. While the child is in the Lab he is free of all outside pressures. His parents never come in with him and are never told how he is doing. Even his regular teachers, to whom he may be emotionally attached, stay out of the picture. Staff members themselves—half a dozen young wives of Yale graduate students—try to be as impersonal as possible.

The "talking typewriter" consists of a standard-size typewriter keyboard with colored keys, a small speaker, an exhibitor (a frame on which printed matter can be displayed) with a red pointer, a projector which resembles a miniature TV screen, and dictation equipment. Blank paper in the typewriter stands ready to take anything the child types, in jumbo type. There is nothing in the soundproof, air-conditioned booth to distract the child's attention from the machine. Only the keyboard is accessible to the child; all the other gadgets are enclosed in plexiglass or in a wooden cabinet behind the typewriter.

The child discovers immediately that this interesting, adult-looking typewriter is his to play with on his own initiative. The younger the child, the more joyous his response.

The game begins when he presses a key. At once a large letter, number, or punctuation mark appears on the paper, and a soft voice names it through the loudspeaker. The same things happen no matter what part of the keyboard he strikes, as rapidly and as often as he desires. (To test his new-found powers, one two-year-old gleefully struck the asterisk key seventy-five times in succession.)

Joyous Discoveries

When the teacher who has been watching through a one-way mirror sees that the child's interest is waning, she switches a control dial. A curtain lifts over the exhibitor and a red arrow points to a single letter. At the same time the machine's voice names it. Puzzled, the child may try to depress a key, but to his surprise it doesn't work. He tries more and more keys, until he finds the right one. Then the key goes down and prints the letter while the voice names it again. As a new letter pops up on the exhibitor, the child faces an exciting puzzle, a game of "try and find me." Every time a number, letter, or punctuation mark appears on the exhibitor, he hunts for it amid the blocked keys until he hits the jackpot.

From stage to stage, the rules of the game keep being changed for the child, who must constantly adapt himself to fresh situations.

Meanwhile he is learning to touch-type without effort. Each set of keys to be struck by a particular finger has its own identifying color, and the group meant for the right hand responds to a slightly different pressure from that meant for the left. He is also learning to recognize different styles and sizes of type as they appear on the exhibitor, and handwritten letters which may be flashed on the projector's screen.

About once a week the child plays with a blackboard and chalk in a booth which has little automated equipment. (Only one "talking typewriter" is fully automated at present, and the children are assigned to booths at random.) Under ordinary circumstances, when you give a child a piece of chalk, he will scribble or draw pictures. But there are horizontal lines on this blackboard which discourage art work, and eventually the child tries to make letters. At this point, the teacher helps by putting a letter on the projector and suggesting that he draw one like it. Soon the child learns to write the letters he has begun to read and type.

The teacher's role depends on the degree of automation in the booths. Sometimes she takes over the machine's voice part, speaking as gently and patiently as the "talking typewriter." Sometimes she operates the exhibitor by hand. When using the fully automated booth, she merely watches the child through a one-way mirror and comes to his rescue if he raises his hand for help. This may happen if the machine gets stuck (until now the Lab has had only an experimental model to work with) or if the child needs a handkerchief or human company.

As the child advances he finds that the exhibitor suddenly shows him a series of letters, such as "CAT." By now he may be able to pick out a "T" right away, but when he tries this the key is blocked. "A" is blocked, too. When he strikes "C" however, the machine responds by typing it and saying, "C." The exhibitor's red arrow, which had been pointing to "C," then moves to the right over "A." As he strikes all three keys in the proper sequence, the machine prints them, names them one by one, and then says, "Cat." From now on, letters appear only in series—but to the child they are still letters, not words. Then one day, although no one has been "teaching" him, the child suddenly realizes that the letters he knows so well determine words. Overwhelmed by the revelation he is likely to run out of the booth ecstatically—a reaction the Lab has witnessed over and over again.

This joy in discovery, Professor Moore believes, is sadly lacking in most methods of early childhood education. "By the time a child is three, he has achieved what is probably the most complex and difficult task of his lifetime—he has learned to speak," he points out. "Nobody has instructed him in this skill; he has had to develop it unaided. In bilingual or multilingual communities, children pick up several languages without accent at a very early age. There's plenty of information-processing ability in a mind that can do that."

I visited his "Responsive Environments Laboratory" a few weeks ago. It is a modest, green, prefabricated structure with a narrow corridor, five cubicles with "talking typewriters" in various stages of automation, and a few offices.

At 8:30 in the morning I watched a very small girl enter the building, trailed by a few slightly older children. After being helped to remove her coat and muffler, she walked over to a long table on which stood open jars of bright-colored paints and let a teacher paint her fingernails different colors, to match the color code on the typewriter keys. Then she went into the automated booth and sat down at a chair facing the typewriter. First she pressed the carriage-return key a couple of times, seeming satisfied with the noise it made and the voice which said, each time, "carriage return." Then she banged on "C" and listened to the machine's response, "C." For a while she hummed a tune. Next she fiddled with a side lever. Finally she began to type a few letters rapidly, glancing up at the characters she produced and alert to the voice which came from the loudspeaker. After eighteen minutes in the booth, she suddenly raised her hand. A teacher came in to help her off the chair. "Bye-bye," said the little girl, and walked out.

She was exactly two years and eight months old. In less than two months she had taught herself all the letters in the alphabet, both upper and lower case, and could also write some of them on the blackboard.

Most children pay little attention to the adults in the Lab—they are too fascinated by the machine. The only exceptions are some older ones who have learned to be careful before they start work at the Lab. Thus one newcomer, a little boy of six, would go into his booth and hesitantly press a few keys, then run out to ask the teacher, "Am I doing it right?" He could not get used to the idea that *anything* he did was all right.

Watching the children in the nursery group, mostly four-year-olds, I saw that several who had been in the Lab no more than four months were writing full sentences.

"Barry is a RAT," one little boy typed in complete, silent concentration. He had ranged all over the keyboard, typed the numbers from 16 to 20 in proper sequence, played with the quotation marks, and written several nonsense words before producing his gem, to which he suddenly added, "and a cat." He was using correct fingering technique. Later on, checking his records, Professor Moore told me that while the boy was bright, he did not test in the "gifted" range, which begins above an IQ of 140. He did have one incalculable advantage however: permissive parents who laid heavy emphasis on intellectual skills, thus giving him much to relate to what he learned in the Lab.

Because of their individual differences, I found it hard to gauge the progress of the kindergarteners, the next group, who had been in the Lab for a year and four months. But the first-graders were impressive. Two of them—aged six—were busy in one of the offices editing a newspaper which they and a few classmates had dictated into the tape recorder and then typed. It contained little stories, poetry, and riddles: "Why is grass like a mouse?—Answer: because the cat'll eat it (cattle)." One poem by a girl of five was entitled "A Duck" and read as follows:

There was a duck,   He could run in a race,
Who could kick.   He would win.
He had good luck,   He would get some lace
Because he was quick.   And a magic pin.

When I met the pint-sized poet she was engrossed in her daily session with the "talking typewriter." From the projector she fluently read a story about Aladdin's lamp. Then she questioned the teacher about the plot and answered the teacher's questions about the meaning of certain words and the story. When she came out of the booth, she sat down with me in an empty office. I asked her whether she wanted to be a poet when she grew up. "No," she replied without hesitation, "I want to be a housewife." Writing poetry was fun, she said, but the really nice part was being able to work on the newspaper "with Jeff," one of the editors. Did she prefer the Lab when a teacher was there, as today? She liked it best when she was alone in it, she replied emphatically, "so I can do *exactly* what I like."

The most advanced children in the Lab are the two young editors. One is Professor Moore's gifted daughter, Venn, who started playing with the "talking typewriter" when she was two years and seven months old and could read first-grade stories before she was three. Jeffrey, who is the same age, joined her in Professor Moore's early experiments at Yale, and now both children read seventh-grade books with pleasure. To test their skill, I opened a copy of *Scientific American* at random and asked them whether they could read it. They did so exuberantly, taking turns. Although they stumbled over some words which they did not understand, they could clearly handle anything phonetically.

The Crucial Years

People have an idealized version of the playpen as happy and *mindless,* Professor Moore observes. "They say, 'Life is hard enough as it is, let's leave the early period alone.' But we're using only half-an-hour a day! And with the 102 children we've seen so far, we have yet to run into one who'll come in, explore the place, and not want to come back. Of course the children still have their sandbox and paints and so on—in fact, the Lab actually allows us to prolong some of these things.

"As traditionally handled now in the reasonably good nursery schools, at least the children are free, though they receive little intellectual stimulation. But comes the first grade, and the game is over. At the very time when he is becoming interested in the wider world around him, the child must divorce himself from such matters and confine himself to squiggles. He must learn the alphabet, learn to print, and because of his low skill, read baby stories that are not appropriate for him. All of this takes so long that many important things are dropped as frills—painting and music, for instance.

"No wonder so many children develop a hatred for intellectual work early in school. Yet intellectual things are as natural as anything else."

The human mind is extraordinarily open between the ages of two and five. The problem, Dr. Moore believes, is not to miss this critical period. Researchers have found that even rats and monkeys have an inborn curiosity which impels them to seek new territory for its own sake. Experiments have also demonstrated that the key to a rat's learning ability is what happens to it during infancy—which lasts only a few weeks. If rats are exposed to a stimulating environment during this crucial period, they acquire skills with ease later. If not, their whole subsequent performance is impaired.

"If animals are comfortable and have free time, then they will explore," says Professor Moore. In human beings, behavioral scientists have begun to recognize this same "competence drive" as a major motivation along with the drives of hunger, thirst, and sex. But often the drive is stifled. "Every year we lose hundreds of thousands of children who have the ability to learn but who don't go on to college," Professor Moore says. "They have made a nearly irreversible decision very early in life, long before they reach the guidance people in the last year of high school."

For this reason he feels that our educational spending habits are topsy-turvy. "If I had a certain sum to spend on twenty Ph.D. candidates and twenty nursery-school children, I'd use most of it on the youngest children," he says. "They're the ones who need it most." But generally, he points out, schools provide only minimum equipment and teachers for nursery school and kindergarten.

"We're going to have to change our whole notion of how much capital investment should go into education, especially in the early years," Dr. Moore says. "If necessary, we can cut down on expense later; older students should be able to make use of more community facilities, and anyway they can do more on their own."

Dr. Moore has recently set up additional experimental centers in Boston, Massachusetts, and Freeport, New York. Another is being established in Cooperstown, New York. He wants to find out whether his methods work equally well with children in other settings and also to explore the problem of cost.

The matter of expense is possibly the major objection voiced by visitors to his Lab. And indeed it does present a problem. The first production model of his fully automated typewriter (called "A.R.E." for "Automated Responsive Environments") cost an estimated $400,000 to develop. Built by the Thomas Edison Research Laboratory of West Orange, New Jersey, it is a cross between an analogue and a digital computer, new enough to have been patented, and small enough to be portable. The computer coordinates the action of the typewriter keyboard, the voice, the dictation equipment, the exhibitor, and the projector. Even on a mass-production basis, this combination would not be cheap. An effort is now being made to develop a low-cost only partially automated device that can do many of the same things.

But even so, the Moore program cannot be a bargain. The "talking typewriter" actually increases the need for skilled teachers. There must be several monitors in the Lab, at least for young children. In addition, regular classroom teachers must be able to deal with unusually inquisitive, individualistic youngsters. This requires teachers who are not wed to routines.

More Fun for Father

At Hamden Hall, as the Lab produced more and more small children who could read, write, and think independently, some teachers were upset. All their past training seemed threatened when first the kindergarten, then the first grade, were reorganized to make use of the children's skills. One dogged conservative simply refused to face facts. Although nearly all her charges could read and take dictation, she insisted on the standard "reading readiness" exercises.

"That's like giving young children a 'talking readiness' test, and not letting them speak until they pass it," scoffs Professor Moore. "It would mean never saying anything in front of a child that he can't understand, when actually he bathes in speech from the time he is born, and eventually catches on to its patterns."

It was Edward I. McDowell, Jr., headmaster of Hamden Hall, who three years ago took the initiative in bringing Professor Moore and his experiment to the school, in which 340 boys and girls attend classes running from nursery through twelfth grade. Like some of the teachers, a few of the trustees have not been happy about the consequences and last year they tried to oust McDowell. With the backing of parents whose children were directly involved in the experiment he fought back and won out.

This year the first-grade class is reading fourth-grade geography books, going on field trips (to a bakery and other nearby points of childhood interest), and enjoying other extras usually called "enrichment." The children are also plodding—with considerably less enthusiasm—through penmanship practice and the standard school workbooks (the latter at third- and fourth-grade level).

Mr. McDowell foresees far more drastic changes in the kind of school that might in the future evolve from these experiments. "It's going to lead to an ungraded school system all the way up the line," he says. "Educationally this is nothing new, but administratively it's quite a problem. It means the children won't stay in the same room all day long; when it's time for math, for instance, they'll have to split up. In general they'll remain with their own age groups. But in reading-writing, math, and science, they will be grouped according to achievement."

Before starting in the Moore program, each child is given a battery of intelligence and projective tests by a clinical psychologist, as well as physical and eye examinations and hearing tests. A speech expert evaluates his ability to make sounds and a sociologist takes a look at his parents and his home. The clinical psychologist checks up on the children at various stages of the program. So far, there have been no negative results, and according to the psychologist the children's Rorschach tests show "greater richness and better balance" as they advance in the program. Some of their parents report that their children become more interesting.

"Now that letters and numbers are her friends, everything has more meaning for her," commented one mother. Another child's father admitted, "I was waiting for my boy to grow up before I spent time with him. Now, I'm sorry when he goes to bed."

Many aspects of the program are specifically designed to give the child an early grasp of reality. When the child learns to read into the recording equipment and then take his own dictation, for instance, he becomes his own judge of what constitutes adequate reading. If his original reading from the projector is unclear, he realizes that he is the source of his difficulties; if he reads well, he will find that he is helping himself. Such objectivity presumably should help children to think better and develop a more adequate "social self."

"However, we keep watching for other, negative consequences," Professor Moore says. "Maybe they will show up in time."

Meanwhile, Dr. Moore hopes that the less gifted children will benefit even more than the brighter ones from their sessions with a "responsive environment." Because they are alone with the machine, those who don't understand quickly need not be embarrassed or suffer from constant comparison with the faster learners. In the standard classroom, the gifted child often supplies virtually all the central principles, interpretations, and key facts; thus slower students are deprived of exhilarating discoveries. This may be one of the reasons why slower students come to resent the gifted child, he suggests: they intuitively associate him with their loss.

A "talking typewriter" has infinite patience. It plays no favorites. It does not hold out bribes or threats, nor need the child feel anxious about losing its love. For these reasons, it seems ideally suited to teaching retarded children and others with severe handicaps.

Last year, five retarded boys and girls who had been rejected by public kindergartens because of their low IQs and behavior problems came to the Lab, tried out the gadgets, and liked them. After seven weeks of work their attitude improved enough for their schools to agree to take them back conditionally. After a year of work in the Lab, all had learned to read simple material. Their IQs ranged from 59 to 72, classifying them as "educable" retarded who, with the best of standard methods and three to four years of painstaking drills, might begin to read around the age of nine. Yet here was a six-year-old boy (IQ 64) typing away, "The goose laid a golden egg." Although it might take them five or six times as long to reach the same stage as a normal child, they made steady progress at their own pace.

Had these five children been institutionalized or simply deprived of further education, they would probably have become wards of the state for the rest of their lives. In this case the cost of the machine was clearly justified.

Professor Moore plans to concentrate his future research on the deaf, the retarded, and others with severe handicaps. The Responsive Environments Foundation, Inc., a nonprofit organization he has set up with Mr. McDowell, will open its doors to such children next fall.

These experiments with children evolved from Professor Moore's earlier work for the Office of Naval Research. For the past nine years he has dealt with the kind of "human higher-order problem solving" involved in mastering artificial symbolic languages. As his emphasis shifted from deductive to inductive processes, his research with adults became more and more difficult. What he needed was a research lab in which an entirely new order of things had to be discovered.

"Rather than create a whole new environment that was strange enough," he said, "I decided to go in for ignorant subjects."

The most ignorant subjects, of course, are newborns. The most practical time to start experimenting was when these children were up and about, at two-and-a-half or three.

Learning Machines or Teaching Machines?

Unlike parrots, young children don't learn item by item, but by overall search—they absorb whole patterns, Dr. Moore believes. Instead of just repeating a word or phrase over and over, they make up their own sentences. This is the key difference between the "responsive environments" approach and usual "programed instruction" or "teaching machine." Some children explore the keyboard systematically, others scatter their efforts— they are not all sent along a pre-set path from A to B to C.

This flexibility may make it possible to program the "talking typewriter" for six languages simultaneously. The teacher can then select the language she wants by the flick of a switch. She can program the projector to show, for instance, a picture of a cat with the word "cat" in a foreign language. After the student has seen the word, typed it, and heard it pronounced, the machine may ask him to repeat it, and then play back his own and the correct pronunciation. If the dials are set correctly, anybody can insert his own program simply by typing and talking into the machine. Unlike other computers, this machine does not require a mathematician to translate commands for it.

All kinds of unfamiliar subjects can be presented in this fashion. A system for teaching basic arithmetic, using an electric calculator, has been worked out in a preliminary way. The Navy and Air Force plan to try out the "talking typewriter" with adult illiterates as soon as enough machines are available. The city of Freeport, New York, has passed a special bond issue to build a new-model "Responsive Environments Laboratory" for its kindergarten and first-grade pupils next year; circular in design, it will consist of ten booths monitored by a yet undetermined number of teachers in the center of the Lab. And Israel—despite the problems involved in converting to a different alphabet—expects to put several machines on trailers in the near future and send them out to far-flung kibbutzes, to help new immigrants learn Hebrew.

Meanwhile the machines which already exist represent a unique "learner-tracking system," in the words of P. Kenneth Komoski, President of the non-profit Center for Programed Instruction, Inc., which is supported by the Carnegie Corporation. Very little is known about how children actually learn; most of our theories on the subject really deal with performance, rather than the learning process. Yet here are some machines—Mr. Komoski prefers to call them "learning machines," rather than "teaching machines" —which keep records of every relevant or irrelevant path their subjects take while learning.

"Suppose we discover that children with certain kinds of background learn in a certain, restricted way," he speculates. "Eventually it may become possible to open up such closed systems and show these children other ways. Studying the tracks they leave, one might figure out some exercises which would help them break out of overly limited patterns of thought."

Even more important is the impact Professor Moore's work may have on programed instruction as a whole, according to Mr. Komoski. "Programing today takes the best we already know about teaching and puts it into a more efficient means of communication," he says. "It makes the students come up with the right answers, but it is very didactic, with all the little pieces in a preconceived sequence. And because of the tremendous commercial activity in the field, a lot of unimaginative programing is being sold—or oversold. Professor Moore's work is the only real attempt, in automated teaching, to keep alive the student's curiosity and ability to deal with new problems."

Tomorrow's Thinkers

If future experiments prove as successful as those to date at Hamden, what passes for early-childhood education in most nursery schools may come to seem a terrible waste. Professor Moore, however, declines to be drawn into the controversy that is almost certain to result. He has wisely steered clear of an area where slogans like "Why Johnny Can't Read" can arouse the nation, where proponents of the "look-see" method of reading instruction can wage a sterile fight for years with teachers of "phonics," and where the very age at which children should be taught reading is an explosive issue.

"We've been trying very hard to develop an adequate technology and test it carefully. We do not advocate that other people use it" he says. "We don't yet have a finished program. We want to keep the atmosphere free for further experimentation." When the Department of Agriculture wished to convince farmers to shift to hybrid corn and contour farming, he points out, "they simply put up a few model farms here and there, where farmers could come and watch. They did not argue." Professor Moore hopes similarly to proceed by example.

The one issue on which this quiet man speaks with undisguised emotion is the need to develop the next generation's inductive processes. "Modern society is evolving so dynamically that we can no longer depend on child-rearing methods which were adequate before," he says. "We have no time. We can't stand pat. We have more new problems today than we can even name, and we must turn out larger and larger numbers of youngsters who can make fresh inductions about our world.

"A new kind of person is needed to handle the present rate of change. This is our chief trouble today: Technological change but intransigent behavior. It's too late for us—our generation can't make it. At best, we are just the transition group."

FRANK RIESSMAN
Professor of Educational Sociology, New York University

30 · THE LESSONS OF POVERTY

• Wherever we look in the United States today, we see criticism of the school system, of the curriculum, of the teachers and administrators. The conformity of the system and the lack of real learning are constantly being attacked. At the same time the middle class in our country is being sharply criticized. Middle-class people are being portrayed as conformists who have lost their spontaneity, their convictions.

These criticisms are widespread. But there is one time when they seldom arise, and this is when the teaching of disadvantaged children is discussed. Suddenly, when we talk about these youngsters, we have a much more idealized picture of our schools and of middle-class life, and suddenly these children are to be made to conform to our suddenly wonderful ways.

I think that some important changes are beginning to take place in the schools and in the middle class. But a great deal has to be done, and I believe that these disadvantaged youngsters, with their own culture and their own style and their own positives, can help us change the middle class, the school system, and the society.

Before they can help, however, these children do need education. Most particularly they need teachers who take a new approach to teaching; and it is tremendously encouraging that the Federal Government, recognizing this, will next summer support several institutes for the training of teachers of the disadvantaged. These institutes, which were authorized by the 88th Congress when it added Title XI to the National Defense Education Act, will be conducted by colleges and universities, under contract with the Office of Education.

If I were to recommend one thing to the people who will be conducting these institutes, it would be this: Show teachers how to meet the disadvantaged on their own ground.

American Education, 1:21–23, February, 1965.

By this I emphatically do not mean that a teacher should compromise his standards or that he should condescend to his pupils. I mean that he should recognize that the culture from which these pupils spring has its own standards and its own sense of values and that he must work within these standards, in fact turn them to educational profit.

Specifically, I believe that the training of teachers for the disadvantaged should do four things for each trainee:

1. Develop in him a genuine interest in these children and a respect for them rather than simply have him acquire some knowledge about them.

2. Expose him carefully and thoroughly to the disadvantaged so that he can free himself of any negative preconceptions he may have had about these people.

3. Show him how to use teaching methods adapted to the learning style of the disadvantaged.

4. Develop in him an effective teaching *style,* as distinguished from method.

In naming these four objectives I am thinking of disadvantaged children who will be taught in integrated, multi-class schools and classrooms. Although my suggestions may be especially suited to low-income children, they should work well also with middle-class children by improving their styles of learning and broadening their general outlook.

Let us consider each of the four in order.

It is extremely important to respect disadvantaged children. It is the key to winning them to education. But in order to respect someone it is necessary to know something positive about him, and I find that too many of the people who talk about respecting these youngsters really see nothing in them to respect. This is why I think we should stress the good things in the culture, behavior, and style of the disadvantaged. We should stress, for instance, the freedom the disadvantaged enjoy from the strain that accompanies competitiveness; the equalitarianism, informality, and humor; the freedom from self-blame and parental overprotection; the children's enjoyment of each other's company; and the enjoyment of music, games, sports, and cards.

However, it is not enough to give people respect and knowledge; it is necessary also to change the *attitude* of teachers. You may think that this is a very difficult thing to do, but actually it may not be so difficult. The way to do it, I think, is by arousing the *interest* of the teacher in disadvantaged people and their culture.

Generally, teachers and other members of the school staff have not been especially interested in the makeup of these youngsters. They have seen the poor, for the most part, as an undifferentiated drab mass. In order to create interest, I would introduce considerable controversy and ferment about the poor and their psychology. The current proposals for providing teachers with a sociological analysis of disadvantaged groups, while valuable, are not sufficient for developing deep interest in and excitement about these people.

The time has come for teacher preparation to include reading of novels, seeing films, viewing art and dance, and hearing music of various low income groups, particularly the Negro and Spanish-speaking groups. So I would recommend, for example, that discussions take place around books like *The Cool World* by Warren Miller and movies such as *Nothing but a Man*. I think also a good deal of discussion about Negro history and Negro contributions in science, art, and engineering should take place in this kind of teacher training.

My second point is that we ought to take more thought in planning the "laboratory" programs we have for teachers. Many preparatory programs tend to stress visits to the homes and neighborhoods of the poor, visits which can actually reinforce existing stereotypes about the disadvantaged. The simple and obvious reason is that teachers, like everyone else, see what they want to see, what they have been prepared by their training to see.

What I am suggesting here is a carefully directed, prepared exposure that will help teachers know *how* to look at the culture of the low-income groups. They won't see simply a family that is broken, for instance, but rather an extended female-based family which is in many ways highly organized, although organized very differently from the traditional family. They will learn to see the way in which functions are delegated and organized in this family, how child rearing is handled, how cooking is assigned, how members of the family take care of the house, and the way responsibility is divided.

The teachers will also have to be taught not to confuse the normal and the pathological. The normal female-based family is not pathological. But pathology does occur in some families. In some middle-class strata, child rearing may have strong traces of parental overprotection, overindulgence, and the like. This may be the norm, just as less direct, less intensive loving is the norm in lower socioeconomic groups. But neither pattern by itself is abnormal, even though the pathologies in both classes may well be related to the normative pattern.

Nor should the focus be on the environment as such—on the crowdedness, the lack of privacy, the lack of economic security. Rather, the focus should be on how these people struggle with this environment, how they have forged a culture in doing this, and how this culture and style can be utilized in the school situation. This calls for much more than "tours" and home visits.

The third point in my suggested program has to do with teaching methods. A number of techniques may have special value for low income children, but I shall confine myself to discussion of two—namely, role playing and the use of "hip" language.

Before I discuss these two techniques, however, let me simply list a few others that seem to hold promise for the disadvantaged:

1. The "organics" technique of Sylvia Ashton Warner (*The Teacher*) should be especially valuable in building upon the interests and potentialities of the youngsters, and should guard against their being "acted upon." (The latter is the current trend in many programs designed for the disadvantaged, who are supposedly "deficit" ridden.)

2. The Montessori System, which places much emphasis on sensory materials and on order, should be particularly congenial to low-income youngsters.

3. Various game techniques—"In the Manner of the Adverb," for example, and Robbins' "Auditory Set" game—may be valuable.

4. Lawrence Senesh's techniques for teaching economics to first- and second-graders seem promising.

The technique we call role playing owes a good deal of its success to the fact that participants feel free of tension. They act out various types of problems. A caseworker interviews a withdrawn client, say; or the manager of a housing project for low-income families interviews a tenant or a prospective tenant. Since they are "only acting," they can safely express their opinions about the situations they are dramatizing and safely try out new solutions to problems.

My own experience indicates that low-income people make an exceptionally positive response to role-play technology. For one thing it is physical, action-oriented. It is *do* vs. *talk,* and low-income people tend to work out mental problems best when they can do things physically.

The verbal performance of deprived children improves markedly in the discussion period following a role-playing session. Ask a juvenile delinquent who comes from a disadvantaged background what he doesn't like about school or the teacher, and you will get an abbreviated, inarticulate reply. But have a group of these youngsters act out a school scene in which someone plays the teacher, and you will start a stream of verbal consciousness that is almost impossible to shut off.

Role playing can have various beneficial results in the teaching of academic material in the school. If an inquiring student should wonder, for example, what Abraham Lincoln would think of our present civil rights policy, let "Lincoln" and "President Lyndon Johnson" stage a debate! The impossibilities of time and space are eliminated, and the civics lesson will be well-remembered.

The second technique I am recommending here—the careful use of "hip" language, sometimes combined with role playing—can be highly effective in teaching the disadvantaged. An article in the Syracuse, N.Y., *Herald-Journal* last November told how such a combination was put to good use in a ninth-grade English class at Madison Junior High School, which is participating in a program for the disadvantaged called the Madison Area Project.

A teacher had complained to Gerald Weinstein, the project curriculum coordinator, that her students "practically fell asleep" when she read a poem titled "The Magic Carpet" from a standard anthology. Weinstein went to the class armed with copies of the poem "Motto," by the Negro writer, Langston Hughes. It goes:

> *I play it cool and dig all jive.*
> *That's the reason I stay alive.*
> *My motto, as I live and learn*
> *Is: Dig and be dug in return.*

The students read the poem. After a long moment of silence—
"Hey, Mr. Weinstein, this cat is pretty cool."
"It's written in our talk."
Discussion centered on the phrase "dig all jive." Weinstein asked the students how many kinds of jive they understood. They claimed that of course they understood all kinds, but when he launched into an abstract essay on the nature of truth, using all the big words he could find, they looked blank.

He asked them to try him with their jive. They threw six expressions at him, and he got five. "According to Hughes, who has the better chance of staying alive?" Weinstein asked, "You or I?" The class had to concede that he did because he dug more than one kind of jive.

The enthusiasm of that class session led the students into more of Hughes' poetry. Later they moved into other kinds of literature in more conventional language.

But the students, the newspaper article pointed out, were not the only ones learning from that exciting class. Weinstein learned, too. He learned the advantage of being familiar with the language of the children he was teaching, the advantage of establishing rapport with them.

I am not suggesting that teachers employ "hip" language in normal conversation with the underprivileged youngster, as a device for attempting to be friendly with the child. This would indeed be patronizing and dangerous. But the use of hip material in a *formal lesson plan* can become an excellent avenue to the style and interests of the disadvantaged.

There is great need for curriculum materials for use with disadvantaged youngsters. Both the Bank Street College of Education in New York City, through its proposed Educational Resources Center, and New York's Mobilization for Youth project have been developing laboratories in which such materials are created and tested.

Such laboratories should be closely related to the federally supported teacher institutes and should contain not only materials but also reports and films of positive experiments in the teaching of the disadvantaged.

The project conducted by Superintendent Samuel Shepard in the Banneker District of St. Louis is especially noteworthy as an experiment of this sort. He has demonstrated that disadvantaged youngsters at the elementary and junior high school levels can be quickly raised to their proper grade level. More comprehensive efforts than Shepard's might produce even more startling results.

Finally, teaching style—

We tend to assume that good teachers ought to be healthy, well-adjusted people. I am not sure it is that simple. I am not suggesting, of course, that we look for sick people and make them into teachers. I am suggesting that we think about the development of individual teacher style and that some of these individual styles may have significant non-healthy components.

In visits to schools in over 35 cities I have found at least one teacher in each school who according to all—children, parents, colleagues, and administrators—was a "good" teacher. These teachers differed vastly from one another in method and point of view. What I am saying is that there is no one best style.

Teachers attending NDEA institutes should have opportunities to observe teachers using various effective styles and to see films of them in action. They should even role play the classroom, the different problems that arise, the discipline problem, the disorder problem. Out of this role play, each will develop his own repertoire.

Only as he works at it—through such methods and procedures as I have suggested here—can a teacher learn to meet the disadvantaged on their own ground. And only as we meet them on their own ground can we hope to realize the contribution which, as I said at the start, the disadvantaged can make to our schools, our middle class, and society.

THE ADOLESCENT
AS A LEARNER

                                • Three points stand out
in the selection by Braham: (1) The peer-group sub-culture exerts a profound influence upon the development of its adolescent members. (2) It
is during this period of development that the ability to reason abstractly
develops. (3) Adolescent peer groups tend to stultify this important aspect
of intellectual development.

    Although the editors are in partial agreement with these statements,
there are certain limitations to this point of view that need to be made
evident to the reader. First, a negative attitude toward intellectual excellence probably is not peculiar to adolescents; it probably exists just as
strongly, though more subtly, throughout the total culture. As a matter of
fact, the average person, and two out of every three fall within this category
intellectually, appears more willing to assist the growth of those who are
below average intellectually than he is to encourage those who are above
average. It is significant that only in times when national survival is at
stake does the general public become concerned with increasing the competence of the intellectually gifted.

    The second limitation to Braham's position is that he appears to include
all adolescents in his statement regarding the intellectually negating influence of their peer groups. In our opinion this is too inclusive and too general. Not all teen-agers are limited by association with their own age group;
sub-groups do exist which promote rather than inhibit intellectual growth.
We feel that there is a greater tendency among high-school students to
favor intellectual pursuits than there was a decade ago. Still, the problem
of intellectual stultification among adolescents demands attention and action
from educators if all youngsters are to benefit maximally from school experi-

ences. Braham's opinion that attempts to deal with this condition must involve groups merits support and application. Since the problem develops because of adolescent attitudes and the pressure exerted on group members, it is certainly in this context that it can be best dealt with. The subject of group processes will be discussed in greater detail in Section XVI. In our opinion this is an educational resource that could be used much more effectively in most classrooms.

It would be easy to believe that the article by Frymier and Wells deals with *the* focal issue in motivation and mental health—the self concept. We will rest the case by saying it is a highly important aspect of effective learning for teachers as well as pupils. The article is clear, direct, and conclusive. It does leave unanswered the question of how the self concept can be enhanced. Before moving on, the reader might do some thinking about this challenge.

MARK BRAHAM
Doctoral Candidate, Stanford University

31 · PEER-GROUP DETERRENTS TO INTELLECTUAL DEVELOPMENT DURING ADOLESCENCE

● This paper is based on the belief that intellectual activity is not just a distinctive characteristic of mankind, but that it is a necessary constituent of his continued evolution. Following the thesis of De Chardin, in *The Phenomenon of Man*,[1] the belief holds that evolution as such has by no means ceased, that contemporary man represents the present stage of evolutionary development, and that the continuing evolution of man is signified by, and requires, the continued development of his intelligence, a process which is facilitated by intellectual activity.

Further, it is held that education is mankind's most operative means to the development of his intelligence, which of all human behaviors is the least instinctual and requires the longest period of post-natal nurture and training until it becomes an effectively functioning organization. However, recent readings in the social psychology of education suggest that the peer-group structure or "sub-culture" as it appears in adolescence is an educationally negating force which legislates against widespread intellectual activities during the intellectually important period of secondary education. Taken over the long run this would seem to be restrictive of personal, cultural and species evolution. This paper represents an attempt to explore this problem, which can be understood as the problem of peer-group deterrents to intellectual development during adolescence.

Educational Theory, 15:248–258, July, 1965. Used by permission of the author and *Educational Theory*, University of Illinois.

[1] Pierre Teilhard De Chardin, *The Phenomenon of Man* (London: Collins, 1959).

Intelligence

By intelligence, we may understand a mode of behaving, found in some degree in the more cerebral animals, but which reaches its most complex and full expression in mankind. Stott defines intelligence in common sense terms:

> as a general quality of personal functioning—that is, adequacy and effectiveness in meeting life situations. The more effectively one characteristically meets life-situations at any stage in his overall development, the "brighter," the "smarter," the "more intelligent" he is judged to be.[2]

Piaget gives a tighter and a more biological definition:

> intelligence is an adaption . . . it is essentially an organization, the function of which is to structure the universe, just as the organism structures the environment.[3]

while Lewin suggests the more psychological conception, as the process of increasing differentiation of the "Life-space."[4]

In these contexts, intelligence appears as a dynamic, adaptive process that functions in human life in the same sense that instinctive adaptability functions in animal life, but at a much higher level of complexity: it provides for the survival, maintenance and maturation of the individual, and taken collectively or socially, his group, his society and his culture.

There is, however, a vast and important distinction between animal and human adaptability. The animal adapts to, assimilates and structures his environment on the basis of a high degree of instinct and a minimum of learning. Man however, is highly deficient in instinct, and requires a lengthy period of post-natal nurture and training to develop his life-sustaining adaptions.[5] This inherent lack of instinctive behaviors provides for the development of non-physical, or mental, patterns of action, which can be applied to the physical problems of life itself.[6] Thus, in mankind,

[2] L. H. Stott, in W. R. Baller, *Readings in the Psychology of Human Growth and Development* (New York: Holt, Rinehart and Winston, 1962), p. 173.

[3] Jean Piaget, in D. Rapaport, *The Organization and Pathology of Thought* (New York: Columbia Univ. Press, 1950), p. 180.

[4] Kurt Lewin, *Field Theory in Social Science*, ed. Cartwright, D., Tavistock, (London: 1955), p. 246.

[5] Eric Fromm, *Man for Himself* (London: Routledge, 1949): "The emergence of man can be defined as that point in the process of evolution where instinctive adaption has reached its limit." p. 39.

[6] Note: not a mind-body dualism, but the emergence of psychological structures out of physiological structures through natural selection. Cf. Sinnott, below.

biological adaption, assimilation and structuring has been transcended in the process of evolution by the psychological modes of cognitive and conceptual activity, which, for example, enable a man to plow a better furrow, or to predict mathematically the appearance of a planet in the heavens.[7]

Intelligence, thus, can be considered as a complex adaptive process, not "an entity or an 'innate capacity,' "[8] nor a "fixed sum,"[9] but as a *behavior* that provides for human development through qualitatively and quantitatively greater transactions with the environment than are possible by instinctive adaption alone.

INTELLIGENCE AS BEHAVIOR

There is an apparent lawfulness about behaviors in general that seems to be applicable to the discussion of intelligence. The first "law" might well be Lewin's: $B = f(P, E,)$; behavior is a function of the person and his environment.[10] It is also a modifier of both. From this standpoint we may regard intelligence as a behavior whose rate, style, and quality of development is a function of the biogenetic constituents of the germ plasm; the developmental state, experience, age, needs and goals of the individual; and the demands, requirements, limitations, possibilities and values of the socio-cultural group to which the individual must adapt, and with which he constantly interacts.[11] Therefore, to paraphrase Lewin, we may hold that

[7] E. W. Sinnott, *Matter, Mind and Man* (New York: Atheneum, 1960): "The hypothesis presented here maintains that psychology, the science of mind, deals with the same material as biology, though at a much higher level. Both are concerned with patterns in protoplasm to which activity conforms." p. 75.

[8] Stott, *loc. cit.*

[9] Gardner Murphy, in *Childhood Education*, vol. 39, No. 8, April, 1963: "Intelligence itself is not a fixed sum which must be rightly invested. The amount of intelligence is flexible, variable and easily coached, molded, guided and given a richer expression. . . ." p. 363.

[10] Kurt Lewin, *op. cit.*: "Behavior and development depend upon the state of the person and his environment. $B = f(P, E,)$ have to be viewed as variables which are mutually dependent upon each other. . . . In other words, to understand or predict behavior, the person and his environment have to be considered as one constellation of interdependent factors." pp. 239–240.

[11] Nancy Bayley, *Encyclopedia of Educational Research*, 3rd. ed. (New York: Macmillan, 1960). "As in development generally, mental growth is a function of an organism in the process of differentiation and organization (both structural and functional) which occurs as the organism interacts with its environment. . . mental development is a dynamic process of interaction. An organism with specific genetic potentialities responds selectively to relevant aspects of its environment and the specific nature of these relevant environmental stimuli have differential effects on the process of growth." pp. 818–821.

"to understand or predict intelligence, the person and his environment have to be considered as one constellation of interdependent factors."

A second "law" is that behaviors are directional,[12] tending towards the survival, maintenance and maturation of the individual within his particular environment.[13] This "law" may also be considered as the "Principle of Maximal Organization":

> (The) Principle of Maximal Organization . . . asserts that an organism acts in such a way as to maximize under existing conditions, and to the extent of its capacity, the amount of organization in the dynamic system represented in its mazeway; that is to say, it works to increase both the complexity and orderliness of its experience.[14]

Of all human behaviors, intelligence would seem to provide the greatest possibilities for increasing the complexity of individual experience, with the consequence of increasing the complexity, and thus the potential efficiency of individual and cultural life.

A third "law" is that behaviors are developmental. A behavior does not begin to operate as a fully functioning system, but follows a general pattern of development from a point of inception, to a state of "adequate" operations. Such a state does not necessarily represent the limits to behavioral development. The limitations to development depend in large part on whether a maturational factor is involved, and the state of "adequate" operation is usually far short of behavioral maturity. If, as in the case of instinctual behaviors, a general maturation point is implicit in the organism, then by definition it is the terminal point for behavioral development. However, if maturation is not involved, as is the case with non-instinctual behaviors, such as intelligence, the potentiality for continued development (increase in complexity of operations) is apparently unlimited. At least,

---

[12] Morton Deutsch, "Field Theory in Social Psychology" in G. Lindzey, ed. *Handbook of Social Psychology* (Reading, Mass.: Addison-Wesley Co., 1954). "The psychological explanation of behavior assumes that all behaviors have directional characteristics. Hence it is concerned with the purposes which underlie behavior and the goals towards or away from which behavior is directed." p. 183.

[13] Cf. Abraham Maslow, *Towards a Psychology of Being* (New York: Van Nostrand, 1962) "Man demonstrates *in his own nature* a pressure toward fuller and fuller Being, more and more perfect actualization of his humanness in exactly the same naturalistic scientific sense that an acorn may be said to be "pressing toward" being an oak tree, or that a tiger can be observed to "push toward" being tigerish, or a horse towards being equine." p. 151.

[14] A. F. C. Wallace, *Culture and Personality* (New York: Random House, 1961), p. 125.

we do not know what the "upper reaches" of intellectual development are, for the research is far too scanty.[15]

The failure of individuals to maximize a potential beyond the state of "adequacy" ("need-satisfaction"), results in behavioral "fixation" or "arrest." When this occurs, the attained patterns of action tend to stylize, then crystalize, and thus become almost totally resistant to further development. From the standpoint of intellectual development, such "fixation" or "arrest" would seem to have negative consequences for both individuals and society alike.

Any attempt to understand, prevent or rehabilitate "arrested" or "fixated" behaviors involves us in the total person-in-environment interaction. Here, two dimensions can be isolated. The first is the *organic dimension,* which includes the bio-genetic "givens" of the individual. The second is the *existential dimension,* which includes the achieved state of the individual and the nature of the environmental forces with which he interacts. From the standpoint of intellectual development, where nurture predominates over instinct, our concern centers on the existential dimension, with the emphasis upon the psychological state of the person and the nature of his social environment.[16, 17]

Intelligence and Adolescence

It is not until pre- and early adolescence that intelligence, viewed as a coordination of sensori-motor, perceptual, cognitive and conceptual activities, appears as a functioning organization.[18] The period between approximately the tenth and twelfth years of a child's life marks a definitive point in his intellectual life, such that the prior years may be considered as the

[15] Cf. Abraham Maslow, *Towards a Psychology of Being, op. cit.,* also, *Motivation and Personality,* for discussions of higher states of cognitive functioning, (New York: Harper, 1954).

[16] Cf. Allison Davis, *Social-Class Influences upon Learning* (Harvard Univ. Press, 1948).

[17] Cf. *Scottish Mental Survey* (London, England: Her Majesty's Stationery Office, 1947).

[18] Cf. W. E. Vinacke, "The Investigation of Concept Formation," in *Psychological Bulletin,* vol. 48, 1951, p. 16.

Cf. Hans Aebli, *The Development of Intelligence in the Child;* (summary of the works of Jean Piaget published between 1936 and 1948), (Minneapolis, Minn.: University of Minnesota, 1950).

Cf. David P. Ausubel, "Implications of Preadolescent and Early Adolescent Cognitive Development for Secondary School Teaching," in *High School Journal,* vol. 45, 1962, pp. 268 ff.

period of intellectual birth, and with adolescence as the period of true intellectual growth. According to Ausubel:

> . . . the most significant development in cognitive functioning that occurs during the pre-adolescent and adolescent years is the gradual transition from a predominantly concrete to a predominantly abstract mode of understanding and manipulating complex relational propositions.[19]

From the moment of its "inception" with the infant's earliest perceptual activity, to the time of its "birth" as coordinated mental organization, intelligence is a function of the person-in-environment interaction. The early mother-child relationship,[20] the fact of an environment that enlarges as perception increases, the love that is given and the demands that are made by the family, the existence of playmates, the requirements of the culture and of teachers for conforming behaviors, all serve to both extend and modify the patterns of a child's thought.

The child begins life ego-centric in consciousness, symbiotically attached to his surroundings, incapable of distinguishing between himself and his environment. He lives in an autistic world where the only reality is himself. He arrives at adolescence, expanded in his mental horizons, easily capable of distinguishing between himself and his surroundings,[21] and able to think dualistically, in terms of subject and object, and black-and-white absolutes in comparison to the monistic thought of early childhood. By the time the child reaches adolescence he has been imbued with a super-ego; he has learned by and large to think as his culture thinks; he holds ideas about the world in common with his class-mates, his gang, club or group, and his referent for judgments about reality is social. He has transcended his infantile ego-centricity and has become totally socio-centric in consciousness; he has become a "good citizen." The emergence of intelligence as a co-ordinated mental organization ready for abstract functioning, and the affirmation of socio-centric thought patterns converge at adolescence.[22] Here is where our problem begins.

The continued development of intelligence through adolescence requires an intellectually stimulating environment. It also requires interest in, and

---

[19] Ausubel, *loc. cit.*

[20] Cf. Erika Fromm and Leonore Dumas Hartman, *Intelligence, a Dynamic Approach* (New York: Doubleday, 1955).

[21] A function of the decentralization of the ego, and the development of socio-centric consciousness.

[22] Morton Deutsch, *op. cit.* Notes: "Adolescence and pre-adolescence is a period of most intensive social impact. Here, from the social-psychological point of view, it would seem, the social environment would have its most potent effect." p. 173.

motivation for, intellectual activities on the part of the adolescent, for where instinct is not operative, the development of a behavior is not innately bound to the achievement of a particular state beyond that of need-satisfaction. Finally, the development of intelligence requires that the adolescent acquire an increasing awareness of his own potentialities for reflective, imaginative, abstract thought. This latter is essential if we are to have creative and capable thinkers who can attain the development and independence of intellect to go beyond the customary patterns of thought and action, and by so doing contribute to the development of all.

The problem, however, is that when intelligence is just beginning to function as a coordinated structure, and requires the most nurturing circumstances, the adolescent meets a major deterrent to its development, that of the intellectually negating adolescent peer-group structure, or "sub-culture." This "sub-culture" represents the adolescent's predominant social environment within the high school, where intellectual activities should be a major concern. By demanding of its members a high degree of conformity to its own non-intellectual standards, the sub-culture manages to suppress intellectual interest and motivation in all but the deviates.[23] The immediate effect can be seen in the 40% of students who drop out of high school,[24] and in the additional 40% who fail to continue with their formal

[23] Cf. James Coleman, "Academic Achievement and the Structure of Competition," in *Harvard Educational Review*, xxix (Fall) 1959, pp. 330–343.

James Coleman, "The Adolescent Sub-culture and Academic Achievement" in W. W. Charters and N. L. Gage, *Readings in the Social Psychology of Education* (Boston: Allyn and Bacon, 1963). pp. 88 ff.

[24] U.S. Bureau of the Census, *Current Population Reports, Population Characteristics*, Washington, D.C., February 4, 1960, as adapted by Krech, Crutchfield and Ballachey, *Individual in Society* (New York: McGraw-Hill, 1962). p. 314.

Education (in per cent)
College, 18.2
High School, 40.8
Less than high school, 38.9.

Cf. also, *International Yearbook of Education*, "United States Educational Developments in 1961–62," Paris, UNESCO, and Geneva, International Bureau of Education, 1962.

Number of Pupils: The following statistics show enrollment figures for the different types of schools for 50 states and the District of Columbia in 1961–62.

Kindergarten up to grade 8 (elementary)
Public Schools (full-time) 28,700,000
Non-Public Schools (full-time) 5,300,000
Other Schools 200,000
                                         34,200,000

(*Footnote 24 continued on next page*)

education beyond graduation. When we add to this the fact that not all high school programs are intellectually stimulating, we end up with both limitation and wastage of adolescent intellectual potential.[25] The "mental cost" to the individual and the nation at large must be considerable.

The result of this loss of intellectual stimulation, motivation and self-realization is that the majority of youth continue on to physiological maturity and become the majority of adults, while yet arrested in their intellectual maturation. Taken over the long run, this would seem to indicate that the modal state of adult intelligence must be placed somewhere within the adolescent stage of development.

THE ADOLESCENT SUB-CULTURE

Our task is not to blame the adolescent for his lack of intellectual interests, but rather, to come to some understanding of the dynamics of his social-psychological situation.

At the risk of repetition this can be roughly described as follows. The child reaches adolescence well versed in the skills of group membership. He has learned how to get along well with others, to do the "accepted" things, and to fulfill a pattern of socially prescribed behaviors.[26] Essentially socially directed with little self-consciousness, he is attuned to acting in concert with others.

As an adolescent, he finds himself in the transitory phase of becoming increasingly independent of parental authority as he moves towards the potential independence of his own adulthood. In this "betwixt and between" period, he turns to his peers for mutual security and support, and utilizes

---

Grades 5 to 12 (secondary)		
Public Schools (full-time)	9,500,000	
Non-Public Schools (full-time)	1,200,000	
Other Schools	100,000	
		10,800,000
Higher Education		
University, College, Professional Schools, Junior		
College, Normal Schools and Teachers colleges		
(degree-credit enrollment)	4,300,000	
		4,300,000

[25] Robert E. Herriot, "Some Social Determinents of Educational Aspiration," in *Harvard Educational Review*, Vol. 33 (2) Spring, 1963, p. 158.

[26] Cf. Jules Henry, "Attitude Organization in Elementary School Classrooms," in W. W. Charters, and N. L. Gage, *Readings in the Social Psychology of Education*, *op. cit.*, pp. 254 ff.

his social skills to become a conforming member of what is by now his own sub-culture.[27] Of this sub-culture, Bienenstok states:

> (it) is essentially intolerant of deviation. It demands almost complete conformity to the dominant concerns and standards of the group. Except for those who have already won high prestige in the group only slight leeway is given for individual variation from the accepted pattern. There seems to be a distinct tendency on the part of contemporaries to suppress any idiosyncratic qualities among themselves. . . .[28]

Some indication of the value orientation of the adolescent sub-culture can be found in Spindler's (1955) survey showing the following characteristics for the ideal American Boy:

> He should be *sociable,* like people and get along well with them; he must be *popular,* be like others; he is to be *well-*rounded, he can do many things well but is not an expert in anything particular; he should be *athletic* (but not a star), and *healthy* (no qualifications); he should be *ambitious* to succeed and have clear goals but these must be acceptable within limited norms; he must be *considerate of others,* ever-sensitive to their feelings about him and events; he should be a *clean-cut Christian,* moral and respectful of God and parents; he should be *patriotic*; and he should demonstrate *average academic ability,* and *average intellectual capacity.*

> The implications seem clear. The keynote to the character type regarded as most desirable, and therefore constituting a complex of values is, *balance, outward-orientedness, sociability* and *conformity* for the sake of adjustment. Individuality and creativity are not stressed in this conception of values. Introspective behavior is devaluated (intellectuals are suspicioned by many). Deviancy, it seems, is to be tolerated only within the narrow limits of sociability, of general outwardness, of conformity ("Artists are perverts"). The All-American Boy is altogether adjusted. . . .[29]

---

[27] Ralph W. Tyler, "The Impact of Students on Schools and Colleges" in N.S.S.E. Yearbook, vol. 60, part II, *Social Forces Influencing American Education* (Chicago: Univ. Chicago Press, 1961). "Students too form their own social systems. Although the systems formed by very young children are transitory and weak, those formed by adolescents and young adults are often quite complex and of great importance to their members, especially so, when the ties to parents and siblings are loosening and they have not yet formed primary families of their own." p. 172.

[28] Theodore Bienenstok, "The Peer Culture of Youth and the School," in W. Baller, ed., *Readings in the Psychology of Human Growth and Adjustment,* p. 496.

[29] George D. Spindler, *Education and Culture* (New York: Holt, Rinehart and

That this value orientation runs through the core of secondary schooling is pointed out by Bredemeier, Toby and Riley (1954) who show that *friendliness, popularity* and *mediocrity* are more highly regarded as values by high status students, than the value of being a good student (83%, 81%, 71% and 46% respectively).[30] Also, Liberty, Jones and McGuire (1963) found that the *Competent Plodder* is most preferred by peers as an academic, behavior and personal model, while the highly *Intelligent-Creative* students are often attributed a negative model value.[31]

The existence of this intellectually negating power-structure of adolescents cannot really have gone unnoticed by the aware educator, but Coleman (1960) believes that its importance has not been sufficiently emphasized, for, he states:

> The theory and practice of education remains focused on *individuals,* teachers exhort individuals to concentrate their energies in scholarly directions, while the community of adolescents divert these energies into other channels.[32]

Coleman's suggestion is that we give serious attention to finding ways of moving adolescent peer-groups collectively towards intellectual interests, rather than to continue the piecemeal picking upon individual students in the hope of diverting them from identifying with their age-mates. Coleman's own findings help to confirm that the predominant concern of adolescents is with the attainment of high peer-group status and prestige. To be a member of the "leading crowd" where having a "good personality" and "being friendly" are essentials outweighs by far any intellectual interests or desires for academic achievement.[33] Coleman concludes:

> The relative unimportance of academic achievement . . . suggests that these adolescent sub-cultures are general deterrents to academic achievement. . . . The implication for American society as a whole

Winston, 1963). (Data gleaned from open-ended questionnaires given to several hundred college students ranging from 19 to 57 years for general conception of the Ideal American Boy), p. 134.

[30] Bredemeir, Toby and Riley, as quoted in Krech, Crutchfield and Ballachey, *Individual in Society* (New York: McGraw-Hill, 1962), pp. 440–441.

[31] Liberty, Jones and McGuire, "Age-mate Perceptions of Intelligence, Creativity and Achievement" in *Perceptual and Motor Skills,* 1963, 16, 194.

[32] James Coleman, "The Adolescent Sub-Culture and Academic Achievement" in W. W. Charters, and N. L. Gage, *Readings in the Social Psychology of Education, op. cit.,* p. 88.

[33] James Coleman, "Academic Achievement and the Structure of Competition" in *Harvard Educational Review,* xxix, Fall (1959), pp. 330–343.

is clear. Because high schools allow the adolescent sub-culture to divert energies into athletics, social activities and the like, they recruit into adult intellectual activities people with a rather mediocre level of ability. In fact, the high school seems to do more than allow these sub-cultures to discourage academic achievement; it aids them in doing so.[34]

Dynamics of Change

Our problem, in sum, is to overcome what amounts to a major obstacle to personal and social intellectual development: the intellectually negating adolescent sub-culture. While not seeing a solution at this point, I should like to counter the two most obvious "solutions" which come to mind as not being solutions at all, but being only expedients, valid perhaps as short-term programs for interim or experimental purposes.

The first is to select out those adolescents with the greatest intellectual potential, and to transplant them into a special culture of their own:

> We suggest that consideration be given to the development of programs which would enable talented adolescents confronted with "negative" peer influences to develop peer relationships with adolescents more likely to exert a positive influence upon their educational aspiration. (Herriott, 1963).[35]

The consequence of such notions simply leads to the development of an intellectual elite, while maintaining a very unintellectual proletariat among the majority of adolescents who are left to their own status quo. All this can do is to perpetuate the problem of an anti-intellectual adolescent sub-culture, with its school drop-outs and the eventually mentally arrested adults. In an age of intellectual need, increasing leisure time and automation, this is something we can ill afford to do.

The second "solution" is probably the one most current among educators. Essentially this involves the attempt to supply special programs for individual, or groups of, students within their usual class or school surroundings, with the hope of speeding them on their academic way. Although this specialized procedure may be academically successful for many students, it fails to do much, if anything, for the majority of adolescents who are immersed in the intellectual restrictedness of their peer culture. If Coleman's findings are correct—that the adolescents who are presently most

[34] James Coleman, "The Adolescent Sub-Culture and Academic Achievement," *op. cit.*, p. 92.
[35] Herriott, *op. cit.*, p. 171.

amenable to intellectual pursuits are not necessarily those who display the highest intellectual potential, as these latter are more likely to be found as members of the "leading crowd"[36]—then the individualized and special grouping procedure may not be encouraging the best, but the second-best students.

The solution that we need to look for, one, let us say, that is the most inclusive, intensive and durational, must be applicable in principle to the largest number of adolescents. It must be one that is capable of fundamentally altering the value orientation of the adolescent sub-culture itself, even though considerable thought, planning, experiment and time will be required. To this end, it is essential to maintain the proposition that intelligence is by nature not a static patterning of behaviors, and that each adolescent, from the "sub-normal" to the "super-normal" is potentially capable of increasing the rate and quality of his intellectual functioning with positive consequences for the whole society.

From this final point of view, there seem to be a number of basic social-psychological propositions that the educator must take into account if he seeks to provide for the continued intellectual development of his high school students. These may be stated as follows:

1. The Psychological Propositions

1.1.   We will fail to understand the dynamics of the total Behavior, Person and Environment $[B = f(P, E,)]$ constellation upon the individual student, if we concentrate upon the activities of the individual alone, without regard to the foundation of these activities in the total social-psychological situation in which the individual is immersed.

1.2.   Peer groups constitute the essential and desired social environment for the majority of adolescents; thus, any contemplated effort to change adolescent behavior must take into account the nature of the peer-group structure to which a given adolescent or group of adolescents belong.

1.3 "The groups to which a person belongs set standards for his behavior, which he must accept if he is going to stay in the group." (Cartwright, 1951)[37]

1.4.   The cost to the individual of deviation from group values and patterns of action (norms) is liable to be ejection from the group, with a subsequent loss of social prestige and self-esteem.

---

[36] James Coleman, in W. W. Charters and N. L. Gage, *op. cit.*, p. 89.

[37] Dorwin Cartwright, "Achieving Change in People: Some Applications of Group Dynamics Theory," in W. W. Charters and N. L. Gage, *op. cit.*, p. 109.

1.5. Every individual seeks to maintain and return to equilibrium, and will if his group attachments are sufficiently strong, seek to maintain and reinforce these attachments if and when they are threatened.

2. The Sociological Propositions

2.1. The adolescent sub-culture can be understood as an informal social organization comprising innumerable psychological groups (classroom groups, neighborhood groups, clubs, gangs, etc.) which hold within and among themselves, common formalized values, attitudes, beliefs and action patterns.[38]

2.2. Every organization, and every group within an organization, comprises a structure which is formed out of the maintained patterns of interaction and communication between the membership, which coordinates the diversity of activities and gives stability to the whole.

2.3. The structure of an organization determines its essential patterning of actions, attitudes, values, beliefs and the status and privileges accorded to the membership. This essential patterning of actions, et cetera, may be understood as the organization's or group's norms.[39]

2.4. Norms tend to be normative over the membership, thus prescribing and proscribing behavior, so that the organizational structure is maintained. An organization can tolerate only a limited amount of deviation lest damage and distortion appear in its structure and its activities be impaired.[40]

2.5. Every organization (1) tends towards a stable equilibrium, and thus seeks a permanence of structure in order to maintain those operations that

[38] Cf. Krech, Crutchfield and Ballachey, *Individual in Society, op. cit.*, "A psychological group may be defined as two or more persons who meet the following conditions: (1) the relations among its members are interdependent. (2) The members share an ideology." pp. 383–384.

"A social organization may be defined as an integrated system of interrelated psychological groups formed to accomplish a stated objective." p. 384.

[39] Cf. Krech, Crutchfield and Ballachey, *Individual in Society, op. cit.*, "The term *group norm* is defined as a rule which states the attitudes and actions expected of members under given circumstances and which specify the consequences of compliance and non-compliance." p. 247.

[40] Herriott, *op. cit.*, "There is . . . a body of evidence which suggests that others in one's social environment perform a normative function as well: Gross (1958) has isolated three basic ideas which appear in most conceptualizations of the term 'role' which he has examined. Namely, '. . . that individuals (1) in *social locations* (2) *behave* (3) with reference to *expectations*' (p. 117). One source of these expectations is seen to be 'others in the group or society' in which a given individual participates[7]" p. 160.

satisfy its purposes; (2) is homeostatic, and seeks to restore itself to equilibrium by control over or ejection of membership, should the possibility of disruption occur in any way.[41]

3. *The Social-Psychological Propositions Underlying Behavior Change*

3.1.   The majority of adolescents identify (a) with a reference group from which they obtain their ideals, goals and aspirations, and (b) a membership group with whom they share common patterns of action. If the membership group is of sufficient attraction and strength, it may also function as the individual's reference group. Peer groups tend to comprise both reference and membership group functions.

3.2.   External change of individual behavior requires that a reference group be established comprising goals, ideals, values and possibilities that become increasingly dominant and satisfying over those held by the membership group in order (a) to warrant individual deviation from, or transcending of membership group norms: (b) to warrant a possible shift in interests and desires on the part of the membership group itself.

3.3.   If the membership group is also the reference group, the individual's value and action system becomes self-sustaining and circular, thus behavior change is impeded.

3.4.   If behavior change is to be complete, the reference group must in time become the new membership group; if behavioral changes are to continue, a new reference group, representing new goals, ideals, values and possibilities must be established, and become prepotent over the membership group; thus a continual "ringing of changes" of behavioral development is possible. While a membership group always asserts the behavioral norms, if growth is to continue, it must not be allowed to remain normative.

3.5.   Since behavioral changes, deviation from, or attempts to transcend group norms may be traumatic, depending upon the strength of the individual, his membership group and his reference group, assistance, encouragement and support must be provided to help individuals through the period of transition, with its moments of conflict, doubt and potential crises. This is of special importance during the period of adolescence and suggests the need for an integrated curriculum-guidance program in the school.

[41] D. Cartwright, *op. cit.*, "Efforts to change individuals or subparts of a group which if successful would have the result of making them deviate from the norms of the group will encounter strong resistance." p. 112.

JACK R. FRYMIER
Professor of Education, The Ohio State University
ROBERT J. WELLS, JR.
Knox County Schools, Mt. Vernon, Ohio

32 · JUNIOR HIGH SCHOOL STUDENTS' MOTIVATION

The Problem

● Motivational theory (3) suggests that the desire to do good work in school is a function of one's concept of self and his concept of others, his attitudes and values, and his openness to experience, among other things. These attributes suggest that motivation is probably a reasonably stable phenomenon which is made up of a number of interrelated personality and social dynamics. Although parents and teachers sometimes assume that motivational patterns are susceptible to change on a day-to-day basis—that is, that children *can be* motivated at some particular point in time by some particular technique or concept—the conceptualizations presently available suggest otherwise. In one study of over 700 junior high school students' motivation to learn, measures of academic motivation were made on two occasions over a period of ten months, during these students' seventh and eighth grade in school. The data clearly indicate that academic motivation is a fairly constant factor, not subject to extensive change over short periods of time (5). Other studies (4, 6) point up the fact that motivational patterns of boys and girls are fundamentally different, too. The concerns explored in this study grew out of considerations such as these (9).

Specifically, do students who differ in terms of academic motivation differ also in self concept, ability, and achievement in school? Further, are there motivational differences between boys and girls? Stated in predictive form, the following hypotheses were posed:

(1) High motivated students will have more positive self concepts than low motivated students.

Guidance Journal, 4:90–95, 1966. Used by permission of The Ohio State University.

(2) High motivated students will be more able academically than low motivated students.
(3) Girls will be more highly motivated than boys.
(4) High motivated students will make higher grades in school than low motivated students.

The Procedures

All of the seventh grade students in one public school in a small central Ohio city were selected for study. These students were tested with Frymier's Junior Index of Motivation (JIM Scale) and Bills' Index of Adjustment and Values (IAV). In addition, data regarding IQ, academic achievement, and sex were procured from the cumulative records for each youngster involved. Complete data were available on 339 students: 185 boys and 154 girls.

Measuring Academic Motivation: The JIM Scale is an 80 item, paper and pencil measure of academic motivation which has been developed by Frymier after extensive studies of more than ten thousand junior high school youth (3, 4, 5, 6, 7). Each student was tested with the JIM Scale and his paper scored in the conventional manner, then all students were listed according to their scores in rank order from high to low. For the purposes of this study, those persons whose JIM Scale scores fell above the median were considered high motivated. Those whose scores fell below the mid-point were considered low motivated.

Comparison According to Self Concept: The self concept of each student was ascertained by administering Bills' Index of Adjustment and Values (IAV) to all 339 students during the last month of the school year, June, 1964. The IAV is a word association test and provides measures of one's feeling about himself, his feeling about other people, and the relationship of these two factors (1, 2). For the purposes of this study, only the self concept score was used. Self concept scores were determined according to Bills' instructions, and then mean scores and standard deviations determined for students in the high motivated group and those in the low motivated group, as defined above. A comparison of the statistical significance of the difference between group means was made by use of the *t* test.

Comparison According to Ability: The California Test of Mental Maturity, Short Form, was administered to all of these students during the September following the other testing sessions. Mean IQ scores and standard deviations were computed for those students who had been identified as high motivated or low motivated, according to the definition above. Following this, a statistical test of the significance of the difference of group mean IQ scores of high and low motivated students was accomplished by use of the *t* test.

Comparison According to Sex: An indication of each student's sex was determined from the permanent records. Mean JIM Scale scores and standard deviations were computed for boys and girls separately, and a statistical test of the significance of difference of mean motivation scores was undertaken by use of the *t* test.

Comparison According to Achievement: The average grade received for the academic year in each subject was determined by review of the permanent records after the completion of the 1963–64 school year. Each of the year-end grades in each subject was then assigned a numerical value (i.e., A = 4, B = 3, C = 2, etc.), and the totals for each student averaged to determine his mean achievement level for the year. These mean achievement levels were then converted back to letter grades. The number of high motivated students who made average grades of A, B, C, D, or F were compared to the number of low motivated students who made similar grades by use of the chi square statistic.

The Results

Table 1 describes the results which were obtained when high and low motivated students were compared on the basis of mean self concept scores and mean IQ scores. From these data it is obvious that students who are high motivated see themselves differently and in more positive terms than students who are low motivated, thus hypothesis number one can be accepted. Likewise, high motivated students differ from low motivated stu-

Table 1. Comparison of High Motivated and Low Motivated Seventh Graders' Mean Self Concept Scores and Mean IQ Scores

Group	N	Mean self concept score	Mean IQ score
High motivated	169	84.18	106.05
Low motivated	170	80.74	98.18
		2.59*	5.43*

* *t* value significant beyond .01 level of confidence.

dents in terms of their average IQ in the predicted direction, also, so hypothesis number two can be accepted, too.

Table 2 describes the comparison of boys' and girls' mean scores on the JIM Scale, a measure of academic motivation. From these data it is apparent that girls made higher JIM Scale scores than boys, thus hypothesis number three can be accepted, also.

Table 2. Comparison of Seventh Grade Boys' and Girls' Responses to a Measure of Academic Motivation (JIM Scale)

Group	N	Mean JIM Scale score	*t*
Boys	185	106.64	5.80*
Girls	154	122.65	

* *t* value significant beyond .01 level of confidence.

Table 3 describes the comparison of high and low motivated groups' distribution of average grades received for the entire year's work. The pattern is unmistakable: High motivated students tend to make higher grades than low motivated students. Hypothesis number four can be accepted.

Table 3. Comparison of High and Low Motivated Students' Achievement as Reflected in Their Average Grades

Group	N	Number receiving average grade of: A	B	C	D	F	Chi square
High motivated	169	16	67	67	15	4	81.20*
Low motivated	170	2	16	72	49	31	

* Chi square value significant beyond .01 level of confidence with 4 df.

Summary

All of the seventh graders (N = 339) in one small Ohio city participated in a study of motivation in relation to self concept, IQ, sex, and achievement in school. From the data reported here it is obvious that boys and girls differ in terms of their academic motivation, and that high and low motivated students differ in terms of their self concept, their ability, and their achievement as reflected in grades received in school.

BIBLIOGRAPHY

1. Bills, Robert E. "Index of Adjustment and Values." Manual. University of Alabama. Undated. (Mimeographed.)
2. Bills, Robert E., Vance, Edgar L., and McLean, Orison S. "An Index of Adjustment and Values," *Journal of Consulting Psychology*, XV (1951), 257–261.
3. Frymier, Jack R. *The Nature of Educational Method*. Columbus: Charles E. Merrill Books, 1965.
4. ———. "Development and Validation of a Motivation Index: Fourth Report." Columbus: School of Education, The Ohio State University, 1964. (Mimeographed.)
5. ———. "Development and Validation of A Motivation Index: Seventh Report." Columbus: School of Education, The Ohio State University, 1965. (Mimeographed.)
6. ———. "Development and Validation of a Non-Verbal Motivation Index: An Exploratory Study." Columbus: School of Education, The Ohio State University, 1965. (Mimeographed.)
7. Frymier, Jack R., and Thompson, James H. "Motivation: The Learner's Mainspring," *Educational Leadership*, XXII (May, 1965), 567–570.
8. Waetjen, Walter B. "The Alleviation of Nonpromotion," *Theory Into Practice*, IV (June, 1965), 115–121.
9. Wells, Robert J., Jr. "The Relationship of Motivation, Intelligence, Acceptance, Self Concept, Sex, Ability Grouping, and Achievement Among Seventh Grade Students." Master's dissertation, School of Education, The Ohio State University, 1965.

CULTURAL INFLUENCES— THE ROLE OF THE SOCIAL SETTING

• Unwelcome as the idea is in democratically oriented America, we must face the fact that people are neither born equal nor do they all have the same opportunity. This is not because the democratic orientation is wrong but because the multiple facets of equality of opportunity have not been critically examined. One of these facets, the educational neglect of a substantial portion of the population, is being examined today.

Schwebel, using national as well as educational history as part of the evidence, shows that our notions about the nature of man and his intelligence influence the way he is treated. If he is thought to be inferior, he is treated as though he were—and he comes to feel that way about himself. If, on the other hand, he is thought to have both ability and potential, he responds accordingly. The pessimistic and limiting idea of man's intelligence is being replaced by an optimistic belief that intelligence can be expanded by use, nurture, and cultivation. The practical implications of this notion are suggested by Schwebel as he condemns the practice of below-standard buildings and teachers for the already disadvantaged child. The practical implications are expanded as he condemns ability grouping, the misuse of intelligence test data, and the restriction of the curriculum for those whose experience limits their readiness.

The humane and hopeful view of man's unknown capacity for growth and improvement is not simply a matter of idle dreaming or the result of a professor's armchair philosophizing. When such orientations as those outlined by Schwebel are put into practice, the results are uniformly gratifying if not downright surprising. The gain he reports—ten points in average IQ for a high-school class—is substantial. Ten points for an individual is not so unusual, but when the ups and downs of a group on successive test administrations result in an average gain of ten points, one is viewing a phenomenon that merits close scrutiny.

It would seem that something can be done. Deutsch asserts that the "momistically-oriented, deintellectualized enclosures" of early childhood education and the "accumulated sacred cows" of school systems represent a point of attack. Certainly, society as a whole must take an active interest, but before "passing the buck" teachers can begin by asking themselves what they can do.

There can be little doubt that public education with its promise of upward social mobility is controlled by the middle class and mirrors its attitudes and values. Indeed, most educational personnel are so imbued with the middle-class point of view that only with difficulty can they see situations from the perspective of those in the lower economic levels. Because their frame of reference has been so thoroughly conditioned by the traditional model of the classroom, conceptualization of anything much different is difficult for them. The sounding of the alarm by Schwebel and Deutsch may be helpful.

Perhaps the best evidence for this has been the middle-class inability to recognize the "moral imperative." Moral, because learning is living and everyone has a right to live as fully and completely as possible. Imperative, because the "social dynamite" mentioned by Conant and typified by the Watts and Chicago incidents can be ignored no longer.

The article by Deutsch is, we think, both realistic and optimistic. The meaning of failure, the causes of alienation, the futility of vocational education as an antidote for the school's inadequacy, the meaning of readiness, the development of sustained curiosity, sex differences in school orientations are all problems that teachers in contemporary schools must face. The problems are not insurmountable. Reading the included selections serves to strengthen the conviction that the know-how to deal with them may merely await implementation. Financially as well as morally we cannot afford to let educational deprivation persist. Perhaps the biggest obstacle we have to deal with is our own inflexibility. Perhaps it is we who need most to change.

MILTON SCHWEBEL
Associate Dean, School of Education, New York University

33 · LEARNING AND THE SOCIALLY DEPRIVED

/ • The "socially deprived" are that portion of the population that was once characterized as being ill-housed, ill-fed, and ill-clothed. To this triad may be added many other forms of deprivation some of which cut deeply to a person's self-respect, and one very specific one, highly relevant to our topic, namely, ill-educated. /

[Further definition is hardly necessary: the socially deprived live "on the other side of the tracks" in the physical and social life of the community. \ If now a large percentage of them are Negro and Puerto Rican, there are still many "white" persons among them. And not many years ago they were Central and Eastern European, and Mediterranean and Oriental peoples. And before that they were Scandinavian, German, and Irish. Differences among these groups are marked, for of course the learning problems of children whose parents fled oppression in Western Europe after active involvement in political movements are hardly identical with those of uneducated European peasants or of former American slaves. But the vast majority of the socially deprived occupied the lowest-paid positions in their country of origin and were encouraged to come to America to serve a similar occupational role. With the passing years and the new waves of immigrants (or of in-migrants to northern urban areas), the language has changed and the skin color and the customs—and the country to which they have come has achieved a new status in the world, and has new conditions and different educational expectations—but the socially deprived retain essentially the same characteristics: lowliest positions, lowest income, highest unemployment rate, poorest housing, poorest education (Wayland, 1963).

Personnel and Guidance Journal, 43:646–653, 1965. Used by permission of the author and the *Personnel and Guidance Journal*.

How numerous are the socially deprived? The estimate depends, of course, on the criteria employed. The Bureau of Labor Statistics suggested an income of $5,970 as a minimum in New York City for a family with two children to maintain "a modest but adequate" standard of living (Haubrich, 1963). It has been estimated that close to half of the families in New York City, and about 70 per cent of Negro and Puerto Rican families, earn less than that amount. These two groups are not suffering from the fact of being Negro or Puerto Rican but from being deprived of adequate employment and income, as has been true of all the groups that occupied this niche in our social structure.

Yesterday's Deprived

And the same may be said about learning. Long before the migration of Negroes to the northern urban areas, when the education of the Negro child was no public problem because he was not being educated, white socially deprived children were having learning problems to a considerably greater degree than children of the higher classes. Long ago these children had the lower mean IQ's, came from families that had had no educational tradition and little formal schooling, where parents were busy trying to provide the necessities for survival, and where family disruption was caused by the new conditions of being unpopular aliens in a strange land. Long ago the socially deprived were accused of being immoral, of making the streets unsafe "for our sisters and daughters," and long ago as now, the higher incidence of anti-social acts reflected deprivation and frustration and not a group characteristic (Handlin, 1951; Handlin, 1959; Wayland, 1963). And as Snygg (1954), the psychologist, has pointed out, long ago as the public high schools began to be opened to the people for whom almost any education, and especially that beyond the 3 R's, was a new experience, educators needed help and turned to experts on learning. First came mass public education, said Snygg, then came Thorndike!

Because the world is constantly in social and physical motion, history never repeats itself precisely as before. The patterns are very similar, however. If the situation seems complicated by race, previously there were other factors like religion, foreign language, and alien culture. And now at least we are aided by advances in our knowledge. Through the investigations of Pasamanick and Knobloch (1960), Harper, Fischer, and Rider (1959), and others in the U. S., and Drillien (1961) and Douglas (1956) in Britain, it is apparent that premature birth is associated with insults that affect learning capacity, and the incidence of prematurity is significantly higher in the lowest social classes. In Brooklyn in 1957, as Freedman and others (1961) have reported, the rate of live premature births was 7.6 per 100 for whites and 15 for Negroes, with an overall rate of 9.1. In the Bedford area of Brooklyn, where both whites and Negroes are clearly socially deprived, the overall rate was 12.9 and in one area, 19.3.

Their Homes

When the school bell rings in the fall and the doors open wide, many of the bright-eyed kindergarteners come to class greatly handicapped, as others have been coming for the past 70 years or so. Their physical conditions of life from the moment of conception have threatened the integrity of the organism; their social conditions of life with its economic insecurity in a hostile world threatened the integrity of the person (Clark, 1955; Mitchell, 1962); the low educational level of the parents, the fatigue and drudgery that frustrate adult learning, have denied their children intellectual stimulation, even though most such parents value education for their young. Handicapped in these ways would it not be the socially desirable thing to provide them with the best possible education today? In the interest of the educational level of the population, of preventive mental health measures, of the prevention of delinquency, surely the best is indicated.

Their Schools

Yet it is very much less than the best that they get. In her study of Big City, a major midwestern industrial center, Sexton (1961) compared the schools in lower- versus higher-income districts. Presumably the educationally handicapped children should have smaller classes. In fact, in this large city school the class size of the lower half of the income distribution averaged two students more than the higher-income group.

One would expect the educationally handicapped children to be assigned the best teachers. It is difficult to evaluate quality of teaching. Sexton's method was to compare the per cent of not fully qualified teachers, those known as "Emergency Substitutes in a Regular Position." In the lower-income group 17.9 per cent of the teachers were such substitutes, in the upper group only 5.5 per cent. In addition the fully licensed teachers in the upper-income schools tended to be more experienced and hence to get higher salaries than the licensed teachers in the lower-income schools.

One would expect the educationally handicapped children to be given the best possible facilities. The buildings used by the lower-income groups averaged about 45 years old; the upper-income schools, about 25 years. When facilities for instruction were evaluated, Sexton found that in most instances they were much more adequate in the upper-income schools. As one of the extreme and significant comparisons, only 2 per cent of the upper-income group schools *lacked* facilities for science teaching, compared with 47 per cent of the lower income group. The investigator made other comparisons which led her to conclude:

> A typical upper-income child, then, goes to a school that is safer, more suitable and adequate for his needs, more attractive inside and out, with much better facilities in most subjects, including science, music, art and library, and also with better lighting, lavatory and other health facilities than the school attended by the average lower-income child (p. 132).

Perhaps the most startling finding of all in Big City was on the percentage of schools in each income group that served free meals or free milk to the needy. In districts where the average income exceeded $9,000, 78 per cent of the schools served free meals or milk to the needy; where the average family income ranged from $3,000 to $5,000, only 58 per cent of the schools made such provision.

The socially deprived in this large city have poorer lighting, lavatory, and other health facilities and have less opportunity for free nourishment in their schools. At the same time in the group of $9,000 income and more, only 7 per cent of the children did not receive health examinations compared with almost 50 per cent in the $3,000–$5,000 group. The per cent of children who received no treatment for diagnosed defects was approximately twice as great in the lower group, and the incidence of rheumatic fever, of diphtheria and TB, while small, was considerably greater in the lower-income group.

The Poor Get Poorer

As if they are not burdened enough, the day they enter the classroom the disadvantaged children are handicapped further by the conditions under which they are educated. And they respond as one would expect: their reading ability is inferior, their achievement poorer, their frustration greater, leading to a sequence of failure, disruptive behavior and drop-out. For a long time—a very long time—it has been the habit to turn to the IQ to explain the inferior performance of lower-class children. But of course they are poorer students—the reasoning goes—for, after all, they do have less intelligence. Their faculties for learning have been limited by the nature of their inheritance, and in their interest they should be assigned to classes with similarly limited ability. Thus, by grouping the children according to ability, the slower ones will not be frustrated by demands that exceed their capacity and the bright children—usually of the upper social-class groups—will not be slowed down. By the use of this educationally indefensible system, known as homogeneous ability grouping, the learning handicaps of the socially deprived children are intensified; the gap between the deprived and the advantaged children becomes widened each year; and the attitude of the lower-class children concerning their own inferiority is only confirmed. Despite the unprecedented breadth of our educational system and the true devotion of many persons to the ideal of universal education, our concepts of learning ability have successfully rationalized a program of schooling that tends to maintain a large group of poorly educated persons and our concepts also prevent major break-throughs in knowledge about the learning process. For the prevailing theory of learning ability sets limits to research as it does to school practice.

How did it happen that we adopted the theory that intelligence is fixed? How?—especially after Alfred Binet, father of the tests already in 1909, deplored the fact that

> . . . some recent philosophers appear to have given their moral support to the deplorable verdict that the intelligence of an individual is a fixed quantity. . . . We must protest and act against this brutal pessimism. A child's mind is like a field for which an expert farmer has advised a change in the method of cultivation, with the result that in place of desert land, we now have a harvest. It is in this particular sense, the one which is significant, that we say that the intelligence of children may be increased. One increases that which constitutes the intelligence of a school child, namely, the capacity to learn, to improve with instruction (Hunt, 1961, p. 13).

Why now, more than a half century later, must we be making the same assertions? Why now must we make strenuous efforts to free our schools and our research of such self-defeating ideas?

Who Should Be Educated?

In his work on the sociology of knowledge Mannheim (1936) explained that men ". . . do not confront the objects of the world from the abstract levels of a contemplating mind as such . . ." (p. 4). Scientists or scholars, they cannot attend to the physical or social world with a bland neutrality. Their perceptions of nature will be shaped by the mainstreams of thought to which they have been subjected. The intellectual activity of man may be broadly categorized as striving either "to change the surrounding world of nature and society or attempt to maintain it in a given condition" (p. 4). The validity of this concept can be found in examining the ideas on man's capacity to learn in any period of history. For example, Plato identified four classes of people. A person's education was to be determined by his class, and so, too, his station in life. This was not surprising from a man who thought democracy was the worst form of government and so distrusted the people that he felt that censors must safeguard their minds from wrong influences. The differential system of education that he proposed had a purpose: to maintain the position of the aristocracy in the declining days of the Athenian city-state, a state founded upon slavery.

In the early part of the 18th century, the Charity School movement arose in England. Its purpose was "to assure loyalty to the Established Church and to quiet the growing discontent among the poor" (Doughton, 1935, p. 60). The poor had little to hope for, because the purpose of the schools was clearly stated to be "to make them loyal church members, and to fit them for that station of life in which it had pleased their Heavenly Father to place them" (Doughton, 1935, p. 399). These were not schools designed to develop the mind, to encourage the social and physical sciences, to help individuals improve their society and their lot. Yet despite the inadequacies of the Charity Schools, one English writer declared:

> There is no Need of any Learning at all for the meanest Ranks of Mankind: Their Business is to Labour, not to Think: Their Duty is to do what they are commanded, to fill up the most servile Posts, and to perform the lowest Offices and Drudgeries of Life for the Conveniency of their Superiors, and common Nature gives them Knowledge enough for this Purpose (Doughton, 1935).

It should be noted that this was an Englishman writing about other Englishmen. The problem was not racial or ethnic but clearly that of the struggle between those who demanded education for the socially deprived and those who resisted such demands. By the end of the 19th century the clamor for improvements had reached a high peak, but was met by a so-called scientific interpretation of human ability. Francis Galton introduced the normal curve distribution to the study of individual differences. By one of the most curious examples of circular reasoning we were led to believe that intelligence is normally distributed. You start with the assumption that this is so; you then devise a test in such a way that the results will distribute themselves to coincide with a normal curve; you look at the findings which are, of course, normally distributed and you conclude that nature has really distributed man's learning ability in this way. And so a test like Binet's, whose author never intended it as a measure of something fixed or unchangeable, has been used as evidence that lower-class children are less well endowed and can benefit only from limited education.

They Can Be Helped

But what happens when such a view of man's learning capacity is challenged? What happens when under the pressure of growing demands for better education for the socially deprived an experimental program of better quality education is introduced? New York City undertook the Demonstration Guidance Project in 1957 (Demonstration Guidance Project, 1961). About 150 socially deprived boys and girls entering the academic program in a high school were given small classes and also remedial and psychological assistance when they needed it. At the end of their senior year they were compared with four preceding classes, and their superiority was clear in each of the following: the per cent who were graduated from high school; the per cent that completed the academic program; and finally the per cent of students that continued their education. And in the process the mean IQ (Pintner) of the experimental class members *rose* from 92.9 in ninth grade to 102.2 in the twelfth.

These results are not surprising. The limits of human learning are really unknown and cannot be gauged by an IQ test or past performance. Confronted with learning problems in children the correct response is not to attribute them to nature or heredity, nor even in some mechanistic sense to environment. The appropriate response is to analyze the causes and eliminate them. Such analysis requires a careful study of the nature of learning in man.

Current theory about the development of mental processes allows us to be optimistic about our capacity to increase vastly the level of education in the nation. Let us examine three major positions.

The Swiss psychologist Piaget (1952) uses the term *schema* to apply to basic intellectual operations. A schema arises as an adaptive measure but only as a consequence of the organism's interaction with the environment. In the processes of assimilating experience the mental structures are developed. ". . . at every level, experience is necessary to the development of intelligence" (p. 362). As one American student of Piaget has recently written: "Structures come into being in the course of intellectual functioning; it is through functioning, and only through functioning, that cognitive structures get formed" (Flavell, 1963, p. 43). The concepts and operations available to an individual, his mind or intelligence, if you will, depend to a considerable degree on the transactions he has with the environment.

The American psychologist Hunt (1961) studied the evidence coming from research on animal learning, from neuropsychology, from programming of electronic computers for problem solving, and from developmental psychology and concluded that "intelligence should be conceived as intellectual capacities based on central processes hierarchically arranged within the intrinsic portions of the cerebrum . . . the assumptions that intelligence is fixed and that its development is predetermined by the genes are no longer tenable." On the contrary, intellectual development grows from the encounters the child has with his environment. And the central task of those interested in the management of child development is to determine the kinds of encounters that will generate optimal development.

The Russian psychologist Leontiev (1963) wrote that the organs of learning ". . . are formed in the child in the course of life. . . ." These are "functional cerebral systems . . . formed in the actual process" of appropriating man's historical experience. Such organs or systems of learning are sometimes inadequately formed or even not formed at all. Such is the case of musical "tone deafness." By analysis of the structure of the processes it is possible to form the underlying functional systems. By this manner Leontiev developed a technique to form the function of normal tone hearing in those diagnosed as tone deaf. The development of adequate mental actions requires careful guidance by adults. First the child is trained in external actions (e.g., separating five blocks from a larger number). Then the external actions are transformed into speech (e.g., counting five aloud), and finally into internal actions (e.g., counting five "in the mind"). Note that these internal mental actions acquired by the child which form the basis of concepts and knowledge first begin with the demonstrated external action and the speech of the adult.

Piaget, Hunt, and Leontiev and the many scientists in the world for whom they speak share the same central position: the mental functions of human beings develop in the process of learning. While mastering the experience of mankind the cerebral systems are formed. They develop into hierarchical structures, with the more advanced systems arising during the course of the child's experience only if earlier formations have provided the foundational elements.[1]

---

[1] Children who count on their fingers, who have not, that is, mastered the operation of *mental* addition, cannot go on to more advanced stages of arithmetic. The placement in a "slow" group is no solution. Instead they need to return to an earlier stage in the mastery of arithmetic in order to develop the ability to count mentally (Leontiev, 1963). Before any such action is taken it is necessary to diagnose the *cause* of their failure to go on to advanced stages. This procedure applies to all forms of learning, to all academic subjects.

The education of the child begins in infancy. Five or six years later those who enter school with inadequately formed or unformed cerebral functions require diagnostic and corrective measures. They must be helped to acquire these functions through the planned actions of teachers who do not just permissively wait around for some predetermined potential to develop. The children must believe that the community wants them to learn. To label them "slow" or "backward" is simply to intensify their deficiencies and to destine them to a man-made intellectual backwardness with all its tragic social consequences. It is true, as Conant (1961) points out, that learning in school is never independent of social conditions. Improvement in the education of the socially deprived requires "an improvement in the lives of the families who inhabit the slums . . . [and] . . . a drastic change in the employment prospects . . ." (p. 147). Conant is very much mistaken, however, when he advocates that the elementary school syllabus be varied according to the socioeconomic status of the children. He is in error when he advocates that slum junior high schools in which half the children read at the fourth grade level or below should not offer algebra or foreign languages. In educating children who have been intellectually deprived, the solution is hardly to deprive them further. Certainly not in the 1960's, unless one really wants to maintain a large group of poorly educated people. For today, scientific data justify this optimistic statement: The socially deprived have the capacity to develop the cerebral functions necessary for advanced learning. Whenever our society shall want high-level universal education, it can have it. When that day comes our governments will provide public nursery schools for all infants and children, and financial support to students of all ages who need such help. They will educate many more teachers, pay them higher salaries to make additional work unnecessary and give them smaller classes. The colleges will teach the teachers to respect man's limitless mental capacities. All students will know that their society wants them to be educated. They will all take the liberalizing academic subjects and they will have jobs to look forward to. There will be problems in learning and teaching—vast and complex problems—but of course a great will to overcome them, especially through research.

Such research is under way. For example, M. Deutsch (1964, 1965) is investigating methods of offsetting the pre-school educational disadvantage of deprived children and the role of social class in development; John (1963), the intellectual development of slum children. C. Deutsch (in press) is studying the quality of auditory discrimination in the same population of children, and its relationship to learning. Thomas, *et al.* (1960), have been identifying persistent styles of behavior in normal children, including reactions to new experience, modes of adaptation, and persistence. These have implications for teacher behavior. Research on reading has challenged static views on learning, as in the case of Moore's (1960) use of the electric typewriter and an electronic storage retrieval system. His work lends support to the conclusions drawn by Fowler (1962) in his critical review of the literature on the capacity of pre-school children to learn to read. Investigations on the etiology of reading disability, as in Delecato's (1959) work on neurological organization, give at least tentative weight to a unifying theory on the relationship between neurological maturation and the sources of learning problems. The major contribution of Piaget, whose work (apart from his name) is still little known here, has been clearly delineated by Flavell (1963) and is available for research and application. Recent studies on the development of the child's mental processes have been reported by Bruner (1964). An evaluation of man's capacity for change is given in Bloom's (1964) important book. Other investigators at home and abroad are analyzing the processes of learning specific subjects, knowledge of which is essential to the improvement of diagnostic and teaching methods. All of these studies are based on an implicit assumption that man can comprehend the laws of cognitive growth and intervene in its development in increasingly effective ways.

It is fitting to conclude this brief analysis by reiterating the following: The socially deprived have the capacity to develop the cerebral functions necessary for advanced learning. Whenever our society shall want high-level universal education, it can have it.

REFERENCES

Bloom, Benjamin S. *Stability and change in human characteristics.* New York: Wiley, 1964.

Bruner, Jerome S. The course of cognitive growth. *Amer. Psychologist*, January, 1964, 19, 1–15.

Bruner, Jerome S. *Studies in cognitive growth.* New York: Wiley, 1964.

Clark, Kenneth B. *Prejudice and your child.* Boston: Beacon, 1955.

Conant, James B. *Slums and suburbs.* New York: McGraw-Hill, 1961.

Delecato, C. H. *The treatment and prevention of reading problems.* Springfield, Ill.: Charles C Thomas, 1959.

Demonstration Guidance Project. Fourth Annual Report, 1961. Board of Education, New York.

Deutsch, Cynthia. Auditory discrimination and learning: social factors. *Merrill Palmer Quart.*, July, 1964, 10, 277–296.

Deutsch, Martin. Social and psychological perspective for the facilitation of the development of the pre-school child. *Merrill Palmer Quart.*, July, 1964, 10, 249–263.

Deutsch, Martin. The role of social class in language development and cognition. *Amer. J. Orthopsychiat.* January, 1965, 35, 78–88.

Doughton, I. *Modern public education, its philosophy and background.* New York: Appleton, Century, 1935.

Douglas, J. W. B. Mental ability and school achievement of premature children at 8 years of age. *Brit. Medical J.*, 1956, 1, 1210.

Drillien, Cecil M. Longitudinal study of the growth and development of prematurely and maturely born children. Part VII, Mental Development 2–5 years. *Arch. Dis. Childh.*, June, 1961, 36, 233–240.

Flavell, J. H. *The developmental psychology of Jean Piaget.* New York: Van Nostrand, 1963.

Fowler, W. Cognitive learning in infancy and early childhood. *Psychol. Bull.*, 1962, 59, 116–152.

Freedman, Alfred M., *et al.* The effect of hyper-bilirubinemia on premature infants. Progress Report, New York Medical College, 1961.

Handlin, Oscar. *The uprooted.* New York: Grosset & Dunlap, 1951.

Handlin, Oscar. *The newcomers.* Cambridge, Mass.: Harvard Univ. Press, 1959.

Harper, Paul A., Fischer, L. K., and Rider, R. V. Neurological and intellectual status of prematures at 3 to 5 years of age. *J. Pediat.*, December, 1959, 55, (6), 679–690.

Haubrich, Vernon F. Teachers for big-city schools. In Passow, A. H. (Ed.), *Education in depressed areas.* New York: Bureau of Publications, Teachers College, Columbia University, 1963.

Hunt, J. McV. *Intelligence and experience.* New York: Ronald Press, 1961.

John, V. P. The intellectual development of slum children: some preliminary findings. *Amer. J. Orthopsychiat.*, October, 1963, 33, 813–822.

Leontiev, A. N. Principles of mental development and the problem of intellectual backwardness. In Simon, B., and Simon, J. (Eds.), *Educational psychology in the U.S.S.R.* Stanford, Calif.: Stanford Univ. Press, 1963.

Mannheim, Karl. *Ideology and utopia.* New York: Harcourt, Brace, 1936.

Mitchell, C. The culturally deprived—a matter of concern. *Childh. Educ.*, May, 1962, 38, 412–415.

Moore, O. K. Orthographic symbols and the pre-school child—a new approach. *Proceedings,* Third Minnesota Conference on Gifted Children, Univ. Minnesota, October, 1960.

Pasamanick, Benjamin, and Knobloch, H. Environmental factors affecting human development before and after birth. *Pediatrics,* 1960, 26, 210–218.

Piaget, Jean. *The origins of intelligence in children.* New York: International Univ. Press, 1952.

Sexton, Patricia. *Education and income.* New York: Viking Press, 1961.

Snygg, Donald. Learning: an aspect of personality development. In *The Kentucky symposium learning theory, personality theory and clinical research.* New York: John Wiley, 1954.

Thomas, Alexander, Chess, S., Birch, H., and Hertzig, M. A longitudinal study of primary reaction patterns in children. *Comprehen. Psychiat.*, April, 1960, 1 (2), 103–112.

Wayland, Sloane R. Old problems, new faces, and new standards. In Passow, A. H. (Ed.), *Education in depressed areas.* New York: Bureau of Publications, Teachers College, Columbia University, 1963.

MARTIN DEUTSCH
Director of the Institute for Developmental Studies, Department of Psychiatry,
New York Medical College

34 · EARLY SOCIAL ENVIRONMENT AND SCHOOL ADAPTATION

• This paper will make no attempt to incorporate the total complex of social institutions involved in school failure, for this can lead only to a loss of the direction necessary to the carving out of relevant and malleable chunks of the problem. For this reason, the focus will be largely on the school, an institution that in itself cannot initiate major social change, but one which can play a determining role in orienting its products. The school is, after all, the only social institution which has some contact with *all* children.

There is variation in the impact of this contact from group to group, fostered through (1) the child's preparation by his parents for entry into school, (2) the general meaning of the school to the economic substance of the community, and (3) the various expectations of the school and the appropriateness of its curriculum for the child. These differences in the interaction among the child, the school, and the community are determined, among other things, by social attitudes toward education, stability of community, the social class and ethnic membership of family, and the sex of child.

Generally speaking, the middle-class child is more likely to have the importance of school imprinted in his consciousness from the earliest possible age. This is not necessarily bad or good for the child or the school, but it is very different from the preparation of the lower social status child. I

Teachers College Record, 66:699–706, 1965. Used by permission of the author and *Teachers College Record*.

have never seen a school curriculum that is organized on the basis of the existence of these differences. Both sets of children are typically asked to climb the same mountain at the same rate, as if they had similar prior experience and training. The lower-class child, because of poorer preparation, is at a real disadvantage in this exercise, although it is the middle-class child who probably has more personal anxiety about the success of his climb. The middle-class child, however, has available to him other avenues for handling the school situation. There is more likely to be contiguity from the school's orientation to his home-and-family orientation. Failure can be interpreted to him in appropriate and familiar terms, and methods of coping with it can be incorporated, increasing the motivation or offering the necessary rewards, incentives, or punishments to effect the desired changes in performance. For the middle-class child, the school is very central and is continuous with the totality of his life experiences. As a result, there are few incongruities between his school experiences and any others he is likely to have had, and there are intrinsic motivating and moulding properties in the school situation to which he has already been highly sensitized.

What Failure Means

For the lower-class child, there is not the same contiguity or continuity, and he does not have the same coping mechanisms for internalizing success or psychologically surviving failure in formal learning. If the lower-class child starts to fail, he does not have the same kinds of operationally significant and functionally relevant support from his family or community —or from the school—that his counterpart has. Further, because of the differences in preparation, he is more likely to experience failure. It may even be that both groups are equally motivated quantitatively; but failure or lack of recognition for the middle-class child may only serve to channel his energies more narrowly, whereas for the lower-class child, it early becomes dysfunctional, converting the original motivation into a rejection of intellectual striving.

Failure in school for the middle-class child can be more personally disorganizing because the continuity of values from home to school insures that such a child will be considered a failure in both places. As already pointed out, however, there are also more resources available for helping the child to cope with the failure and to recover from it, and to mitigate its degree.

For the lower-class child, school failure may result in less personal upset or disturbance but may be more final, both in the recovery of adequate functioning in school and in occupational choices. Such failure may have the result of gradually but effectively alienating the child from the school and the structure of opportunities associated with it. In addition, though lower-class parents may or may not be opposed to the specific act involved in the child's leaving school prematurely, they may have made clear to the child their own negative affect in response to their personal experiences with social institutions. Particularly the minority-group lower-class parent is likely to explain, rationalize, and attribute job and economic frustration, both correctly and incorrectly, to impersonal societal institutions. He may thus identify, accurately and inaccurately, these same institutions with his child's troubles in school. Such negative attitudes can rapidly, though perhaps inadvertently, be generalized to the whole school-learning process. This kind of constellation has particular significance where the school system operates as a bureaucratic mechanism, isolated from the community and unable to counteract the consequences of inadequate preparation for functioning in the school factory. So the school, at the time the child decides to leave it, has little influence with either the child or the parent, and even if it did, it is frequently just not programed for interpreting its own processes to children or adults from outside the middle class.

Call for Prevention

Thus, if the school is to influence the continued attendance of children, the influence must begin and the channels for its transmission must be opened well before failure and dropout problems arise.[1] This brings us to the first contact of the child and his parents with the school. The process of alienation or, on the other hand, of increasing rapport, begins here. It is at this level that certain crucial questions must be asked: First, is the child intellectually and psychologically ready for the school experience, for the specific curriculum, and for the demands of comprehension, communication, motor control, and timing made by the school? The reference here is not to specific "readiness" as the term has been characteristically

[1] Of course, not all dropouts are school failures (and there might even be instances when high-performance creative children *should* drop out of school—but that is another paper), but the evidence suggests that the majority are. Similarly, of course, all dropouts are not lower-status children. But again, the majority are, and I would postulate that with middle-class children there is a higher incidence among dropouts of psychological malfunctioning, while with lower-status children, it is more likely to be associated with socio-cognitive dissonance, and general problems of communication.

used in educational circles but, rather, to the socio-cognitive preparations and anticipations of the child for this new experience. Next, are the parents helped to become aware of the school's purpose, the nature of its demands on the child, and how they—even if uneducated—can play a meaningful role in the education of their child? Is the school accessible to these parents? In other words, is it a place which stimulates embarrassment for their ignorance and fear of its power, or is it a center for comfortable relationships and a sharing of their interest in their child?

In this interaction among three elements, what about the school itself— the third element? Is it a structure that the community can be proud of and where the staff can share this pride? Does it have teachers and administrators who see a challenge, or are they interested only in securing discipline and in surviving the day? Do they have some understanding of the social backgrounds of their children and the temporary educational limitations that may have been imposed by these backgrounds? Is there a reasonable amount of staff stability, particularly in the early years? And is there some attempt to adjust the curriculum and primers to current life realities?

Lower-Class Alienation

The answers to these questions we all really know. The experiences of the child from the disadvantaged background simply do not prepare him for successful school performance. The teacher has, more often than not, *not* been trained in the sociology of learning; and also, more often than not, her training fails to give her a sense of challenge in teaching children, particularly those who start out with handicaps. Usually, she prefers, both by training and personal inclination, the immediately bright, responsive child who also most likely places a type of demand on her professional skills which is more congruent with the orientation of her training. The schools are likely to be underequipped, closed to the children for afterschool experimentation with extracurricular books and arts and crafts, and closed to the community as evening centers for learning and socializing. Nobody is responsible for explaining to the parents how they can help or be important factors in the education of their child, and the whole process of their child's education—even for the few who become active in the PTA —remains foreign and alien to them. Often, their contact with the school carries a condescending quality. The early curriculum is likely to be unfamiliar and experientially discontinuous, while the primer, despite all criticism, is still most likely to be boring, repetitious, suburban, and altogether too white.

What have been stated here, of course, are some of the major problems of getting a grip on children from social and cultural backgrounds which do not participate in the middle-class values of the school. These problems are raised not because it is now fashionable to identify them as the source of all of our current social difficulties but because they define human realities we are just beginning to face in relation to our educational ideals. We cannot avoid the necessary focus on the early relationship among the child, the family, and the school, and on the transition between the pre-school environment and the school. These factors are crucial if we mean what we say about universal education and educational opportunity.

Considering all these combinations, factors, and circumstances, it is amazing that as many children as do still find sufficient relevance in the school experience to remain. Parenthetically, it must be noted that the real occupational expectations of lower-class children are more congruent with their homes and their community experiences than they are with the school setting. It may be that only as school is perceived as more functionally relevant to adult occupations that early negative experiences can become decreasingly influential in the decision to leave school. Here is not meant the Conant solution of simply more vocational high schools but, rather, the *same opportunity distribution for all populations,* regardless of subgroup membership.

There are many possible avenues through which solutions for these problems could be evolved. But none of them exists independently, and any successful solution must involve a confluence of institutional changes on the level of the child, of the curriculum, of teacher preparation, adequate economic support for schools, and community-school bridges with two-way traffic. Nevertheless, there are certain possibilities for social intervention on the child-focused level that may open individual escape hatches and that may require only minimal changes in the structures and processes of current school operation. The most important of these areas of social intervention, and one that comes least into conflict with existing institutionalized barricades to change, is that of an intensive, highly focused pre-school training program.

Ripeness Is All

From present data, it cannot be said definitely that there is any direct relationship between early school experience and the school dropout; but I hypothesize a very strong relationship between the first school experiences of the child and academic success or failure, and that the more invariant the school experience is, the more important is the early experience to the academic success of the child. I also hypothesize that children who have had preschool and kindergarten experience are more likely to cope appropriately with the kinds of things the school demands intellectually than are children who have not had this kind of previous experience. This would be particularly true for children from lower socio-economic groups, and it would be most true for children who come from the most peripheral groups in our society.

For example, what happens when a child from these groups comes to school for the first time in the first grade? If he has not had experience with books, with the kinds of perceptual and developmental demands that are made by the school, and with the kinds of language skills implicit in the nature of the communication that comes from the teacher to the child, then that child's chances of starting to fail within the school situation are greatly enhanced. It is common in the first grade for a teacher to talk to the class for a period of ten minutes or so. Yet very often these children have never before experienced a ten-minute-long speech sequence coming from an adult to a child. So in school, at the very beginning, the child experiences "foreign" information coming in at a rapid rate, requiring complex auditory differentiations for which life has not suitably programed him. What is likely to happen in this process, and fairly immediately, is that the youngster will start to look upon school as a place where he doesn't understand and where he experiences debilitating failure. Perhaps more important, the teacher often starts to build in expectations of the child's failing. It is probable that, at a very early age, the child perceives this expectation of failure. And the children who are most likely to have these expectations directed toward them are children who come with the fewest aptitudes for fulfilling a middle-class set of values. They tend to be the most poorly dressed, to have a dialect, to come to school somewhat late, and, in general, not to fit naturally into the kinds of middle-class constraints and constrictions that are established within the school system.

The child who comes to school with very few of the kinds of intellectual cognitive structures that it demands will be basically the most susceptible to this process of failing, and he will be the least likely to start communicating with the teacher. The critical question, then, is whether a child can at least begin the educational process by learning the basic skills. In order to accomplish this for children from socially marginal backgrounds, some kind of antecedent experience to compensate for the inadequacies within their homes and in their intimate social environments would be highly likely to help them achieve a positive adjustment to the demands of the school. (The use of the term "adjustment" here is not meant to imply adjustment to the social aspects of the school process, or to the conformity pressures of the school. Such questions are beyond the scope of this paper.)

Leveling Upward

A good preschool program would attempt to bring the lower-class child to a kind of parity with the preparation for school that the home, community, and at least relative affluence characteristically give to the middle-class child. Such programs could only be set up after intensive training of teachers and staff to work on the problems of communicating with parents as well as developing methods and techniques for compensating the youngsters for a narrowness of experiential variation. The attempt would be to enrich those developmental areas most functional and operative in the school situation, thereby establishing both cognitive and attitudinal continuity between the preschool and school years. Hopefully, because the child is most responsive to acquiring basic skills at pre- and early-school ages, these skills can be fostered with reasonable readiness, and their acquisition can thus help lay the basis for a reduction in school failure experiences and for an increase in school success. The skills involved include, for example, the visual and auditory perception which underlies reading, language abilities, spatial and temporal orientation, general information, familiarity with books, toys, and games, and the development of a sustained curiosity. In addition, the attempt must be made to engage the child as an active participant in the learning process rather than as a passive recipient of a school experience.

School vs. Home?

In facilitating the learning process in underprivileged youngsters, the school must expect frequently to do a portion of the job traditionally assigned to the home, and the curriculum must be reorganized to provide for establishing a solid base for the special learnings that are necessary.

It is important to emphasize that the early training recommended here is not a matter of inculcating middle-class values but, rather, of reinforcing the development of those underlying skills that are operationally appropriate and necessary for both successful and psychologically pleasant school learning experiences. The fact that these skills are almost routinely stimulated in middle-class homes does not mean that in content they are middle class. For instance, there is nothing fundamentally culturally loaded in a good or poor memory, but it can be awfully important in preparing for an examination.

Another question must also be considered: How are the child's first anticipations developed toward the school? It is often stated that among Negro parents there is low motivation toward school accomplishment. I have not found this so. I've found a great degree of motivation, but a lack of understanding of how instrumentally to make these aspirations operative for the child. The problem, then, is to interpret for the child the kind of behavior that will make it possible for him to function well and to cope with the school's mechanisms. One way this could be handled is through a direct relationship between the teacher and the community. For example, there are some communities where the school is seen as a major and central resource center. Where it is kept open in the evening, there are library books that can be taken out, and the school can be favorably perceived as a place of social transition. When the school is a real part of his life and of his community, the child can more normally enjoy the opportunity some day to decide if he wants to move toward a learning experience consistent with the demands of the school, if he wants to stop with a lower level of education, or if he wants to seek advancement in some type of vocation with skills less closely related to the requirements of formal schooling.

To return more directly to the problem of anticipations toward the school, there is reason to believe that the sense of failure that often develops at an early stage projects itself through the total experiences of the persons—not only temporally, in terms of his reaction to the demands of the school, but also in terms of his whole concept of self-identification, of a positive self-concept, of the development of a sense of dignity. This sense of dignity, I think, is closely related to how much money, how much concern, and how much institutional modification we are willing to invest in education. In neighborhoods where most schools have practically every window broken, there are some protected schools which are beautifully kept. There is a reciprocal feedback, as if the institution and the children were working with and cooperating with one another, and there is a sense of mutual respect that goes along with it. Here too, of course, is where teacher training in community sociology and mental health becomes a very important issue.

Horizons and goals are stimulated early in life; and if the parents have had low ceilings because of impoverished experiences, having known job insecurity, humiliating negotiations with welfare agencies and landlords, and the like, there is not much left to give the child a sense of identifying himself with goals that entail initiative and disciplining. This problem, in a larger context, is societal and has its analogous aspects in the routinized existence of much of the middle-class, rigid schedules, automated work, and cities and suburbs that share an ugly sameness and drabness. Sometimes the excitement to be sparked in a child must reach his subjective self, his imagination and individual poetry. After this, he may make discriminations and differentiations not seen by his peers in the external world. This development of the inner self, which can certainly start soon after the development of language, can be an intrinsic part of the preschool experience and, possibly, a basis for much later motivation.

Female Dropouts

It is often in school that another element of the dropout problem, related to a different type of discrimination, takes form—and is regularly ignored. There is a special complex of difficulties associated with the female dropout. Typically, discussions of dropouts deal with all cases as an undifferentiated totality or concentrate on males without recognizing that many of the factors responsible for high dropout rates among Indian Americans, Negro Americans, etc., are similar to those operating on girls. At some undefined point, our social expectations as reflected through our teachers become differentiated with respect to intellectual behavior in boys and girls. This is probably not always a conscious distinction, but males of any social class are more or less expected to have to use their intellects in the business of preparing to make a living. For females, this assumption is less likely to be made, and the antecedent attitudes are probably manifested in the preschool and kindergarten. I know of no data here, but there is no other known area of strongly ingrained social attitudes and expectations which is completely discontinuous with earlier, though not necessarily discernible, orientations. It seems improbable that these sex-related expectations would develop only in the later school years. A high proportion of female school dropouts, then, are apt to be intellectually average girls who enjoy, proportionate to the boys, more academic success but still feel that intellectual development and their personal futures go along divergent paths. With society increasingly needing skilled people, the distinction between male and female intellectual roles must be explicitly eliminated early in the learning process if the later effects are to be minimized and if school is to offer the same potential to children regardless of sex.

The emphasis voiced here on the preschool program as a means of accommodation between the school, the child, and his family represents, it is felt, a necessary approach to the dropout problem. It is beyond our present scope to examine it from the other end of the continuum: the problem of the motivation of the high school student to join the labor force when the opportunities available to him may not be numerous or productive. Further, the high incidence of minority-group dropouts makes necessary a consideration of prejudice in employment patterns. But these are broad societal problems, to be attacked and solved in the social arena. And even if they were solved, the individual problems of the unprepared child coming into the unpreparing school would assume even greater importance. Developmentally, it would seem that preschool experience is one of the first areas in which to approach the problem, and one in which there may be less resistance.

There seems to be a great need currently to discuss all problems thoroughly, to investigate their causes, and to delineate all possible solutions; and then to implement only those solutions that have been rendered sufficiently sanitary that they represent no threat to the status quo. The danger to the approach discussed here is that it will be put into the context of the stress-free, allegedly supportive, momistically-oriented, deintellectualized enclosures where much of early childhood education is both considered and carried out. If such takes place, social experimentation would be sterilized and useless. But if social scientists and educators undertake relevant projects jointly, in a spirit of experimentation and with bovicidal collaboration against the accumulated sacred cows, the possibilities of humane success are greatly enhanced.

GROUP PROCESSES IN THE CLASSROOM

• Despite much talk about individual differences, the traditional ratio of teachers to pupils is one teacher to 25–35 pupils. Nevertheless there is surprisingly little treatment of groups and group dynamics in most educational psychology texts. In this section two articles and a review of a book are presented to initiate some study of groups from the standpoint of the practical educational psychologist—the teacher.

We definitely hold with the second of Boocock's hypotheses that those who are accepted and secure in their interpersonal relationships are more likely to have positive attitudes in other areas, and that freedom from anxiety and conflict will exert a positive effect on academic achievement. In terms of Maslow's arrangement of human needs into a hierarchy of prepotency, a person must feel security and belongingness before his major concern can be his need for learning or cognition.[1] In terms of the developmental task approach that holds that if certain competencies are not adequately developed at certain ages, achievement in subsequent tasks will be impeded, establishing or maintaining competence in interpersonal and social relationships is listed for substantially more of the ages than is gaining academic information.[2] It is not so much a question of what is most important in school as it is a question of what comes first. As students cannot be expected to write effectively without reading skills, so individuals cannot be expected to learn effectively before some social interaction skills

---

[1] Abraham H. Maslow, *Motivation and Personality* (New York: Harper and Brothers, 1954), pp. 80–106.

[2] R. J. Havighurst, *Developmental Tasks and Education,* 2nd ed. (New York: David McKay Company, Inc., 1952), 100 pp.

and a sense of belonging and identification with the group have been accomplished. Children develop in a holistic and integrated manner. If any aspect—physical, psychological, social, or intellectual—does not keep pace, the growth of all other aspects is impeded.

In their preoccupation with the academic and their neglect of the emotional and psychological facets of development, schools have tended to overlook groups and the possibilities for learning and teaching which they offer. Each classroom constitutes a potential human-relations laboratory. It has individuals interacting with one another in close proximity, in situations that can be easily observed. The sociometric devices advocated by Gronlund serve a useful function, but they usually stop with the identification of the isolate or problem student. Groups of youngsters, on the other hand, can provide a means not only of recognizing and analyzing self-defeating behavior patterns but of substituting new behaviors and validating their results in terms of group reactions. Teachers, because of their close contacts with youngsters, are in a better position than anyone else to facilitate and direct this process. Since knowing how to maintain effective interpersonal relationships is so crucial to the success and happiness of individuals, teacher-preparing institutions should include the development of some expertise in the dynamics and processes of groups. Teachers who do not have preparation in this area should seriously examine the increase in professional competence that it could give to them.

Runkel's review of the latest book by the Sherifs expresses high praise. We hope the reader of this volume will be encouraged to read the one by the Sherifs. In his review, Runkel reflects the notion that there is still much to learn about groups. Hence, this and the other selections are presented as an incentive to further study.

S. S. BOOCOCK
Research Associate, Department of Social Relations, the Johns Hopkins University

35 · TOWARD A SOCIOLOGY OF LEARNING: PEER GROUP EFFECTS ON STUDENT PERFORMANCE

(Part 3 of a four-part article.)

• Before turning to groups and institutions outside of the school, I shall consider the educational implications of a sub-system which is in a sense both inside and outside the school—i.e., "youth culture," the "adolescent society," the "adolescent sub-culture," or "peer group," to mention a few of the names given to this contemporary phenomenon.[1] The peer group is interesting structurally in that while its membership is made up almost entirely of high school and college students, it is not part of the formal organization of the school system.

Although Waller pointed as early as the 1930's to the basic conflict between the values and interests of the larger adult society which teachers represent and the things which are interesting and meaningful to children

Sociology of Education, 39:26–32, 1966. Reprinted by permission of the author and the American Sociological Association.

[1] While these terms are generally used interchangeably, this phenomenon can be considered on different levels, from the small friendship groups in particular schools to the general, and national, phenomenon, whose products and symbols (e.g., clothes, hair styles, music) are recognizable in almost any part of the United States.

Note also that some of the measures discussed in the last chapter under the topic of value climates are really measures of peer group opinion and thus relevant to this section also.

(Waller, 1932, Chapter 9), widespread debate and systematic analysis of youth culture has been relatively recent. Parsons (1962) sees it as an inevitable reaction to the "strains" in contemporary American society, in which rising levels of expectations for children are combined with permissive child-rearing practices and progressive educational methods. Coleman's adolescent society is a reflection of a highly industrialized society, in which the family has lost many of its former functions, especially those which made it a self-sufficient economic unit. Thus "the child can no longer help the family economically; in turn the family has little to offer the child in the way of training for his place in the community" (Coleman, 1961, p. 3).

There has also been disagreement over the structure of these informal youth groups. Smith (1962) sees them in terms of a series of transitory group memberships through which the young person progresses, from one-sex gangs to cliques increasingly oriented toward the opposite sex and culminating in marriage and the establishment of new families. To Smith, adolescent sub-group activities are an integral part of the normal progression toward adulthood. Eisenstadt, on the other hand, feels that one reason why the integration of young people into the larger community is so problematic in modern societies is that not only does the youth group, "whatever its composition or organization, usually stand alone," but also that it "does not constitute a part of a fully institutionalized and organized series of age groups" (Eisenstadt, 1962, p. 38).

Virtually all the analysts agree, however, on the existence of such a culture, distinct from, if not entirely independent of, adult culture and institutions.[2] What makes it of concern to educators and relevant to the topic of this paper is that—

—*the student's peer group seems to have tremendous influence upon his attitudes toward and behavior in school;*

—*this powerful influence seems often to work at variance with the learning-achievement goals of the school.*

Probably no study of adolescent sub-groups has created more interest and controversy than Coleman's, already discussed [earlier in the original article, of which the present selection is Part 3] under the topic of value

[2] There are a few dissenters. Elkin and Westley, 1955, see little conflict between parents and children and little evidence of any kind of separate youth culture. However, their conclusions are based upon a very small sample of cases in a rather atypical (upper middle class, professional and business, Canadian) suburb where parents and children seemed to participate in an unusually large number of joint activities.

climate, and it is worth reformulating some of the major findings within the framework of this section.

Coleman's thesis is that not only do high school students as a whole hold academic achievement in low esteem relative to athletics and other activities peculiar to their own culture, but that peer groups in many schools "exert a rather strong deterrent to academic achievement," actually working against the formal goals of the school system (Coleman, p. 265). No matter what the value climate of the schools, the social elites were less favorable to the "brilliant scholar" value than the non-elites (although the grade averages of the former tended to be higher). Students identified as athletic stars received more sociometric status than scholars, although the athlete-scholar usually received the most of all. And in schools where anti-intellectualism was especially strong among the leading crowds, those who were willing to take an intellectual role were not those with the highest intelligence, but those willing to work at a relatively unrewarded activity (Coleman, p. 265).

Finding no relationship between per pupil expenditure and achievement of students according to their abilities, Coleman concluded that no amount of money poured into school facilities will be really effective unless students value scholastic excellence. His recommendation was rather to apply the structure of activities that are highly supported by young people (e.g., interscholastic athletics) to the classroom.

Coleman's book has had strong supporters and vehement critics. My own reservations can perhaps be summed up by saying that many of the findings are inconsistent with consistency theory. For example, the members of leading crowds tended to value academic performance less but get better grades than the non-elites; the same was true of girls as compared to boys; academic values were not high in schools (such as Executive Heights) in which the highest proportions of students planned to attend college. That is, both on the individual and system levels there seems to be an inconsistency between the values of groups of respondents and their subsequent behavior. Three possibilities are suggested: the validity of Coleman's measures of value climate can be questioned; the peer culture may not be the only, or the strongest, influence in certain areas, such as academic performance; a lot of youngsters are under a lot of strain as a result of inconsistency between their stated values and their actual behavior.

On the college level, the most intensive recent examinations of peer influence upon academic commitments were the studies of Vassar College students, sponsored by the Mellon Foundation and directed by Nevitt Sanford (cf. Sanford, 1956; Freedman, 1956; Sanford, 1959; Bushnell, 1962). Questionnaire data and diaries (in which respondents recorded all their activities for several one-week periods) were collected from all students over a five-year interval. In addition, a sample drawn from one class was intensively interviewed and tested; an anthropologist was a kind of participant observer of the student culture; and some studies of alumnae were conducted.

Sanford and his associates found peer group influences operating in much the same way as those described by Coleman, although the pressures were perhaps more subtle. There was a distinct student culture. Girls resisted acculturation on the faculty's terms, not by rebelling against studying and achievement in general (good grades were, in fact, generally respected) but by resisting wholehearted commitment to scholastic achievement at the cost of satisfactory social relations with friends. The goal of the student culture was a pleasant campus life, with agreeable interpersonal relations and a minimum of conflict and soul-searching in connection with course work. Certain student norms—e.g., proscriptions against close relationships with professors or · excessive amounts of time spent on studying—functioned to maintain the relatively unruffled status quo that students thought desirable. It is interesting that the "scholar," one of several sudent "types" developed by Sanford, tended to be found among girls who had suffered "early and persistent awkwardness in social relations with peers" (Sanford, 1959).

The study by Hughes, Becker and Geer of student culture in a Kansas medical school acts as a kind of replication of the Vassar studies. Peer group effects showed up even more clearly in this setting because of the intense pressures placed on students by the formal requirements of medical training. The student culture was perceived to have two major functions: "first, to provide modes of adaptation that make the pressures of the school tolerable and not too upsetting to the individual student, and, second, to provide support for patterns of behavior which, though they are in the interest of the students as they see it, may be at variance with what is desired by the faculty and administration" (Hughes, et al., 1962, p. 466). Thus students reach informal agreements on what *all* of them will learn in preparation for exams (Hughes, et al., p. 525), and informal norms direct which and how many case summaries out of the total assigned by professors will actually be completed and turned in (Hughes, et al., pp. 527–528).

A striking thing about these three studies is their similarity to studies of informal factory work groups, such as the Hawthorne Study Bank Wiring Room experiments. In each case the small informal group is not part of the "official" system and is sometimes not even recognized by it. It is characterized by close ties of a "primary" sort, and has a great deal of control over the productivity of its members in respect to the goals of the formal organization.

A rather different approach to the analysis of peer group influence on the college level was taken by Wallace (1965), who compared the post-graduate aspirations of an entire freshman class of a midwestern college at three times during the school year. Wallace found that the proportion of freshmen wanting to go on to graduate or professional school after graduation rose at each subsequent measurement, bringing the freshman profile ever closer to the aspiration pattern of the upper classes. Even with measures of previous academic achievement and future occupational ambition held constant, the aspiration climate created by the freshman's older peers seemed to account for an appreciable amount of his aspiration change.

There were also some interesting interaction effects among the three factors. For example, peer influence seemed to be most powerful among those students with the *lowest* past academic achievement. Wallace interprets this finding as suggesting that "the rise in low academic rank freshmen's graduate school aspirations may have had more to do with their social attitudes toward, and experiences in, college than with their expectations of graduate school success" (Wallace, p. 384), and that the student who is weaker academically is also the one most likely to be susceptible to and to conform to peer group pressures. A similar pattern was found in connection with socio-economic ambition, with a greater rise in post-graduate study aspirations being expressed among freshmen who chose relatively low status occupations for themselves when they entered college.

A major distinction of the Wallace study is in the conceptualization of peer group influence. The Coleman-type analysis seeks to characterize the climate of a given school by locating it in one cell of a multidimensional property space, and its location on each dimension is determined by the expressed attitudes of the entire student body (or a representative sample of it). The Wallace study uses a technique, originally set forth by Peter Rossi, by which *each student* has an "Interpersonal Environment" score, obtained by having him check all the names he or she recognizes from a list of the entire student body (freshmen and non-freshmen). For each student, the measure "estimates that part of the total student-body with which he had direct or indirect contact sufficient to remember the names of its members" (Wallace, p. 378).

Wallace's method of measuring aspiration climate suggests that the very notion of climate may be more complicated than the Coleman type of measure implies. In a system as large as many schools are (the college

Wallace studied had a student body of 1,051), there may be two or more sub-groups each holding different sets of values. Thus a student who seems to be a deviant from the values of the student culture may be deviating from those of the most visible or "leading" clique but may be well integrated into his own sub-group. And even if one can distinguish a single—or at least a dominant—value climate, Wallace's conceptualization suggests that it may affect different students differently, depending upon which other members of the system they have contact with.

One of the reasons it is important to understand the dynamics of peer group influences and values is that people care so much about being liked and respected by their peers. A large portion of the work in the field of sociometry has centered around the measurement of peer group status. Two opposing hypotheses can be formulated relating sociometric status to learning. One hypothesis would predict a negative correlation, based on the reasoning that high achievement is an alternative or a compensation for unsatisfying interpersonal relations. The other hypothesis would predict a positive correlation, on the grounds that the student who feels accepted and secure in his interpersonal relationships will have a positive attitude in other areas as well and will be free of conflict and thus able to concentrate on school work.

Research evidence seems to favor the latter hypothesis slightly. In a review of studies of elementary school children Gronlund (1959) found positive correlations between achievement test scores and sociometric status ranging from .14 to .36, and these correlations tended to get stronger when comparisons were made between only the highest and lowest status groups. Ryan and Davie (1958) got similar results in a study of four Connecticut high schools, and concluded that social acceptance, at least in terms of their rather crude measure, accounted for "a small portion of grade variance" (Ryan and Davie, p. 102). Buswell (1953) found that the correlations tended to disappear when intelligence was controlled, I.Q. and achievement being themselves highly related. Buswell attributed the small original correlation to a tendency for children to over-choose others who are pretty similar or *slightly* above them in achievement and intelligence rather than greatly superior.

The lack of striking correlations lead Gronlund and Ryan and Davie to conclude, as Coleman did, that social acceptance is not a uniform factor but depends upon the character of the school and its component parts. "School achievement is probably most closely related to sociometric status where such achievement is highly valued by the group. . . . Thus, when the relation between school achievement and sociometric position is being considered, the level of achievement of the choosers as well as that of the chosen must be considered" (Gronlund, pp. 195–196).

In conclusion, while the true strength and nature of peer group influences are not yet known, it seems clear that educational programs that work against peer values are doomed to failure. The best thing to do with such a potentially powerful force is to use it, and the search for areas of agreement between youth and adult culture and for methods of teaching that retain the structure and channel the energies of student friendship groups seems a very fruitful kind of research. Student tutoring programs, team projects, and academic games are a few modes of instruction designed to use such groups to further learning goals.

REFERENCES

Bushnell, J. H. "Student Culture at Vassar." In N. Sanford (ed.) *The American College*. New York: Wiley, 1962, 489–514.

Buswell, M. M. "The Relationship between the Social Structure of the Classroom and the Academic Success of the Pupils." *Journal of Experimental Education*, 22 (1953), 37–52.

Coleman, James S. *The Adolescent Society*. New York: Free Press, 1961.

Eisenstadt, S. N. "Archetypal Patterns of Youth." *Daedalus*, 91 (Winter, 1962), 28–46.

Elkin, Frederick, and William A. Westley. "The Myth of Adolescent Culture." *American Sociological Review*, XX (Dec., 1955), 680–684.

Freedman, M. "The Passage Through College." *Journal of Social Issues*, 12 (1956), 12–28.

Gronlund, Norman E. *Sociometry in the Classroom*. New York: Harper, 1959.

Hughes, E. C., H. S. Becker, and B. Geer. "Student Culture and Academic Effort." In N. Sanford (ed.) *The American College*. New York: Wiley, 1962, 515–530.

Parsons, Talcott. "Youth in the Context of American Society." *Daedalus*, 91 (Winter, 1962), 97–123.

Ryan, F. J., and J. S. Davie. "Social Acceptance and Academic Achievement among High School Students." *Journal of Educational Research*, 52 (1958), 101–106.

Sanford, N. "Personality Development during the College Years." *Journal of Social Issues*, 12 (1956), 1–71 (entire issue).

Sanford, N. "Motivation of High Achievers." In O. D. David (ed.) *The Education of Women*. Washington, D. C.: American Council on Education, 1959, 34–38.

Smith, Ernest A. *American Youth Culture*. Glencoe, Ill.: Free Press, 1962.

Wallace, Walter L. "Peer Influences and Undergraduates' Aspirations for Graduate Study." *Sociology of Education*, 38 (1965), 377–392. This complete study has been published as: *Peer Groups and Students' Achievement*. Chicago: Aldine, 1965.

Waller, Willard. *The Sociology of Teaching*. New York: Wiley, 1932.

NORMAN E. GRONLUND
Professor of Educational Psychology, University of Illinois

36 · SOCIOMETRY AND IMPROVED SOCIAL RELATIONS IN THE CLASSROOM

● The sociometric technique has been widely used in school settings to study the social acceptance of individuals and the social relations of group members. Although its greatest use has been at the elementary school level, it is finding increasing use at the high school level. The simplicity of the technique and the variety of purposes served by the results have made it a welcome addition to the other evaluation procedures used in the classroom.

In using the sociometric technique, the teacher simply asks the students to choose a given number of companions for some group situation or activity. For example, students may be requested to select seating companions, laboratory companions, fellow committee members, or the like. Their choices are written on a slip of paper, or a specially prepared form, and turned in to the teacher for analysis and for use in rearranging the group.

The basis for choice on a sociometric test should be a natural part of the ongoing classroom activity and the students should be assured that their choices will be put into effect. If five choices are allotted for a particular situation, it is usually possible to satisfy at least two choices for each student. Since the reliability of sociometric results has been shown to increase up to the five-choice limit, and not beyond that number, five choices seems to be a good number to use with each sociometric question.[1]

The High School Journal, 48:391–395, March, 1965. Used by permission of The University of North Carolina Press.

[1] Gronlund, Norman E. *Sociometry in the Classroom.* New York: Harper & Row, 1959.

In analyzing sociometric results each choice should be given a value of one regardless of level of choice. There seems to be no logical basis for assigning weights to the various levels and the use of one point for each choice simplifies the analysis. The social acceptance of each student is determined by simply totaling the number of choices received. The social relations of the group members can be revealed by plotting the results in the form of a sociogram. This is a graphic representation of the choices made by each individual. It is especially useful in detecting cliques, cleavages, and similar social patterns existing in the group structure.

Sociometric results have been found to be surprisingly stable from one time to another, from one choice situation to another, and from one group to another. Wertheimer[2] studied the sociometric status scores of 200 high school students who stayed in the same home room classes over a two-year period and reported considerable stability over that period of time. Results obtained 20 months apart correlated .69 for boys and .62 for girls. A study by Gronlund and Whitney[3] has cast light on the extent to which classroom social status can be interpreted as a measure of general social acceptability. They asked students in 12 home room classes to choose the *classmates* they most preferred as seating companions, and then to choose from *throughout the entire school population* those students they most preferred as fellow classmates in their home room the following year. On the first choice situation all choices were, of course, confined to pupils within the same classroom. On the second choice situation, approximately 40 per cent of the choices went to pupils in classes other than those in which the choices were given. Despite the relatively large percentage of choices passing *between* classrooms on the second choice situation, the students' sociometric status scores correlated .72 over the two situations. In other words, the students' social acceptance in the classroom was significantly related to their social acceptance throughout the school. A further analysis of the results indicated that students who were isolated (i.e., received no choices) in the classroom tended to remain social isolates when choices were made on a school-wide basis. Studies such as these tend to support the significance of classroom sociometric results.

There are a number of specific ways that sociometric results can be used by the classroom teacher. These can best be described in terms of diag-

[2] Wertheimer, R. R., "Consistency of Sociometric Status Position in Male and Female High School Students," *Journal of Educational Psychology*, 48:385–390, 1957.

[3] Gronlund, N. E. and Whitney, A. P., "Relation Between Pupils' Social Acceptability in the Classroom, in the School, and in the Neighborhood," *School Review*, 64:267–271, 1956.

nostic, therapeutic, and evaluative uses. All of the uses have implications for improved social relations and, hopefully, a resulting salutary effect on learning.

Diagnostic Uses of Sociometric Results

The major value of the sociometric test as a diagnostic tool resides in its ability to identify problems which originate from, or are influenced by, the social structure of the group. Such problems include the socially isolated student, social cleavages along racial, religious, or social lines, and small clique structures which may have an undesirable influence on group functioning. Sociometric results do not indicate why these social patterns exist nor what to do about them, but they do provide a good starting point for further study. The choices to and from individuals also provide clues to group rearrangement which might have a beneficial effect on the social relations of the group members.

In analyzing sociometric results, it is important to interpret the data in light of all other information known about the students. A socially isolated student, for example, may be busily pursuing his own individual interests and have little need for a circle of friends, or he may be so desperately unhappy in his social isolation that he is unable to concentrate on his school work. Similarly, a student may be socially isolated because he is shy and withdrawn, because he is hostile and aggressive, or simply because he differs from the other group members in some way (e.g., race, religion, or social class). To obtain full meaning from sociometric results, consideration must be given to a student's need for social interaction, his personal characteristics, and the social forces operating in the group. Social relations are the product of numerous factors interacting in complex ways and simple interpretations are seldom adequate.

In addition to their use in identifying social relations problems per se, sociometric results can also aid in a fuller understanding of other types of classroom problems. The social acceptance and social relations patterns of the retarded reader, the slow learner, the difficult discipline case, the truant, and the like, can aid in analyzing their difficulties and possibly provide clues for remediation. Difficulties in social relations both contribute to and are affected by problems of learning and adjustment in other areas of development.

Therapeutic Uses of Sociometric Results

The most direct contribution of sociometric results to improved social relations can be seen in the arrangement and rearrangement of classroom groups along sociometric lines. Through sociometric grouping each student is given a position in which he feels psychologically comfortable, and consequently one that provides him with the greatest opportunity for developing satisfying social relations. There is some research evidence to support the claim that the sociometric arrangement of classroom groups has a beneficial effect on social interaction, but most of the studies were done at the elementary school level.

One study,[4] using high school students, is of interest because it involved the sociometric grouping of an entire freshman class. In the spring of the year, all freshmen were asked to indicate their preferences for classmates in their home rooms the following year. The home room classes for the sophomore year were then arranged by placing each student in the home room which satisfied the largest number of his sociometric choices. A follow-up sociometric test at the end of the sophomore year indicated a general increase in the students' social acceptance scores over those obtained a year earlier. Although this study was of the "action research" type, without a control group for comparison, the findings suggest that sociometric grouping at the high school level may be of therapeutic value.

When arranging sociometric groups, consideration also should be given to factors other than the students' choices. It may, for example, be desirable to break up a clique that is having a disturbing influence on the class or to provide for greater social interaction between subgroups formed along racial, religious or social class lines. Such adjustments can be made within the framework of sociometric choosing, and, of course, any promises made to the students concerning the number of choices they will have satisfied must be kept. Where sociometric groups are formed in a mechanical fashion (i.e., on the basis of sociometric choices alone), there is the danger that clique formations and social cleavages will be further increased; resulting in a detrimental rather than a beneficial influence on students' social relations.

Evaluative Uses of Sociometric Results

Another use of the sociometric test is in evaluating the influence of various school practices on students' social relations. Probably the most common use in this regard is in evaluating special programs designed to improve social relations. The effectiveness of our efforts to integrate racial groups in the classroom, for example, can be partially determined by noting changes in the number of sociometric choices passing between members

---

[4] Amundson, C. L., "Increasing Interpersonal Relationships in the High School with the Aid of Sociometric Procedures," *Group Psychotherapy*, 6:183–188, 1954.

of the different groups. Similarly, we can evaluate the success of programs aimed at improving social interaction between social classes, religious groups, rural-urban students, and the like.

Sociometric results can also contribute to an evaluation of programs not directly concerned with improving students' social relations. If ability grouping is used in the school, for example, sociometric data can help us determine if a social cleavage is developing between the various ability groups. In a like manner, we can determine the social effect of different teaching techniques, promotional practices, special classroom activities, and the like. Although numerous other factors must be considered in evaluating a particular practice, whether it has beneficial or detrimental effects on students' social relations is an important consideration.

A study by Forlano[5] illustrates one of the many ways that sociometric data can be used for evaluation purposes. He measured changes in students' social acceptance scores in core and noncore classes and found that core classes contributed to greater gains in interpeer acceptance. While no one would claim that the main objective of core classes is to improve students' social relations, the finding is of significance in an over-all evaluation of the influence of core classes on student development.

In summary, the sociometric test is easily administered, it provides a fairly stable and general measure of social relations, and the results can be used for diagnostic, therapeutic, and evaluative purposes. Despite the apparent usefulness of sociometric results, however, they provide no panacea for our educational problems. The modern classroom teacher will use many diagnostic techniques, a variety of grouping methods, and a wide array of evaluation procedures. The sociometric test is simply a useful adjunct— one which directs special attention to students' social relations.

[5] Forlano, George, "Peer Acceptance in Core and Noncore Classes," *The Journal of Educational Research*, 57:431–433, 1964.

PHILIP J. RUNKEL
Associate Director, Center for the Advanced Study of Educational Administration,
University of Oregon

---

37 · CONFORMITY AND DEVIATION: Review of REFERENCE GROUPS: EXPLORATION INTO CONFORMITY AND DEVIATION OF ADOLESCENTS

A review of a book by Muzafer Sherif and Carolyn W. Sherif

Reference Groups: Exploration into Conformity and Deviation of Adolescents by Muzafer Sherif and Carolyn W. Sherif. New York: Harper and Row, 1964. 370 pp.

● Amid the current frenzied discussion of whither our youngsters, this book returns us to the firm ground of observable events. It shows us how to take a close and long look at adolescent behavior; a close look in the sense of actual observations of adolescents interacting with each other, and a long look in making sound interpretations of what we have observed. It deserves to become a handbook both for those who work directly with youth and for researchers into social organization. In fact, one of the important contributions of this book is the strong bridge it builds between those who work with youth on the one hand and the social scientists on the other. For school people, social workers,

---

The Educational Forum, 30:103–109, November, 1965. Used by permission of Kappa Delta Pi, an Honor Society in Education, owners of the copyright.

and other practitioners, the Sherifs lay out in bold relief the knowledge of the adolescent's world which the practitioner must have if he is to accomplish what he has set out to do. For the social scientist, the Sherifs make very plain the special characteristics of the world of the adolescent which those who plan research into that world must take into account. This book will, I hope, become a standard fixture on the shelves both of those who work with youth and of those who study society.

At many places in their book, the Sherifs pit their findings (and the findings of other research) against current popular notions about adolescent behavior. Their arguments for their conclusions are cogent and their illustrations often colorful. I shall quote some of their comments about some of the current notions they discuss, but there is not space here to convey adequately the style of the book, which is at the same time sober and lively.

Are adolescent groups (cliques, gangs, clubs) pervasive throughout our society or do they occur only in certain segments of the society? The Sherifs studied twelve adolescent groups distributed over three levels of neighborhood and two types of cities. After displaying the data and giving numerous illustrations, they conclude that adolescent groups having important influence on the behavior of their members arise in all segments of society. They comment that

> The structure and functions of adolescent groups in respectable and affluent social strata are glossed over. . . . For various reasons related to the resources of their parents, their actions do not usually get counted in social statistics. For these reasons, the usual adult reaction to youthful misbehavior of groups in "favored" areas is one of surprise (p. 237).

> The resources of youngsters in more favored neighborhoods really make it much simpler to interact regularly in private and to keep forbidden activities secret (p. 238).

Are adolescent groups composed of pathological types? One might suppose that the Sherifs, as social psychologists, would be loathe to say *yes* to such a question, and so they are. The Sherifs hold the great bulk of delinquent behavior to be a result of normal group processes in special settings. Evidence for this point of view is to be found throughout the book, culminating in Chapters 11 and 12. Here is a comment on method and a summary statement.

> Lacking [adequate] data, a competent social worker characterized one of the boys we studied as "not only *anti*-social, but completely *a*social." She had observed and interviewed him at a recreation center

whose adult personnel was a special target for members of the boy's group. They took particular delight in outrageous behavior in the presence of these adults. This "asocial" boy happened to be the recognized leader of the group, and frequently displayed a strong sense of responsibility, loyalty, and protectiveness toward its members. Conversely, we have observed numerous instances in which "Sunday best" manners were adopted for the benefit of an adult "investigator" or a teacher. After this display of sweet reasonableness, the adult would be unable to understand how the boy could participate in some of the activities of his group (p. 117).

In fact, as the evidence in this book shows, the importance of group formations in socially undesirable behaviors by youth almost precludes great importance to individual pathology as a causative factor. Being a responsible, reliable member of a group, who can be counted upon by others even in secret and dangerous activities, is simply not possible for any period of time if one is severely disturbed emotionally, subject to acute anxieties, depression, persecution, or other such symptoms (p. 279).

Sometimes the remark is heard that youngsters can belong to delinquent groups only because they have no conscience. Although social scientists are likely to become impatient with such a remark, it is nevertheless worth rebutting. The Sherifs do so in a way which is instructive not only for the layman but for social scientists whose vision becomes restricted by the blinkers of their own particular specialties.

> [The] classic conception of conscience is almost wholly a negative one—applicable to problems of "resistance to temptation" and "guilt" but not at all to those "positive qualities which become ideals to be attained in their own right. . . ."

If discussions of adolescent morality and conscience are to square with the facts, two lines of factual evidence have to be considered in addition to the obvious fact that life is not wholly made up of avoiding temptation or feeling guilty.

First, there is ample evidence, contrary to Freudian notions, that psychological development continues throughout life and that, in particular, the adolescent period is characteristically a period of change. . . .

Second, the individual's standards of right and wrong behavior are not derived simply from representatives of adult society (parents, teachers, church, mass media of communication), and even these are filtered, reinforced, or contradicted in interactions among those of his peers who count for him. Thus, "conscience" is not a set of prescriptions divorced from his continuing psychological development. It is the warp and woof of his very conception of himself in relation to others who *count* in his eyes, woven in the course of interactions with them . . . (p. 181).

What, then, produces these adolescent groups? The Sherifs take the view that the maturing inner urges of the adolescent and the motivations into which these urges are converted by the larger society very often fail to find adequate satisfaction in the activities which the larger society typically provides or permits adolescents. The next postulate in the argument is that one of the deep-laid human urges is to have a place of one's own in one's own group. Together these conditions lead to the universal human practice of seeking within group life the statisfactions for a great portion of our motives.

> Individuals do not form groups of their own choosing just to be, mechanically, one of a set. . . . They come together and interact with strongly felt urges and with desires experienced as their own, whether these be desires to be accepted as a person in one's own right, desires to gain social distinction, sexual urges, wishes for desirable objects and instrumentalities, desires for exciting leisure-time activities, searches for recognition, or desires to prove themselves apart from adult supervision (p. 243).

Most of the remarks made or quoted so far could apply to most any kind of small human group having some stability. Part of the current concern about adolescent groups, however, is that many engage recurrently in violence. Why does this happen? Drawing upon their previous work, the Sherifs find among urban adolescent groups the same conditions of intergroup competition which they found in their earlier experimentation— conditions powerful in producing not only strong solidarity within groups, but also hostility and violence between groups.

It is often said that members of adolescent groups typically turn to violence in an eager search for excitement. But the Sherifs take pains to point out that they found no evidence that the typical group member enjoyed conflict.

> *A major concern of every group studied which engaged in violence against other groups and their members was avoidance of conflict* (p. 230).

Some people feel that the rank and file of a group showing objectionable behavior may be the dupes of a "ringleader"—that they are being led astray by a Svengali. The Sherifs disagree. Far from being carefare and able to bend the members of the group to his every whim, the leader must be a focus and catalyst for the ideas and desires of the group. Although the leader typically must stand high in some of the abilities and characteristics valued in the group, he need not embody in himself the acme of what every group member would like to be. This is impossible on the face of it, since there are not that many paragons to go round. Rather, the leader must exhibit enough desirable qualities and skills to be an example of solidarity; beyond that, he must be able, above all, to originate the effective initiative to move the group—and its members along with it—toward the goals and satisfactions they all cherish. Indeed, the exercise of this "effective initiative" is the Sherif's definition for leadership—or so I interpret the discussion in Chapter 7.

The Sherifs' discussion of popular explanations of adolescent behavior reminds one that psychologists and other social scientists very often remark to each other that they know, after all, very little about human behavior and have discovered very few principles that are new. Faced with great expanses of what they wish they knew but don't, and struggling with the many unanswered questions which their research orientations teach them to ask, this plaint from social scientists is understandable. Yet the list of popular explanations dealt with by the Sherifs should reveal this complaint to be parochial, probably stemming from the tendency of experts to talk chiefly with each other. In conversing with each other, the social scientists give hardly a thought to the knowledge they all share while debating their differences concerning the problems upon which they all fervently wish to make inroads. But while the social scientists argue with each other, the lay public goes on believing and acting upon the sort of primitive and inadequate notions which the Sherifs tick off in their book.

One of the great difficulties which social scientists encounter in trying to understand the complexities of human behavior is that of being restricted by existing methodologies to studying only a portion of the world within which humans actually move. If it were demanded that I pick out one thing as the chief contribution of this very rich book, I should claim it to be the Sherifs' exhibition of how they brought into concert three realms or levels of influence in elucidating adolescent behavior: (1) the influences from within the small group itself, (2) those from the immediate environment of the group—the neighborhood, for example—and (3) those from the broader American culture impinging upon the youth. The following quotation gives a capsule example of the way the Sherifs bring into mutual illumination the influences from the various levels of social organization.

1. When the neighborhood and the larger setting abound and are saturated with examples of fast success;

2. When one feels that he utterly lacks things that others like him have in abundance as he sees them in the neighborhood, at school, in the movies, on TV, on the covers of books in the drugstore;

3. When he is caught in a depriving or frustrating home situation, or has to suffer a life with parents whose world is at variance with his;

4. When he comes to feel that the world owes him a car, nice things to wear, money to spend, girls to entertain;

5. When, to top it all, he feels that he is looked down upon as inferior because of his origin, race, or religion;

6. When he finds that the line of work he is good in brings no recognition or holds no future promise (pp. 297–298).

This book is colorful; even dramatic. I must, therefore, confess that my first reaction to Chapter 12 was one of keen disappointment when I found that the cavalry was not riding to the rescue. The Sherifs do not lay out a cookbook plan for dealing with delinquency, nor even a skeleton set of prescriptions. They do, it is true, state unequivocally one overriding principle:

> The cardinal point is to ensure throughout (whatever the activities) the youth's feeling of having a *function* in their initiation, development, and execution. . . .

Beyond this, the Sherifs take pains to urge a multipronged attack on the problem, to be preceded by research just as many-sided so as to develop the knowledge necessary to mount effective local actions programs. But if the Sherifs do not provide us with a plan to take to the city council, they do give us in Chapter 12 a penetrating analysis of the crucial weaknesses of techniques currently popular for dealing with juvenile delinquency, and they do give us, in the book as a whole, a firm and promising framework within which to build new efforts.

This much must suffice to suggest the manner in which the book explains the formation, maintenance, and change of adolescent groups. Before closing, however, I must say something about the methodology which the Sherifs used in their study, since it has important lessons for all of us.

Chapter 6 explains the methods by which groups in the various neighborhoods and cities were found, the methods by which observers were established in positions to make their repeated observations, and the rationale for these procedures. The Sherifs make clear, as it has rarely been made clear elsewhere, that when we are seeking information about the behavior of individuals in groups, we must be prepared for the observer or the questioner to have a strong effect—not merely a noticeable effect but in most cases a radical effect—upon the very interaction processes which he is trying to witness. This is only to be expected, for the usual observer becomes, if not actually a member of the group itself, at the very least a significant part of the group's social environment; in either case, inevitably altering the communication dynamics from what they would be were he not present. Obviously, this applies as much to the occasional forays for information on the part of teachers, social workers, and other practitioners as it does to the more systematic explorations of the social scientist.

Particularly, in seeking information about human behavior within its social web (and we often forget how much of human behavior is of this sort) the Sherifs disdain the more common techniques which hope for "interviewer rapport." A nutshell example is provided by the Sherifs when they tell of an observer who had been accepted by a group with full trust as an ordinary feature of their immediate environment, but whose interaction possibilities with the group were radically altered, even though relations continued to be friendly, when group members discovered him to be an "outsider."

> One observer in City B was a policeman whose duties never took him into the neighborhood where he observed. He successfully concealed this fact from the group until after his observations were completed. Sometimes later, they saw him in a downtown area in his uniform. Afterward, he returned to their neighborhood to see what their reactions were. Although these boys had never done anything more "delinquent" than smoke cigarettes smuggled from the grocery store owned by the father of one of the members, they told him they never would have let him into their affairs if they had known his occupation. As they talked, two boys occupied themselves by drawing derogatory pictures of a policeman on the sidewalk with a piece of chalk. Others questioned him about his occupation, saying that since he was a policeman they were glad that they liked him anyway (p. 232).

The Sherifs established their observers as ordinary, unexceptional parts of the immediate neighborhood environment of the group to be observed; close enough so that they were frequently invited to go along on activities of the group but not so close that they became actual members of the group competing for status with the others. Full details of how this was achieved are given in Chapter 6 and in the appendix of the book.

Ordinarily, an experimental design would call for observing a group in which no observer was present in order to ascertain whether, indeed, the effects of the observer were negligible. Given the difficulty of observing a group without using an observer, the Sherifs built into their design some checks of a different sort, but quite as convincing. One example is that of sharing secrets. Every one of these groups engaged in some activities which they kept secret from all but their own group members and their closest associates—from all other groups and particularly from authorities. All the groups studied, however, engaged in such activities freely in the presence of their observers.

It cannot be claimed, of course, that the observers had no effect whatever on communication patterns within the group, nor upon the interpersonal events through which group roles and statuses were maintained or changed. The Sherifs make an excellent case, however, for claiming that intragroup processes remained very little different if at all, from those which normally include trusted individuals belonging to the immediate social environment. It should be clear, by the way, that this technique is not that of the usual "participant-observer." The observers used by the Sherifs in no case tried to become "un-noticed" nor did they allow themselves ever to be perceived as "observing."

No claim is made, of course, that social scientists have been unaware of the effect of observers on the behavior being observed. The Sherifs, indeed, make reference to the laboratory experiments which have been performed on exactly this effect. The large virtues in the Sherifs' discussion are (1) that the phenomena they studied enable them to display the very great magnitudes which this effect can reach and (2) that they show so unarguably that their technique for avoiding this effect was successful in their kind of study.

As to the style of the book, the professional social scientist will perhaps miss the usual plethora of tables and the detailing of significance tests to which he is accustomed in research reports. However, there are sufficient tables and charts to display the shape of the data and, whenever statistics are compared, the nature of the tests and the level of confidence are adequately indicated. Although specific descriptions of data are interwoven with theory, further hypotheses, and insightful illustrations, the Sherifs have made it easy for the attentive reader to tell when they are moving from one kind of statement to another.

I found one feature of the book irritating and frustrating; the index is abysmally inadequate.

PROGRAMED
LEARNING AND
AUTOINSTRUCTION

• The issue of whether machines will replace teachers appears to have either solved itself with the passing of time or to have been tabled for the moment as insoluble. At any rate, the argument has subsided from the pitch of a few years ago and seems to have progressed to a consideration of how programed materials and techniques can be used to supplement and complement rather than supplant conventional instructional methods. Periodical educational literature tends to relate to the concerns which are paramount at the time. In this respect, the dates of the included selections are significant. The issue was on its way to solution in 1963, and the question of practical application was already being dealt with.

When Pressey argues that an important benefit of silent reading—the recognition of structure—is destroyed when the material is put on a teaching-machine roll in serial order, he seems to be evaluating programing as a replacement rather than as a supplement. He also apparently has linear, not intrinsic, programing in mind.

In the opinion of the editors, Crowder's distinction between linear and intrinsic programing is an exceedingly valuable contribution. It eliminates the need for espousing and implementing any particular theory of learning and enables educators to apply what works when it is indicated. Both programing and autoinstruction then can be used for the "adjunct instruction" that Pressey felt would help to facilitate meaningful learning.

Now that the threat of the teaching machine and programed instruction as teacher replacements has subsided and it is possible to view them more objectively, the following contributions to the learning process seem to have been made.

1. Individualization of instruction is possible to a greater degree. With autoinstructional materials the learner can study at his own rate. Regular classroom presentation can be complemented and enriched for the gifted youngster, while the learner who fails to comprehend as rapidly as his classmates can fill in the gaps in his understanding on his own. In regular teaching situations, large classroom quotas and full schedules generally prevent adequate attention to either of these badly needed functions.

2. The emphasis that programed learning puts on reward and reinforcement of specific learnings and on the necessity for learning in sequence has caused educators to look more critically at teaching procedures. As Stolurow indicates, programed learning may eliminate from instructional materials much of the hack writing and many of the ineffective methods by providing a means of determining what works and what does not.

3. Programed materials provide the learner with the opportunity to take charge of, and to be responsible for, his own learning. Furthermore, his progress is more readily apparent and his sense of having done it himself is enhanced. When a student takes responsibility for his own learning and no longer feels that it is up to the teacher to *make* him learn, then one of the greatest obstacles to his gaining an education is removed.

4. Teaching machines, programed textbooks and autoinstructional devices add variety to learning experiences. Youngsters can bring new enthusiasm to an old task when they are using the new approach provided by programed materials. The attraction of manipulating a machine may provide the increase in motivation that makes the difference.

We agree that autoinstructional devices are here to stay, but we see them as a means to the end of good instruction rather than as the totality of teaching itself. Like all tools, they only increase the effectiveness of those who know how to use them.

SIDNEY L. PRESSEY
Professor Emeritus, The Ohio State University

38 · TEACHING MACHINE (AND LEARNING THEORY) CRISIS[1]

● For several years now, all over the country, learning theorists have been programing books and other matter into numerous little "frames" each consisting of a very easy question or statement with space for writing a one or two word "constructed" response, to be verified by turning a page or turning up a "teaching-machine" roll. One learned by responding (the theory was) and the more responding the more adequate the learning. In preparing each question the effort was not so much to contribute to a larger meaning as to assure that the student "emitted" the desired response, on the ground that he learned by making correct responses and an error would tend to recur. Multiple-choice questions are not used, because they involve the presentation of wrong alternatives, and also call merely for discrimination. All this has seemed plausible theoretically, and hopes have been high for extraordinary educational advances.

Not Gain but Confusion

Instead, evidence has been accumulating that the above hypotheses on which the programing was being based were, *for human learning of meaningful matter*, not so! Such learners dealing with such materials may profit by seeing not only what a thing is but what it is not, may profit by mistakes, may learn to recall from learning to discriminate. Further, some

Journal of Applied Psychology, 47:1–6, 1963. Copyright © 1963 by the American Psychological Association, and reproduced by permission.

[1] This paper was presented in modified form at the St. Louis meetings of the American Psychological Association, August 31, 1962.

half-dozen investigators have reported that as much may be learned in a given time simply by reading, as by reading *and* responding (Pressey, 1962; Silberman, 1962). In short, these theorists have independently discovered what educators have known about and been investigating for over 40 years —silent reading! Further, as programed matter has been used over a period of time, it has been realized that for skimming for main ideas, for review— for any use except that initial go-through—the programed book is almost impossible and the teaching-machine roll entirely so. Mostly, even for the first go-through, they are unsatisfactory, because most important matter to be learned has structure, which the programing destroys except the serial order, and most important learning is integrative and judgmental, so requires a looking about in what is being studied; for all such purposes a teaching machine seems about as hampering as a scanning device which required that one look at a picture only 1 square inch at a time, in a set order. Much seems very wrong about current attempts at autoinstruction.

A possible basic factor is suggested by Hilgard (1956) when he questions

> the generalization from comparative studies that there are no differ-
> ences, except quantitative ones, between the learning of lower
> mammals and man. . . . It is strange that the opposite point of
> view is not more often made explicit—that at the human level there
> have emerged capacities not approached by the lower animals, in-
> cluding other primates. . . . Language in man is perhaps the clearest
> of the emergents which carries with it a forward surge in what may
> be learned. . . . There are probably a number of different kinds of
> learning, following different laws. [Further, in man] the ceiling of
> ability itself may be modified by training. [Thus after acquiring]
> appropriate linguistic or mathematical tools [he can solve problems
> previously impossible] (pp. 460–461).

Surely that now taken-for-granted but really marvelous skill, silent assimila-
tive reading, is such a tool. Also more important than often recognized
are a variety of skills and strategies in learning usually grouped together
as methods of study.

With Hilgard's position the writer would agree. He would say that the
learning theorists have with notable vigor and consistency applied "generalizations from comparative studies" to problems of learning in school,
and that the results have shown, more adequately than ever before, the
unsatisfactoriness of those generalizations for that purpose. For a learner
with reading-study skills, conventional textual matter orders and structures its contents in paragraphs and sections and chapters, exhibits that
structure in headings and table of contents, makes all readily available in

index with page headings and numbers. The learner thus has multiple aids to the development and structuring of his understanding. If need be he can, with a flick of the finger, move about in the material; he can skip the already known, turn back as a result of a later felt need, review selectively. As a way to present matter to be learned, the average textbook may not be best. But thousands of frames on a teaching-machine roll or strung through a programed book would seem close to the worst. To make a very bad pun, the programers have "framed" the textbook. Instead of trying to improve their programs, they might better consider very broadly how best to present matter for learning. The opinion is ventured that the best will be found closer to texts than to their programs.

But did not Socrates so teach the slave boy? The boy could not read. What about the often-cited skillful tutor? He assumed that the student had done some reading. However, both Socrates and the tutor did further learning by asking questions. The writer would contend that neither simply presented an idea and then reinforced it. Brownell's (1928) early research regarding primary school children's learning of arithmetic here seems relevant. Simply telling them that $2 \times 3 = 6$ did *not* bring about real learning of that number combination. These sturdy little empiricists had not merely to be *told*; they had to be *shown*, as by putting out two sets each of three pennies and demonstrating that they did indeed count to six. They had similarly to verify, and to differentiate, that $2 + 3$ was 5 and $3 - 2$ was only 1. As Piaget (1954) and others have described, children gradually develop a number system, also cognitive schema as of space, causality; and they do this not by so crude a rote process as the accretion of bit learnings stuck on by reinforcements, but by progressive processes of cognitive integration and clarification.

Moreover, such clarification is commonly by differentiation, and multiple-choice items involve just such processes. The three-choice question $2 \times 3 = 1$, 5, or 6 differentiates the correct answer from answers got by wrongly subtracting or adding. In this one concise little item are thus packed three arithmetic processes and three number combinations, and study of the item might well involve all six issues, with autoinstructional dealing with the item clarifying of all. The point will be returned to.

But first a brief summary of the position so far. The past decade has seen an extraordinary "boom" in autoinstruction; most of this work has been dominated by concepts of operant conditioning deriving directly from animal experimentation and has become stylized in terms of initial presentation of tasks in numerous frames with immediate constructed response. Because thus so special in origin and nature, as well as yielding often question raising results, a basic critical review of current autoinstructional concepts seemed called for. Doubts have been raised as to whether human learning of meaningful material can be adequately accounted for by animal based theory, programed matter is satisfactory for such learning, and reinforcement adequately accounts for the process (Gagné, 1962).

But Where from Here?

When in doubt about such a theory-dominated situation, it is sometimes well to pull back and see whether a very practical analysis may helpfully reconstrue issues. If this be done, an obvious early question is this: what is the best way *initially* to present matter to be learned? The programers have been cutting it into little pieces each responded to, but now recognize that one may learn from reading without responding. Then how big may the piece be? The writer has stressed that the bigger piece may have structure which should be made evident, and that first consideration as well as review or selective use may make it desirable that the learner can move about freely in the material. Perhaps it would be granted that a questioner who interrupted the reading of this paper should be asked to wait until it was all before him—that it would be then that the discussion could be most profitable. Surely it will be granted that the paper can best be understood if seen in print so that one can glance about and see headings; rather than if heard, when one cannot thus study—as one cannot study a teaching-machine roll. So the suggestion is: that the initial presentation might most often best be a very well organized and well written substantial statement much like a chapter in a good textbook! And the autoinstruction should follow and should be like a series of questions in a very good discussion of such a chapter.

Some "autopresentation" might be helpful: a teaching-machine roll might picture two groups each of three pennies and then six and so make clear to the child mind that 2 × 3 does make six. *After* his number system has been somewhat established, there may be automatized drill. The printed word "house" may be thus associated with a picture of one. Sundry sorts of detail-learning and of drill may be dealt with piecemeal. But mostly (the writer believes) initial presentation of what is to be learned will be in field trip, demonstration or experiment, or most commonly a substantial unit like an incisive textbook chapter, *not* all mixed up with autoinstruction. The "autodiscussion" would follow, and its function would be (to paraphrase a statement in Ausubel's 1961 review) to enhance the clarity and stability of cognitive structure by correcting misconceptions, and deferring the instruction of new matter until there had been such clarification and elucidation.

In difficult matter such as a science text or industrial or military training manual, bits of autoinstruction may be needed more frequently; each step in the solution of a difficult problem may need such autoelucidation. But the manual or text need not be fragmented into thousands of frames. Problems may be explicated in autoinstructional matter supplementary to the text; and there, or perhaps every 3 or 4 pages in the book, clusters of autoexplicating queries may keep check on understanding. But a book's structured coherence and orderliness of presentation, and its convenience for overview, review, and reference, can be kept.

If the autoinstruction is thus to *follow* presentation of what is to be learned, then (like a good tutor or teacher) it will deal only with issues which need further clarification or emphasis. Such adjunct autoelucidation will *not* cover everything, may jump from one point to another or even back and forth. It will be very much shorter than present "programs," which attempt both to present matter to be learned and autoinstruct about it in the same aggregate. Being so different, such supplemental autoinstruction might well be given a different name, as autoelucidation or explication.

But how would matter for adjunct autoinstruction or explication be selected? Experienced teachers would have many suggestions as to points needing special elucidation. They would be indicated in published research regarding pupils' learning of and difficulties in spelling, arithmetic, algebra, composition, science, and history. Additional research, for development and trial of such elucidative material, would suggest more items and better ways of presenting them. Some could be cleared up by making the initial presentation more lucid. But some students would still have difficulty with some items; perhaps those troubling 10% of the pupils or more would be dealt with in the adjunct autoinstruction.

The items should usually there appear (the writer is convinced) as multiple-choice questions with only such wrong alternatives as express common misunderstandings and a right answer notably clear. There is evidence that, contrary to theoretical inference, students do, after autoinstruction with such items, *less* often make the so-labeled mistakes, more often get things right, and transfer or generalize so that the gains appear on recall and yet other types of end tests (see for instance Jones, 1954; Lumsdaine & Glaser, 1960, pp. 52–93). Only half the students in a class may get such an item right on a pretest, but almost all of them do so on an end test a month later. In striking contrast, the perverse requirements of the orthodox programer make any such effectiveness impossible: the item is initially supposed to be so easy that at least 95% pass it, errors cannot be identified as such because they must not be shown, and right statements are limited to such as the student can be maneuvered into hastily formulating himself. And orthodox improvement consists of making the items yet easier! In contrast, improvement of such an item as here urged would involve making wrong alternates clearer expressions of common misconceptions and the right more clearly right so that gains would be yet greater. In addition, the ease of checking objective items, with immediate indication of correctness (as by instant change of color of the check mark on a "chemo-card" or turn to next question on a key machine) makes possible going through many more items in a given time—so presumably more learning.

Range of Evaluations

But what of the argument that orthodox programs have been found greatly to save time, so that for instance a college course was finished in the first 2 months of a semester, or an industrial training course similarly shortened? Independent study plans have made possible marked reduction of time in class without any such programs (Baskin, 1960). The average class and the average business training session may be very time wasting and otherwise inefficient, and a number of alternatives may be shown to be better. In a college or secondary school course with several sections, it should be feasible to have one or more taught in conventional fashion, one or more use an orthodox program, a similar number try what the writer has called adjunct autoinstruction, another venture a planned independent study procedure, and outcomes on a carefully made final examination compared. If so made, such examinations can yield some analysis of outcomes: does one method or another bring more recall, transfer, application? Experiments of this type under the writer's direction have shown adjunct auto-instruction superior to conventional classes in all these respects.

These experiments also showed the adjunct materials very useful in planned independent study: in a room set aside for such use and having all the readings, laboratory material, and adjunct autoinstructional sheets available but looked after by an assistant, the students came in and worked when they wished, in small groups or individually, consulting the assistant when they so desired. All finished the 11-week course within 6 weeks. All did well on midterm and final examinations. But informal reports and interviews indicated yet other values, as gains in ability to work independently—though the students became better acquainted than in formal classes! The opportunity to save time was motivating. Several of these students took another course by independent study during the second half of the quarter.

More broadly, appraising experiments involving considerable numbers of students with different instructors over considerable periods of time—preferably a whole school or business training course—have yet other values. Methods have to be tolerable in long continued and routine, not simply brief and special, use. In the work just described, the best all-purpose "teaching machine" was judged to be a 3 × 5 chemo-card having 30 lines each of four squares: on this answer card the student checked his choice of answer to each of 30 four-choice questions on a teach-test sheet, using a special red ink which instantly turned black when he marked in the right answer-box (because of an invisible chemical printed there). The student kept trying on each question until this color-change feedback told him he had the correct answer. For remedial review he had only to note where his red marks were, the sum of them was his error-score; the instructor had only to note where he saw most red on the cards for a given day to see where some corrective discussion might be desirable, and for both him and the students the cards were a compact easily-filed record.[2] In the writer's adjunct autoinstructional procedure, everything except the cards could be used over and over again, easily returned to again as for review. For long-continuing flexible use and re-use, it seemed apparent that a text or business manual plus perhaps 50 adjunct autoinstructional sheets (and some chemo-cards) was far more practicable than that manual or text cut up into 3,000 frames on a teaching-machine roll (with the machines) or strung through a programed book.

Resumé and Recommendations

Teaching machines and programed materials are now being used all over the country in schools and colleges and in industrial and military training. Manufacture and sale of such products are a major enterprise of many publishers and equipment makers. Ambitious young people are embarking on careers in such work. The whole subject has become an accepted topic of everyday talk. However, there is disturbing evidence that current auto-instruction is *not* up to the claims made for it, that the current "boom" might be followed by a "bust" unfortunate for those involved—and for

[2] Yet more convenient autoinstructional cards are possible. Instead of a pen with special ink, only a pencil may be needed; a mark with it, or a stroke of its eraser, breaks through an overprint to reveal a "c" underneath when the right answer is found. For 30-item 3-choice teach tests, a device little larger than a stop watch, and less complicated, may both teach and keep score. An apparatus little larger than an electric desk clock may both teach and provide selective review.

psychology. This paper is first of all a plea that to guard against such a danger the whole situation be soon given close critical inspection, and not merely to assure (as is now being attempted) that programs are good; but critically to consider whether the whole current concept of programing may be at fault, and an almost totally different approach than now orthodox to all ideas about autoinstruction be called for.

The archvillain, leading so many people astray, is declared to be learning theory! No less a charge is made than that the whole trend of American research and theory as regards learning has been based on a false premise— that the important features of human learning are to be found in animals. Instead, the all-important fact is that human has transcended animal learning.[3] Language, number, such skills as silent reading, make possible facilitations of learning, and kinds of learning, impossible even for the apes. Autoinstruction should enhance such potentials. Instead, current animal derived procedures in autoinstruction destroy meaningful structure to present fragments serially in programs, and replace processes of cognitive clarification with largely rote reinforcings of bit learnings.

An "adjunct autoinstruction" is urged which keeps, makes use of, and enhances meaningful structure, the autoinstruction serving to clarify and extend meaningfulness. Texts, manuals, laboratory exercises, instructional moving pictures and television would be kept (though often improved), and the autoinstruction would aid in their use and increase their value. The materials would be perhaps only a tenth as bulky as present programs; and being objective, their use could be greatly facilitated by automating devices.

Evaluations should not merely (as is now projected) compare the merits of various "orthodox" programs. Those should be compared with such adjunct autoinstructional materials as here advocated. Adaptability should be compared for use with other media as books and movies and other methods as guided independent study. Convenience and cost for continuing general use should be hard-headedly appraised. The prediction is

[3] For this conclusion there is no less evidence than the whole history of civilization! Basically more significant than Skinner's brilliant research regarding animal learning may well be the almost forgotten finding of Kellogg and of Cathy Hayes that even if an ape be raised in a home like a child, it can never learn to talk. Far more remarkable than Skinner's pigeons playing ping pong is the average human scanning a newspaper—glancing about to find matter of interest to him, judging, generalizing, reconstruing, all in silent reading without overt respondings or reinforcings. Most remarkable of all is it to see learning theorists, hypnotized by the plausibilities of a neat theory, trying to teach that human as if he were a pigeon—confining his glance to the rigid slow serial peep show viewing of innumerable "frames" each demanding that he respond and be reinforced.

ventured that in all respects adjunct autoinstruction will be found far superior: time and work saving will be great yet more will be accomplished —courses often completed in half the usual time, years saved but nevertheless more accomplished in school and college, industrial and military training tasks reduced perhaps a third in length and all with great time and trouble saved instructional staffs. Then at long last the "industrial revolution" in education may come about which the writer predicted (Pressey, 1932) just 30 years ago. Further, somewhat as the practical testing movement from the first world war on greatly stimulated and aided research and theorizing regarding abilities, so autoinstruction may get research on learning out from under its long dominance by comparative psychology and confinement in the laboratory and evolve vigorous new theory.

REFERENCES

Ausubel, D. P., and Fitzgerald, D. Meaningful learning and retention: Intrapersonal and cognitive variables, *Rev. Educ. Res.*, 1961, 31, 500–510.

Baskin, S. *Quest for quality: Some models and means.* Washington, D. C.: United States Department of Health, Education, and Welfare, 1960.

Brownell, W. A. The development of children's number ideas in the primary grades. *Suppl. Educ. Monogr.*, 1928, No. 35.

Gagné, R. M. Military training and principles of learning. *Amer. Psychologist*, 1962, 17, 83–91.

Hilgard, E. R. *Theories of learning.* (2nd ed.) New York: Appleton-Century-Crofts, 1956.

Jones, R. S. Integration of instructional and self-scoring measuring devices. *Abstr. Doct. Dissert., O. State U.*, 1954, 65, 157–165.

Lumsdaine, A. A., and Glaser, R. *Teaching machines and programmed learning.* Washington: National Education Association, 1960.

Piaget, J. *The construction of reality in the child.* New York: Basic Books, 1954.

Pressey, S. L. A third and fourth contribution toward the coming "industrial revolution" in education. *Sch. Soc.*, 1932, 36, 668–672.

Pressey, S. L. Basic unresolved teaching machine problems. *Theory Pract.*, 1962, 1, 30–37.

Silberman, H. F. Self-instructional devices and programmed materials. *Rev. Educ. Res.*, 1962, 32, 179–193.

NORMAN A. CROWDER
Technical Director, Educational Sciences Division, U. S. Industries, Inc.

39 · ON THE DIFFERENCES BETWEEN LINEAR AND INTRINSIC PROGRAMING

● Many present discussions of programed learning do not clearly distinguish between linear and intrinsic programing. This is understandable in view of the history of the field, but it is quite unfortunate. Any attempt to view linear and intrinsic programing as mere technical variants of the same method, or to derive both techniques from the same basic rationale, seriously impedes an understanding of the field.

Linear and intrinsic programing have nothing in common historically, having arisen in different contexts and in response to different circumstances. They have nothing in common theoretically, but rather rely for their expected effectiveness on different rationales and make different and, in fact, diametrically opposed assumptions about the nature of the learning process. The materials produced following the different methods have only superficial similarities, and what similarities appear may be misleading, as will be discussed below. As a matter of fact, the common use of the word "programing" is coincidental, the word originally having been used in a somewhat different sense by writers of the two schools. It is the purpose of this paper to make these basic differences quite clear.

One Problem, Two Different Solutions

The objective of both schools of programing is to produce materials that permit efficient individual study by a student independent of an organized

Phi Delta Kappan, 44:250–254, 1963. Used by permission of Phi Delta Kappa.

study group and without the continuous intercession of a live instructor. Now, materials technically suitable for independent study, e.g., textbooks and reference materials, have been in use for many years. The educator may then well ask why proponents of programed instruction expect their materials to be more effective than are the conventional materials. The answers given by theorists of the two schools of programing are quite different. The linear theorist will describe a particular model of the learning process which he believes is accurate and general enough for practical educational use. He will then show how materials prepared by the linear method follow the requirements of this specific learning model, and hence should, in use, promote efficient learning. In the case of linear programing it is fair to say that the specific learning theory came first; the techniques used derive directly from the theory.

For intrinsic programing the situation is the reverse. The intrinsic programing theorist will not point to a specific learning model, but will rather describe a technique which, in common-sense terms, appears to permit inanimate materials to assume some of the educational functions that have previously required a live instructor, or tutor, for each student. Thus, while the linear programer is exploiting a particular theory, the intrinsic programer is exploiting a particular technique. The linear programer is, in effect, claiming to have discovered something about the learning process which he is putting to practical use with his materials; the intrinsic programer does not claim to have discovered something about learning, but rather to have developed a new technique that allows allows some rather old ideas about teaching to be more effectively implemented.

Basic Linear Theory and Technique

The learning model used in linear programing is basically a conditioning model. Briefly, it postulates that a desired change in behavior, defined as learning, can best be brought about by inducing and then rewarding the desired behavior, in much the same manner as a dog is trained. As a partisan of intrinsic programing, I would be decently diffident about drawing the parallel between linear programing and animal training were it not for the fact that the linear theorists place such emphasis on the derivation of their method from experiments with animals, and the parallel does serve to illustrate the technique. Thus the linear materials are designed to cause the student to emit the behaviors defined as the subject matter to be learned, piece by piece, rewarding each instance wherein the student emits the desired behavior.

The format of linear materials is by now familiar to most educators. Following a very short presentation of new material, the student is required to emit a response, usually the writing of a word. He then compares his response to the correct response (which he discovers by appropriate manipulation of the materials, such as turning to the next page) and, if his response matches the correct response, he feels thereby rewarded, and the act is thus "learned." *In linear programing, the student's response is considered an integral part of the learning process; the response is induced in order that it may be rewarded and learning thus occur.* In the strict application of linear theory the question of how the student is induced to emit the correct response is irrelevant; the important thing is to get response emitted in order that it may be rewarded and thus "learned."

Linear programs make no explicit provision for errors by the student, since errors are, by linear theory, simply irrelevant to the learning process. If a student makes an error, i.e., emits the wrong response, the program has at best wasted his time, at worst he may harmfully have practiced an incorrect response. Hence linear programs, if properly constructed, are refined to the point where erorrs occur very infrequently, and may be neglected. The task of a linear program is to get the student to emit, in response to the given stimuli, the responses that have been defined as constituting the behavior to be learned. An error on the part of a student is considered a fault on the part of the program.

From the above theoretical considerations, the characteristics of linear programs—very short steps, a high degree of redundancy and prompting leading to very easy "questions"—follow directly. The student response is ordinarily a "constructed" response, as it was early believed by the linear theorists that "thinking" a response could not properly be called "behavior" and thus could not be brought within the purview of the theory. "Thinking" is still a little awkward for the theory to handle, but experiments in which students, instructed to merely think the response, learned as well as students required to write out the response, have forced some reconsideration of this issue.

In summary, linear materials are built on the assumption that a conditioning model is appropriate for educational use, and the techniques employed are derived from that model. The student is confronted with a series of stimuli which, building from the presumed known or previously learned responses, cause him to emit new responses (or old responses to new stimuli); the emission of the desired responses is rewarded by the student's discovering that he was correct, and the desired responses are thus learned. Errors by students on a fully developed program are so few that their occurrence may be neglected.

Basic Intrinsic Theory and Technique

Intrinsic programing makes no assumptions about the nature of the learning process that have not been common educational coin for some time. Furthermore, as suggested above, intrinsic programing is not a theory about how education should be conducted. It is a technique for preparing written materials that will accommodate quite a range of educational purposes. Accordingly, the technique will be described before the theoretical issues.

The technique is based on this simple fact: The student's choice of an answer to a multiple-choice question can be used automatically to direct him to new material; the student who chooses one alternative can automatically be directed to different material than that to which a student choosing a different alternative is directed. One use that can be made of the technique is to include in ordinary expository text questions that are automatically administered, scored, and appropriate remedial action automatically taken if indicated.

In the simplest "scrambled book" or Tutor Text (TM) format the student is given a short discussion of the material to be learned, followed by a multiple-choice question designed to test the point just discussed. Each answer alternative has a page number beside it. The student chooses what he believes is the correct answer to the question and turns to the page number given for that answer. If he has chosen correctly, the page to which he thereby comes will contain the next unit of material to be learned and the next question, and so on. If he has chosen an incorrect answer, the page to which he thereby comes will contain a discussion of why the answer chosen is incorrect, and, following this discussion, an instruction to return to the original question page to try again. He will not come to the next unit of new material until he has chosen the correct answer, of course, although in choosing incorrect answers he will come upon new discussion of the old material.

The pages in a Tutor Text are randomly arranged; that is, the page numbers given with the answer choices are not consecutive or in any other obvious order. Thus the student cannot ignore the question and routinely pass to the next page of material; he must commit himself to one of the answer choices, or else choose blindly, but he cannot ignore the question and pass to the "next page" of instruction, since the "next page" is not the sequentially numbered next page, but the page whose number is given with the right-answer choice.

The basic intrinsic programing technique, then, amounts to nothing more than the inclusion of multiple-choice questions in relatively conventional expository text and the use of these questions to continually check the student's progress through the material and to furnish specific remedial material as it is required. *In intrinsic programing the questions serve primarily a diagnostic purpose, and the basis of the technique is the fact that the diagnosis so made can be promptly utilized to furnish specific remedial material to the student.*

The inclusion of the question and its answer choices in each page of expository text brings about changes in both text style and format that the skillful program writer will use for a variety of auxiliary purposes. Thus the question may be used to draw the student's attention sharply to the key point of a paragraph; solutions to problems may be suggested by way of the answer choices provided with the question; answering the question may provide the student with useful practice with the concept involved, and so forth. I mention these auxiliary uses of the question to make the point that the material from which the student is to learn includes the expository text, the question, the answer choices provided, and the remedial material provided for each of the wrong answers. In other words, one does not prepare an intrinsic program merely by chopping up expository text into paragraphs and providing a multiple-choice question for each paragraph. However, the fact that a skillful writer will make the structural features of the format serve useful auxiliary ends, just as any competent craftsman will get the most from a technique, should not divert attention from the fact that the primary purpose of including the questions is diagnostic, the diagnosis being desired in order that prompt remedial action may automatically be taken.

Basic Differences in Theory

The basic differences in theory between linear and intrinsic programs should now be manifest. Indeed, it would be a shorter task to detail the similarities than to discuss the differences, since the differences cover almost every point of theory and technique. The linear theorist assumes that human learning is sufficiently well described by a conditioning model to allow the requirements of that model to be the overriding consideration in preparing educational materials. The intrinsic programing theorist considers the direct application of such a model to human learning to be naive. The linear programer assumes that the student will learn only those responses on which he can be given rewarded practice; the intrinsic programer does not pretend to know in detail *how* the student learns, but is interested in *whether* he learns. Hence one writes items to exercise the student, the other writes questions with a diagnostic purpose in mind. The linear programer is distressed if an item draws erroneous responses while the intrinsic programer regards a question that everyone passes as a waste of space.

The writer of intrinsic programs is no more committed to any specific theory of learning than is the writer of any other type of expository writing as primarily an art; he may have very specific detailed rules he follows in writing; if he really believes that grossly redundant text with words left blank now and then communicates better than conventional prose, he could even prepare the expository part of the text in the form of a linear program. The distinguishing feature of an intrinsic program is not theoretical; it is the structural feature of including diagnostic questions throughout the exposition, and providing remedial material for those who fail the questions.

The Question of Self-Pacing

It is often stated that all programs are self-pacing in the sense that the student proceeds through them at his own best rate. A moment's reflection will show that linear and intrinsic programs are self-pacing in entirely different degrees. A linear program is self-pacing in the sense that some students read faster than others, but all must read the same material. An intrinsic program provides different amounts and kinds of material for individual students, based not on prior estimates of the student's needs or on his self-evaluation as he goes through the program but on his demonstrated performance in choosing answers to the questions.

The matter of adapting programed material to the needs of the individual student is, of course, of primary importance in preparing material for individual use. The central feature of intrinsically programed materials— the fact that each piece of material seen by the student, whether it be new or remedial material, depends on his performance on the previous question —is intended to serve this end of adapting the material to the manifest needs of the individual student.

Why Should Students Make Errors?

It is a current shibboleth that "when the student makes an error, the fault is in the program." This is a seductive half-truth and as such proposes a solution that conceals the bulk of the problem. Certainly no one would propose to write materials systematically designed to lead the student into errors, and anyone would prefer programs on which no student made an error *if this could be achieved without other undesirable results.* To see what undesirable results we must concern ourselves with, consider how we would proceed to write a program on which no student will make an error. We can produce virtually error-free programs if we are careful never to assume knowledge that the most poorly prepared student does not have, never to give more information per step than the slowest can absorb, and never to require reasoning beyond the capacity of the dullest. The inevitable result of such programs is that the time of the average and better than average student is wasted, and what is more important, the subject matter itself, no matter how dignified and characteristically human are its antecedents, must be reduced to fragments appropriate to the conditioning model of learning.

It seems to me that the linear model makes the most pessimistic possible set of assumptions about the student. Material prepared in the intrinsic format, on the other hand, makes the most optimistic assumptions and lowers them only when and if the particular student, by making errors, demonstrates that he cannot learn from material written at a higher level of abstraction. It certainly seems to me that it is consonant with our educational goals that the pressure of the program should be upward, allowing the student to deal with the material on the highest level of abstraction of which he is capable, rather than downwards, forcing all students to plod through a path designed for the least able. We are free to apply such upward pressure in an intrinsic program because we can automatically make provision for those who cannot stand the pace.

The Question of "Response Mode"

A great deal has been made of the presumed differences in the psychological process involved in constructing an answer in a linear program and those involved in choosing one of several alternatives to a multiple-choice question in an intrinsic program. Such discussion usually tacitly assumes that the function served by the question is the practice function considered important in the linear model, wherein the theory would predict that the constructed response would serve this practice function more efficiently. Experiments with linear programs have shown that multiple-choice questions in linear programs seem to work as well as constructed response questions, which would suggest that either the theory was wrong, or, what seems to me to be more likely, it simply did not describe accurately the function served by the question.

As I have indicated, I believe the practice consideration is irrelevant, particularly in intrinsic programs. We use multiple-choice questions for the purely practical reason that we think of the questions as primarily serving a diagnostic or testing function, for which the multiple-choice question is directly useful while the open-ended question is not. The choice of an answer to a multiple-choice question can be translated into a discrete physical act, such as turning to a particular page in a book, or pressing a particular button on a machine, whereby appropriate new or remedial material is automatically selected. In the present state of the art, no practical device that will respond differentially to written or open-ended questions is available, except in certain very specialized applications.

In any discussion of response mode, the question of whether having multiple-choice questions does not permit the student to practice errors is sure to arise. Again, the point is relevant to the training of pigeons, but it seems to me irrelevant for serious educational work with human beings. We expect the student to give the right answer to a question because he has understood the material he has just read on the point in question, not because he has given the response in question more often than he has given another response. For pure rote material the point may be relevant, but for most material of interest to educators there is presumably a reason behind the correct answer to a question, not merely a statistical history of frequency of responses.

The Question of Machines vs. Books

Nowhere does the confusion of linear and intrinsic programing produce more mischievous results than in the discussion of the relative merits of programs presented via "teaching machines" versus those presented in book form. In a linear program, the material is not responsive to the student's activity, i.e., each student comes to the same "next step" in the program, whether he has given the correct response, an incorrect response, or no response at all to the previous item. Since there is no control of the programed materials required in a linear program, it is hardly surprising to find that it seems to make little difference whether the material is presented via book or machine.

An intrinsic program, of course, varies the material presented to each student on the basis of the student's response to each question. It may be desired to direct the student to specific remedial material, through remedial subsequences, or even back through an entire lesson. All of this can be done in book form, or rather, one can suggest it to the student in book form; in the machine format, as in the AutoTutor® teaching machine, the desired excursions on the part of the student can be made automatic and mandatory.

The effect of the machine is to increase the responsiveness of the program; obviously it will not be of importance unless the programer has written a responsive program.

Summary

Linear and intrinsic programing, while having some superficial similarities, are basically different in approach, intention, and rationale. The linear technique is an attempt to adapt a simple conditioning model of learning to educational use; the intrinsic programing technique exploits the possibility of letting the student's choice of answers to questions included in the text direct him to new or remedial material as appropriate. The two techniques impose different restrictions on the program writer; the author has argued that the conditions imposed by the intrinsic programing format are consonant with a variety of desirable educational objectives, while the conditions imposed by the linear model are undesirably restrictive.

LAWRENCE M. STOLUROW
Professor of Psychology and Education, University of Illinois

40 · LET'S BE INFORMED ON PROGRAMED INSTRUCTION

● Education is not just in transition, it is in crisis. The question facing us is whether this crisis is to be met by evolutionary means by professionals from within their own ranks or by revolutionary means by outsiders.

Programed instruction represents one radical departure from present practice. It is not accepted by many educators, but it does enjoy enthusiastic support from some. Before the rest of us accept or reject it, we need to know something about it.

If we fail to inform ourselves and meet this situation head-on with the best we have, the rascals will take over. Who are the rascals? They are the industrial and business people who see education as a market and the demand for programs as a "pie" to be divided among themselves. Education is one of our biggest businesses and it has not yet yielded to the Madison Avenue heel. Hopefully, it won't. But many Madison Avenue moguls look upon education as their new frontier. They see, on the one hand, the millions of minds thirsty for educational sustenance, and, on the other, the scarcity of mentors. Demand without supply makes their greedy pulse rise with great visions of profit, and hiding behind them are hordes of hack writers waiting for the signal to pick up pen and plagiarize.

A significant change is under way from the art of education to the technology of education. Under these circumstances, we need to develop our technological arm rather than let it be developed by others. It is in this spirit that I would like to treat programed learning and teaching machines.

The problem of instruction can be treated as a systems concept. The process of education requires an engineering approach. While teachers do

Phi Delta Kappan, 44:255–257, 1963. Used by permission of Phi Delta Kappa.

not normally think of themselves as engineers, in a larger sense whatever they do when they plan and carry out instruction is a type of engineering. In other words, the teacher's task is to design and develop an educational environment within which students can learn efficiently.

From this point of view, the various media such as educational television, films, tape recordings, language laboratories, and teaching machines are to be examined in terms of the instructional functions they perform.

The more functions a teacher performs, the *more adaptive* he can be. The same is true of a machine. Films and television are less adaptive than teaching machines, for they perform few individualizing functions. They are pre-programed, so to speak, and all students are presented with the same displays, in the same order, and at the same rate. With programed learning materials, either in printed book form or presented by means of a machine, the students move at their own rate. In addition, with programed instruction most, if not all, of the instructional process is individualized. Different students are presented with different materials, depending upon their behavior. These materials are presented at different rates, depending upon the student's rate of progress.

It is interesting to note that studies conducted so far, using simple mechanical devices, do not report data to support the need of a machine. The general finding is that either the text presentation comes out ahead in providing equivalent instruction in less time or is the machine's equal in efficiency. Thus there is no objective evidence from research to support the need for a machine to assist student learning. On the other hand, there is a requirement to use teaching machines for research, for program development, and for the study of teaching strategies. The primary factor that makes instruction effective is the program, and the design and development of the program is critical at this time.

This finding that the machine itself does not produce any measured increment in learning makes one ask, "Should machines be used?" The answer can be "yes" or "no," depending upon what you want the system to accomplish.

If you want simply to improve instruction at minimal cost, you do not need a machine. A purchase based solely on the *hope* of improved student performance should not be made. You should not buy a machine simply because you feel that it will increase the amount students will learn from a program. The existing programed materials alone when used in book form will teach as well as when used in a machine.

A teaching machine purchase could be justified on economic grounds, provided it is part of a computer-based system. It also could be justified as a research tool to be used in developing programed learning materials. For instruction, a teaching machine can pay off economically if it can handle a large number of students simultaneously, and if it can reduce student data faster and get scores back to the instructor and students more rapidly. However, to do this you need a system that is capable of providing individualized instruction to a very large number of students at one time. The cost has to be less this way than it is when one teacher or teaching assistant hands out printed materials to groups of twenty-five to thirty students.

Some Machines NOT Here to Stay

The small, free-standing mechanical devices are *not* here to stay. They take a lot of time to set up so that each student can go to his machine and pick up today where he left off yesterday. Furthermore, the small mechanical devices require personnel to process the data they produce. Depending on the number of students and the length of the program, a large number of detailed records of students' responses have to be read. With programs consisting of thousands of frames, studied by hundreds of students, a large amount of time will go into the analysis of their errors even when the error rate is low. Few schools, if any, could afford the data processing personnel costs even if they could find warm bodies to do the job. Data processing costs can be cut at the expense of information about student performance; however, this may be a way to solve a problem of data reduction for the schools, but not for the person developing a program. The results of studies do not clearly indicate that student's errors tell one very much about student capability after he has completed a program that was well developed. The real payoff for the school is the student's performance on a test given at the end of programed instruction. Thus, with a developed program for students like those you intend to use it with, it is only necessary to give such a test and score it. Errors made in taking the program need not be examined with a developed program, except where there is reason to question its suitability for your students. If suitability is to be looked at, then you should collect error data on one or more sections of the program and compare your findings with the error data reported by the development group. This is a useful thing to do with an early part of a program as a calibration procedure in deciding whether all of it might be used with benefit to your students.

The comparative studies of overt and covert response indicate that students do as well or better if they are required to read the program without making any overt responses, when the program is teaching them something new. This means that one could provide students with printed programed material and let them read it through at their own rate. After that, they could be given a test and decisions made regarding what to do next. If this procedure were followed, the data suggest that the students would learn as much and would learn in less time than if they were required to make an overt response to every step.

The studies of program sequences suggest that with linear programs the logic built into the sequences may or may not be critical in determining the amount learned. For the most part, students seem to learn about as much with a scrambled order as with a tightly developed sequence. However, these studies have led to the realization that a large amount of material does not require careful sequencing throughout. Examination in several areas will show that textbook authors differ in the sequences they use. Thus, for more material than we realize, there is little reason to become too concerned about minor variations in sequence. Certainly, some concepts and many skills require a specific sequence of materials, if they are to be learned efficiently. Learning the alphabet is a good example of the need for a specific order. However, many more materials do *not* require one, and only one, sequence. If a sequence is not critical, then what difference does it make to the student if he gets one or another? The data comparing sequenced with mixed orders suggest that the students learn about the same amount, but different sequences may make different demands upon the students' abilities.

The obvious implication of these data is that we should be sure that the expenditure required to prepare a particular sequence is justified. The same thing holds for hardware. You may not need a machine that can accommodate branching sequences. If you do not, there is no need to pay a great deal for branching capability. Certainly, one could not justify a large expenditure for a branching capability if it would be used only 5 per cent of the time. Before buying devices, you want to determine carefully whether it is worth a million dollars to you or whether you might be better off putting the money into more programs.

These are only some of the practical issues that have arisen in connection with decisions about teaching machines and programed instruction. The data are quite clear in indicating that a wide variety of persons can and do learn from programed materials as well as they do from reading texts or from being taught by a live teacher. Our ability to generalize from comparative studies is limited because in them the best possible programs were obviously not used, since we do not yet know how to prepare them. Furthermore, we do not know whether the teachers and/or texts used were the best or poorest that were available. Consequently, before we can make an interpretable comparison we have to know the relative quality of each example of the media being compared, so we can know whether each is typical, or the best, of its type. Furthermore, knowledge of their effectiveness in achieving the same instructional objectives is not enough. It is also necessary to know their relative efficiency in doing this.

Programing Here to Stay, but Form Will Change

In my view, programed learning is here to stay. However, the forms it will take are anybody's guess at the moment. Even if no other use is made of it than to develop instructional materials, I think it safe to say that it will eliminate from instructional materials much if not all of the hack writing and the ineffective methods more justified as "artistry." Playing by ear, which is what we have had to do up to now, can produce both effective and ineffective materials without discriminating between them. The method of programed instruction, however, does provide a means by which the effectiveness of the product can be determined.

MENTAL HYGIENE AS AN ASPECT OF EDUCATIONAL PSYCHOLOGY

• It is unnecessary for us to be told that there is a relationship between mental health and success in school. The author of the first article in this section concerns herself with the nature of this relationship, adding thoughtful qualifications to the common view. It will be necessary for the reader to bear in mind Dr. White's definition of the "clinic model" and the "educational model" of personality. And here the educator may find that he has been living with an ambiguously defined set of educational goals. Do you agree with the editors that education should be directed toward self-realization and developing one's unique capacities? Then do you find that your classroom activities have been pointed toward another, and diametrically opposed, direction? Is the goal for personality development in which you believe the clinical or educational one?

White's article might have been grouped with the selections we have placed under the heading of motivation. It might also have been placed with those dealing with the cultural setting for learning. In short, we see the article as bringing together several facets of educational psychology. One might pursue in detail and independently some of the ideas so casually presented; e.g., "The poor . . . relate problems to external causes and pressures, in the face of which they feel helpless. Identifying problems outside the self, they cannot be helped by a service presuming that there is 'the necessary raw material for change' in the client-clinician relationship."

The article on dropouts by Millard gets to the focal problem of the relationship of mental health and education—the feelings and attitudes of the individual learner. While others talk of socioeconomic status, peer influences, cultural disadvantage, and parental attitudes as the cause of dropouts, Millard makes it clear that it is the reaction of the pupil to such phenomena that is the real concern of educators. He sees mental health as a problem that must be more realistically regarded by teachers and their co-workers in the field of psychology, psychiatry, and social work. Because "good education involves good mental hygiene," more attention must be given to experiences that will help the pupil create the ability to tolerate educational demands.

MARY ALICE WHITE
Teachers College, Columbia University

41 · LITTLE RED SCHOOLHOUSE AND LITTLE WHITE CLINIC

● The values advocated by the mental health movement in the school setting often conflict with educational values. It would be fair to say that the mental health movement has revered warmth of feeling; spontaneity; insight; a high interest in others, particularly peers; the ability to communicate, especially one's feelings; warm parents; freedom to exercise judgment; warm teachers, and democratic classrooms. The same movement has been against: being compulsive; competitive striving; intellectualism; being either thing- or achievement-oriented; being emotionally unresponsive, as well as being angry or passionate; being a loner; not confiding in others; teachers who are curriculum-oriented; the regimentation of school life; group tests; red tape; and vice-principals in charge of discipline. Many of these are precisely the values revered by educators committed to the "cognitive" cause.

The purpose of this paper is to evaluate some of the theories and evidence relevant to proposals made by a movement much concerned with strengthening mental health in childhood—and therefore drawn increasingly toward our schools. It is also my purpose to point out certain dilemmas which arise when I contemplate broadened mental health programs in the schools.

Views and Biases

Let me define my points of view toward mental health and education, so that my biases will be clear. I start with the conviction that mental illness is tragic, and that its incidence should be reduced by whatever humanitarian methods are available or can be invented. Whatever similar

Teachers College Record, 67:188–200, 1965. Used by permission of the author and *Teachers College Record*.

means can be demonstrated to increase mental health is another goal. At the same time, I am committed to the importance of education in our public schools, by which I mean essentially the acquisition of knowledge and of cognitive skills. This is not to say that education should not include many other things. I simply mean that no impairment should take place in the acquisition of knowledge and of cognitive skills as the result of other goals. A final bias of mine, probably the most influential, is that I am addicted to evidence as the basis for judgments.

Therefore, if we are to propose mental health programs, or accept them, I would suggest we weigh the evidence we have. The literature on mental illness is huge; the literature on mental health, minute. There are enormous holes in our knowledge, a lack of good longitudinal studies, an inability to find good measures of either mental health or of illness. What *is* known at the present time about the prevalence of mental illness?

The evidence to date suggests a strong negative relationship between the incidence of adult mental illness and socioeconomic status in both the United States and Great Britain. Since socioeconomic status, or SES, is positively related to intelligence, the corollary must be added that mental illness and intelligence may also be negatively related. To be more precise, several studies (3, 4, 7, 8, 23) suggest that the lower the social class, the higher the prevalency rates of mental illness, particularly the psychoses, and most particularly schizophrenia. Quite an argument goes on in the literature as to whether the environmental conditions of the lower class produce these results, or whether mentally ill adults drift down the class structure as a consequence of their illness. Pasamanick (17) has published several studies suggesting that poor health care and nutrition in lower SES mothers result in complications of pregnancy, which, in turn, lead to subtle neurological deficits in their children which are related to school maladjustment. There is, too, the old argument that the heredity and constitution of lower class members are somehow inadequate, physiologically and mentally, resulting in inadequate coping behavior. This latter interpretation was strongly suggested by Langner & Michael (8) who failed to find more stresses in their lower class adults, but did find that they used less socially appropriate coping mechanisms in this class as compared with the higher classes.

Problems of Method

There are, of course, terrible methodological problems here that make the most ardent student of epidemiological data shrink from forming firm opinions. Who gets labelled mentally ill, by whom, and against what criteria? This is such a disturbing question that there are times when one wonders if the diagnosis of mental illness is just another social class judgment. It would not be surprising, if this were so, that more of such judgments are applied to those lower in the social order by those who are higher.

Nevertheless, such studies provoke the question as to whether there are some conditions in childhood which disfavor the children of lower SES and might lead to the association of mental illness with social class in adults. It is quite clear today that one of these possible conditions is education itself.

Let us look briefly at what we know about the epidemiology of mental illness in children. As we do, let us bear in mind that mental illness in children is judged quite differently than it is in adults. It is essential to remember that children rarely seek help for emotional disturbance on their own. They are brought or referred by an adult who has made the decision. This adult is quite likely to be a member of the school staff, and increasingly so as our mental health programs expand in the schools. Further, children are not usually judged mentally ill by the types of behaviors used as criteria for adult mental illness. An adult, for example, has a number of choices about his job, his neighborhood, and the sub-culture to which he belongs. He can choose, unless he lives in a ghetto and is impoverished, to seek out that sub-culture which is most harmonious to him. For a child, there is essentially one set of norms for all, and these are school norms. True, schools vary in their criteria of acceptable behavior, but not, I believe, to the extent that they do for adult sub-cultures. Another point for us to remember is the peculiar nature of the school. A child is not only asked to behave according to certain school standards; he is also asked to *learn*. We do not judge mental illness in adults by their rate of learning.

School-Oriented Criteria

What I am suggesting is that studies of mental illness in children are a very different matter than those for adults, because the criteria applied are very largely school-oriented criteria—more uniform and more involved with learning than they are for adults. The difference in the criteria used for determining mental illness in children may therefore produce differences in rates which are a function of these criteria. In addition, we have the problem of age changes, so that children present more developmental differences than do adults; and even here, there are sex differences in these developmental stages.

With all these reservations in mind, what do we know about the spectrum of mental illness in children? First, diagnoses of severe mental illness are quite rare. In out-patient clinics, the rate for diagnosed schizophrenia in childhood is as rare as 9 per 100,000 for boys, and 3 per 100,000 for girls (20), compared with adult rates of 34 per 100,000. Yet we find that the total rate of all out-patient treatment for children is 16% higher than that for adults; that there is a peak for boys between 9 and 14 years, and between 14 and 16 for girls; and at every age, there are almost twice as many boys admitted as girls. This sex differential equalizes after about 18 years of age. Curiously, not only are boys referred twice as often as girls for all mental illnesses, but boys are seen within the school environment as having two to three times as many problems of all kinds over girls: reading, speech, behavior problems, vision, language disorders, and emotional problems (1).

When one searches for studies of the variables associated with diagnosed mental illness in children, we find a good deal of information about the variables related to school maladjustment, but little about mental illness in children as defined by admission to a mental health facility.

Institutionalized Children

One of the few studies in this area is that by Bloch & Behrens (2), which makes somber reading. These authors studied the characteristics of some 960 children referred to residential treatment centers in New York State in 1956. These centers were designed to treat severely disturbed children in a residential setting. Among the mental health professions, such children are usually considered to be mentally ill. The authors found that the demographic characteristics of this group were as follows: The ratio of boys to girls was 5:1; their families were unstable, riddled with pathology, poorly educated, and subsisting on a marginal income, often with public assistance. Less than one quarter of these children had lived only in their natural homes; forty per cent had lived in four or more homes or institutions and been in touch with a variety of social agencies which, early in the children's lives, had diagnosed, rediagnosed, referred, and placed them, without giving them anything we would term treatment. Finally, "most of these children first expressed their difficulties in school and were referred to agencies or professional persons for this reason. . . . Behavioral difficulties in school were reported for 65% of these children; 52% had learning difficulties; 34% had reading problems; and 30% were excessively truant."

We can dismiss this study as dealing with a collection of society's orphans; but it is a little hard to do so when we realize that, whether such children should be labelled as mentally ill or not, they are the ones being treated for mental illness. By the criteria used in epidemiological research, they form part of the population treated as though they were mentally ill. We are justified, therefore, in taking note of their low socioeconomic status and all the other familiar characteristics of those whom we term the culturally deprived. Unfortunately, no intelligence data was reported, but a likely guess is that it was below average for the group as a whole.

This study suggests the possibility that institutionalized mental illness in children may be like that of adults in its negative relationship to social class, and possibly to intelligence. Unfortunately, we have no comparable data on which to evaluate such an important hypothesis.

School Maladjustment

Let us turn now to the data concerning school maladjustment in children. The distinction between mental illness and school maladjustment in children is a fuzzy one, but they are not synonymous. From school maladjustment comes a sub-population of referrals to private practitioners and agencies, from which some children are placed in mental hospitals and in residential treatment centers. But not all school maladjustment is referred, and not all is institutionalized.

We have two major methodological problems here. First, who is making the judgment of emotional disturbance and how qualified are the judges? Second, not all school maladjustment is in the area of what we label mental illness. A lot of behavior which is seen as undesirable by the school is more likely to be classified as deviant, predelinquent, acting out, antisocial, or sociopathic. If such children are referred, they may be handled as either mentally ill or delinquent, with a confusing and sometimes overlapping type of placement or treatment. The distinction between a child who is primarily emotionally disturbed and acting out, and one who is delinquent with an accompanying emotional disturbance, is probably a distinction created by the nature of his immediate acts which have led him either to a mental health agency or to a law enforcing agency.

This may seem a trivial point; but it is not, if we are interested in understanding more about school maladjustment in children. Some of the children seen as school maladjusted may turn up later, as adults, in two quite different locations in society—jail, or the mental hospital. Unfortunately, adult studies of mental illness rarely take this into account, for the criminal and the insane are treated as separate populations. Again, however, we need to remember that children are very different from adults in that they are a reservoir of many things which they may become as adults—dead, physically ill, mentally ill, soldiers of fortune, alcoholics, criminals, expatriates, successful, happy, unhappy, productive, or forgotten. Children disappear into varied sub-populations as adults and become very hard to locate and count. One of these—the deviant sub-population—may show a possible relationship between what we call school maladjustment and adult antisocial or criminal lives. If we restrict ourselves only to adult mental illness, we may be missing a significant point about the potential predictability of childhood difficulties.

In the studies of school maladjustment, then, the evidence says to me that the ability to adjust to school—that is, the ability to learn; to produce; to pass to the next grade; to be liked by one's peers; to achieve on achievement tests; to be considered well adjusted by one's teachers; to go on to further education—is positively related to the social class of the child's family and to the child's tested intelligence. The inability to adjust to school—which means the poor learner, the poor reader, the behavior problem, the truant, the drop-out, the discipline problem, the emotionally disturbed, the peer rejected, the child referred by the classroom teacher for school maladjustment—is associated much more frequently with the child whose family is of lower social class status and the child with lower tested intelligence (25).

There is a third variable here, that of sex, which some of us think has an unknown but not constant relationship with social class and IQ. Boys are poorer school achievers than girls up to some point in high school. Boys from the lower class seem more severely handicapped than are such girls in their ability to make a good school adjustment, so sex may be a third interacting variable here whose role in combination with SES and IQ we do not yet understand. One possible explanation for this phenomenon is that of the physiological vulnerability of the male sex to what may be the neurological hazards of lower class reproduction. Another may be the poorer language ability of boys, which, added to the deficit of SES and IQ, may make school much harder sledding for a boy as compared with his sister. Other theories have emphasized the complacent behavior of girls, the bias of female teachers, and differences in expected sex roles.

Seeds of Illness

At this point we might ask: But isn't the term school maladjustment a deceptive term? Since it obviously involves educational achievement, we know that intelligence will play a major role, and we know intelligence and social class are positively correlated. But what has school maladjustment to do with adult mental illness, or mental health?

O'Neal and Robins (14) have done a series of interesting follow-up studies on children who were seen in an out-patient clinic in the 1920's. Their findings for their control group are particularly relevant here. As controls, they picked children who were matched with their experimental subjects for sex, race, age, residence and IQ. In addition, the control group had to be making a normal adjustment in school. Normal adjustment meant they had no extensive school absences, had not repeated a grade, had no recorded disciplinary actions, and had an IQ of 80 or better. What surprised the authors in their follow-up thirty years later was the striking amount of mental health in this control group. On the other hand, the experimental subjects, who had been seen at the mental health clinic, showed a high proportion of adult sociopaths and of adult mental illness. This suggests that a reasonably good school adjustment may have some positive relationship to later adult adjustment.

One of their later studies (18) bears on the earlier question raised about school maladjustment and later deviant behavior. When the authors followed up the group of children at the clinic who had been antisocial, they found that these children, as adults, had moved down the occupational ladder from the occupational position held by their fathers. This drift hypothesis, mentioned in relation to mental illness, now appears connected to deviant behavior. Does this suggest the possibility that both adult mental illness and deviance follow a similar downward course, and that both may arise in the children's population of what we call school maladjustment? Roff (19) has reported another possible relationship between school adjustment and adult deviance. He found that reliable predictions could be made about bad conduct in service based on school reports of children who were mean, disliked by their classmates, and antagonizing to other pupils.

An even more interesting addition to the relationship between adult and school adjustment is the massive longitudinal Nobles County study. The major conclusion was that few predictions of later adjustment held up, except that of intelligence. A more detailed examination of those later deemed delinquent, outstanding, or emotionally disturbed, showed IQ and SES to be the best predictors. Unfortunately, the follow-up period reported was only four years, meaning that the oldest school child in their original study was only about 20 years of age. This is really not a measure of adult adjustment, but of extended school adjustment. However, it is interesting to note that SES and IQ were predictors of three things: outstanding adjustment, which was really outstanding college achievement; emotional disturbance as identified by community agencies; and delinquency as defined by court records. This is quite similar to Havighurst's (6) findings in River City.

Is it true, then, that low IQ and SES both contribute to emotional disturbance and to delinquency? (An even sharper question is: Are they really different social disorders?)

Schools as Classifiers

So much then for some glimpses into the little we know about mental illness in children. If a relationship exists between mental health and school adjustment, and it seems as though it well might, then it may simply be a function of the school as a public institution. Since almost all children attend school for ten years or more, it is hardly surprising that those who can get through this first stage of life successfully are likely to go on to a more successful later adjustment, than those who don't. Schools have been referred to as the great mobility agent in our society. From the point of view of maladjustment, we might say that they also are the great classifying agent. If a child does not succeed in school, a large number of possible pathways are closed to him; and new ones open, most of them through the social agencies. These agency routes may lead to a large proportion of such children being labelled mentally ill, deviant, mentally retarded, or any other term for which we have agencies and institutions acting as receivers of the classified.

The tendency of the school to classify and label makes problematic its role in determining who is seen as mentally well or ill. The problem here is whether the schools are acting unreasonably in seeing as maladjusted those who don't adjust to school—or whether there is some truth to the position that whatever it takes to succeed in school contains the ingredients of what we call mental health. Let me stress how important it is to see this difference clearly.

If we argue that the schools have rather rigid standards of behavior, are essentially middle class and narrowminded in their insistence on education as a virtue, then we might logically argue for a more broadminded social institution, flexible in its response to various sub-cultures and classes, and open to a number of goals beside that of learning. This, of course, is part of the present argument being used today on behalf of the culturally deprived, and we are busy devising new techniques for them. These new techniques, however, are largely concerned with learning—the acquisition of knowledge, particularly language, and of cognitive skills, particularly concepts. Most of those working in the area of cultural deprivation seem quite convinced that the education of these children must be improved.

They are not asking the schools to lower their educational efforts but, in fact, to intensify them. This position seems rather consistent with what I outlined as Position B, that whatever it takes to succeed in school is important to adult adjustment.

But Position A says that the schools are really the villain of the piece—middle class, rather female, rigid, and overvaluing book learning—what may be termed the "little red schoolhouse syndrome," a highly ethnocentric one.

Dilemmas of Ethnocentricity

There is another type of ethnocentricity, however, which is basic to the dilemma presented here. This is the one that the mental health movement has brought with it to the school. Let me give you an example: One mental health project with a school staff (13), reports that the project ". . . encountered a variety of defenses such as denial, projection, avoidance of commitment, and over-volubility. Many of these are prevalent partly because the culture of the schools, with its emphasis on rightness, on form, and on infallibility, encourage them." The implication here is that the values commonly associated with education are ones which may lead to mentally ill mechanisms. The more relevant question is whose set of values are better—the schools' or the clinicians'—and for what?

It should not be necessary for me to point out the particular values of the mental health professions. We are aware of the halo we have placed on being person-oriented, rather than thing-oriented; on being warm; on being in touch with our feelings; on being democratic rather than authoritative; on being flexible rather than rigid. We need to be aware of the ethnocentricity of some of the values the mental health movement advocates in the school setting—and of the fact that they are often in conflict with educational values.

If the school has been rightly charged with the syndrome of the "little red schoolhouse," the mental health movement should accept the charge that it suffers from the syndrome of "the little white clinic." For the values of the movement are derived from clinical experiences which have been almost entirely with the sick end of the population continuum, and with only that group which was continued in therapy.

To be successful in psychotherapy as we know it today, an individual requires the following skills (or the ability to develop them): verbal ability; the ability to form concepts; a sense of historical time and order; intelligence; and a belief in man's ability to solve many of his own problems. It seems apparent then that much of what is required for successful participation in therapy is similar to what is required for successful school adjustment. So why is there any dilemma here, except for the fact that education and psychotherapy assume two distinct avenues to somewhat different goals?

It is hard to delineate the exact areas where mental health values clash with educational values, partly because a clear picture of the mental health goal for personality is hard to find. Presumably, the goal is a happy and self-realizing person, which education would not reject. But somewhere along the way the paths divide; and we find, in actual practice at least, the clinician emphasizing the importance of feelings over intellect, of personality expression over achievement, and of self-awareness over social commitment. Educators, on the other hand, tend to place intellectual activities higher than feelings, achievement over personality expression, and social responsibility—if not commitment—over self-awareness. In practice, these represent two personality models operating in the schools.

A Clash of Values

There is one point where the characteristics of the two models overlap: We fail to treat successfully the same group of people we fail to teach successfully. Hollingshead and Redlich (7) show that lower SES patients receive less psychotherapy and more somatic therapies than do higher SES patients in hospitals. They attribute this to differences in social class background in the middle class therapist and his patient; and it may be asked whether more severe diagnostic labels are not applied for a similar reason.

There is a high attrition rate in out-patient psychotherapy: as high as 45% in New York (25). In child psychiatric clinics in a large city (4) 59% of the patients seen at intake did not complete treatment; and the question has been raised as to whether the high professional status of the agency may not have been served by such a selection process rather than the needs of the clients. This may sound familiar to those of us who have been told that the standards prevailing in the schools are unreasonable and arbitrary, irrelevant to the needs of the deprived.

Overall and Aronson (16) attribute the swift termination of clinic treatments to the fact that lower SES patients base their expectations on a medical model built on previous agency contacts and quite different from the one the therapist has in mind. These patients are seen as having behavioral patterns which are foreign, even repugnant, to those who interview them. They show a lack of parental responsibility, ambition, marital stability, and educational goals; and they seem to hold no realistic expectations about the service which the agency can or should render.

Schneiderman's observations (21), it happens, might be applied to deprived children entering the first grade in the schools with expectations utterly different from those the teachers expect. The poor, he says, relate problems to external causes and pressures, in the face of which they feel helpless. Identifying problems outside the self, they cannot be helped by a service presuming that there is "the necessary raw material for change" in the client-clinician relationship. The poor, in addition, order speech and thought according to their own rules. They describe how the world looks narrowly, from their particular vantage points; and the context in which they speak may not be clear to the listener. Their organizing ideas are hard to define, and the resulting vagueness expresses itself in apparently disso-ciated comments "which may leave the listener wondering what is going on."

The teacher, expecting children to come to school eager to learn, may be in a position similar to the child who arrives with a different set of expectations: that school is a necessary evil; that education has not helped anyone in his neighborhood get anywhere; and that the behavior required in school makes no sense and need not be accepted. It seems to me that very little translation is needed to see that those who are failures in the "little white clinic" are likely to be failures in the "little red schoolhouse" as well.

We have failed to educate successfully the same group of people we have failed to treat successfully. The schoolhouse has admitted its failure and is striving to find new educational methods. The clinic is now recognizing its failure and seeking new therapeutic strategies.

The Need to Choose

The dilemma is, which way is more effective? Should we teach them or should we promote mental health? Which goal is more appropriate, and to what? Which method is more effective, and toward what goal? If we insist on thinking of mental illness as a disease—like t.b., cholera, or measles—then we will want to launch public health teams into the swamps of our schools to identify, isolate, decontaminate, build up immunities, to vaccinate and develop antibodies. The evidence on mental illness, as I read it, suggests that what we call mental illness is not usually a physical disease, but more likely a social disorder, arising from complex combinations of conditions, acting upon individuals with inadequate, or socially inappro-priate, coping techniques. Mental illness is a social definition, not a medical one.

How, then, shall we resolve this dilemma? The first issue for each of us to decide is which goal is more appropriate to what. If we argue for the mental health goal—the psychiatric hero—we must be aware that his characteristics may be very inappropriate to lower class life. By giving a child from this population the characteristics of the sensitive, perceptive, verbal, feeling, and self-aware psychiatric hero, would we be helping him to cope with the realities of lower class life? Do we not have to be keenly aware that as society changes—and I believe the society of young people in this country is changing dramatically toward social commitment and action— that the personality model may also need to change?

I am troubled by the very implication that one kind of personality is better than another. To me, this is not only ethnocentric, but dogmatic. I question whether I have the right to instill my psychiatric hero into the value system of a child, or his parents, simply because I prefer it, or simply because this model has proved to be therapeutically successful with certain patients. I think I have to ask myself a deeper question, which is: Are there personality models other than the therapeutically successful one, which are also successful in the social order? I believe there are, partly because I have seen them around me, but also because they have been documented in MacKinnon's work on creative talent (10). This leaves me in the position of being a personality pluralist, I suppose, in that I think there is more than one personality style which is desirable, or appropriate, or successful.

The same problem exists, however, if we weigh the educational model. Perhaps it is not so insistent on personality style as the psychiatric model, but it is one-sided in its emphasis upon the value of intellectual effort, of achievement, of striving, of rising in the social order, of compliance to school authority, and of application to work.

In the final analysis, those who favor the educational model will argue that, without education in today's society, there is little realistic chance of success in our social order. This seems to be a strong argument in favor of the educational model. The importance of the therapeutic model as successful in the social order is not proven, but those who favor it would reject such a test of success. They would argue, I think, that being psychologically at peace with oneself and self-realizing is not something that can be measured by educational or occupational achievement. This brings us right back to the start of our argument as to whether or not position in the social order, by which we mean social class, is positively related to that which we call mental health.

As long as we have a society that does regard educational, occupational, and economic achievement as good things, we will be left with criteria for mental health which are very similar to the criteria for the social order.

It is inescapable, as I see it now, to define mental health apart from social judgment, and that judgment always involves what a society sees as desirable.

Fallible Techniques

As far as the techniques we use in evaluating our clients, we are all well aware of the shaky ground upon which we operate. Every time we use observations of children to arrive at diagnosis or opinions, we realize, as Miller (12) found, that the more pathological the child, the less reliable our judgments. We recognize the inaccuracy of the histories that mothers give us (11). When we move into the school and observe in classrooms, we check our impulse to laud the democratic classroom over the autocratic one, for we realize that its value may not have been demonstrated, largely because of methodological problems (24). When we use teacher judgments of children who are disturbed, we check our impulse to rush in, diagnose, and refer, because we suspect that there are two chances in three that these same children will not be seen as disturbed in two years by another teacher (15).

If we are honest, we have to admit that we cannot demonstrate the validity and reliability of our techniques. That is no reason not to use them, until we have better ones, but it is a very good reason to use them with great caution and humility. It is also a very good reason not to substitute them for any other technique which has performed better.

Those who favor the educational model will insist on this very point. They will argue, I believe, that bad as our teaching techniques are, bad as our evaluation measurements are, bad as our educational research has been, that educational techniques are more reliable than those of mental health. They would argue that it is true no one can really define a good teacher, or even good teaching, but no one can do this in therapy either. It is true no one knows what a mark really means, or whether ungraded schools are really better for some things than graded ones, or whether new math has not produced a set of new problems while curing some old ones —in fact, whether the effects of innovation can be measured at all.

The Relevance of Values

But they will argue that educational techniques can measure whether or not a child can respond correctly to a question (I did not say "knows"); they can measure his spoken and reading vocabulary; they can predict, rather reliably, a child's future educational achievement by no later than sixth grade, and possibly as early as the fourth grade; and this is no mean feat. Where else in human behavior are our predictions as accurate as they are in the educational behavior of children? Granted, there are some built-in reasons why this is so, and maybe they are wrong, but our instruments are more accurate than any of the predictors I know in the field of mental health, social behavior, political behavior, or economic behavior.

In essence, then, each of us will choose the particular model of personality which he prefers in light of his own values, training, and experience. I have no quarrel with those who choose the mental health model or the educational model, as long as we are both aware that the reason for our choice stems from our value system, but *not* from any strong evidence that one is superior to the other against criteria acceptable to both sides. Those who believe primarily in mental health as a goal will argue for the model of the psychiatric hero. Those who believe primarily in education will argue for the educational model. I would think there are other models of the moment—the creative model, the socially committed model—each of which will have its own adherents.

I will, however, raise strong objections whenever the mental health movement knocks at the door of the public school to insist that its personality model should be chosen, because it is better, or more scientific, or more modern, or more anything else that implies it is better. Educators tend to be impressed by professional people who sound technical and knowledgeable, and are inclined to buy their wares as superior to anything the school can offer. Educators tend to forget that the school has some rather good techniques, compared with the mental health movement, for schools are so busy defending themselves from public attack that they get used to being apologetic about even those things which they do rather well.

My second objection to accepting the "little white clinic" syndrome into the public school stems from the "public" in public schools. Public schools are just that, the property of the nation, the institution which belongs more to everyone than any institution I know in our society. Until one understands the thoroughly responsive nature of the public school to the values of our society—its fads, its witch hunts, its desire for excellence, its desire for endless innovation, for economy, for morality but not religion—one does not understand the "public" in the public school. On these grounds, that of the public responsibility of the school, I would raise objection to the imposition of any one personality model upon the nation's children, particularly a model that has arisen from a very special endeavor called psychotherapy, by a very special set of people called clinicians who work with a very, very special set of people called patients who are not at all representative of the nation's children in a setting which has not been given the charge of raising the nation's children according to the goals determined by that society.

My dilemma is only partially resolved, as you can see. I am unwilling to give up the educational model with its "little red schoolhouse" syndrome for the mental health model of the "little white clinic," because I think both are imperfect; but to my mind, the evidence at the moment favors the retention of the educational model.

Both models need to change. I hope we can broaden the educational model to be more responsive to cultural differences. To do so without impairing whatever it may be that is similar between educational achievement and adult success will be most difficult, unless, of course, we change the rules for success in the social order. Schools cannot be held responsible for a lack of jobs, or lack of opportunity for upward mobility. The schools merely reflect many of the ugly facts of society. The process of education has to lead its participants to something they want in order for them to want to be educated.

As for the little white clinic, it has a great opportunity to change, much more so than the public schools. It can innovate almost at will, without going through a school board and without submitting a budget to a public vote. It can discover new strategies of personality change which are meaningful to the particular people involved. I would suggest that a profitable effort for the clinician would be to ask what procedures the public schools have tried with these same groups, and learn how these have failed, and in the last sixty years, how many have succeeded. Over the last century, the public schools in this country have effected an unprecedented upward social mobility movement. They have received children from dire poverty, from a myriad of cultures, tongues, nationalities, and religions, and have exposed them to the little red schoolhouse. It may be an ethnocentric syndrome; but the astounding thing is that it has worked for many millions. Perhaps there is something there which the mental health movement could study with profit.

To the school staff I recommend more earnest study of the learning and the teaching processes. The proper study of the schools is education, and there is much to be studied. For my own specialty, that of school psychology, I predict in the next few years the flowering of that long-delayed romance between psychology and education.

Recommendations

To both the school and the clinic staff, I recommend more earnest study of the epidemiology of maladjustment, including both mental illness and deviance; an attempt to differentiate between incompetent coping techniques and socially inappropriate coping techniques; a reexamination of the notion that educational or social mobility equals neuroticism; the exploration of wildly imaginative educational and therapeutic methods, including those which offend our values, such as autocratic advice and public residential schools; an examination of therapy as an educational process as well as education as a therapeutic process; and a continuing concern with the conflict in values between the feeling-oriented mental health model, and the intellect-oriented model of education.

To the extent that we continue to place the school as the public doorway to the great society, I suspect we will continue to find that education will be positively related to the social criteria of success, adjustment, and of achievement—that is, to various definitions of mental health. As long as the school is the doorway, we will continue to find that whatever recipe makes for school success tends to correlate with the recipe for mental health in this society. As long as this is true, I think the choice of who can do the most for mental health—the school or the clinic—will have to be answered in favor of the school.

But as I said when I started, my bias is obvious. I am incurably addicted to evidence on the basis for opinion, particularly when it comes to advocating change in our public schools.

REFERENCES

1. Bentzen, Frances, "Sex ratios in learning and behavior disorders," *Amer. J. Orthopsychiat.*, 1963, 33.
2. Bloch, D. A., and Behrens, Marjorie L., *A study of children referred for residential treatment in New York State*, Albany, N.Y.: New York State Interdepartmental Health Resource Board, 1959.
3. Brooke, E. M., "National statistics in the epidemiology of mental illness," *J. Mental Science*, 1959, 105.
4. Frumkin, R. M., "Occupation and major mental disorders." In A. M. Rose (Ed.), *Mental health and mental disorder*, New York: Norton, 1955, pp. 136–160.
5. Gordon, S., "Are we seeing the right patients?" *Amer. J. Orthopsychiat.*, 1965, 35, 131–137.
6. Havighurst, R. J., Bowman, P. H., Liddle, G. P., Matthews, C. V., and Pierce, J. V., *Growing up in River City*, New York: Wiley, 1962.
7. Hollingshead, A. B., and Redlich, F. C., *Social class and mental illness: A community study*, New York: Wiley, 1958.
8. Langner, T. S., and Michael, S. T., *Life stress and mental health*, New York: Free Press of Glencoe, 1963.

9. MacKinnon, D. W., "The nature and outline of creative talent," *Amer. J. Orthopsychiat.*, 1965, 35, 99–105.

10. MacKinnon, D. W., "Personality and the realization of creative potential," *Amer. Psychol.*, 1965, 20, 273–281.

11. Mednick, S., and Shaffer, T. B. P., "Mothers' retrospective reports in child rearing research," *Amer. J. Orthopsychiat.*, 1963, 33, 457–461.

12. Miller, L. C., "Q-sort agreement among observers of children," *Amer. J. Orthopsychiat.*, 1964, 34, 71–75.

13. Newman, Ruth G., "Educational technical assistance," *Amer. J. Orthopsychiat.*, 1964, 34, 137–139.

14. O'Neal, Patricia, and Robins, L. N., "The relation of childhood behavior problems to adult psychiatric status: a 30 year follow-up study of 150 subjects," *Amer. J. Psychiatry*, 1958, 114, 361–369.

15. Onondaga County School Studies. *Persistence of emotional disturbances reported among second and fourth grade children.* Mental Health Research Unit, Syracuse, N.Y.: N.Y. State Dept. of Mental Hygiene, Sept., 1964.

16. Overall, Betty, and Aronson, H., "Expectations of psychotherapy in patients of lower socio-economic class," *Amer. J. Orthopsychiat.*, 1963, 33, 421–430.

17. Pasamanick, B., "Epidemiologic investigations of some prenatal factors in the production of neuropsychiatric disorder," In P. H. Hoch, and J. Zubin (Eds.) *Comparative epidemiology of the mental disorders*, New York: Grune & Stratton, 1961, pp. 260–275.

18. Robins, L. N., Gyman, H., and O'Neal, P., "The interaction of social class and deviant behavior," *Amer. Sociol. Rev.*, 1962, 27, 480–492.

19. Roff, M., "Childhood social interactions and young adult bad conduct," *J. abn. soc. Psychol.*, 1961, 63, 333–337.

20. Rosen, Beatrice M., Bahn, Anita K., and Kramer, M., "Demographic and diagnostic characteristics of psychiatric clinic outpatients in the U.S.A.," *Amer. J. Orthopsychiat*, 1964, 34, 455–468.

21. Schneiderman, L., "Social class, diagnosis and treatment," *Amer. J. Orthopsychiat.*, 1965, 35, 99–105.

22. Sechrest, Lee, "Studies of classroom atmosphere," *Psychol. in the Schools*, 1964, 1, 103–117.

23. Srole, L., Langner, T. C., Michael, S. T., Opler, M. K., and Rennie, T. A. C., *Mental health in the metropolis: The midtown Manhattan study*, Vol. 1, New York: McGraw-Hill, 1962.

24. White, Mary Alice, and Harris, M. W., *The school psychologist*, New York: Harper & Brothers, 1961, pp. 92–118, 149–183.

25. Woodward, L. E., Patton, R. E., and Pense, Cynthia, "The value of statistical reporting in the planning and revising of community mental health programs," *Amer. J. Orthopsychiat.*, 1961, 31, 292–319.

THOMAS L. MILLARD
Assistant Professor of Sociology, Montclair State College, Upper Montclair,
New Jersey

42 · SOME CLINICAL NOTES ON DROPOUTS

● The spiraling rate of
dropouts is profoundly disturbing to those of us in education who believe
that such waste in human resources is indefensible; and that salvaging this
precious resource is a challenging and urgent task for education, and one
in which mental health has a vital interest.[1]

If real progress is to be made in reducing this problem to a tolerable
level, educational strategy must reflect a widening recognition and acceptance of not only the community's social and vocational agencies, organizations and individuals concerned about and competent in lending assistance,

Journal of Secondary Education, 39:343–347, 1964. Used by permission of the
author and the *Journal of Secondary Education.*

[1] Actually, the percentage of school dropouts has not risen, though the number
of dropouts was greater in 1960 than in 1950. As an example, for the 17-year-old
group, dropouts declined from 32 per cent in 1950 to 24 per cent in 1960. But
because of the rapid increase in numbers of this age group, the number of dropouts
rose from 670,000 to 698,000.

Despite the increasing number of high school graduates, the Population Reference Bureau, a non-profit research and educational agency, estimates that during
the 1960's about 7.5 million youngsters will drop out of school. Nearly a third
of them—about 2.3 million—will have an eighth-grade education or less. And
when this is viewed against the current 15.9 per cent unemployment figure for
out-of-school, unskilled youth, it makes a cogent argument for greater educational
activity, plus other programs that stimulate youth employment and training.

That this may suggest an even more massive educational and social problem
for the future is seen in the fact that high school enrollment will increase 30 per
cent in the next decade. The enrollment of 12.7 million youngsters in the fall
of 1964 will become 16.3 million by the fall of 1974.

but of education's own resources, specifically its mental health services, in its practical and strategic position within the school setting for observing and understanding the sequence of events that leads to early school leaving.

From this writer's clinical experience, a substantial number of children become school dropouts because they are either unable or unwilling to test their learning abilities (or to be more specific their ability for mastering feelings of defeatism) and therefore overcompensate for their feelings of inadequacy or failure by withdrawal of self from the educational environment.

Finding themselves drifting further and wider from the main educational experience of their peers, such children, out of sheer need for self-preservation, make sweeping use of denial and flight, which in effect is an attempt to dilute the experience, i.e. devalue or minimize its importance, thus reassuring the person of his ability to control the emotions attendant with self-inadequacy.

Supposedly, by not displaying feelings like his contemporaries in similar circumstances, he is emancipated from the learning requirements and demands of educational relationships—where warmth and sympathy make him obligated to be conforming, and shame and embarrassment are supposed to make him feel guilty and hence strive to do better.

By means of dropping out, the individual attempts, consciously or unconsciously, to master unpleasant or intolerable feelings by blunting, then nullifying them, denying them, repressing or suppressing them.

Then too, he may resort to realignment of these feelings from the specific social or learning activity causing them, and link them to some innocent or neutral object, for example, downgrading his school performance with the rationalization, "Those kids are jerks. Who wants to go to school with them?" or "They (whom he can't identify) didn't like me and I can get a job anyway," and so on, all of which suggests a facade for his intense feelings of hostility and self-pity.

Such responses to stressful situations may well be a matter of deep-rooted emotional discord.

A disturbing problem one constantly encounters with prospective dropouts is their inability (or perhaps unwillingness) to draw realistic inferences from what is happening to them as well as what is happening to others who have dropped out of school.

Not only will these youngsters not learn from what they have seen or heard about the risks and problems of the dropout, but they will counter these efforts with such an illusory and illogical self-confidence that it is best described as the product of a narcissistic personality complete with magic and wish-fulfillment fantasies.[2]

Fantastic notions of self-marketability and ideas of exceptionalism to current employment practices pervade their thinking.

Thus, for example, the fact that other dropouts are unable to find employment has no implication for his decision, but the fact that another youngster has found employment represents a resounding rebuttal to adult intervention and a source of strength for his argument of "exceptionalism." "Well, my friend found a job and if he can find one, so can I."[3]

Such responses characterize one of the chief deficiencies in the dropout's personality—namely, the inability of the ego to differentiate and single out his own contribution to this dilemma, and this is as tragic to report as the much mentioned' poverty breeding cycle.

For many dropouts, this psychological phenomenon of non-perception of their own share in the events of their lives can be seen as purposeful denial, of trying to ward off guilt and self-inquiry, the kind of personal introspection which is neither painful nor pleasant but which is necessary for successful living.

To understand the dropout syndrome, we must see the dropout process

[2] This is an important point but it is hardly surprising in view of our high-success value orientation. Everyone must succeed, hence failing in school is a very serious matter, both socially and psychologically; it leaves one with a feeling of defenselessness, a feeling of inadequacy and failure.

All children invest something of themselves in the learning process. Failing in school means, in a sense, that this invested portion of oneself has failed.

Consequently, there is a need to find some less difficult and complex task, something easier and less demanding that can restore his nearly shattered concept of himself and, since for these youngsters, there is still a sub-cultural identification in "toiling with the hands," they view employment as one area in which investment of natural strength rather than formal learning is the common denominator of acceptance and success.

Hence the idea of work has an irresistible attraction to frustrated youngsters. The proposed solution in dropping out helps the youngster to reduce some of his anxiety because it removes the threat to his self-concept. But, unfortunately, it does not help him to make any positive moves to cope with the real problem.

[3] Such reaction is perhaps understandable if only because each individual with his own set of cultural-personal expectations tends to view his environment, which certainly includes the performances of others, differently from every other person. In effect, each individual infuses a certain measure of himself into what he perceives and hears. Psychologically, he "projects" something of his own bias, needs and viewpoints into the actions and attitudes of other people. For the prospective dropout, this is a natural outcome of his attempt to interpret or react to his environment.

as part of a life-long defensive and adaptive scheme for the individual, rather than a specific act, and it is characterized by undue emphasis on denial, repression and flight.

But in seeking an understanding of this phenomenon, it is well to remember that dropout behavior cannot always be adjudged socially abnormal.

For some children, the very act of withdrawing from an emotionally-laden situation with its attendant frustrations and anxieties is a safety valve by which the individual seeks to consolidate his ego strengths in coping with the specific emotional predicament.

Whatever the ultimate explanation for school dropouts may be, it is quite evident that school specialists in mental health must play a much larger and more responsible role in its final formulation.

It is well to remember that today's modern school is no longer a place where only the acquisition of basic skills and knowledge are fostered, it also is, in fact, a social agency of that community licensed to minister to all of the varied and complex needs of child development, not the least of which is mental well-being.[4]

Mental health then, and its direct application cannot be viewed in residual terms, an isolated entity apart and separate from the total school effort at socializing the youngster for meaningful and responsible membership in society.

Early school leaving is symptomatic of a more basic disorder in social adaptation and functioning and the conclusion seems inescapable that where we have failed to muster our full resources on behalf of the child, so that he

---

[4] But this fact, unfortunately, is only flickeringly evident in token programs on mental health in the curricula and the even more slow recognition and accept-ance of psychiatry, psychology and social work as legitimate educational services. According to the Joint Commission on Mental Illness and Health, an interdisciplinary survey authorized by the Congress in 1956, the concept of mental health held by school administrators is far from ideal. The promotion of mental health and its maintenance in the school setting has not been fully appreciated to the extent that it should. For an illuminating discussion on this and other problems in mental health, see *Final Report, Action for Mental Health* (Basic Books) 1961. However, great strides have been made in strengthening the resources of special education. The National Defense Education Act has been a godsend in the recruitment of professional staff for the gifted, and many states have encouraged additional facilities and services for the retarded, as well as for the emotionally disturbed and socially maladjusted. For more on this, see Henry P. David, "Public Mental Health, Child Welfare, and the School: Some Implications of the Joint Commission Report," *The Welfare Reporter*, Vol. 14, No. 1 (January, 1963), pp. 16–20.

may cope effectively with today's society, to that extent we have failed in promoting mental health.

While, unfortunately, there are no magical formulas for the universal management of all children, especially for potential dropouts, we can nevertheless make more effective use of good mental hygiene practices through the establishment of psycho-educational conditions that shore up feelings of reassurance and support for the academically unresponsive child.

In this view, good education involves good mental hygiene.

As we attempt to cope with the infinite and complex variations to these problems, there is no question that mental health can add new dimensions in differentiating and organizing socio-psychological phenomena in terms of cause and effect on the individual.[5]

As Lindgren suggests, the things, situations, and events that attract the greatest amount of attention are those that are perceived as threats to our self-concepts and self-esteem.[6] The big problem, of course, is how to change "threats" into "challenges." When things appear threatening to us, we have the feeling of helplessness and vulnerability—in other words, anxiety.[7]

As one looks at present-day society, the first thing that impresses us is the tremendous cultural complexity that confronts the individual, creating peculiar and special problems for him.

[5] Then too, school-oriented mental health can contribute new awareness on the image and meaning of education for the individual. For as the task of continually organizing and reorganizing frames of references and systems of sub-cultural expectations develop meaning, we are able to formulate new insights into, and achieve a new objectivity about educational ways of doing things.

[6] For a discussion on the development of the self-concept as part of a larger task in organizing and classifying the sensations, impressions, and ideas that crowd into our consciousness, see Henry Clay Lindgren, *Meaning: Antidote to Anxiety* (New York: Thomas Nelson and Sons, 1956).

[7] Anxiety is an important factor in human adaptation and functioning—this fact, no one disputes, but there is much controversy regarding attempts to assess or measure it. Especially pertinent for a discussion of this point are: Seymour B. Sarason et al., *Anxiety in Elementary School Children: A Report of Research* (New York: John Wiley and Sons, 1960); Paul H. Mussen, ed., *Handbook of Research Methods in Child Development* (New York: John Wiley and Sons, 1960); Carol N. Zimet and Glen A. Blackbill, "The Role of Anxiety in Psychodiagnosis," *Journal of Clinical Psychology*, Vol. 12, No. 2 (April, 1956), pp. 173–177; Irwin G. Sarason, "Empirical and Theoretical Problems in the Use of Anxiety Scales," *Psychological Bulletins*, Vol. 57, No. 5 (September, 1960), pp. 403–415. For a comparative strategy in assessing anxiety, see Arnold H. Buss et al., "The Measurement of Anxiety in Clinical Situations," *Journal of Consulting Psychology*, Vol. 19, No. 2 (April, 1955), pp. 125–129.

These forces in varying degrees are seen in the general instability created by rapid social change and it is this phenomenon as it has meaning for the child that must become the specialized concern of psychiatry, psychology and social work.[8]

To understand the dropout problem then, mental health must be brought more into the investigation and treatment of the basic causes of early school leaving. The usual explanations as offered by these youngsters cannot be accepted, because they are rational ations covering up more basic and fundamental conflicts.

Unmanageable hostility toward classmates or teachers, disinterest in learning or truancy are but surface descriptions of school difficulty.

Far more fundamental forces are fear and anxiety, feelings of inferiority, hatred, aggressiveness, guilt and other mental disorders that prevent youngsters from assembling a well-organized and stable personality able to relate itself in a more positive way with those influences interacting with it.

"Mental health" which has offered some of the most satisfactory explanations of how these influences lead individuals to give up and quit school can shed new light on ways of preventing these young people from early school leaving by assisting in programs that build up their hopes and natural wants through reassuring and supportive experiences that enable these children to tolerate more comfortable educational demands.

Today mental health is increasingly becoming associated with those forces in society which recognize the close interrelation between individual welfare and social welfare, and which seek to create a social environment conducive to the development of the fullest social and psychological potential of the person.

In this respect, only as we begin to move more in a common awareness, will mental health and education be closer to the answer.

It cannot be said too often that for wholesome development, every child needs to attain good social adjustment as well as full use of his potential talents. The one must not be sacrificed to the other. This is essential for vocational success as well as for personal well-being.

Indeed, the newer trends in education all flow from recognition of this principle. That there is an urgent concern for every child to fully realize

---

[8] The usual arrangement for school mental health services consists of the psychiatrist, psychologist and psychiatric social worker. So closely interwoven is the work of these disciplines, and so similar their basic goals that they are often referred to as a "clinical team," and in many of the school districts where mental health services exist, they do function as a clinical team.

his potential is in evidence. And in no area has this concern been carried further than in the establishing of mental health services in school programs.

Thus today, the first concern of our better schools is the development of the child—the "whole child." Such schools seek to provide a good environment for self-discovery.

From the standpoint of mental hygiene, a good school system is one that provides ample auxiliary and supporting services for the satisfaction of these needs.

TEACHER PERSONALITY AS A FACTOR IN LEARNING

• "As the teacher, so is the school" is a truth that is sometimes difficult to face, but it does seem to be an inescapable fact that methods, standards, curricula, and organization are secondary to the personality of the teacher. The subject of educational psychology will be most effective when it results in the teacher's asking, "What can I do about making myself a more significant person?"

We believe that the relationship between the teacher and students is more important for effective learning than the information presented and the techniques used. Although it is widely accepted that the kind of a person the teacher is, or his personality, determines the quality of these relationships, this is the factor which receives the least attention when ways of improving the educational process are considered. Candidates for teacher education rarely are screened in terms of their ability to maintain effective interpersonal relationships. Teacher-preparation curricula seldom provide the aspirant with help in dealing with personality patterns that may be detrimental to his effectiveness as a teacher. In-service programs for improving teacher competence are seldom organized around the objective of improving teacher personality.

Skinner postulates that to teach, one must communicate. This cannot be done unless someone listens. When a student cannot accept the teacher as a person because the teacher has failed to make him feel accepted, he tends to reject on a total basis. Not only is it difficult for him to like the teacher, it is difficult for him to accept much of what the teacher represents or projects. Subject matter, structure and discipline, and the "oughts" and "ought-nots" of the middle-class value system are likely to be rejected. Skinner's "escalation of counter-attacks" in response to what he regards as "aversive control" is descriptive of what happens.

Teachers and schools do not consciously defeat themselves by promoting classroom conditions and relationships that operate to negate instruction. This is often done through the failure of teachers to understand themselves. One does not always communicate what he thinks he does, and he is not always perceived as he believes himself to be. People are often not aware of how unsuccessful they are in hiding their emotional reactions from others. Because it is essential for teachers to know what emotion they communicate to students, they have an obligation to explore and understand their emotional make-up and the way in which it affects others.

The article by Haas does not refer to teachers, but two focal concerns of the schools are dealt with—social class and the personality of the professional. With almost half of the school-age children belonging to the lower social class and with virtually all teachers coming from the middle class, the implications of Haas's presentation are clear. The reader will only have to substitute the word *teacher* for *psychiatrist, therapist, doctor,* or *social worker* to make the selection apropos.

Jersild advances some practical and worth-while suggestions for personal and professional growth in this respect. We urge teachers in all stages of preparation and practice to consider his message thoughtfully and thankfully. This may well be the next big breakthrough in education and human relationships!

B. F. SKINNER
Edgar Pierce Professor of Psychology, Harvard University

43 · WHY TEACHERS FAIL

● The most widely pub-
licized efforts to improve education show an extraordinary neglect of
method. Learning and teaching are not analyzed, and almost no effort is
made to improve teaching as such. The aid which education is to receive
usually means money, and the proposals for spending it follow a few,
familiar lines. We should build more and better schools. We should recruit
more and better teachers. We should search for better students and make
sure that all competent students can go to school or college. We should
multiply teacher-student contacts with films and television. We should
design new curricula. All this can be done without looking at teaching itself.
We need not ask how those better teachers are to teach those better students
in those better schools, what kinds of contact are to be multiplied through
mass media, of how new curricula are to be made effective.

Perhaps we should not expect questions of this sort to be asked in what
is essentially a consumer's revolt. Earlier educational reforms were proposed
by teachers—a Comenius, a Rousseau, a John Dewey—who were familiar
with teaching methods, knew their shortcomings, and thought they saw a
chance to improve them. Today the disaffected are the parents, employers,
and others who are unhappy about the products of education. When teachers complain, it is as consumers of education at lower levels—graduate
school authorities want better college teaching, college teachers work to
improve high-school curricula, and so on. It is perhaps natural that consumers should turn to the conspicuous shortcomings of plant, personnel,
and equipment rather than to method.

It is also true that educational method has not been brought to their
attention in a favorable light. Pedagogy is not a prestigious word. Its low
estate may be traced in part to the fact that under the blandishments of

Saturday Review, 40 (No. 42) :80–81, 98 ff., October 16, 1965. Reprinted by
permission of the author and the *Saturday Review.*

statistical methods, which promised a new kind of rigor, educational psychologists spent half a century measuring the results of teaching while neglecting teaching itself. They compared different methods of teaching in matched groups and could often say that one method was clearly better than another, but the methods they compared were usually not drawn from their own research or even their own theories, and their results seldom generated new methods. Psychological studies of learning were equally sterile—concentrating on relatively unimportant details of a few typical learning situations such as the memory drum, the maze, the discrimination box, and verbal "problems." The learning and forgetting curves that emerged from these studies were never useful in the classroom and came to occupy a less and less important place in textbooks on educational psychology. Even today many distinguished learning theorists insist that their work has no practical relevance.

For these and doubtless other reasons, what has been taught as pedagogy has not been a true technology of teaching. College teaching, indeed, has not been taught at all. The beginning teacher receives no professional preparation. He usually begins to teach simply as he himself has been taught, and if he improves, it is only in the light of his own unaided experience. High-school and grade-school teaching is taught primarily through apprenticeships, in which students receive the advice and counsel of experienced teachers. Certain trade skills and rules of thumb are passed along, but the young teacher's own experience is to be the major source of improvement. Even this modest venture in teacher training is under attack. It is argued that a good teacher is simply one who knows his subject matter and is interested in it. Any special knowledge of pedagogy as a basic science of teaching is felt to be unnecessary.

The attitude is regrettable. No enterprise can improve itself to the fullest extent without examining its basic processes. A really effective educational system cannot be set up until we understand the processes of learning and teaching. Human behavior is far too complex to be left to casual experience, or even to organized experience in the restricted environment of the classroom. Teachers need help. In particular they need the kind of help offered by a scientific analysis of behavior.

Fortunately such an analysis is now available. Principles derived from it have already contributed to the design of schools, equipment, texts, and classroom practices. Programmed instruction is, perhaps, its best known achievement. Some acquaintance with its basic formulation is beginning to be regarded as important in the training of teachers and administrators. These positive contributions, however, are no more important than the light which the analysis throws on current practices. There is something wrong with teaching. From the point of view of an experimental analysis of behavior, what is it?

Corporal punishment, which has always played an important role in education, provides one clue. As H. I. Marrou says in *A History of Education in Antiquity*: "Education and corporal punishment appeared as inseparable to a Hellenistic Greek as they had to a Jewish or an Egyptian scribe in the time of the Pharoahs. . . . When the men of antiquity thought back to their schooldays they immediately remembered the beatings." The cane is still with us, and efforts to abolish it are vigorously opposed. In Great Britain a split leather strap for whipping students called a taws can be obtained from suppliers who advertise in educational journals, one of whom is said to sell 3,000 annually. (The taws has the advantage, shared by the rubber truncheon, of leaving no incriminating marks.)

The brutality of corporal punishment and the viciousness it breeds in both teacher and student have, of course, led to reform. Usually this has meant little more than shifting to noncorporal measures, of which education can boast an astonishing list. Ridicule (now largely verbalized, but once symbolized by the dunce cap or by forcing the student to sit facing a wall), scolding, sarcasm, criticism, incarceration (being "kept after school"), extra school or home work, the withdrawal of privileges, forced labor, ostracism, being put on silence, and fines—these are some of the devices that have permitted the teacher to spare the rod without spoiling the child. In some respects they are less objectionable than corporal punishment, but the pattern remains: the student spends a great part of his day doing things he does not want to do. If a teacher is in any doubt about his own methods, he should ask himself a few questions. Do my students stop work immediately when I dismiss the class? (If so, dismissal is obviously a release from a threat.) Do they welcome rather than regret vacations and unscheduled days of no school? Do I reward them for good behavior by excusing them from other assignments? Do I punish them by giving them additional assignments? Do I frequently say, "Pay attention," "Now remember," or otherwise gently "admonish" them? Do I find it necessary from time to time to "get tough" and threaten some form of punishment?

The teacher can use aversive control because he is either bigger and stronger than his students or able to invoke the authority of parents or police who are. He can coerce students into reading texts, listening to lectures, taking part in discussions, recalling as much as possible of what they have read or heard, writing papers, and so on. This is perhaps an achievement, but it is offset by an extraordinary list of unwanted by-products traceable to the basic practice.

The student who works mainly to escape aversive stimulation discovers other ways of escaping. He is tardy—"creeping like snail unwilling to school." He stays away from school altogether. Education has its own word for this—"truancy"—from an old Celt word meaning wretched. A special policeman, the truant officer, deals with offenders by threatening still more aversive consequences. The dropout is a legal truant. Children who commit suicide are often found to have had trouble in school.

There are subtler forms of escape. Though physically present and looking at teacher or text, the student does not pay attention. He is hysterically deaf. His mind wanders. He daydreams. "Mental fatigue" is usually not a state of exhaustion but an uncontrollable disposition to escape, and schools deal with it by permitting escape to other activities that, it is hoped, will also be profitable. The periods into which the school day is broken measure the limits of successful aversive control rather than the capacity for sustained attention. A child will spend hours absorbed in play or in watching movies or television who cannot sit still in school for more than a few minutes before escape becomes too strong to be denied. One of the easiest forms of escape is simply to forget all one has learned, and no one has discovered a form of control to prevent this ultimate break for freedom.

An equally serious result which an experimental analysis of behavior leads us to expect is that students counter-attack. If the teacher is weak, the student may attack openly. Physical attacks on teachers are now common. Verbal attacks in the teacher's absence are legendary. When the teacher is present, attacks may take the form of annoyance, and students escape punishment by annoying surreptitiously—by groaning, shuffling the feet, or snapping the fingers. A "tormenter" was a surreptitious noise maker especially designed for classroom use.

Counter-attack escalates. Slightly aversive action by the teacher evokes reactions that demand severer measures, to which in turn the student reacts still more violently. Escalation may continue until one party withdraws (the student leaves school or the teacher resigns) or dominates completely (the students establish anarchy or the teacher imposes a despotic discipline.)

Vandalism is another form of counter-attack that is growing steadily more serious. Many cities maintain special police forces to guard school buildings on weekends. Schools are now being designed so that windows cannot be easily broken from the street. A more sweeping counter-attack comes later when, as taxpayers or alumni, former students refuse to support educational institutions. Anti-intellectualism is often a general attack on all that education represents.

A much less obvious but equally serious effect of aversive control is plain inaction. The student is sullen and unresponsive. He "blocks." Inaction is sometimes a form of escape. Rather than carry out an assignment, the student simply takes punishment as the lesser evil. It is sometimes a form of attack, the object of which is to enrage the teacher. But it is also in its own right a predictable effect of aversive control.

All these reactions have emotional accompaniments. Fear and anxiety are characteristic of escape and avoidance, anger of counter-attack, and resentment of sullen inaction. These are the classical features of juvenile delinquency, of psychosomatic illness, and of other maladjustments familiar to the administrations and health services of educational institutions.

In college and graduate schools the aversive pattern survives in the now almost universal system of "assign and test." The teacher does not teach, he simply holds the student responsible for learning. The student must read books, study texts, perform experiments, and attend lectures, and he is responsible for doing so in the sense that, if he does not correctly report what he has seen, heard, or read, he will suffer aversive consequences. Questions and answers are so staple a feature of education that their connection with teaching almost never occasions surprise. As a demand for a response that will meet certain specifications, a question is almost always slightly aversive. An examination, as a collection of questions, characteristically generates the anxiety and panic appropriate to avoidance and escape. Reading a student's paper is still likely to be called "correcting" it. Examinations are designed to show principally what the student does *not* know. A test that proves to be too easy is made harder before being given again, ostensibly because an easy test does not discriminate, but more probably because the teacher is afraid of weakening the threat under which his students are working. A teacher is judged by his employers and colleagues by the severity of the threat he imposes: he is a good teacher if he makes his students work hard, regardless of how he does so or of how much he teaches them by doing so. He eventually evaluates himself in the same way; if he tries to shift to nonaversive methods, he may discover that he resists making things easy as if this necessarily meant teaching less.

Proposals to add requirements and raise standards are usually part of an aversive pattern. A well known educator has written: "We must stiffen the work of our schools . . . we have every reason to concentrate on [certain subjects] and be unflagging in our insistence that they be really learned . . . Senior year [in high school] ought to be the hardest . . . [We should give] students work that is both difficult and important, and [insist] that it be well done. . . . We should demand more of our students." These expressions were probably intended to be synonymous with "students should learn more" or possibly "teachers should teach more." There may be good reasons why students should take more mathematics or learn a modern language more thoroughly or be better prepared for college or graduate school, but they are not reasons for intensifying aversive pressures. A standard is a level of achievement; only under a particular philosophy of education is it a criterion upon which some form of punishment is contingent.

Most teachers are humane and well disposed. They do not want to threaten their students, yet they find themselves doing so. They want to help, but their offers to help are often declined. Most students are well disposed. They want an education, yet they cannot force themselves to study, and they know they are wasting time. For reasons which they have probably not correctly identified, many are in revolt. Why should education continue to use the aversive techniques to which all this is so obviously due? Evidently because effective alternatives have not been found. It is not enough simply to abandon aversive measures. A Summerhill is therapeutic not educational. By withholding punishment teachers may help students who have been badly treated elsewhere and prepare them to be taught, but something else is needed if they are to teach. What is that something else, and why has it not yet solved the problem?

A child sees things and talks about them accurately afterward. He listens to news and gossip and passes it along. He recounts in great detail the plot of a movie he has seen or a book he has read. He seems to have a "natural curiosity," a "love of knowledge," and "inherent wish to learn." Why not take advantage of these natural endowments and simply bring the student into contact with the world he is to learn about? There are practical problems, of course. Only a small part of the real world can be brought into the classroom even with the aid of films, tape recorders, and television, and only a small part of what remains can be visited outside. Words are easily imported, but the verbal excesses of classical education have shown how easily this fact may lead to a dangerous overemphasis. Within reasonable limits, however, is it not possible to teach simply by giving the student an opportunity to learn in a natural way?

Unfortunately, a student does not learn simply when he is shown or told. Something essential to his natural curiosity or wish to learn is missing from the classroom. What is missing, technically speaking, is "positive reinforcement." In daily life the student looks, listens, and remembers because certain consequences then follow. He learns to look and listen in those special ways that encourage remembering because he is reinforced for recalling what he has seen and heard, just as a newspaper reporter notes and remembers things he sees because he is paid for reporting them. Consequences of this sort are lacking when a teacher simply shows a student something or tells him something.

Rousseau was the great advocate of natural learning. Emile was to be taught by the world of things. His teacher was to draw his attention to that world; but otherwise his education was to be negative. There were to be no arranged consequences. But Emile was an imaginary student with imaginary learning processes. When Rousseau's disciple, Pestalozzi, tried the methods on his own flesh-and-blood son, he ran into trouble. His diary is one of the most pathetic documents in the history of education. As he walked with his young son beside a stream, Pestalozzi would repeat several times, "Water flows downhill." He would show the boy that "wood swims in water and . . . stones sink." Whether the child was learning anything or not, he was not unhappy, and Pestalozzi could believe that at least he was using the right method. But when the world of things had to be left behind, failure could no longer be concealed. "I could only get him to read with difficulty; he has a thousand ways of getting out of it, and never loses an opportunity of doing something else." He could make the boy sit still at his lessons by first making him "run and play out of doors in the cold," but Pestalozzi himself was then exhausted. Inevitably, of course, he returned to aversive measures: "He was soon tired of learning to read, but as I had decided that he should work at it regularly every day, whether he liked it or not, I determined to make him feel the necessity of doing so, from the very first, by showing him there was no choice between this work and my displeasure, which I made him feel by keeping him in."

The failure of "showing and telling" is sometimes attributed to lack of attention. We are often aware that we ourselves are not listening or looking carefully. If we are not to punish the student for not looking and not listening, how can we make him concentrate? One possibility is to make sure that there is nothing else to be seen or heard. The schoolroom is isolated and freed of distractions. Silence is often the rule. Physical constraints are helpful. Earphones reassure the teacher that only what is to be heard is going into the student's ears. The TV screen is praised for its isolation and hypnotic effect. A piece of equipment has been proposed that achieves concentration in the following desperate way: the student faces a brightly lighted text, framed by walls which operate on the principle of the blinders once worn by carriage horses. His ears are between earphones. He reads part of the text aloud and then listens to his recorded voice as he reads it again. If he does not learn what he reads, it is certainly not because he has not seen it!

A less coercive practice is to make what is to be seen or heard attractive and attention-compelling. The advertiser faces the same problem as the teacher, and his techniques have been widely copied in the design of textbooks, films, and classroom practices. Bright colors, variety, sudden change, big type, animated sequences—all these have at least a temporary effect in inducing the student to look and listen. They do not, however, *teach* the student to look and listen, because they occur at the wrong time. A similar weakness is seen in making school itself pleasant. Attractive architecture, colorful interiors, comfortable furniture, congenial social arrangements, naturally interesting subjects—these are all reinforcing, but they reinforce only the behaviors they are contingent upon. An attractive school building reinforces the behavior of coming in sight of it. A colorful and comfortable classroom reinforces the behavior of entering it. Roughly speaking, these things could be said to strengthen a positive attitude toward school. But they provide merely the setting for instruction. They do not teach what students are in school to learn.

In the same way audiovisual aids usually come at the wrong time to strengthen the forms of behavior that are the principal concern of the teacher. An interesting page printed in four colors reinforces the student simply for opening the book and looking at it. It does not reinforce reading the page or even examining it closely; certainly it does not reinforce those activities that result in effective recall of what is seen. An interesting lecturer holds his listeners in the sense that they look at and listen to him, just as an interesting demonstration film reinforces the behavior of watching it, but neither the lecture nor the film necessarily reinforces listening or listening in those special ways that further recall. In good instruction interesting things should happen *after* the student has read a page or listened or looked with care. The four-color picture should *become* interesting when the text that accompanies it has been read. One stage in a lecture or film should be interesting only if earlier stages have been carefully examined and remembered. In general, naturally attractive and interesting things further the primary goals of education only when they enter into much more subtle contingencies of reinforcement than are usually represented by audiovisual aids.

It is possible that students may be induced to learn by making material not only attractive but memorable. An obvious example is making material easy. The child first learns to write in manuscript because it resembles the text he is learning to read; he may learn to read material printed in a phonetic alphabet; he may learn to spell only words he will actually use; and so on. This sort of simplification shows a lack of confidence in methods of teaching and often merely postpones the teacher's task, but it is sometimes a useful strategy. Material which is well organized is also, of course, easier to learn.

Some current psychological theories suggest that material may be made memorable in another way. Various laws of perception imply that an observer "cannot help" seeing things in certain ways. The stimulus seems to force itself upon the organism. Optical illusions are often cited as examples. These laws suggest the possibility that material may be presented in the form in which it is irresistibly learned. Material is to be so "structured" that it is readily—and almost necessarily—"grasped." Instructional examples are, however, far less persuasive than the demonstration offered in support of them. In trying to assign an important function to the material to be learned, it is particularly easy to overlook other conditions under which learning actually occurs.

No matter how attractive, interesting, and well structured material may be, the discouraging fact is that it is often not learned. Rather than continue to ask why, many educational theorists have concluded that the teacher cannot really teach at all but can only help the student learn. The dominant metaphor goes back to Plato. As Emile Bréhier states it in *The Hellenic Age*, "Socrates . . . possessed no other art but maieutics, his mother Phaenarete's art of delivering; he drew out from souls what they have in them . . ." The student already knows the truth; the teacher simply shows him that he knows. The archetype is the famous episode in the *Meno* in which Socrates takes an uneducated slave boy through Pythagoras's theorem for doubling the square. In spite of the fact that this scene is still widely regarded as an educational triumph, there is no evidence that the child learned anything. He timidly agrees with various suggestions, and he answers leading questions, but it is inconceivable that he could have reconstructed the theorem by himself when Socrates had finished. Socrates says as much later in the dialogue: "If someone will keep asking him these same questions often and in various forms, you can be sure that in the end he will know about them as accurately as anybody." (Socrates was a frequency theorist!)

It must be admitted that the assignment was difficult. The boy was starting from scratch. In this little book, *How to Solve It*, Polya uses the same technique in presiding at the birth of the formula for the diagonal of a parallelepiped. His students make a more positive contribution because they have already had some geometry. But any success due to previous teaching weakens the claim for maieutics. And Polya's promptings and questionings give more help than he wants to admit.

It is only because mathematical proofs seem to arise from the nature of things that they can be said in some sense to be "known by everyone" and simply waiting to be drawn out. Even Socrates could not argue that the soul knows the facts of history or a second language. Impregnation must precede parturition. But is it not possible that a presentation that has not seemed to be learned is the seed from which knowledge grows to be delivered by the teacher? Perhaps the intellectual midwife is to show the student that he remembers what he has already been shown or told. In *The Idea of a University* Cardinal Newman gave an example of the maieutic method applied to acquired knowledge. It will stir painful memories in many teachers. A tutor is talking with a candidate about a bit of history—a bit of history, in fact, in which Plato's Menon lost his life.

> "What is the meaning of the word *Anabasis?*" says the Tutor. The Candidate is silent. "You know very well; take your time, and don't be alarmed, *Anabasis* means . . ."
> "An ascent," says the Candidate.
> "*Who* ascended?"
> "The Greeks, Xenophon."
> "Very well: Xenophon and the Greeks ascended. To what did they ascend?"
> "Against the Persian king: they ascended to fight the Persian king."
> "That is right . . . an ascent; but I thought we called it a *descent* when a foreign army carried war into a country? . . . "Don't we talk of a descent of barbarians?"
> "Yes."
> "Why then are the Greeks said to go up?"
> "They went up to fight the Persian king."
> "Yes; but why *up* . . . why not *down?*"
> "They came down afterwards, when they retreated back to Greece."
> "Perfectly right; they did . . . but could you give no reason why they are said to go *up* to Persia, not *down?*"
> "They went *up* to Persia."
> "Why do you not say they went *down?*"
> "They went *down* to Persia."
> "You have misunderstood me. . . ."

Newman warned his reader that the Candidate is "deficient to a great extent . . . not such as it is likely that a respectable school would turn out." He recognized a poor student, but not a poor method. Thousands of teachers have wasted years of their lives in exchanges which have been no more profitable—and all to the greater glory of maieutics and out of a conviction that telling and showing are not only inadequate but wrong.

Although the soul has perhaps not always known the truth nor ever been confronted with it in a half-forgotten experience, it may still *seek* it. If the student can be taught to learn from the world of things, nothing else will ever have to be taught. This is the method of discovery. It is designed to absolve the teacher from a sense of failure by making instruction unnecessary. The teacher arranges the environment in which discovery is to take place, he suggests lines of inquiry, he keeps the student within bounds, and so on. The important thing is that he should tell him nothing.

The human organism does, of course, learn without being taught. It is a good thing that this is so, and it would no doubt be a good thing if more could be learned in that way. Students are naturally interested in what they learn by themselves because they would not learn if they were not, and for the same reason they are more likely to remember what they learn in that way. There are reinforcing elements of surprise and accomplishment in personal discovery that are welcome alternatives to traditional aversive consequences. But discovery is no solution to the problems of education. The individual cannot be expected to rediscover more than a very small part of the facts and principles that have already been discovered by others. To stop teaching in order that the student may learn for himself is to abandon education as a medium for the transmission of the accumulated knowledge and wisdom of a culture.

There are other difficulties. The position of the teacher who encourages discovery is ambiguous. Is he to pretend that he himself does not know? (Socrates said Yes. In Socratic irony those who know enjoy a laugh at the expense of those who do not.) Or, for the sake of encouraging a joint venture in discovery, is the teacher to choose to teach only those things that he himself has not yet learned? Or is he frankly to say, "I know, but you must find out" and accept the consequences for his relations with his students?

Still another difficulty arises when it is necessary to teach a whole class. How are a few good students to be prevented from making all the discoveries? When that happens, other members of the class not only miss the excitement of discovery but are left to learn material presented in a slow and particularly confusing way. Students should, of course, be encouraged to explore, to ask questions, to study by themselves, to be "creative." When properly analyzed, the kinds of behavior referred to in such expressions can be taught. It does not follow, however, that they must be taught by the method of discovery.

Effective instructional practices threaten the conception of teaching as a form of maieutics. If we suppose that the student is to "exercise his rational powers," to "develop his mind," to learn through "intuition or insight," and so on, then it may indeed be true that the teacher cannot teach but can only help the student learn. But these goals can be restated in terms of explicit changes in behavior, and effective methods of instruction can then be designed.

In his famous four idols, Francis Bacon formulated some of the reasons why men arrive at false ideas. He might have added two special Idols of the School that affect those who want to improve teaching. The Idol of the Good Teacher is the belief that what a good teacher can do, any teacher can do. Some teachers are, of course, unusually effective. They are naturally interesting people, who make things interesting to their students. They are skilful in handling students, as they are skilful in handling people in general. They can formulate facts and principles and communicate them to others in effective ways. Possibly their skills and talents will someday be better understood and successfully imparted to new teachers. At the moment, however, they are true exceptions. The fact that a method proves successful in their hands does not mean that it will solve important problems in education.

The Idol of the Good Student is the belief that what a good student can learn, any student can learn. Because they have superior ability or have been exposed to fortunate early environments, some students learn without being taught. It is quite possible that they learn more effectively when they are not taught. Possibly we shall someday produce more of them. At the moment, however, the fact that a method works with good students does not mean that it will work with all. It is possible that we shall progress more rapidly toward effective education by leaving the good teacher and the good student out of account altogether. They will not suffer, because they do not need our help. We may then devote ourselves to the discovery of practices which are appropriate to the remaining—what?—ninety-five percent of teachers and students.

The Idols of the School explain some of the breathless excitement with which educational theorists return again and again to a few standard solutions. Perhaps we should regard them as merely two special cases of a more general source of error, the belief that personal experience in the classroom is the primary source of pedagogical wisdom. It is actually very difficult for teachers to profit from experience. They almost never learn about their long-term successes or failures, and their short-term effects are not easily traced to the practices from which they presumably arose. Few teachers have time to reflect on such matters, and traditional educational research has given them little help. A much more effective kind of research is now becoming possible. Teaching may be defined as an arrangement of contingencies of reinforcement under which behavior changes. Relevant contingencies can be most successfully analyzed in studying the behavior of one student at a time under carefully controlled conditions. Few educators are aware of the extent to which human behavior is being examined in arrangements of this sort, but a true technology of teaching is imminent. It is beginning to suggest effective alternatives to the average practices that have caused so much trouble.

KURT HAAS
Associate Professor of Psychology, State University College, New Paltz, New York

44 · THE MIDDLE-CLASS PROFESSIONAL AND THE LOWER-CLASS PATIENT

• Unpalatable as the concept of relatively distinct and meaningful socioeconomic class differences may be to the professional working in the mental health area, these differences should nevertheless be reckoned with. It must be realized that members of one class may not actually understand what members of another class need or want, what values they cherish, and what facets of society and family are dear to them.

Psychiatrists, psychologists, social workers, and other professional personnel working in a mental health setting are almost invariably from the large and powerful American middle class. Although the middle class also produces its shares of patients—in some instances a disproportionate share —many mental health workers are confronted with lower-class patients. In fact, since mental health facilities are typically maintained by state or local government funds, many more lower-class patients are probably in contact with mental health professionals than with any other single class of medical specialists.

Because of the frequently different class membership of the mental health professional and his patients, the two often fail to communicate with one another. The psychiatrist, for example, fails to understand what, in his patient's story or behavior, is really important to the patient himself. The patient, in turn, frequently fails to comprehend the nature of the questions (or their importance) evolving from the psychiatrist's middle-class back-

Mental Hygiene, 47:408–410, 1963. Used by permission of the author and The National Association for Mental Health, Inc.

ground. Consequently, the lower-class patient listens with faint heart and half an ear to the psychiatric intonations, and the psychiatrist hears with cynical and paternal indulgence the recital of the lower-class patient.

To a considerable extent, the communication failure may be traced to the different values and attitudes typical of the two classes. The middle class is oriented toward thrift, work and achievement. Undoubtedly, the middle-class professional has attained his status through hard work, serious study and intelligent planning.

His intellectual ability and motivation have provided him with the rewards of prestige and recognition as well as a stable and comfortable income. The middle-class professional shares with his fellow socioeconomic group members a distaste for strongly expressed emotion. He shuns aggression and hostility, and physical combat is, of course, completely repugnant. Sexuality is clinically admissible but is carefully circumscribed lest it be abused or too openly flaunted. The middle class is clean, well-shaven, neatly dressed, moderate and temperate in its habits; it respects authority and pays homage to the significant symbols of state and church; it respects the institutions which it has carefully constructed, and it seeks a virtuous and successful existence.

Although adhering to some of the values of the middle class, the lower class places much less emphasis on education, for example, than does the middle class and as a consequence, is very unlikely to have finished or to have continued beyond high school. Neither is the lower class especially impressed with achievement through hard work, solvency through thrift, etc. Cleanliness, order, and thrift are not as valued by the lower class as by the middle class.

The lower-class father who earns a living doing day labor, working on a monotonous assembly line, etc., cannot be expected to feel that his source of income is a matter of pride or respect. The lower class frequently works very hard indeed; physically, the work may be brutally difficult, but its rewards are slim, its continuance questionable, its justification coming only when the work day is over.

The lower-class child is much less restricted in expressing impulse or strong feeling. Aggression, physical combat, hostility and emotionality are permissible in larger degree than in the middle class. Physical punishment, for example, is frequent.

For the lower class, material rewards are few and recreational opportunities are limited. Possibly as a consequence, basic and immediate physical needs are more likely to be sources of satisfaction for the lower class than for the middle class. Alcohol can provide a kind of quick escape for the lower-class male; this, the middle class professional finds difficult to understand. As the studies on male sexual behavior by Kinsey and his associates dramatically illustrated, sexual stimulation is far more direct and extensive in the lower class than in the middle class. In language as well as behavior the lower-class child, for example, evidences degrees of sexual sophistication the middle-class parent finds horrifying.

These sketchy descriptions cannot do justice to the different standards and values of the lower and middle class. They provide only a glimpse of the extensive and complex inter-class differences. In view of these cultural differences, however, the middle-class professional should be guided by remembering the following.

It is a hopeless job for the middle-class professional to attempt to change the entire structure of a home, a family or a way of life. The lower-class patient cannot be turned into a middle-class psychiatric image. He cannot be taught sobriety when alcoholic indulgence is a way of life; thrift and achievement have little meaning for a lower-class family whose job status varies from day to day. Expression of sexuality, illicit pregnancy and profanity are related to a way of life, not necessarily pathognomic, and are not particularly influenced by middle-class moralizing.

The mental health worker is too ready to label as a psychiatric case many a lower-class patient whose behavior is not particularly inappropriate in a lower-class family context. Worse, however, efforts at rehabilitation keep middle-class rather than lower-class goals in mind.

Much has been said about the intricacies of the patient-doctor relationship in general. Unquestionably, almost every such lower-class, middle-class contact is filled with misunderstanding and disappointment. The psychotherapist may focus on sexual and emotional inhibition and control. These his patient willingly talks about, but he is really little concerned; chances are he has suffered from fewer inhibitions than has his psychiatric mentor. The therapist may explore the relationship of alcoholism to deep-seated personality traits and needs. Again, the lower-class patient co-operates, but, frankly, he recognizes these are the psychiatrist's needs, not his own. The patient drinks because all of his friends do; sometimes more, other times less. It depends largely on environmental circumstances.

The lower-class patient beats his wife, abuses his children, pilfers from his employers. The middle-class therapist may long seek the wellsprings of this kind of behavior within his patient's personality or in parental circumstances. He fails, however, to look in the proper place; namely, the lower class and its accustomed way of life. The lower-class patient is fatigued, lacking in ambition, sullen and depressed. His behavior, again, can only be understood in its context. It is simply of no use to treat these symptoms as though they were found in a well-educated middle-class housewife.

The part played by the professional in the mental health area needs careful consideration. The lower-class patient needs to be understood and treated, not as a group of symptoms but as a single human being emerging from a culture which, in many ways, is different from and frequently in conflict with the background and understanding of the middle-class professional. In fact, the lower-class patient, *just like all other patients,* seeks to be understood in terms of his own *needs* and his *own* accustomed way of life.

REFERENCES

1. Hollingshead, A. B., *Elmstown Youth: The Impact of Social Classes on Youth* (New York: John Wiley & Sons, Inc., 1949).
2. Warner, W. L., M. Meeker, and K. Eells, *Social Class in America* (Chicago: Science Research Associates, 1949).

ARTHUR T. JERSILD
Professor of Psychology and Education, Teachers College, Columbia University

45 · THE VOICE OF THE SELF

• In a recent study of a group of representative teachers, all but one reported a variety of personal problems. This lone exception said that he was not a bit anxious: He was never troubled by his anger; and his love life, social life, and work life were all okay. He had no personal problems. He did, however, have ulcers.

Every teacher, but particularly the typical neophyte, has personal problems. Some of them he openly admits having, but others he probably does not reveal even to himself.

The study I have mentioned brought information from about 200 teachers who had sought help in achieving self-understanding. Many of them spoke of attitudes which had interfered with their effectiveness as beginning teachers and which had persisted even after they had finished their apprenticeship.

Anger is one of the most common, pervasive, and difficult emotions in the teacher's life. From early childhood the restraints on showing anger or even feeling it are so powerful that many individuals lose touch with their anger. They fail to realize that unaccountable spells of the blues, feelings of fatigue, and headaches may be anger in disguise.

A large proportion of the teachers in the study mentioned finding it difficult if not impossible to know their own minds and assert their rights. As a rule, teachers do not tend to be aggressively self-assertive. Even veteran faculty members sometimes accept extra assignments meekly and allow themselves to be harassed without openly protesting. They may, however, store up the anger they feel, perhaps without even noticing it.

One source of anger is vulnerability growing out of the universal need to be approved and liked. This need is especially strong in a person who is

NEA Journal, 54 (No. 7): 23–25, October, 1965. Reprinted by permission of the author and the NEA Journal.

feeling his way a bit uncertainly and who needs reassurance concerning his worth. Teachers in the study said that their need to be liked sometimes placed them at the mercy of their pupils.

Another condition that prevails frequently among teachers is anxiety. Everyone is anxious; the circumstances that produce anxiety are as numerous and varied as the predicaments and desires that arise in the course of human experience. The anxieties of teachers are as diverse as the anxieties of people in general. Some special conditions exist in the teaching profession, however, that may in distinct ways express or give rise to anxiety.

Anxiety springs from a condition of inner conflict. It is especially likely to prevail if a discrepancy exists between a teacher's avowed motives and the motives that actually impel him. When such a discrepancy occurs, the teacher is, in a sense, acting in a devious fashion—playing false with others, with himself, or both.

A teacher is likely to feel anxious if he uses the teaching situation to satisfy needs in his own life while trying to convince himself that everything he does is for the welfare of his pupils. One teacher reported that, as a beginner, she encouraged her pupils to be dependent upon her, to view her as a precious person. She got a great deal of satisfaction because many of them cried when they said goodbye to her on the last day of school.

Then this young woman examined her motivation. She decided that she had been fostering dependence to gratify her need for power or to be assured of her adequacy—that her reasons had been devious. She changed her tactics and encouraged independence. Instead of having the last day resemble a wake, she made a gay event of it. She ended her account by saying that she felt much happier now that she was more honest with her pupils and herself.

A teacher feels that he is being false to himself if he claims that he is a soft disciplinarian because he believes that children learn best in a free and permissive atmosphere when his softness actually springs from fear of giving offense by being firm.

By the same token, he feels false to himself if he claims that he is strict because pupils learn more from a tough teacher, when his true motivation is a need to dominate others.

A sensitive teacher becomes anxious if he is a partner in, or a silent spectator of, practices which he regards as wrong. The more idealistic his aim, the more inevitable is a hiatus between that aim and what he is able to do. If he must convince himself that everything he does is right because he is unable to accept himself as one who compromises between what he would like to do and what he can do, he is in a false position and anxiety results.

The beginning teacher often sees himself as on trial before his pupils, his colleagues, and his supervisors, and, what is likely to be the toughest trial of all, before himself.

As a beginner, he is a learner, and as such, he is bound to make mistakes, but he castigates himself for these mistakes more than a realistic appraisal of the situation would warrant.

Self-criticism becomes a scourge when a beginner is constantly dissatisfied with his work even though it is satisfactory to others. He makes himself a failure in his own eyes by imposing standards he cannot fulfill, by seeking perfection he can never reach.

If teachers are to cope with their own problems and live up to their potentialities, they must grow in self-understanding. Both teacher-preparation institutions and in-service activities could and should do far more than they usually do to help teachers to take stock of themselves, to get a thoughtful conception of their worth, and to overcome barriers within themselves. What knowledge is more fundamental than knowledge of self?

From an academic standpoint, awareness of self is necessary if a person wishes to appreciate and to help his pupils appreciate the richness of many of the scholarly disciplines. We do not really grasp the truths embodied in history and literature unless we can appreciate them through an awareness of how they relate to ourselves. Napoleon remains a wooden soldier unless we can perceive him in the light of Napoleonic tendencies within ourselves. Hamlet comes alive only when we realize a kinship between his doubts and conflicts and our own.

From a humanitarian point of view, knowledge of self is even more important. Most persons move through childhood into adult years with a burden of emotional problems. Self-knowledge not only helps an individual to understand himself; it helps him understand others, too. The best way to learn about what lies hidden in the secret self of someone else is to inquire, "What lies hidden within me?"

The voice of the self, usually silent and yet sometimes audible to the inner ear, speaks a universal language. The closer any human comes to knowledge of himself the more he is in touch with a core of humanity which he shares with all others.

Knowledge of the self does not flow through the channels of instruction we usually employ in the training of children or the preparation of teachers. In most fields of scholarship, an interested, able learner can appropriate all that men's minds have wrought through generations of labor. For example, the learner can use a map without having been a pioneer explorer. But in the sphere of self, each person is an explorer almost from birth.

The most intimate and decisive aspects of learning pertaining to the self are in the domain of attitudes and emotions. If an individual is to grow in self-understanding, it is essential for him to examine these—to face them thoughtfully rather than blindly.

How can teachers-in-training or teachers-on-the-job do this? Currently, intensive psychotherapy or psychoanalysis represents the most systematic efforts in this area. Group therapy, under the guidance of a professionally trained person, is another means. These methods are available only to a few, however, and many do not want or need prolonged and costly therapy.

A resource short of such intensive methods can be cultivated in every teacher education institution and in every sizable school faculty. I refer to work groups in which the participants mutually seek to help one another explore the realm of feeling. Almost all members of such groups report that they receive great benefit from the activity.

Many practical considerations and psychological limitations are, of course, connected with work of this sort. Membership in such groups must be voluntary. A certain amount of leadership is required, at least in the beginning. Members must be committed to the idea of examining their attitudes rather than of showing how smart they are. They must have or acquire enough courage and trust to share states of mind that ordinarily are not aired in the presence of others.

Persons who use this approach, particularly for the first time, will have to undertake a good deal of groping and exploring, feeling their way at the beginning. Arrangements should be made with a minimum of fanfare, without fancy promises, and without any pretension that this is the same as a professionally supervised therapy group.

Participants should be allowed to move at their own pace. It needs to be understood that everything is confidential and that the participants are all seeking self-understanding.

One of the fascinating features of this kind of group work is that it almost invariably involves facets of the mind that usually are ignored in the academic setting, including fantasies, dreams, vagrant feelings and thoughts, and the ability latent in all of us to let the mind roam in a process of free association. Trickles of anger, fear, tenderness, and other feelings that often are barely noticed can be made articulate and can be examined.

Another reward of effective group work is the spirit of trust, sympathy, and comradeship that gradually builds up. Sometimes the very persons who have most annoyed each other establish strong bonds of affection.

A reservoir of friendliness and good will is present in any group of decent people. Often, however, feelings of kindness and compassion are hidden until a person has had an opportunity to voice his anger without being punished or rejected or has had an opportunity to reveal his fears without being called a coward.

In a genuine search for self-understanding, the accounting methods differ from those we ordinarily apply in everyday life; the uncovering and sharing of weakness often leads to previously unfound strength. The greatest kind of courage is not the courage to banish fear but to acknowledge it.

When a person delves into himself, he is likely to discover that the things which alienate him from others are outweighed by the worth of his own humanity and by his kinship with others.

The greatest reward of knowledge of self is growth in compassion—compassion which leads a person not just to say dutifully, "I am my brother's keeper," but to feel, "I am my brother's brother." If, through self-study, beginning teachers can reap this reward more fully, they and all mankind will be blessed.

EVALUATING FOR FUTURE GROWTH

• Whether the grading system employed by the schools enhances rather than inhibits the purposes of education has been a topic for discussion and even argument for a number of years. Alexander is one of those who question its efficacy. His is a rather sweeping indictment. He finds that not only do grades operate to discourage learning, but they may also have far-reaching psychological consequences on the student—the development of negative self-regarding attitudes, failure expectancies, and anxieties.

Why is such a practice continued? How can a practice that may well limit rather than promote personal and educational growth be condoned by school systems? One of the reasons is indicated by Jarrett: grades are expected by parents and the culture. We have grown so accustomed to them that they have become ends in themselves rather than a means to an end. They have come to be values in themselves rather than a means of evaluating. The diploma is more highly esteemed than the knowledge that is gained. Perhaps this distortion of the evaluative process is the crux of the problem. Somehow or other our evaluating seems to have got mixed up with our valuing. We are prone to see the student with high grades as being worth more as a person than the student whose grades are low. Worse yet, each may see himself as worthy or unworthy in proportion to his grades. As Alexander points out, the process is self-reinforcing. Those who doubt themselves are less able to achieve and thus come to doubt themselves even more. In a sense they are denied the freedom to risk, to try and to be mistaken, lest they be forced to think even less of themselves.

Although some schools have experienced a degree of success at eliminating grades by instituting a system of teacher-parent conferences, there is a possibility that grades are more the whipping boy than the culprit. Perhaps it is the evaluating attitude rather than the measuring standard that requires examination and change. It is our experience that whenever one puts himself in the position of judging another, he puts conditions on the relationship they can have. In effect, he sets certain standards which the other person must meet in order to be acceptable to him. One can value another and place no restrictions upon him. He cannot evaluate without becoming a part of the other person's problem. Think carefully about this. How has it been with you?

EUGENE D. ALEXANDER
Administrative Director, Child Guidance Center, Harrisburg, Pennsylvania

46 · THE MARKING SYSTEM AND POOR ACHIEVEMENT

● Today with the tremendous mass of students being exposed to our education system we are deeply and sincerely concerned about the standards of our education. We are afraid that the level of learning is approaching mediocrity. In a desperate effort to bolster our standards, we become more strict in our marking system and we emphasize the test situation as a means of discouraging those students unable to compete. We see marks as an incentive to study and learning. We feel that the student will work harder and learn better in order to obtain higher grades. We see marks as a method of reward for the better student and as a means of "realistic" evaluation for all students. Unfortunately the relationship of marks with ability and interest in learning is not so simple. In fact there are a great number of influences affecting achievement that have no relationship at all to ability and interest in learning. There is some evidence that, for many people, marks become a barrier to learning and are seen more as punishment for poor achievement than as a reward for successful accomplishment.

Factors Related to Poor Achievement

Of the large number of factors related to poor achievement, some are part of the immediate school experience, but many are outside the control of the school situation. McMillan found that children showed more success and less failure when (a) they were female rather than male, (b) their parents had more education, (c) their parents came from a higher educa-

The Teachers College Journal, 36:110–113, December, 1964. Reprinted by permission of the author and The Teachers College Journal, Indiana State University, Terre Haute.

tional level, (d) they were high in socioeconomic status, (e) parents had higher incomes, (f) they had not moved in 10 years, (g) they belonged to a relatively small family. Kurtz (1951) found that under-achievers more often came from homes with unhappy emotional climate, had fewer friends and these friends had a less favorable attitude toward school than over-achievers, felt inferior and unhappy, preferred non-academic to academic tasks, had minimum ambition and did not have high prospects for themselves, a feeling shared by their teachers. Walsh (1956) compared 20 low achieving boys from grades 2 to 5 with 20 adequate achieving boys with equal ability. She examined their attitudes toward themselves by analyzing the roles projected in a boy doll with which they played. The low achievers consistently differed from the adequate achievers in portraying the boy doll as restricted in action; unable to express his feelings appropriately and accurately: being criticized, rejected or isolate; and acting defensively through compliance, evasion or negativism. Alexander (1963) discovered that for 10th grade students there was a significant relationship of expressed self-concept and self-acceptance with marks when the effect of intelligence was partialled out. From his data he concluded that a student's self-perception could be an important factor in school achievement and often operated independently from intelligence. Stevens (1956) found that academically unsuccessful students showed poor self-insight into their intellectual abilities and showed poor self-acceptance. Tallent (1956) in examining 9th graders observed a direct relationship between behavior control and intellectual achievement. The controlled group was superior on concentration, and tasks demanding a high order of conceptualization. The impulsive group was superior on sensory-motor speed and coordination and tasks with very little intervening mental manipulation.

Baer (1956) reported that children entering school at a later age consistently achieved better than children of the same IQ entering earlier. Spivak (1956) found that children in self-contained 7th and 8th grades achieved significantly better than youngsters from a departmental organization. This difference was maintained throughout the ninth grade when all students entered a departmental situation. Malpass (1953) observed a significant relationship between perception of school and end of semester grades. Youngsters with a better perception of school received better grades. Bond (1952) found that reading was an important factor that presented itself as an obstacle to low ability pupils. Repeated failure led to a "don't care attitude" and the students learned to retreat when confronted with a problem situation. They were fearful about achieving and this impeded studying.

Thus, developmental factors, socioeconomic factors, emotional climate in the home and peer relationships all relate to school achievement, but are relatively outside the school situation. Teacher-pupil relations, perception of school and basic ability are close to the school situation. Poor self-concept, self-rejection, anxiety, poor self-control and feelings of powerlessness are reflections of the individual's inner life. As can be seen, there are many characteristics and influences that have absolutely nothing to do with the school environment, yet which very profoundly relate to the student's performance. There are many influences inside the school situation that relate to achievement yet are not academic in nature. All of these the student brings with him as he faces the evaluative experience and this experience leaves him with no alternative other than success or failure. Let us examine what actually takes place in the poor achievement or failure situation.

Failure Leads to More Failure

Smith (1952) experimentally induced the belief of failure by verbal instructions and found that throughout a series of 15 trials there was an impairment of learning whether actual failure took place or not. Osler (1954) gave 15 classrooms of students an arithmetic test. She then divided the students into groups matched for ability, age, and scores on the arithmetic test. She randomly assigned these groups to treatment conditions. She informed one group that they were among the lowest 10% on the test. She informed another group that they were among the most successful students on the test, and she gave another group no set at all. She then administered an arithmetic test comparable to the first test. She found that the students in the success and control groups did significantly better than students in the failure group. In both these studies it was not actual failure that led to poor achievement, but the feeling of failure that the individual had. The individual perceived himself as a failure so he functioned as a failure.

Failure Leads to Defensive Action

Van Holt (1955) discovered that *under neutral conditions, achievement is related to imaginal and creative processes, but that under failure conditions, achievement is related to emotional processes and their control.* Thorne (1954) compared a low self-acceptance group with a high self-acceptance group after an induced failure situation. The low group raised their self-evaluation in the task while the high group lowered their ratings. *Those with low self-acceptance became so preoccupied with loss of self-*

esteem that they could not make a realistic evaluation of their performance.
Diller (1954) found that after a failure experience, self-attitudes are not
positively correlated with attitudes toward others. A disrupted pattern of
attitudes appears. An individual may either raise his self-esteem while lowering his esteem of close friends, or he may lower his own self-esteem while
rating his close friends higher. Martine (1953) examined the self-concepts
of college students after placing them in a relaxed situation and later placing them in a situation where they were pressured to achieve. He found
two groups that did poorer under pressure. One of these groups was successful in the relaxed situation though doing poorly under pressure. They
had the need to achieve but this need was blocked by conflict and anxiety
over either succeeding or failing. "They probably have experienced considerable failure. Possibly, competition leads to anxiety over the possibility
of failure which in turn causes further disorganizing emotion and consequent failure." Another group did poorly under both relaxed and pressured
situations. *"These individuals have the motive to succeed, but fear of failure
is so strong that anxiety results in an avoidance of response, which disallows
even the imagination of positive striving for achievement."*

Thus, under pressure of failure, people tend to get so involved in anxiety
over their feelings about themselves that their efficiency of achievement
suffers.

The Picture of the Poor Achiever

Putting this information together, a clear picture slowly emerges. The
key concept is the student's own self-perception. A student enters the
academic situation with a certain self-concept which may be good or poor,
depending on his previous experience and environment. Success and failure
operate on this self-concept either to enhance or to depreciate it. Generally
speaking, the poorer the early environment the greater the need for a, good
school experience and the more difficult it is to get one. Much of this
depends on the pupil-teacher relationship. Of course it is more difficult for
the teacher to give the poor ability student a good experience than to give
one to a good student.

When the student experiences failure he begins to perceive himself as
a failure and his achievement drops. This seems to be operative with high
as well as low ability students. As this feeling of failure increases, the
student becomes defensive. He becomes more involved in protecting his
self-concept than in achieving. This may take the form of depreciation of
the academic situation, increased involvement with non-academic experi-

ences, devaluation of others and hostility toward them, or, more subtly, an involvement with the rote aspects of learning at the expense of creativity. Pressure only leads to greater defensiveness or poorer achievement. The culmination of repeated failure is "an avoidance response which disallows even the imagination of positive striving for achievement."

Thus, the self-concept and achievement interact with mutual effect. That is, poor achievement leads to a depreciation of the self-concept which leads to continued poor achievement; and, to a lesser extent, good achievement leads to an enhancement of the self-concept which leads to better achievement. One of the best defenses that the poor achiever can use to escape this cycle is to devaluate or de-emphasize the academic situation so that achievement becomes unimportant to the maintenance of the self-concept. It is then possible for him to maintain an adequate self-esteem in spite of his poor performance in the school situation. At its worst this may lead to a depreciation of thinking and learning in general.

With this picture in mind, it is now much easier to understand some of our typical poor-achievers. There is the hostile aggressive student who maintains a "good" self-concept by being "tougher than the other guy." There is the congenial student, often of high ability, who never gets his homework done or never pays attention in class. He then can protect his self-esteem by telling himself that he is failing not because he is an incapable student, but because he doesn't do his work. There is the average student who tries and tries and gets nowhere because he "knows" he is a failure. There is the student who doesn't even try because he is convinced that he is a failure from the start. More subtly, there is the student who maintains high marks because he can regurgitate but who is unable to think creatively. And on and on.

To call the poor achiever lazy, to say he has no motivation is just to describe the symptom. The student is trying to maintain a good self-concept. The individual can not live with himself unless he can see himself as worthwhile. He will avoid or defend himself from any situation that threatens his self-esteem. If feelings of repeated failure in the academic situation threaten his self-concept, he will avoid or protect himself from experiences that stimulate this feeling. The only way in which he will meet a situation head on and try to achieve is if it enhances his self-esteem and does not give him feelings of failure.

Helping and Hindering the Poor Achiever

Thus, to help the poor achiever we can either strengthen his self-esteem by helping him see that he is a worthwhile individual no matter what his past experience, or we can give him successful experiences of achievement so he can see that he is not a failure. In evaluating any method we must ask ourselves if that particular experience will enhance the student's self-concept. If it doesn't, we must reject it. The same method can meet with success or failure, depending on the total situation in which it is applied. It is the human interpersonal relationship between teacher and pupil that determines whether the method is a success or failure. If conditions such as an impossible home environment or rigid marking system act as obstacles it will make it very difficult for the teacher to give the pupil feelings of self-esteem and success.

Low marks function more as a threat of failure than as a motivation for improvement. As often as not they are actually punishment for previous failure, poor past environment or emotional difficulty. As a student continues to get low marks he begins to perceive himself as a poor achiever. As he perceives himself in this light he begins to function this way, no matter what his ability. He may decide that school is too threatening to his self-concept and may discount school so it is no longer important enough to be a threat.

Tests do not help to motivate the poor achiever, either. They represent the failure situation and are to be avoided and feared by him. They only raise his anxiety and increase his poor self-concept. Tests may motivate the good achiever, but often only to memorize and repeat rather than think and originate.

Nor is external pressure the answer to poor achievement. It leads to anxiety and blockage in some students and almost complete immobility in others. For some a relaxed situation with understanding guidance and support may help, but others need even more than this.

For the severe poor achiever direct counseling may be the only answer. Only through exploration of his self-concept can he begin to see himself in a more worthwhile light. Only then can he begin to believe that he does not have to continue to be a failure.

The low-ability pupil is defeated before he begins. He can seldom hope to obtain an average grade. School is one failure experience after another. The havoc wreaked on his self-concept can be imagined. Special consideration and often a special program are necessary if he is to have the opportunity to feel successful.

The marking system with its normative criteria leads continually to more difficult goals for the poor achiever. He can see no progress. It represents continued failure. The only way he can begin to experience some success is under a system with more obtainable goals. Perhaps the most realistic criteria are his previous experiences. He can see that he is not really a failure.

The most surprising thing that research points out is that even students with skills and ability tend to continue to fail after they experience failure. Thus, of equal importance to teaching skills is the supportive role of the teacher. A good deal of her time must be spent believing in, and supporting her students. She must support them to exploring in their own way and not in terms of what she decides they should explore, for rejection of the student's own initiative in itself implies failure on his part. Inflexible direction can lead to the most dismal failure of all—the A student who functions brilliantly in a structured situation but is so dependent on external approval that he is unable to produce anything really creative. Conforming is his protection against feelings of failure.

An educational system that evaluates its students on their ability to memorize, recall and repeat is actually penalizing the students whose talents are expressed in the unique and original. Often such students appear as poor achievers when evaluated by the usual marking criteria. Any system that substitutes extrinsic incentive for intrinsic motivation creates conditions for conformity, manipulation and control. A student does not have the opportunity to learn to evaluate himself independently. He actually depends on the judgment of others. The evaluation situations that he faces are imposed upon him and he automatically reacts to them without searching deeply within himself. A failure experience and being a failure are often felt to be synonymous when judged extrinsically. When a person has the opportunity to establish intrinsically his own conditions of experience, failure acts to give the individual insight into the limitations of his abilities. He more willingly exposes himself to the anxieties of the unknown and in not having to protect his self-esteem, he does not interpret a failure experience as a failure of himself.

Our society is often accused of anti-intellectualism. Maybe the extrinsically imposed testing and evaluative functions of our educational system are partially to blame. Perhaps this attitude, to some extent, is an avoidance response and a defense feeling of failure engendered when individuals had been confronted previously with intellectual experiences.

REFERENCES

Alexander, Eugene D., "The Relationship Between Self-Concept, Self-Acceptance and School Marks" *Dissert. Abs.* 1963, 23:3229.

Baer, Clyde, "A Comparison of the School Progress and Personal Adjustment of Underage and Overage Students of Comparable Intelligence During Eleven Years of School." *Newsletter,* Division of Sch. Psychologists, A.P.A., Vol. 10 #2 Winter 1955–6.

Bond, Jesse A., "An Analysis of Factors Adversely Affecting Scholarship of H. S. Pupils." *J. of Ed. Res.* 46:1–15, Sept. 1952.

Diller, Leonard, "Conscious and Unconscious Self-Attitudes After Success and Failure." *J. of Per.* Sept. '54, 23:12.

Kurtz, John J., Swenson, Esther J., "Factors Related to Over-Achievement and Under-Achievement in School." *Sch. Rev.* 59:472–80, Nov. 1951.

Malpass, Leslie F., "Some Relationships Between Student's Perception of School and Achievement." *J. Ed. Psy.* 44:475–82, D1953.

Martine, John George, "Relationship Between the Self-Concept and Differences in the Strength and Generality of Achievement Motivation." *Dissert. Abs.,* 1953, 13:877..

McMillan, R. T., "School Acceleration and Retardation Among Village Children in So. Oklahoma."

Osler, Sonia F., "Intellectual Performance as a Function of 2 Types of Psychological Stress." *J. Exp. Psy.* 47:115–121, 1954.

Smith, George Joseph, "Influence of Failure, Expressed Hostility, and Stimulus Characteristics on Verbal Learning and Recognition." *Dissert. Abs.* 1952, 12:600.

Spivak, Monroe L., "Effectiveness of Departmental and Self-Contained Seventh and Eighth Grade Classrooms." *Sch. Rev.* 64:391–6, D'56.

Stevens, Peter H., "An Investigation of the Relationship Between Certain Aspects of Self-Concept Behavior and Students' Academic Achievement." *Dissert. Abs.* 1956, 16:2531–2.

Tallent, Norman, "Behavioral Control and Intellectual Achievement of Secondary School Boys." *J. of Ed. Psy.* 47:490–503, D'56.

Thorne, Robert Bernard, "The Effects of Experimentally Induced Failure on Self-Evaluations." *Dissert. Abs.* 1954, 14:1817.

Van Holt, Jr., Henry William, "A Study of Personality Processes Under Neutral, Failure and Success Condition." *Dissert. Abs.* 1955. 15:1660.

Walsh, Ann M. *Self Concepts of Bright Boys with Learning Difficulties.* New York: Teachers College, Columbia University, 1956.

CALVIN D. JARRETT
Southern High School, Graham, North Carolina

47 · MARKING AND REPORTING PRACTICES IN THE AMERICAN SECONDARY SCHOOL

> • I cannot say with Ovid—

"Jamque opus exegi, quod nec jovis ira nec ignes, nec poturit ferrum, nec edax abolere vestustas." *

The increased attention which has been given to the improvement of marking and reporting practices may be accounted for in two ways: (1) traditional practices are obviously inconsistent with democracy in education, and (2) the solution of the problem appears to be so simple.

The acceptance of a democratic philosophy of secondary education and the continued use of aristocratic and selective devices and practices in marking present one of the interesting inconsistencies in our educational thinking and practice. The idea that secondary education is for everyone is generally accepted. Few people any longer argue that educational opportunity should be restricted on the basis of wealth, intelligence, or any other such factors. Yet most schools continue to use a marking system which encourages and selects those of greater scholastic ability and discourages and eliminates those who do not have what it takes to do successfully the things which the school expects them to do.

Why Do We Mark and Report?

The purposes of marking and reporting might be grouped under three headings: administration, information, and motivation. Marks are used to determine whether a student has passed or failed, whether he should be

Peabody Journal of Education, 41:36–48, July, 1963. Used by permission of the author and the *Peabody Journal of Education*.

* "I have already finished the work, which neither the wrath of Jupiter nor fires, nor sword, nor devouring age has been able to abolish."

promoted or retained, and whether he should be graduated. They are reported in transferring the student from one school to another. They are used as a basis for advising the student in the selection of his elective courses and in deciding whether he should be recommended for college. They are used by the college in deciding whether the student should be admitted. Marks are used to inform the student and his parents of his achievement, progress, and success and failure in his schoolwork. They are used to stimulate the student to greater effort and to encourage those who learn much or who try hard, and to punish those who learn little or who put forth little effort. They are also used as a basis for deciding the awarding of honors and in determining eligibility to participate in extra-class activities. It is remarkable how the use of five simple letters, A, B, C, D, F, can be made to serve such a variety of purposes . . . if they really do![1]

A study by the United States Office of Education in 1932 of 258 selected schools revealed that there were eleven purposes recognized as being served by marks. The purposes are listed in the following table.

	Frequency	
Purpose	Number	Per Cent
1. Keeping parents informed of pupil's progress	224	95
2. Furnishing a basis for promotion	238	92
3. Furnishing a basis for graduation	212	82
4. Motivating pupils	194	75
5. Furnishing a basis for the awarding of honors	190	74
6. Furnishing a basis for guidance in the election of subjects	158	61
7. Furnishing a basis for guidance in college recommendation	155	60
8. Furnishing a basis for determining extent of participation in extracurricular activities	133	52
9. Furnishing a basis for guidance in recommendation for employment	113	44
10. Furnishing a basis for awarding credit for quality	100	39
11. Furnishing a basis for research	50	19

A similar study made at the present time would probably reveal that teachers still use marks for most of the purposes listed above.[2]

[1] Wrinkle, William L., and Gilchrist, Robert S., *Secondary Education for Democracy,* Farrar and Rinehart, Inc., New York, 1942. Page 417.

[2] Jacobson, Paul B., *The American Secondary School,* Prentice-Hall, Inc., New York, 1952. Pages 374–75.

The major problem in the classroom use of marks and grades is not so much the question of how marks and grades should be computed or even of which marking or grading system should be used. Much more important is the discovery of means of keeping teachers, students, and parents from attaching too much importance to marks. There are classes which are conducted as though the mark which students receive was the most important outcome of the day's work. The overemphasis on marks interferes seriously with the quality of the learning activities in school. The teacher who has his pencil constantly poised for making entries in his marking book can hardly encourage students to regard the classroom discussion as an opportunity to air their doubts and to seek the answers to troubling questions. When test marks are overemphasized, students tend to limit their study activities to preparing for likely questions on the test, to the neglect of other materials. Every teacher has experienced the let-down in class morale that follows the administration of so important an examination as the mid-term test and knows how impossible it is to many schools to attempt to accomplish anything more once the students know that the grades for the term have been computed.[3]

Many parents, teachers, and pupils still consider evaluation primarily as a means of assigning marks. Reporting to parents on this basis is the relatively simple process of sending home a mark for each school subject. Not only is such a system wholly inadequate as an evaluation program, but it also has serious implications for the learning process: pupils tend to work for marks rather than for real achievement. This becomes a menace to the development of self-direction on the part of the pupil and to his continued self-education beyond the years of formal schooling. Marking is only a narrow phase of the total evaluation of growth. In most instances, marks give but an extremely limited picture of what is happening to the child in school. Much more evaluation than is used for marking purposes must go on in the classroom.

Marks, in order to show progress, should reflect individual growth. Competitive marking and relative ranking deny known psychological facts regarding individual differences in ability, interests, and home background by assuming that all types of pupils learn the same things in the same way and at the same time. Each child should be evaluated in terms of his own abilities and interests rather than compared with others who may differ markedly. Equal achievement does not necessarily indicate equal abilities

---

[3] Rivlin, Harry N., *Teaching Adolescents in Secondary Schools*, Appleton-Century-Crofts, Inc., New York, 1948. Page 445.

or effort. Undue emphasis upon competitive marks also frequently results in bad morale and conditions of poor mental hygiene in the classroom.[4]

Competitive American life has stressed getting ahead, and in turn differences among individuals have come to the fore. In turn, the American high schools have emphasized getting ahead, pitting one student against the other in each class, ranking the entire class at the end of the grading period, and at the end of the four years designating the valedictorian, the salutatorian, the first ten, and innumerable other ranks in the graduating class.

While teachers and students in the average high school are still bartering in facts and marks, the educational journals are full of attempts to produce new systems of marking and home reporting. The student of secondary education hears more and more of "judging the child against his own capabilities," of "judging one's participation in group life," and of similarly enlightened statements for the report card. There can be seen a definite tendency to eliminate the dual system of subject-report and citizenship-report, and in the merger to shift attention from achievement in specific subjects over to progress in different desirable phases of living.

The ultimate result of this promising undertaking can hardly be predicted now. It is in keeping with the reorganization of the learning experiences themselves, and stem back into the theory of individual differences and individual worth. The eventual outcome will depend not a little upon the answers to the three questions: (1) Can the school shift the student's endeavor from the earning of marks, and at the same time still administer its work on the quantitative basis of earning credits and units for a diploma? (2) Can it go off the A-B-C-D-F gold standard without losing the confidence of the influential patron who has known nothing else? (3) Can it work out its new system in accordance with its preconceived purposes of the school without having to effect an unsatisfactory compromise with the college admissions office?[5]

A number of years ago many public schools discarded the percentage system of school marks and in its place substituted letter grades. During the transition period some schools atttempted to set up a system of equivalents to enable parents to interpret the letter grades. For example, one school reported to parents that a grade of A was equivalent to 96 through 100 per cent; B, 88 through 95 per cent; C, 80 through 87 per

---

[4] Anderson, Vernon E., Grim, Paul R., and Gruhn, William T. *Principles and Practices of Secondary Education*, The Ronald Press Company, New York, 1951. Pages 266–67.

[5] Spears, Harold. *Secondary Education in American Life*, American Book Company, New York, 1941. Pages 373–74.

cent; D, 70 through 79 per cent; F, below 70 per cent. Gradually this practice decreased as parents became familiar with letter grades.

More recently, there has been a movement to eliminate the idea of marking, because of its tendency to emphasize the making of marks over the more fundamental values of learning. Some schools use other schemes than letter marking in their elementary schools but retain the letter plan for secondary schools because the secondary school pupils have been accustomed to it through the elementary grades. At present the movement is growing to substitute a sound basis for recording pupil achievement in place of the very questionable practice of letter marks.

Current plans of marking are reported by Billett in his summary of the marking system found in 258 selected school systems. The table below reveals that letters or other symbols, such as the numbers, 1, 2, 3, 4, 5, were used as marks in 81 per cent of the 258 schools studied. Percentages were still used in 26 per cent of the schools, some schools using both plans. Billett found that most schools with letter or number grades used five grades, either A, B, C, D, and F or some other series of five letters, or five numbers, either 1, 2, 3, 4, and 5 or the Roman numerals I, II, III, IV, and V. Some schools, however, had only two grades: pass and fail.[6]

Forms in Which Marks Are Issued	Frequency	
	Number	Per Cent
Letters or others symbols	210	81
Percentages	67	26
Class ranks	25	9
Percentile ranks	7	3
Written records or logs of pupil's progress	4	2
Accomplishment quotients	2	1
Sigma scores	2	1

Obviously, while a general discussion of schools marks may help the student (and teacher, too, probably), a detailed analysis and discussion of the individual student's marks—especially the low marks—will probably be even more beneficial to him. This analysis may be made by asking each student to write down all of the possible reasons or explanations for his lowest mark. If he has several low marks, he should work first on only one in order to see the problem clearly and completely. Later he may analyse his other marks in the same manner.

[6] Umstattd, J. G. *Secondary School Teaching*, Ginn and Company, New York, 1953. Pages 417–18.

After the student writes out his reason on a sheet of paper, he thinks seriously about each one, and crosses out those which appear to be the least logical and justifiable. The remaining reasons may then be discussed by the entire group. In order to avoid personalities, the papers may be collected or exchanged. Many of the reasons listed will be quite similar, and these may be grouped or classified and discussed, with variations, at one time. In but few instances, after such a discussion, will the student be able to blame the teacher for his low mark. Naturally, the emphasis should be on a careful and fair diagnosis that will help to prevent a low mark the next time.

Another device, somewhat similar to that above, is to have the student check the possible reasons for his low mark on a mimeographed sheet. And, of course, between reports the group may discuss the entire list of reasons. The following are suggestions on such a list:

1. Lack of attentiveness.
2. Poor sight, teeth, etc.
3. Undernourishment; illness.
4. Ineffective study habits.
5. Loss of sleep.
6. Lack of adequate preparation.
7. Irregular attendance.
8. Outside work and activities.
9. Carelessness in work.
10. Lack of parental interest.
11. Poor study surroundings.
12. Too much radio, TV, automobile, etc.
13. Lack of personal confidence.
14. Dislike for the teacher.
15. Trouble with parents, friends.
16. Making trouble in class.
17. Too heavy a schedule.
18. Dawdling, daydreaming.
19. Too many extracurricular affairs.
20. Failure to ask for help.[7]

One way in which many schools seek a greater degree of specificity in their marks of pupils is by the establishment of "citizenship marks" as separate from scholastic marks. Thus, on a report card, "citizenship" is listed along with the school subjects in which pupils are rated with a percentage mark or with a letter symbol. There is difference of opinion among the

[7] McKown, Harry C., *Homeroom Guidance*, McGraw-Hill Book Company, Inc., New York, 1946. Page 254.

schools as to the value of the citizenship mark. A number of schools which have tried it have abandoned it, primarily on the ground that "citizenship," while distinguished from scholastic achievement, is nevertheless too vague and general to be honestly marked with a single symbol. A confusing factor, too, is the extent to which, in actual usage, a "citizenship" mark is only the old "deportment" mark under a new name. Unless the term is carefully described and defined, citizenship, to many teachers means roughly "obedient and respectful," or perhaps, "cooperation," without reference to the source of authority or the purposes of the cooperative activity. Under such conditions, citizenship marks are not likely to help to develop the kinds of citizens a democracy requires.[8]

Achievement in Relation to Ability

By giving mental tests and standardized educational tests in several subjects the achievement quotient (AQ) may be found. This is done by dividing a pupil's educational age (EA) by his mental age (MA). It shows, in general, within the limits of the test, the relation of achievement to mental ability. Thus, if two people of unequal ability in the same class should make the same score in a subject, the higher mark would be awarded the one with the lower ability since he achieved all that his mental ability showed that he could, while the other did not.

The AQ shows to what extent a pupil is achieving as much as he can. It supplies information valuable in pupil guidance. It affects marks indirectly, but to use it as an element in marking would not be limited to achievement alone. To use it would be confusing and to secure the AQ for all pupils would scarcely be feasible.[9]

Until recently school achievement quite generally was graded on a scale of 100 points. It was not uncommon to hear the announcement at the time of graduation that the valedictorian had won by a margin from close competitors. His nearest competitor had something like a grade of 97⅝, while the victor edged out his rival by a flat 98 per cent grade. In consequence the naive assumption has prevailed that the valedictorian in reality was the undoubted intellectual superior of his class.

One reason for the disfavor into which this system of grading has fallen is the theoretical assumption, implicit in the plan, that school accomplish-

[8] *Learning the Ways of Democracy,* Educational Policies Commission, (NEA) 1940. Page 401.

[9] Reinoehl, Charles M., and Ayer, Fred C., *Classroom Administration and Pupil Adjustment,* Appleton-Century-Crofts, Inc., New York, 1940. Pages 293–94.

ment can be measured in minute degrees from complete absence of the thing the instrument is set to measure to perfection. Psychologically it is inconceivable that any student in a class who had put forth any effort would not have learned something, yet it is possible for a student to take a new type of essay examination, fail all questions, receive a grade of zero, and still have a considerable fund of knowledge of the subject. It is equally impossible to measure perfection. To try to do so on a scale of 100 is misleading. A grade of 95 in the first year of high school biology cannot mean that the student lacks just five per cent of complete knowledge of biology, or even of perfect knowledge of the first-year course. The further weakness of the assumption of an absolute scale is the evidence from experience and experimentation that when an arbitrary passing mark is set, say 70 or 75, it consciously affects the grades given a class. The teacher tends to pass about the same number of students, whether the passing mark be placed arbitrarily at 60 or 75.

Another serious objection to the percentage plan is the inability of the teacher to measure with such refinement assumed by the 100 per cent scale. It is a generally accepted fact among students of the subject that man's ability to shade differences in categories of judgment is very limited, and normally does not exceed a range of over ten divisions. A range of five is most widely approved.[10]

Many studies have been made of teachers' marks as bases for appraisal of school work. Practically all studies show extreme variations in teachers' marking, not [only] among the different teachers but also between the marks given by the same teachers on the same examination or test at different times. Apparently some teachers are traditionally and by principle or habit "hard markers" while others are very consistently "easy." It might happen, therefore, if a given student chanced for several terms to come under the direction of one of these hard markers, his work would be appraised as only average or perhaps inferior. But if this same student were to be transferred suddenly to classes taught by easy markers, his work might be appraised as better than average or even as superior. Such a situation is accounted for by the fact that teachers do not use the same criteria when marking papers. For example, one mathematics teacher counts nothing for "effort" or for "method," another counts partial credit for "method" but none for "effort," a third does the reverse, a fourth gives partial credit for both, so on through the possibilities in the situation. The use of the teacher-made objective tests helps correct the situation, and the use of standardized

---

[10] Bossing, Nelson L., *Progressive Methods of Teaching in Secondary Schools*, Houghton Mifflin Company, Boston, 1935. Pages 684–85.

tests helps even more. But there still remains the problem of trying to appraise honest effort with correct method, which, as has been shown, is attempted by some schools through taking student traits into account in one way or another.

Some of the facts which the good teacher has clearly in mind and takes into account in assigning marks are: (1) the native ability of the individual student; (2) individual achievement as shown by tests, examinations, and the like; (3) individual achievement as shown by performance of assigned work; (4) group rank of the student in intelligence; (5) group rank of the student in achievement; (6) growth of the student in power and in ability to advance. All of these have important bearing upon teacher judgment in assigning marks.[11]

Many schools help parents interpret grades and report cards more accurately. But grading children on a comparative basis in subject achievement only is still widely practiced; and in some instances the letter grades in the various subjects are the main entries on the report cards. The report cards in turn are the principal public relations link between the teacher and parent, school and community. And what may be desirable characteristics of a reporting system from the standpoint of developing good public relations?

1. A reporting system should produce excellent child-teacher relations. Toward the end of the reporting period, Miss Blytt's best estimate of Bill's progress was: Speaking: Excellent progress with usual teacher help. Listening: Average progress with usual help of teacher. Reading: Slow progress with much teacher help. Spelling: Slow progress with much teacher help. Composition: Slow progress with much teacher help.

Reporting the progress as suggested in the five areas might have avoided the confusion and feeling of failure. Instead of a failure, wanting to quit school, Bill would want to continue to learn under the helpful guidance of Miss Blytt. The relationship would be a pleasant one between the child and his teacher. Good relations between Miss Blytt and Bill would result from the suggested report.

2. The reporting system should produce excellent parent-teacher, home-school relations. Mrs. Jones noted the C which Mary received in the required United States History. There was no other indication of Mary's progress toward any objectives of citizenship. So Mrs. Jones wondered what the C meant. Did it mean that Mary is or will be a commercial or lower-grade citizen? With Mary as with Bill, Mrs. Jones wondered what the school was

[11] Williams, L. A., *Secondary Schools for American Youth*, American Book Company, New York, 1944, 1948. Pages 331, 336.

doing for her child. And in a telephone conversation she was asked by her neighbor, Mrs. Smith, how the children were getting along in school.

"I am not sure," replied Mrs. Jones.

"And how do the children like their new teacher?" asked Mrs. Smith. Being uncertain but hoping for the best, Mrs. Jones commented, "All right, I guess."

3. The reporting system should include the important objective toward which the school program is directed. The report card did not tell Mr. and Mrs. Jones that Mary followed the safety regulations of the school, took good care of materials and other school property, used her time well in independent study, worked at learning tasks consistently, and was developing many interests. It did not tell the parents that Bill worked well with his classmates, respected them as individuals, was friendly and courteous to them, and kept himself neat and in good health. So these children's growth toward some of the most important objectives of education was not reported.

Besides objectives closely related to the subject fields, how many other similar to those listed above should be included in the reporting system?

So to maintain and enhance good relations, teachers must make sure that teachers, children, and parents understand the reports.

So it is not only what is reported, but how it is reported that leads to good relations between children and teachers, home and school. Printed information which supplements the report card, meetings with larger groups of parents, small group meetings between the teacher and parents, individual conferences between teacher and parents, telephone conversations, the sending home of samples of children's work—these and other procedures are useful and necessary in a good system of reporting.

There is no one technique or report form that works best in all schools, at all grade levels, in all areas of school work, with all teachers. However, when the reporting system, with accuracy and with full respect for each child and each parent as a worthwhile individual, indicates that the children with few exceptions are making progress, the areas in which they are making progress, and what the teachers are doing to help the children, more parents may work zealously to double the amount of funds which will apparently be needed to maintain, not improve, the present quality of education being provided for American children.[12]

Current tendencies in reporting to parents seem to be (1) less frequent

[12] Klausmeier, Herbert J., "Grading, Reporting, and Public Relations," *The High School Journal*, The University of North Carolina Press, Vol. 40, January, 1957. Pages 147–50.

reporting for all pupils; (2) more frequent reporting in cases of exceptionally good or exceptionally poor performances; (3) ratings on many more traits and abilities than formerly; (4) making the reports more and more descriptive; and (5) reporting data for the purpose of furthering pupil growth.[13]

There are many unanswered questions and unsolved problems in this field, some of which appear impossible of experimental or objective solution by means and methods at present available. The question of the effects of marks upon those to whom they are given, not merely in learning in the relatively near future but upon a much broader basis, is very important and merits much study. Much opinion has been expressed, but few facts are available. The reliability of semester marks should be investigated by having two or more equally competent persons observe, examine, and rate all the work done by a group of pupils during that time by comparing marks. The whole question of whether standards for marking should be uniform and fixed or adapted to the group should be attacked more thoroughly than it has been but much of the attack must be by clear, critical thinking rather than the use of objective data. Finally, more attention should be devoted to learning what results are obtained from programs of improvement in the marking system. People are slow about doing away with the things that they have always known. I guess the best way to secure our educational aims is through education itself. Let's educate the educators. This can sometimes be a slow process!

REFERENCES

Anderson, Vernon E., Grim, Paul R., and Gruhn, William T., *Principles and Practices of Secondary Education*, The Ronald Press Company, New York, 1951.

Bossing, Nelson L., *Progressive Methods of Teaching in Secondary Schools*, Houghton Mifflin Company, Boston, 1935.

Jacobson, Paul B., *The American Secondary School*, Prentice-Hall, Inc., New York, 1952.

Klausmeier, Herbert J., "Grading, Reporting, and Public Relations," *The High School Journal*, The University of North Carolina Press, Vol. 40, January, 1957.

Learning the Ways of Democracy, Educational Policies Commission, (NEA), 1940.

[13] Rivlin, Harry N., *Encyclopedia of Modern Education*, Philosophical Library, New York, 1943. Pages 667–68.

McKown, Harry C., *Homeroom Guidance*, McGraw-Hill Company, Inc., New York, 1946.

Reinoehl, Charles M., and Ayer, Fred C., *Classroom Administration and Pupil Adjustment*, Appleton-Century-Crofts, Inc., New York, 1940.

Rivlin, Harry N., *Teaching Adolescents in Secondary Schools*, Appleton-Century-Crofts, Inc., New York, 1948.

Rivlin, Harry N., Ed., *Encyclopedia of Modern Education*, Philosophical Library, New York, 1943.

Spears, Harold, *Secondary Education in American Life*, American Book Company, New York, 1941.

Umstattd, J. G., *Secondary School Teaching*, Ginn and Company, New York, 1953.

Williams, L. A., *Secondary Schools for American Youth*, American Book Company, New York, 1944, 1948.

Wrinkle, William L., and Gilchrist, Robert S., *Secondary Education for American Democracy*, Farrar and Rinehart, Inc., New York, 1942.

JAMES H. RICKS, JR.
Assistant Director, Test Division, The Psychological Corporation

48 · ON TELLING PARENTS ABOUT TEST RESULTS

• Like any other organization dealing with people, a school has many confidences to keep. School administrators, teachers, and especially guidance workers inevitably come to know items of private information. A gossip who carelessly passes such information around abuses his position and his relationship with his students. It is both right and important that some kinds of information be kept in confidence.

What about test results? Do they belong in the category of secrets, to be seen only by professional eyes and mentioned only in whispers? Or is their proper function best served when they become common knowledge in the school and its community? (In some towns, names and scores have been listed in the local newspaper, much like the results of an athletic contest.)

We think neither extreme is a good rule. Sometimes there is reason to make group data—figures such as the average and the range from high to low—generally public. Seldom should individual results be published except for the happy announcement of a prize won, a scholarship awarded, and the like. But short of general publication, school guidance workers face a particularly important question: Should parents be told their children's test results?

Hard questions, often, are hard because they deal with genuinely complicated problems. Simple "solutions" to such questions are likely to be a trap rather than an aid if their effect is to divert our attention from the difficulties we truly face. Simple rules or principles, on the other hand, can be of real help as one tackles complex problems and situations. This article

Test Service Bulletin (The Psychological Corporation), No. 54, December, 1959.

will present some rules that we have found useful in facing questions such as—

"What should I say when a mother wants to know her son's IQ?" "Should we send aptitude test profiles home with the children?" "We feel that parents in our school ought to know the results of the achievement tests we give, but then it's hard to explain the discrepancies between these and the teachers' grades."

No single procedure, obviously, can be appropriate for every kind of test. Nor for every kind of parent. To Mr. Jones, a well-adjusted and well-educated father, a report of his daughter's test scores may enhance his understanding of her capacities and of what the school has been giving her. To Mr. Green, a somewhat insecure and less knowledgeable man, the identical information may spark an explosion damaging to both child and school. And the counselor or teacher often has no sure way of knowing which kind of person he will be reporting to.

Two principles and one verbal technique seem to us to provide a sound basis for communicating the information obtained from testing. The two "commandments" are absolutely interdependent—without the second the first is empty, and without the first the second is pointless.

The first: PARENTS HAVE THE RIGHT TO KNOW WHATEVER THE SCHOOL KNOWS ABOUT THE ABILITIES, THE PERFORMANCE, AND THE PROBLEMS OF THEIR CHILDREN.

The second: THE SCHOOL HAS THE OBLIGATION TO SEE THAT IT COMMUNICATES UNDERSTANDABLE AND USABLE KNOWLEDGE. Whether by written report or by individual conference, the school must make sure it is giving *real* information—not just the illusion of information that bare numbers or canned interpretations often afford. And the information must be in terms that parents can absorb and use.

Few educators will dispute the first principle. It is in parents that the final responsibility for the upbringing and education of the children must lie. This responsibility requires access to all available information bearing on educational and vocational decisions to be made for and by the child. The school is the agent to which parents have delegated part of the educational process—but the responsibility has been delegated, not abdicated. Thoughtful parents do not take these responsibilities and rights lightly.

The parents' right to know, then, we regard as indisputable. But, to know what?

Suppose that, as a result of judicious testings, the school knows that Sally has mastered social studies and general science better than many in her ninth grade class, but that few do as poorly as she in math. In English usage she stands about in the middle, but her reading level is barely up to the lower border of the students who successfully complete college preparatory work in her high school. The best prediction that can be made of her probable scores on the College Boards three years hence is that they will fall in the range which makes her eligible for the two-year community college, but not for the university. She grasps mechanical concepts better than most boys, far better than most girls. Looking over the test results and her records, her experienced teacher recognizes that good habits and neatness of work have earned Sally grades somewhat better than would be expected from her test scores.

All of these are things Sally's parents should know. Will they know them if they are given the numbers—Sally's IQ score, percentiles for two reading scores, percentiles on another set of norms for several aptitude tests, and grade-placement figures on an achievement battery?[1]

Telling someone something he does not understand does not increase his knowledge (at least not his correct and usable knowledge—we are reminded of the guide's observation about the tenderfoot, "It ain't so much what he don't know, it's what he knows that ain't so that gits him in trouble"). Transmitting genuine knowledge requires attention to content, language, and audience. We have already referred to some of the characteristics of parents as an audience. Let's look at the other two elements.

Content means that to begin with, *we* must ourselves know what we are trying to get across.

We need to know just what evidence there is to show that the test results deserve any consideration at all. We need equally to know the margins and probabilities of error in predictions based on tests. If we don't know *both* what the scores mean *and* how much confidence may properly be placed in them, we are in trouble at the start—neither our own use of the information nor our transmission of it to others will be very good.

Content—what we are going to say—and *language*—how we are going to put it—are inseparable when we undertake to tell somebody something. In giving information about test results, we need to think about the general content and language we shall use and also about the specific terms we shall use.

To illustrate the general content-and-language planning: a guidance director may decide that he wants first to get across a sense of both the values and the weaknesses of test scores. One excellent device for his purpose would be an expectancy table or chart. Such a chart can make it clear to

---

[1] The implied "No" answer to this question does not, of course, refer to those few parents trained in psychometrics—perhaps even to a point beyond the training of the school staff. Parents include all kinds of people.

persons without training in statistics that test results are useful predictors *and* that the predictions will not always be precise. Local studies in one's own school or community are of greatest interest. But the guidance director who lacks local data may still find illustrative tables from other places helpful in preparing parents and students to use test results in a sensible way.

Specific terms used in expressing test results vary considerably in the problems they pose. Consider, for example, the different kinds of numbers in which test results may be reported.

IQ's are regarded as numbers that should rarely if ever be reported as such to students or to their parents. The reason is that an IQ is likely to be seen as a fixed characteristic of the person tested, as somehow something more than the test score it really represents. The effect, too often, is that of a final conclusion about the individual rather than that of a piece of information useful in further thinking and planning. Few things interfere more effectively with real understanding than indiscriminate reporting of IQ scores to parents.

GRADE PLACEMENT scores or STANDARD SCORES of various kinds are less likely to cause trouble than IQ scores are. Still, they may substitute an illusion of communication for real communication. Standard scores have no more meaning to most parents than raw scores unless there is opportunity for extensive explanations. Grade placements *seem* so simple and straightforward that serious misunderstandings may result from their use. As noted in a very helpful pamphlet,[2] a sixth-grade pupil with grade-placement scores of 10.0 for reading and 8.5 for arithmetic does not necessarily rank higher in reading than he does in arithmetic when compared to the other sixth-graders. (Both scores may be at the 95th percentile for his class—arithmetic progress much more than reading progress tends to be dependent on what has been taught, and thus to spread over a narrower range at any one grade.)

PERCENTILES probably are the safest and most informative numbers to use PROVIDED their two essential characteristics are made clear: (1) that they refer not to per cent of questions answered correctly but to per cent of people whose performance the student has equalled or surpassed, and (2) who, specifically, are the people with whom the student is being compared. The second point—a definite description of the comparison or "norm" group—is especially important in making the meaning of test results clear.

---

[2] Katz, M. R. *Selecting an Achievement Test.* E. & A. Series No. 3, 1958 (Page 26). Available free from Educational Testing Service, Princeton, New Jersey.

Much more can be said about the kinds of numbers used to convey test score information. Good discussions can be found in a number of textbooks.[3] But a more fundamental question remains— *are any numbers necessary?*

We intend nothing so foolish as suggesting a ban on the use of numbers in reporting test results. But we have been struck repeatedly by the fact that some of the very best counselors and many of the best written reports present numerical data only incidentally or not at all.

Along with the two "commandments" at the beginning of this article, we mentioned a verbal technique. Generally, we dislike formulas for writing or speaking. This one, however, seems to have advantages that outweigh the risks attending its suggestion. It's just a few words:

"YOU SCORE LIKE PEOPLE WHO . . ." Or, to a parent, "Your son (or daughter) scores like students who . . ."

The sentence, of course, requires completion. The completion depends on the test or other instrument, the reason for testing, and the person to whom the report is being given. Some sample completions:

> ". . . people who are pretty good at office work, fast and accurate enough to hold a job and do it well."
> ". . . people who don't find selling insurance a very satisfactory choice. Three out of four who score as you do and become insurance salesmen leave the job for something else in less than a year."
> ". . . students who find getting into liberal arts college and getting a B.A. degree something they can attain only with extra hard work. On the other hand, they find a year or two of technical school interesting and they probably do well in the jobs to which that leads."
> ". . . students who are disappointed later if they don't begin a language in the ninth grade and plan to take some more math and science. It's easier to head toward business later if you still want to than to go from the commercial course into a good college."
> ". . . students who don't often—only about one out of four—manage to earn a C average their freshman year at State."
> ". . . students who have more than average difficulty passing in arithmetic—you [*or, to a parent,* he] may need some extra help on this in the next few years."

Many more samples will come readily to mind. The most important thing to note is that a satisfactory report combines two kinds of information:

---

[3] See, for example, Chapters 17 and 18 in *Measurement and Evaluation in Psychology and Education,* by Thorndike and Hagan (New York: Wiley, 1955), or pages 556–563 and 584–588 in *Appraising Vocational Fitness,* by Super (New York: Harper, 1949).

1) the test results of the individual person, and
2) something known about the test or battery and its relationship to the subsequent performance of others who have taken it.

Also, a satisfactory completion puts the school or the counselor out on a limb, at least a little. Some variant of "That's not so!" or, more politely, "How do you know?" will be the reaction in some cases, probably less frequently voiced than it is felt.

Well, let's face it. The decision to use a test at all is a step out on a limb. Some limbs are broad and solid and the climber need feel little or no anxiety. Some are so frail that they offer only hazard, with the bait of an improbable reward. We climb out on some limbs of medium safety because there is evidence of a real chance that they will help us, and those whom we test, toward a worthwhile goal.

The words of the formula need not actually be used in each case. Sometimes percentiles, grade placement scores, or a profile may be what the parents should receive. But it is well to try first mentally stating the meaning of the results in the language suggested above. If this proves difficult or discomforting, a warning signal is on—reporting the numbers is likely not to be constructive in the case at hand!

The audience of parents to which our test-based information is to be transmitted includes an enormous range and variety of minds and emotions. Some are ready and able to absorb what we have to say. Reaching others may be as hopeless as reaching TV watchers with an AM radio broadcast. Still others may hear what we say, but clothe the message with their own special needs, ideas, and predilections.

The habit of using the formula, and of thinking a bit about what answer to give if the response is a challenging or doubting one, puts the interpreter of test scores in the strongest position he can occupy. In the case of achievement tests, it requires him to understand why and how the particular test or battery was chosen as appropriate for his school and his purpose. In the case of aptitude (including scholastic aptitude or intelligence) tests, it requires him to examine the evidence offered in the test manual and research studies to back up the test's claim to usefulness. And it reminds him always that it is in the end *his* thinking, *his* weighing of the evidence, *his* soundness and helpfulness as an educator or counselor that is exposed for judgment—not the sometimes wistful ideas of the test author or publisher.

The school—or the counselor—*is* exposed for judgment when telling parents about the abilities and performances of their children. The parents have the right to know. And knowledge in terms they can understand and absorb is what the school must give.

REPRESENTATIVE TEXTS CORRELATED WITH *Readings*

Representative Texts Correlated with *Readings*

(See table on facing page)

Bernard, Harold W. *Psychology of Learning and Teaching*, 2d ed. New York: McGraw-Hill Book Company, 1965.

Cronbach, Lee J. *Educational Psychology*, 2d ed. New York: Harcourt, Brace and World, Inc., 1963.

Crow, Lester D., and Alice Crow. *Educational Psychology*. New York: American Book Company, 1958.

Frandsen, Arden N. *Educational Psychology*. New York: McGraw-Hill Book Company, 1961.

Garrison, Karl C. *Educational Psychology*. New York: Appleton-Century-Crofts, Inc., 1964.

Lindgren, Henry C. *Educational Psychology in the Classroom*. New York: John Wiley and Sons, 1962.

McDonald, Frederick J. *Educational Psychology*. San Francisco: Wadsworth Publishing Co., 1959.

Sawrey, James M., and Charles W. Telford. *Educational Psychology*, 2d ed. Boston: Allyn and Bacon, Inc., 1964.

Smith, Louis M., and Bryce B. Hudgins. *Educational Psychology*. New York: Alfred A. Knopf, 1964.

Sorenson, Herbert. *Psychology in Education*. New York: McGraw-Hill Book Company, 1964.

Readings Related to Chapters in Representative Texts*

Chapter	Bernard	Cronbach	Crow	Frandsen	Garrison	Lindgren	McDonald	Sawrey	Smith	Sorenson
1	1, 2, 3	1, 2, 3	2, 3	1, 2, 3, 4	2, 3	2, 3	3, 27, 28	1, 2, 3	2, 43, 45	27, 28
2	4, 5, 6	43, 44	4, 12, 14, 43, 45	5, 6	1, 6	17, 18	43, 44, 45	6, 17, 21	20, 21, 22	17, 22
3	7, 8	11, 12, 42	6, 18, 22	29, 30, 31	18, 22, 28	22, 28	18, 19	18, 19, 22	27, 28	18, 24, 36
4	9, 10, 11	18, 19, 28	28	20, 21, 22	20, 21, 22	17, 24, 30, 34	23, 24, 25, 26	4, 5, 6	30, 31, 33	2, 34
5	16	4, 5, 6	18, 22	17, 18, 37	15, 16, 17	35, 36	4, 5, 6	9, 10, 11	23, 41, 42	43, 45
6	12, 13, 14	23, 24, 28	9, 24, 25, 26, 42, 46	23, 24, 26	30, 31, 33, 34	26, 41, 42	7, 8, 15, 16	12, 13, 14	24, 36, 37	20, 21, 48
7	15, 17	20, 21	17, 18, 28, 33, 34, 37, 44	11, 12, 13	1, 23, 43	7, 38, 39	29, 30	15, 16, 20	36, 44	9, 10, 11
8	18, 19	17, 33	10, 20, 21, 31, 48	9, 10, 42	7, 8, 39	4, 13	31, 32	7, 8	12, 13, 14	16, 18, 37
9	20, 21	13, 22	10, 48	40, 43, 45	18, 22, 29, 38, 42	20, 21, 23	12, 40	23, 24	4, 5, 6	30, 33, 44
10	22	7, 8	27, 28	7, 8	18, 22, 43	25, 43	9, 10, 11	25, 26	7, 8, 10	23, 24
11	23, 24	9, 10	9, 13, 34, 37	23, 33, 35	10, 11	12, 13, 29	13, 14	41, 42	15, 16, 17	19, 27, 41
12	25, 26	15, 16, 38, 39	4, 13, 22, 26, 39, 42	41, 42	27, 31, 37	24, 34, 37	41, 42	27, 30, 31	18, 29, 32	11, 26, 31
13	27, 28	35, 36, 37	9, 11, 23	14, 33, 36	46, 47	1, 31, 32	35, 36, 38, 39	28, 29, 37	9, 11	13, 29
14	29, 30	29, 30, 31	4, 5	25, 32, 43	46, 47	8, 46, 47	46, 47	46, 47, 48	25, 26, 40	32, 38, 39, 40
15	31, 32	14, 44	17	46, 47, 48	36, 48	20, 48	37, 48	31, 32	1, 38, 39	25
16	33, 34	46, 47, 48	9, 10, 11		13, 17, 30, 33, 43	10, 11, 17	20, 21	33, 34, 35		7, 8
17	35, 36, 37	25, 27, 43	7		9, 27	19, 27	17, 33, 34			1
18	38, 39, 40	41, 45	46, 47		19, 24, 31	4, 12, 14, 27, 43, 44, 45	2, 22			46, 47
19	41, 42		36, 46, 47		12, 14, 24, 25, 44, 45					
20	46, 47, 48		48							
21	43, 44, 45		15, 16, 17, 33, 34							

* The numbers in the first column refer to *chapters* in the texts listed on the facing page. The numbers in the columns under the authors' names designate the *readings* in this volume that correlate with the chapters.

AUTHOR INDEX

SUBJECT INDEX